Encyclopedia of

MULTICULTURALISM

Encyclopedia of

MULTICULTURALISM

Supplement

Volume 8

Mfume, Kweisi – *Wyatt v. Strickley*
Index

Editor

SUSAN AUERBACH

Marshall Cavendish
New York • London • Toronto

Project Editor: R. Kent Rasmussen
Production Editor: Cynthia Breslin Beres
Research Supervisor: Jeffry Jensen
Photo Editor: Karrie Hyatt
Acquisitions Editor: Mark Rehn
Layout: James Hutson

Published By
Marshall Cavendish Corporation
99 White Plains Road
Tarrytown, New York 10591-9001
United States of America

∞ The paper in these volumes conforms to the American National Standard for Permanence of Paper for Printed Library Materials, Z39.48-1984.

Library of Congress Cataloging-in-Publication Data

Encyclopedia of multiculturalism. Supplement / editor, Susan Auerbach.
    p. cm.
    Includes bibliographical references (p. 1767) and index.
    Contents: v. 1. A. Philip Randolph Institute–Business and corporate enterprise; v. 2. Mother Cabrini–Estonian Americans; v. 3. Ethnic and minority group names–Inner city; v. 4. Daniel Ken Inouye–Mythology, American Indian; v. 5. Names and name changes–Six Nations; v. 6. Slavery–Zoot-suit riots.
    1. Pluralism (Social sciences)—United States—Encyclopedias. 2. Multiculturalism—United States—Encyclopedias. 3. Ethnology—United States—Encyclopedias. 4. United States—Ethnic relations—Encyclopedias. 5. United States—Race relations—Encyclopedias.
    I. Auerbach, Susan, 1956-
    E184.A1E58   1993
    306.4′46′0973—dc20   93-23405
    Supplement   CIP
    ISBN 0-7614-7096-4 (set)   AC
    ISBN 0-7614-7063-8 (volume 8)

First Printing

Contents

Encyclopedia of
MULTICULTURALISM

Mfume, Kweisi (Frizzell Gray, b. Oct. 24, 1948, Baltimore, Md.): U.S. congressman and president of the NATIONAL ASSOCIATION FOR THE ADVANCEMENT OF COLORED PEOPLE (NAACP). Born Frizzell Gray, Mfume had a difficult childhood and fathered five sons out of wedlock before he even reached the age of twenty-two. He then turned his life around and took the Ghanaian name Kweisi Mfume, meaning "conquering sons of kings." In 1979 he began his political career by winning a seat on the Baltimore city council. Seven years later he was elected to the first of five terms to the U.S. House of Representatives. There he served on three congressional committees and became chairman of the CONGRESSIONAL BLACK CAUCUS. In February, 1996, he accepted the leadership of the troubled NAACP, the nation's oldest and largest civil rights organization.

As president of the NAACP Mfume hoped to build consensus and coalition among activist groups as well as to reinvigorate the organization itself. He set as immediate priorities encouraging voter registration and involving youths in civil rights struggles. After his first year in office, he was criticized for having done "little to restore the spiritual and legislative luster" to the NAACP. He responded that he planned more activism and that no issue would be beyond the scope of NAACP lobbying efforts, such as police brutality and substandard education.

In 1996 he published an autobiography, *No Free Ride: From the Mean Streets to the Mainstream.* —*Maria L. Alonzo*

Migrant Health Act (1962): U.S. federal legislation establishing government funding for health services for migrant workers. Signed by President John F. Kennedy

Kweisi Mfume shortly after his installation as president of the NAACP in late 1995. (Reuters/Win McNamee/Archive Photos)

Migrant farmworkers harvesting peas near Nipomo, California, in 1989. (AP/Wide World Photos)

in September, 1962, the Migrant Health Act provided funds to be used as grants to create health services for migrant farmworkers in the United States. Because such workers typically lacked permanent residences in the counties in which they worked, they often did not have full access to public health care. The federal act particularly benefited many Mexican and Mexican American farm laborers working in the United States. Federal legislation was necessary to implement the reforms because employment of many migrant workers involved matters of interstate commerce.—*Alexander Scott*

Militias: Privately organized and operated paramilitary groups, many of which operate outside of the law to advance extremist political agendas. During the 1990's, a number of self-proclaimed "militias" emerged in the United States. They frequently employed various forms of domestic terrorism against minority groups and gov-

ernmental agencies. Militia groups have typically claimed authority stemming from the Second Amendment to the U.S. Constitution, which states:

> A well regulated Militia, being necessary to the security of a free State, the right of the people to keep and bear Arms, shall not be infringed.

The guarantee of the right to "keep and bear arms," has been construed as permitting militias to stockpile all types of weapons, irrespective of federal and state laws against private ownership of certain kinds of weapons. Indeed, militia groups have typically viewed federal and state authorities to be "enemies" of the United States, and their laws to be null and void by dint of their supposed unconstitutionality. Numerous conspiracy theories have undergirded this view. These have included claims that the federal government is in league with the United Nations to implement a totalitarian "New World Order"; that international Jewish bankers have taken over the U.S. government; and that the government has been coopted by racial minority groups. Militia members have seen such theories as justification for their use of terrorism against authorities and members of minority groups.

The notion of "multiculturalism" is scorned by members of most militia groups, who understand it to mean the emasculation of the United States, undermining of traditional American values, or oppression of white people, particularly males. Thus it is not surprising that many militia groups are associated with WHITE SUPREMACISM.

One of the first modern militia groups to gain notoriety was the Militia of Montana, founded in 1994 by an anti-Semitic white supremacist. Since that time,

militia groups have rapidly sprung up across the United States. Some estimates have placed the numbers of persons involved in militias much higher than 10,000 (some estimates have been as high as 40,000); many of the groups known to government authorities have ideologies based on RACISM or XENOPHOBIA.

The combination of paranoia, attitudes of moral superiority, and antigovernment beliefs has led many militia groups to engage in acts of DOMESTIC VIOLENCE and terrorism. They have viewed their causes as "armed resistance" against an illegitimate and authoritarian government. Many members have also clearly resented the political, social, and economic gains made by minorities and women in the late twentieth century.

Militias have attached great—almost mythical—importance to their clashes with authorities. For example,

The devastating bombing of Oklahoma City's federal building on April 19, 1995, has been seen as an act of revenge perpetrated by militia terrorists. (AP/Wide World Photos)

the federal government's assault on the stronghold of white supremacist Randy Weaver in Idaho in 1992 has been compared to Japan's bombing of Pearl Harbor in World War II. The federal government's siege of the BRANCH DAVIDIANS in Waco, Texas, in 1993 has also been held up as evidence of the government's war against its own citizens. The 1995 bombing of the federal building in Oklahoma City, Oklahoma, which killed 168 persons, is only the most heinous of numerous acts of domestic terrorism that have simultaneously provoked and "avenged" federal law enforcement efforts.

SUGGESTED READINGS. The subject of modern militias has attracted considerable attention in newspapers and news magazines. Many articles on the subject are listed in the *Reader's Guide to Periodic Literature.* For incisive discussions of aspects of the movement, see Alan W. Bock, "Weekend Warriors: Is the Militia Movement a Threat?" *National Review* (May 29, 1995); June Jordan, "In the Land of White Supremacy," *The Progressive* (June, 1995); and Kenneth S. Stern, "Militia Mania: A Growing Danger," *USA Today* 124 (Jan., 1996).—*Steve D. Boilard*

Military, homosexuals in: During the 1990's the question of whether homosexuals should be allowed to serve in the U.S. military became a prominent national political issue. After having increasingly asserted their rights as U.S. citizens, homosexuals were more openly claiming the right to serve in the armed forces without fear of being dishonorably discharged because of their sexual orientation. Many leaders in the military and their supporters asserted, however, that the presence of avowed homosexuals in the military would lead to unacceptable morale problems and an erosion of military efficiency.

Contrasting Legal Rationales. Homosexuals claimed that they were "persons" within the meaning of the FOURTEENTH AMENDMENT's words and thus entitled to EQUAL PROTECTION of the law, as promised by that section of the Constitution. As citizens, homosexuals argued, they should not be excluded from military service since there was no concrete evidence that their sexual orientation would diminish their capacity as soldiers, sailors, or airmen. Further, they contended that it was wrong to ban their participation simply because other persons were offended by their sexual orientation or lifestyles. They amplified this view by reminding the government that they were not only U.S. citizens, but also taxpayers, entitled to participate fully

in institutions they were required by law to support with their taxes.

Leaders in the armed forces and their supporters argued that the nature of military organizations required members of the same sex to live and work in such close quarters that mixing homosexuals and unsympathetic heterosexuals might lead to violent conflicts, loss of morale, and loss of efficiency in an institution critical to the nation's security.

Homosexuals in Military History. Evaluations of this issue depend partly on changing interpretations over time. Because the word "homosexual" itself was not even coined until around 1871, behavior that in the twentieth century would be labeled homosexual would have been described using different words in the past. However, homosexual behavior—by whatever name—has existed in virtually all military systems throughout recorded history. Indeed, some armed forces of the past encouraged homosexual behavior, believing that it enhanced military morale and efficiency. Behavior now called homosexual was considered the highest form of love in ancient Greek city-states, such as Athens and Sparta. The famous Spartan infantry, in particular, applauded homosexual behavior because of the belief that it increased the soldiers' bravery since they were fighting alongside persons they loved intimately.

Many modern historical scholars have shown that homosexuals fought in the U.S. armed forces in all major American wars without impeding military efficiency. Military officials have not denied that this was true, but assert that homosexual behavior in the military was hidden from public view. What they have most strongly objected to is the efforts of homosexuals to seek open recognition of their sexual orientation. Military officials have acknowledged that they cannot stamp out all homosexual behavior, even under their preferred policy, but insist they ought not to give public recognition or acceptance to such behavior. Military supporters have also admitted that many Western European countries—including members of the North Atlantic Treaty Organization—have admitted avowed homosexuals into their armed forces, and that U.S. military personnel have successfully fought alongside European homosexuals without apparent loss of morale or efficiency.

The Recent Controversy. The question of admitting homosexuals into the military became a major national issue after late 1992, when president-elect Bill Clinton announced that he would issue an executive order re-

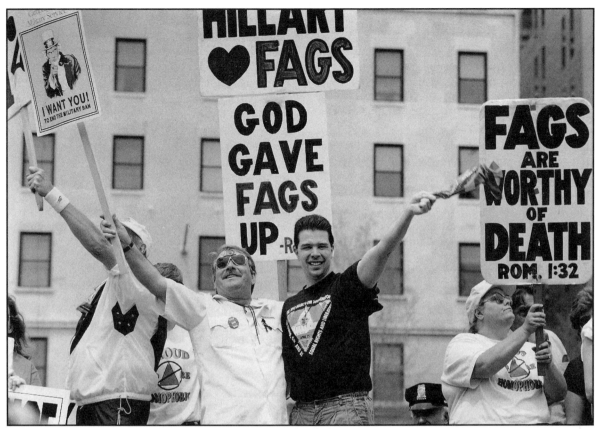

Gay demonstrators march in Washington, D.C., in early 1993 to protest the military ban on homosexuals. (AP/Wide World Photos)

versing the policy banning homosexuals in the armed forces. Military leaders quickly objected; with their political allies forming a majority in the Congress, they threatened to override Clinton's announced policy. After lengthy negotiations, the president and the Congress announced a compromise known as the "DON'T ASK, DON'T TELL" policy. This policy directed military officials not to ask recruits if they were homosexuals and not to take active steps to search out homosexuals for discharge, so long as homosexual servicemen themselves did not publicly declare their sexual orientation.

On the surface, this compromise appeared to restore the situation prior to WORLD WAR I, when the military first began asking recruits about their sexual orientations, excluding those who admitted being homosexuals, and discharging homosexual servicemen who were later discovered. Although the U.S. Supreme Court upheld civil laws against homosexuality in *Bowers v. Hardwick* (1986), homosexuals continued to assert their rights, using the logic of the Fourteenth Amendment to lend credence to their position.

SUGGESTED READINGS. An objective source of legal cases and other materials on issues including homosexuals in the military can be found in William B. Rubenstein's *Lesbians, Gay Men, and the Law: Cases and Materials* (2d ed., 1996). An attempt at a balanced treatment of legal issues affecting homosexuals is Morris A. Kaplan's *Sexual Justice: Democratic Citizenship and the Politics of Desire* (1997). Books advocating the right of homosexuals to serve in the armed forces are numerous. Andrew Sullivan's *Virtually Normal: An Argument About Homosexuality* (1996) argues that religious conservatives and liberals should accept homosexuality as normal in American culture and allow homosexuals full rights to marry and to enlist in the military. Lois Shawver makes a similarly strong argument in *And the Flag Was Still There: Straight People, Gay People and Sexuality in the Military* (1994). *Gay Rights, Military Wrongs: Political Perspectives on Lesbians and Gays in the Military* (1996), edited by Craig A. Rimmerman, collects essays arguing for the right of homosexuals to enlist in the armed forces.—*Richard L. Wilson*

Milliken v. Bradley (1974): U.S. Supreme Court decision relating to the use of BUSING to achieve school integration. This case arose out of a federal district judge's decision to require busing to establish racial balance within DETROIT, Michigan, metropolitan area schools. The district judge found de jure SEGREGATION within Detroit city schools because the city's school officials had maintained a dual, or racially segregated, school system since the Supreme Court's 1954 BROWN v. BOARD OF EDUCATION decision that had mandated school DESEGREGATION. There was, however, no finding of de jure segregation within any of the fifty-three small school districts immediately surrounding Detroit. Nevertheless, the district judge ordered busing across district lines to promote racial balance within Detroit itself and the larger metropolitan area.

On July 25, 1974, the Supreme Court reversed the lower court's decision, holding that the school districts neighboring Detroit should not be required to bus students simply because the city of Detroit could not be desegregated to reflect the racial composition of the greater metropolitan area.—*Jerry A. Murtagh*

Million Man March (1995): WASHINGTON, D.C., event organized by NATION OF ISLAM leader Louis FARRAKHAN. Held on Monday, October 16, 1995, the march attracted hundreds of thousands of African Americans, mostly men, from throughout the United States. According to Farrakhan, the march was undertaken "to convey to the world a vastly different picture of the black male, and to publicly proclaim to the global community that the black man is prepared and moving forward to unify our families and build our communities." In preparation for the event Farrakhan asked leaders of all religious faiths to declare October 16, 1995, as a "Holy Day of Atonement and Reconciliation." It was to be a day of fasting and prayer, and the "first time since the institution of slavery that black people would have declared a Holy Day for our people."

The day of the march opened with a sunrise prayer service on the Washington Mall, where a minister urged the growing crowd to pull together, as bands played music and participants chanted, "Long live the Million Man March!" Participants then began assembling near the Capitol Building, forming a dense chain of humanity extending west to the Lincoln Memorial. The day-long event attracted speakers who emphasized the need to eliminate violence, drugs and other social problems within black neighborhoods. Among speakers' recurrent themes was the urgent need for men to play stronger roles in black families.

Organizers and government observers disagreed on how many people participated in the march. The Nation of Islam claimed that the number was 1.5 million, while the U.S. National Park Service put the number at 875,000. However, either number compared favorably with the estimated quarter of a million people who participated in Martin Luther KING, JR.'S MARCH ON WASHINGTON in 1963.

Filling the area between the Washington Memorial and the Capitol Building, most participants in the Million Man March watched speakers on huge television screens. (AP/Wide World Photos)

Despite the predominantly upbeat mood and positive themes emerging from the march, many Americans, including some prominent black leaders, expressed ambivalence about its value, in part because of controversy surrounding Farrakhan and in part because of the omission of women from the name of the event. A flamboyant and inflammatory speaker, Farrakhan, was often criticized for his anti-Semitic remarks, as well as his negative comments regarding Roman Catholics and homosexuals. Further criticism fell upon the march's lead organizer Benjamin CHAVIS, who had been recently ousted as director of the NATIONAL ASSOCIATION FOR THE ADVANCEMENT OF COLORED PEOPLE for his alleged mismanagement of funds.

Before the march many critics had accused Farrakhan of race baiting, while his supporters had pointed to his positive messages of self-reliance and family values. Among the eighty public speakers and supporters at the march were civil rights activist Jesse JACKSON; Washington mayor Marion BARRY; poet Maya ANGELOU; Tyneta Muhammad, the widow of Nation of Islam founder Elijah MUHAMMAD; Betty Shabazz, the widow of MALCOLM X; and ROSA PARKS, whose refusal to surrender her bus seat to a white man in 1955 had helped launch the CIVIL RIGHTS MOVEMENT.

Among those who openly opposed the march were U.S. Congressman John L. Lewis; Mary Frances Berry, chairperson of the U.S. COMMISSION ON CIVIL RIGHTS; Michael Meyers of the New York Civil Rights Coalition; and retired general Colin POWELL, who said he did not want to lend credibility to Farrakhan.

President Bill Clinton was not in Washington at the time of the march; he was at the University of Texas at Austin, where he delivered a speech charging both black and white Americans to "clean our house of racism." The president blamed the "stubborn persistence of racism" and a lack of candidness in conversations among blacks and whites for continuing racial divisions. He supported the rally's goals of commitment to self-reliance and strong families, but in an apparent subtle allusion to Farrakhan, he also urged Americans to avoid divisiveness.

Despite initial concerns by some Washington residents about potential unrest due to the semipolitical nature of the gathering, no serious crowd-control problems developed. Reporter Jack White called the march "one of the most dignified events I have ever witnessed," adding that it "will go a long way to changing the minds of people who still have an open mind about black people."

In October, 1997, a year after the Million Man March, hundreds of thousands of African American women gathered on Philadelphia's Benjamin Franklin Parkway to call attention to issues of health care, education, unemployment, and crime. (Reuters/Jay Gorodetzer/Archive Photos)

A year later many members of the black community commemorated the first anniversary of the Million Man March with special events. Meanwhile, film director Spike LEE released a feature film, *Get on the Bus*, about eighteen men who ride a bus together to attend the march; they begin their journey as strangers but emerge, three days and two thousand miles later, as brothers.

The success of the Million Man March moved many African American women to stage a similar event in 1997. On October 25, 1997, hundreds of thousands of women gathered in Philadelphia for what was billed as the Million Woman March.

SUGGESTED READINGS. *The Million Man March* (1995), a photograph album with text by Michael Cottman, provides a fascinating graphic overview of the march. For a critical study of Louis Farrakhan, see

Prophet of Rage: A Life of Louis Farrakhan and His Nation (1996), by Arthur J. Magida.—*Lorenzo Chavez*

Mills v. Board of Education of District of Columbia (1972): U.S. federal district court case involving the rights of mentally retarded, emotionally disturbed, and hyperactive children. After several such children were denied admission to District of Columbia public schools and no provisions for alternative educational placement were made, supporters of the children filed a civil suit. The federal district court ruled that the District of Columbia Board of Education had to provide adequate education for these children, basing its decision in part on the due process clause of the Fifth Amendment to the U.S. Constitution. The court further ruled that if funds were not available to finance all needed programs, such fiscal concerns could not be allowed to affect children with mental and emotional disabilities more severely than other children.—*Glenn Canyon*

Minimum wage laws: Legislation forbidding payment of wages that fall below specified levels. The first minimum wage laws in the United States were passed by individual states, beginning with Massachusetts in 1912. Coverage under early state laws was limited to women and children because employer opposition was too strong to permit passage of laws guaranteeing minimum wages for adult males. Moreover, a "protective" principle could be shown which had constitutional approval not equally available toward adult males.

Federal minimum wage policy began in 1933 with Congress' passage of the National Industrial Recovery Act (NIRA). Each of the 585 codes of fair competition adopted under the NIRA contained minimum wage provisions. The act's minimum wage levels varied among industries, but most were at least thirty cents per hour. About a fourth of the codes provided for lower minimum wage levels for women. However, the NIRA itself was ruled unconstitutional in 1935.

A permanent federal minimum wage program was created by the Fair Labor Standards Act of 1938. This law called for minimum wage levels to rise from an initial twenty-five cents to forty cents an hour, beginning in 1945. No differentials were permitted between men and women; however, a large proportion of female workers were excluded by exemptions for trade and service jobs. For most industries, the law also forbade interstate shipment of goods produced using workers under the age of sixteen.

The inflation of the 1940's lifted actual wages well

Most fast-food service employees earn the minimum wage. (James L. Shaffer)

above the minimum. Congress responded by raising the minimum wage in 1949 and numerous times thereafter. During that period minimum wage levels were generally around 40 to 50 percent of the national average for wages. Large increases in coverage were mandated in 1961 and 1967. Coverage of private non-farm employment rose from about 61 percent in 1950 to 69 percent in 1961, 83 percent in 1967, and 86 percent in 1978. Most sectors with concentrated female employment were also finally covered. By 1977 coverage of domestic service reached 64 percent of workers, other services 74 percent, and retail trade 79 percent. State laws extended coverage still further.

In 1996 the federal minimum was increased, reaching $5.15 an hour, effective September 1, 1997. An estimated twelve million workers were earning less than that figure in 1996; however, only 11 percent of these workers were sole breadwinners of families with children, while 35 percent were young people living with their parents.

Actions to enforce the minimum wage against employers paying low wages can be initiated either by affected workers or the government. Workers earning less than the minimum wage can sue employers for the amounts they should have been paid and collect additional damages of equal amounts. The Wage-Hour Division of the Department of Labor can initiate actions against employers, seeking either civil or criminal penalties. In actual practice, however, enforcement against small firms has always been loose, and some employers have found loopholes in the law to avoid full compliance. For example, restaurants have been permitted to claim the tips waiters expect to receive as part of their wages. Even after passage of the 1996 federal legislation, actual minimum wages could be as low as $2.13 an hour for employees whose tips were expected to raise their overall incomes to the new $5.15 per hour minimum.

SUGGESTED READINGS. *Myth and Measurement: The New Economics of the Minimum Wage* (1995), by David Card and Alan B. Krueger, claims that increases in minimum wage levels have not decreased employment levels. *The Economics of Legal Minimum Wages* (1981), edited by Simon Rottenberg, contains twenty-eight essays on different aspects of minimum wage laws; some of these essays are highly technical. John M. Peterson's *Minimum Wages: Measures and Industry Effects* (1981) is especially good on the extensions of coverage.—*Paul B. Trescott*
(updates original entry; vol. 4, p. 1154)

In an earlier time a white Texan such as Senator Phil Gramm—pictured here early in his political career with his Korean American wife, Wendy, and their sons—could not have hoped to succeed in politics after marrying an Asian. (AP/Wide World Photos)

Miscegenation: Mixing of members of different racial groups through sexual union or marriage. The term miscegenation was first used in the United States in 1864. Before then, a word derived from metallurgy, "amalgamation," was commonly used to describe the merging of races.

Early American leaders emphasized the promise of assimilation for U.S. citizens but did not envision an amalgamated country. Many eighteenth and nineteenth century European scientists assumed that RACE was an immutable biological category and that Caucasians were superior to other groups. Hence, many racial theorists stressed the importance of racial purity, using scientific RACISM to justify practices such as SLAVERY and beliefs about the inherent intellectual and moral inferiority of nonwhites. Although ideological definitions of race were discredited in the twentieth century, early racial theorists believed that races should not be allowed to mix.

During America's colonial era, white leaders attempted to control interracial unions by enacting AN-TIMISCEGENATION LAWS, especially in the South. Slavery, however, made enforcement of antimiscegenation laws difficult and raised the problem of defining the mixed race offspring of unions between masters and slaves. Within the plantation slave system white masters commonly made their female slaves concubines—a practice that unlike interracial marriage was not criminalized. Questions about whether their mulatto children should be classified as black or white were answered by individual states; however, white public opinion, supported by legal cases, eventually defined as "black" all persons with any trace of African ancestry. In 1920 the U.S. BUREAU OF THE CENSUS dropped all mixed-race categories from its racial classification terminology.

Other nonwhite groups were also marked for containment. For example, an Arizona antimiscegenation statute outlawed marriages between whites and "negroes, mulattoes, Indians or Mongolians," providing fines and imprisonment for offenders. In 1916 an advocate of EUGEN-ICS named Madison Grant published *The Passing of the Great Race*,

Richard and Mildred Loving shortly before they challenged Virginia's antimiscegenation law in the case that led to the U.S. Supreme Court's landmark Loving v. Virginia *decision.* (AP/Wide World Photos)

a book arguing that intermarriage between whites of Western European origin and members of "biologically inferior" groups—which included Asians, Jews, and Southern and Eastern Europeans—would endanger the survival of the "great race." Grant and others helped persuade Congress to pass IMMIGRATION LEGISLATION with national origin quotas that sharply limited immigration from non-Western European countries. It was not until 1965 that the national origin quota laws were repealed, and it was not until 1967, in the case of *Loving v. Virginia*, that the Supreme Court declared antimiscegenation laws unconstitutional.

Although antimiscegenation beliefs have often been associated with white racism, some members of nonwhite minority groups who

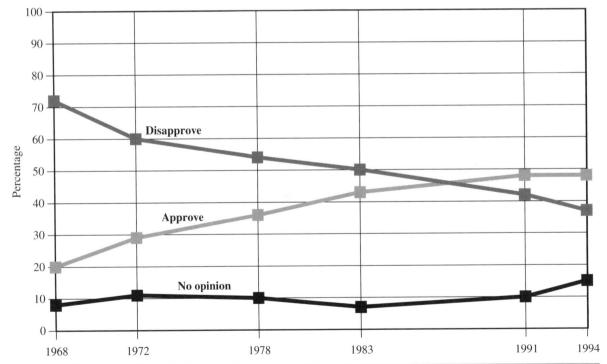

Changing American Opinions on African American-White Marriage

Source: The Gallup Poll: Public Opinion, 1994 (Wilmington, Del.: Scholarly Resources, 1995).

Interracial Marriages in the United States

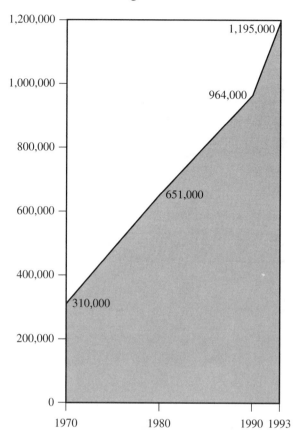

Source: Newsweek, Feb. 13, 1995.

wish to preserve group identity have also opposed miscegenation.

SUGGESTED READINGS. Both Naomi Zack's *Race and Mixed Race* (1993) and F. James Davis' *Who Is Black? One Nation's Definition* (1991) examine the issue of miscegenation, focusing on black and white relationships. Lawrence R. Tenzer includes public opinion surveys in *A Completely New Look at Interracial Sexuality: Public Opinion and Select Commentaries* (1990).—*Sandra K. Stanley*

Misogyny: Hatred of women by men. Misogyny is often expressed through RAPE or other male acts of violence against women. It can also be expressed in subtle ways, such as holding women in low regard, ridiculing them, or treating them as sex objects.

Misogyny has a long history, and it has been a constant theme in many human cultures. The ancient Greek myth of Pandora, for example, holds that the first woman was a beautiful but deceitful creature who brought all evils, including disease and old age, on humanity by opening a forbidden jar. In the Jewish and Christian tradition, Eve, the first woman, tempted Adam to eat forbidden fruit which led to their being cast out of Paradise. Many Christian thinkers have claimed that all women have been guilty of the sin of Eve. Some critics of the contemporary ROMAN CATHOLIC Church have maintained that the church's restriction of the priesthood to unmarried males is the product of a heritage of misogyny.

Throughout history, misogyny has had clear connections to warfare, since rape and mistreatment of women are common in war. For example, during West Pakistan's nine-month occupation of Bangladesh in 1981, West Pakistani soldiers raped an estimated 400,000 women. In 1992 international news services began to report on camps in Bosnia organized by the Serbian military for the mass rape of Bosnian Muslim women. During the VIETNAM WAR American soldiers frequently raped Vietnamese women. Critics of the U.S. military maintained that the military encouraged this victimization of women by using sexuality to spark aggression. Recruits in boot camps, for example, were often ridiculed as "ladies" or "pansies" by drill sergeants.

Misogynistic themes have often been found in pornography and even in the mainstream mass media. Pornographic films, magazines, and literature have often portrayed women in painful or humiliating circumstances. Film critics Gene Siskel and Roger Ebert have also criticized horror films, claiming that they often display and encourage misogynistic violence.

Explanations of misogyny have tended to be evolutionary, psychological, or cultural in character. Evolutionary theories have maintained that aggression has become a part of male sexuality because aggressive, power-seeking men are more likely to mate and produce offspring. Psychological theories, generally influenced by the thinking of Sigmund Freud, have traced misogyny to men's relationships with their mothers. In particular, it has been argued that boys need to distance themselves from their mothers in order to establish themselves as male. As a consequence, women have come to be perceived as threats to male identity. Cultural theories, such as feminist approaches, have argued that misogyny is a result of a culture of male power, or patriarchy, which requires that women be subordinated to men. From this point

Many people, particularly feminists, have charged that pornography is a manifestation of misogyny because of its crude disrespect for women. (AP/Wide World Photos)

of view, misogyny is similar to racial PREJUDICE, since it is the attitude of members of a dominant cultural group toward members of a dominated cultural group.

SUGGESTED READINGS. Andrea Dworkin's *Pornography: Men Possessing Women* (1989) presents a radical feminist interpretation of pornography as misogyny. *The Way Men Think* (1990), by Liam Hudson and Bernadine Jacot, argues that men bear permanent psychological wounds from the experience of breaking away from their mothers. Matt Ridley's *The Red Queen: Sex and the Evolution of Human Nature* (1993), holds that a tendency to be aggressive toward women has been instilled in men by Darwinian natural selection.—*Carl L. Bankston III*

Miss Saigon controversy (1990): Protest mounted by ASIAN AMERICAN actors, writers, and others against the employment of a white actor in the lead role of the New York production of the hit London musical *Miss Saigon*. The controversy prompted an industry inquiry into inequities faced by nonwhite American actors.

American theater history has a long tradition of white actors wearing "yellowface" makeup depicting stereotyped Asian characters. White actors applied yellow greasepaint to their faces, drew exaggerated "slanted" eyes, and dainty bee-stung lips, and delivered their lines with exaggerated Asian accents, emphasizing confusion between *l* and *r* consonants.

Miss Saigon, a modern musical adaptation of Giacomo Puccini's opera *Madama Butterfly* (1904) set in Southeast Asia during the Vietnam War, became a big hit when it was staged in London during the late 1980's. In 1990, when the play's British producer, Cameron Mackintosh, began planning a Broadway production of *Miss Saigon*, he found himself at the center of an angry debate because he planned to use his London star, Jonathan Pryce, in the lead role of the Eurasian "Engineer." Articulating the position of the Asian American theater community were playwright David Henry Hwang, actor B. D. Wong, and Tisa Chang, the artistic director of New York's Pan Asian Repertory Theatre.

Miss Saigon was charged with presenting deplorable images of both male and female Asians, depicting Asian women as exotic and sexually available and Asian men as obsequious and untrustworthy. Mackintosh countered that his production would employ thirty-four Asian American actors, but opponents of the production asked whether it was work worth having. Those who opposed Mackintosh also held that Asian Americans had been unfairly overlooked for leading roles for which they were ethnically appropriate, and that they objected to being relegated to the

Lea Salonga, the Filipina singer to whom Cameron Mackintosh gave the female lead in the New York production of Miss Saigon. *(Archive Photos/Saga/Frank Capri)*

chorus. Mackintosh defended his choice of Filipina newcomer Lea Salonga as Kim in the leading female role, pointing out that he had personally auditioned more than twelve hundred Asian American women for the role and had found none capable of handling its difficult singing requirements.

The male lead in *Miss Saigon* had gone to British film star Jonathan Pryce, who had created the role of the Eurasian "Engineer" for the British production. In Pryce's case, Mackintosh was forced to explain why it was acceptable for a European to play a Eurasian character. Pryce had also worn prosthetic latex eyepieces to give the appearance of epicanthic eyefolds. When told that these were offensively reminiscent of a century of yellowface characterizations, Pryce and Mackintosh agreed to remove them for the American production.

Despite the angry and protracted debate, Actors Equity Association, the professional actors' union, ultimately agreed to compromise in the name of creative freedom by allowing Mackintosh to choose his own cast. *Miss Saigon* went on to become one of the most commercially successful Broadway musicals of the late twentieth century. However, the controversy succeeded in focusing industry and public attention on issues of casting discrimination and the need for nonwhite actors to secure dignified work in the entertainment business.

SUGGESTED READINGS. Ronald Takaki's *Strangers from a Different Shore* (1989) provides a comprehensive overview of Asian populations emigrating to the United States. Philip Kan Gotanda's play *Yankee Dawg, You Die!* (1992) depicts the struggle of Asian American actors to confront prejudice. Edward Behr and Mark Steyn's *The Story of Miss Saigon* (1991) describes *Miss Saigon*'s creative process from its beginnings in 1986 through the 1990 controversy. —*Randy Barbara Kaplan*

Mommy track: Alternative career path for working mothers. In 1989 Felice N. Schwartz, the founder of Catalyst, an organization that works on career and leadership development of women, wrote in *Harvard Business Review* that half of all women who take MATERNITY LEAVE return to their jobs late or not at all. Because the resulting upsets in corporate personnel staffing and training programs can be expensive, Schwartz proposed that companies adopt two career tracks for women employees: a career-primary track and a career-and-family or "mommy track." She stressed the importance of employers' identifying career-primary women early so they can remove barriers to their advancement to the top. To do this, she suggested that companies identify career-primary women employees early; give them the same opportunities as men to develop and contribute to company profitability; accept them as valued members of management teams; recognize that the business environment is more difficult and stressful for women than it is for their male peers.

According to Schwartz, most women are career-and-family types, who want to pursue serious careers and participate actively in raising their children. High performing career-and-family women can be major players in their companies; however, Schwartz advised executives that they must plan for maternity leave, provide flexibility for these women to take time off, and take active roles in helping to make family supports and high-quality, affordable CHILD CARE available to all women employees.

Some of Schwartz's suggestions were immediately accepted as sensible; however, she did not explain how women should be identified and categorized or explain what might happen to women who decide to switch tracks. Nor did she address an implicit assumption be-

Felice Schwartz on the eve of her retirement from her research firm, Catalyst, in mid-1993. (AP/Wide World Photos)

hind her proposal that has caused an uproar: Namely, that it is always women who bear responsibility for their families, and that it is women who must choose between families and careers. Schwartz did not suggest that men should also choose one track or the other.

Schwartz's article prompted thousands of responses. *Business Week* announced that across the country, female managers and professionals with young families were leaving the fast track for the mommy track, although there was no proof of this. In her 1991 book *Backlash*, Susan FALUDI wrote that mommy track women were, in reality, a minority of women in the workplace. In 1984 a survey found more women preferring high-pressure jobs with advancement possibilities than low-pressure jobs without such possibilities. Another survey, in 1990, found that 70 percent of the women questioned regarded the mommy track as discriminatory and merely another excuse to pay women less than men.

Schwartz herself eventually changed her views on this subject and denied having ever supported the mommy track option; however, her revised views fell on deaf ears. The concept of the mommy track has continued to be touted as one of the most important management strategies of the twentieth century.

SUGGESTED READINGS. Susan Faludi's *Backlash* (1991) discusses the mommy track and other women's issues, particularly in relation to media portrayals. Felice Schwartz's "Management Women and the New Facts of Life," in *Harvard Business Review* (Jan.-Feb., 1989), explains her original conception of what has come to be known as the mommy track.—*Kate Peirce*

Morissette, Alanis (b. June 1, 1974, Ottawa, Canada): Canadian ALTERNATIVE MUSIC vocal artist. One of three children and a twin, Morissette, is the daughter of Hungarian parents who settled in Canada after the Soviet occupation of Hungary in 1956. At the age of eleven she began her entertainment career on the popular Canadian television program *You Can't Do That on Television.* She used the money she earned from television to finance her first single recording, "Fate Stay with Me," which sold two thousand copies. A Canadian music company that saw promise in her work produced her first albums, *Alanis* (1991) and *Now Is the Time* (1992).

Embarrassed by her early recordings, Morissette moved to Los Angeles in 1994 to begin her singing career anew. The result was the eclectic thirteen-song pop album *Jagged Little Pill* (1995). Containing songs

Alanis Morissette at a news conference in Ottawa in early 1996. (Reuters/Peter Jones/Archive Photos)

written by Morissette herself, this album stressed the theme of lost love. The following year the album earned Morissette four Grammy Awards.—*Jeri Kurtzleben*

Morning-after pill: Postcoital contraception medication. The so-called "morning-after pill" is technically not a single pill, but a dose of hormones taken to prevent pregnancy after unprotected sexual intercourse. Women who have had unprotected midcycle sexual intercourse may use birth control pills or high doses of estrogen or progestin to prevent pregnancy. The closer to the time of intercourse these drugs are taken, the more effective they are. Researchers believe that the hormone treatment affects the uterine (womb) lining so that developing embryos cannot implant. Nausea and vomiting are common side effects. In cases in which such treatments fail, the long-term effects on fetuses are unknown. (The French drug RU-486, sometimes called the "abortion pill," is one of several varieties of morning-after pills.)

Some groups have objected to postcoital contraception on moral grounds because they regard it as equivalent to ABORTION. Others believe that this option

should be offered to all women who have been subject to RAPE. Some women have had limited access to postcoital contraception because of lack of money, transportation, access to health care, or knowledge of its availability.—*Rebecca Lovell Scott*

Mossop v. Attorney General of Canada (1993): Canadian litigation involving the rights of gay couples. By a 4-3 vote the Supreme Court of Canada dismissed a plaintiff's claim that an employer's denial of a day of bereavement leave to attend the funeral of his intimate partner's father constituted discrimination on the basis of "family status," in contravention of the CANADIAN HUMAN RIGHTS ACT. The court did, however, imply that a finding of wrongful DISCRIMINATION might have been made if the plaintiff had instead filed his suit citing provisions of the CANADIAN CHARTER OF RIGHTS AND FREEDOMS.—*Christopher E. Kent*

Mothers Against Drunk Driving (MADD): Nonprofit victim advocacy organization established in 1980 by Candy Lightner, a California mother whose thirteen-year-old daughter had been killed by a hit-and-run drunk driver. During its first two decades this grassroots organization evolved into a highly visible and proactive agency with more than six hundred American chapters and affiliates in Canada, Great Britain, Australia, and New Zealand. Despite its name, MADD counts male and female members of all ages among its ranks. The only requirement for membership is a commitment to stopping drunk driving and supporting the victims of this violent crime.

After its formation, MADD played leading roles in the passage of more than 2,300 drunk-driving laws at the federal, state, and local levels. Among the best known of these efforts was passage of a national minimum age drinking law in 1984 and the "zero tolerance" provision of the National Highway Systems Law. This provision, passed in 1995, made it illegal for all persons under the age of twenty-one to drive with any measurable amount of alcohol in their systems.

In seeking support for tougher drunk-driving legislation, demanding equitable treatment for victims, and creating public awareness of the necessity of eliminating the lethal combination of drinking and driving, MADD has challenged popular notions that drunk-driving mishaps are merely "accidents" for which offenders should not be held accountable. MADD has worked to develop a public perception of drunk driv-

Candy Lightner (left), the founder of MADD, with U.S. senator Richard Lugar and Transportation Secretary Elizabeth Dole joined together in 1983 to call for a national drinking age of twenty-one. (AP/Wide World Photos)

ing as a violent crime that results from voluntarily choosing to consume alcohol and choosing to get behind the wheel of a motor vehicle. MADD has therefore urged drinkers of legal age to designate nondrinkers to be responsible for driving them after they drink.

MADD's support for victims has included crisis intervention when families lose loved ones, assistance during the grieving process, and guidance through the criminal justice system by trained MADD victim advocates. The organization has also provided information, publications, and referrals. A unique aspect of MADD victim advocacy was the development of the "V.I.P." or "Victim Impact Panel," in which DWI (driving while intoxicated) survivors tell their stories of loss to offenders who have been ordered by judges to attend the panels as part of their sentencing.

MADD has also sponsored a National Candlelight Vigil of Remembrance and Hope every December to commemorate DWI victims, honor their loved ones, and educate the public about the necessity of stopping drunk driving. The magnitude of the problem can be seen in the statistics: According to the National High-

way Traffic Safety Administration, two of every five Americans will be involved in an alcohol-related crash some time in their lives. Although MADD has been instrumental in lowering the numbers of deaths and injuries from drunk driving crashes, DWI remains the most commonly committed violent crime in the United States, an indication of the laxity with which intoxicated driving has continued to be perceived.

SUGGESTED READINGS. Earl A. Grollman's Straight *Talk About Death for Teenagers* (1993) presents strategies for adolescents experiencing the grieving process. Rabbi Harold S. Kushner's popular *When Bad Things Happen to Good People* (1981) posits a philosophy for interpreting the nature of suffering. *Color of Justice* (1990), by Brian Ogawa, describes the impact of violent crime on ethnically diverse populations.
—*Randy Barbara Kaplan*

Mothers of East L.A.-Santa Isabel (MELA-SI): Southern California community support organization. Formed in May, 1984, MELA-SI was organized solely to fight construction of a state prison in the Boyle Heights district of EAST LOS ANGELES. After Roman Catholic parish, school, and neighborhood watch groups within the community rallied behind this cause, MELA-SI filed a suit that forced the state to adhere strictly to imposed guidelines concerning the project.

After achieving that victory, MELA-SI began involving itself in battles with corporations, government officials, and others who have threatened communities in CALIFORNIA. It has sponsored programs such as GRAFFITI abatement, hiring local students to paint over graffiti-ridden walls in East Los Angeles. It has also hired students to canvas East Los Angeles neighborhoods to educate residents about lead-poisoning dangers within their homes. MELA-SI's neighborhood beautification program has brought together community groups, local politicians, and officers of the city police department to clean streets, cut trees, and trim weeds. Other MELA-SI sponsored programs have included water conservation and child immunization programs.

In 1994 MELA-SI established a scholarship fund that awarded 110 needy students more than $60,000 in scholarship money during its first three years. MELA-SI has also been dedicated to bolstering and empowering communities through knowledge and understanding of economic, environmental, political, and social issues.—*Andrea E. Miller*

Mount Pleasant riots (1991): Civil disturbances in the WASHINGTON, D.C., area involving conflicts between African Americans and Latinos. In May, 1991, tensions fueled largely by economic competition between African American and Latino residents of the Washington suburb of Mount Pleasant exploded into violence after a black policewoman shot a Latino man who had been arrested for drunkenness. Widespread fighting between members of the two ethnic groups erupted. After the mayor of Washington ordered police to exercise restraint, many police officers simply stood by as rioters looted and committed arson. Despite complaints about police passivity, no one was killed in the disturbances, and only twelve injuries were reported. However, property damage caused by the riots exceeded two million dollars. —*Alexander Scott*

Mukherjee, Bharati (b. July 27, 1940, Calcutta, India): Teacher and novelist. Born into a Bengali Brahmin family, Mukherjee was educated in Calcutta. After receiving a master's degree from the University of Baroda, she came to the United States to attend a writing work-shop at the University of Iowa, where she earned an M.F.A. degree in 1963. That same year she married an American writer of Canadian descent with whom she moved to Canada in 1966. She taught at McGill University and earned a Ph.D. degree in English and comparative literature from the University of Iowa. In 1972 she became a Canadian citizen. Eight years later she returned to the United States and became a permanent resident.

While teaching at various institutions, Mukherjee began publishing fiction. The characters in her books are often educated emigrants from India. Her first novel, *The Tiger's Daughter* (1971), recounts the culture shock of a Calcutta-born woman returning to India after several years as a student in the United States. In *Darkness* (1985), a collection of stories, Mukherjee paints a bleak picture of racism in Canada. *The Middleman and Other Stories* (1988), which established Mukherjee as a major author, celebrates immigrant life in the United States. With her Canadian-born husband Clark Blaise, Mukherjee co-authored *Days and Nights*

Publication of Jasmine *earned Bharati Mukherjee a National Book Critics Circle Award for Fiction in 1989.* (Tom Victor)

in Calcutta (1977) and *The Sorrow and the Terror: The Haunting Legacy of the Air India Tragedy* (1987), both nonfiction. Her other books include the novels *Wife* (1975), *Jasmine* (1989), and *The Holder of the World* (1993).—*Edward A. Malone*

Multiculturalism Act (1988): Canadian federal law. Enacted by parliament in July, 1988, this act was designed to promote a policy of MULTICULTURALISM throughout Canada by combatting RACISM and DISCRIMINATION based on race and culture.

Canada officially embarked on a policy of multiculturalism in 1971 at the suggestion of the federal government's Royal Commission on Bilingualism and Biculturalism. The Multiculturalism Act was intended to ensure all Canadians the freedom to promote and pursue their individual cultural heritages. The law's intent to introduce multiculturalism into every aspect of Canadian life and culture has made Canada the world's first officially multicultural society. Canada is the only nation fully to embrace a policy of multiculturalism on the federal level. The provisions of the Multiculturalism Act are mandatory for all departments of the Canadian government, and its implementation is overseen by Canada's secretary of state.

Changes in the ethnic composition of Canada's peoples moved Canada toward its multicultural policy. The country's population became significantly more ethnically diverse after World War II. In response to this change, Canada's political policy has evolved to provide freedom and safety for all ethnic and minority groups. The legislative actions most strongly demonstrating Canada's commitment to multiculturalism have been the CANADIAN CHARTER OF RIGHTS AND FREEDOMS (1982), the EMPLOYMENT EQUITY ACT OF 1986, and the Multiculturalism Act. In 1991 the federal government formed a department of Multiculturalism and Citizenship.

Canada's policy of multiculturalism allows Canadians of all ethnic backgrounds full representation while enabling government and private institutions to enact nondiscriminatory policies. The Multiculturalism Act guarantees all Canadians the full rights and privileges of citizenship, while outlawing the denial of rights to members of any ethnic or minority groups. The law requires federal government departments to promote understanding and respect for all ethnic or minority groups.

Some aspects of the Multiculturalism Act have been controversial. Although most of its provisions have been accepted by a majority of Canadians, many Canadians have expressed concerns that the act endangers national unity by promoting ethnic divisions instead of union. Other critics have charged

The Multiculturalism Act was written to enable all Canadians, such as these members of Toronto's Chinese community, to preserve their traditional cultures while enjoying their full rights as citizens. (Dick Hemingway)

that the policy has not helped to solve problems of racism or provided a national identity for Canada's citizens. Despite such criticisms, many people have called Canada a "role model" for the world because it is leading the way to a national society that values and protects the rights of all its peoples.

SUGGESTED READINGS. *Being and Becoming Canada* (1995), edited by Charles F. Doran and Ellen R. Babby, is an informative source on multiculturalism in Canada. J. W. Berry and J. A. Laponce provide deeper research findings on Canadian culture in *Ethnicity and Culture in Canada: The Research Landscape* (1994). *Multiculturalism in Canada* (1988), by Jean R. Burnet, gives good background information on Canada's policy of multiculturalism.—*Kimberley H. Kidd*

Museum of Tolerance: Educational center in LOS ANGELES, California, that opened in 1993. Dedicated to exploring issues of intolerance arising in contemporary, daily life, and HOLOCAUST history and interpretations, the museum is a branch of the Simon Wiesenthal Center, a Jewish human rights organization. The museum's 165,000 square-foot complex houses several permanent exhibitions: the Tolerancenter and Holocaust Section, and the Multimedia Learning Center. The latter contains interactive computer workstations that offer access to some five thousand subjects related to the museum's themes. Video testimony, photography, and archival information can be accessed immediately via touch-screen technology. In addition to these permanent installations, the museum has an exhibit area for the museum's archives, an exhibit gallery, an auditorium, and a theater. These facilities have presented special exhibitions on a variety of tolerance and Holocaust-related issues, as well as films and lectures. The museum has received national and international acclaim and has been well attended.—*Sheila Golburgh Johnson*

Mutual assistance associations (MAA): Organizations of Southeast Asian REFUGEES living in the United States who help fellow refugees adapt to American life. An MAA is a type of mutual aid society, an association formed by members of an ethnic or racial group to provide economic and social support to group members. MUTUAL AID SOCIETIES AND ORGANIZATIONS have a long history in the United States. Many immigrant groups that arrived in the nineteenth century formed societies to provide one another with loans, to share information and skills, and to maintain a sense of cultural identity. After the Civil War African Americans were

especially active in creating their own mutual aid societies. Modern immigrants to the United States have continued the tradition of maintaining mutual aid societies such as rotating credit associations, which pool funds to make capital for starting businesses available to ethnic group members. MAAs, however, have been unique among mutual aid societies because they have received U.S. government recognition and financial support.

Origins of Mutual Assistance Associations. When the first major waves of Southeast Asian refugees—who were overwhelmingly Vietnamese—began arriving in the United States in the spring of 1975, they initially had little direct involvement in their own resettlement. The federal government placed them in refugee camps in California, Arkansas, Florida, and Pennsylvania, and later relocated them in communities where American families, religious organizations, or community agencies had agreed to act as their sponsors. Responsibility for receiving and resettling the refugees was in the hands of a number of voluntary agencies, including the U.S. Catholic Conference, the American Council for Nationalities Service, Episcopal Migration Ministries, and the International Rescue Committee.

As increasing numbers of Vietnamese, Laotians, and Cambodians settled in the United States in the late 1970's, the earlier arrivals began forming societies to help their newly arriving compatriots. Many of the voluntary agencies encouraged this form of self-help. By 1980 Southeast Asians in the United States had formed an estimated 260 mutual aid associations. These associations were usually led by previously arrived refugees who had become fluent in English. Their ability to find jobs for new arrivals and help them deal with American institutions helped Southeast Asians deal with what was to them the largely alien world of American society.

The U.S. Congress' passage of the REFUGEE ACT OF 1980 laid a foundation for a system of government-subsidized self-help organizations for refugees. Among its provisions, the Refugee Act established funds for programs and services that served refugees. It also created the Office of Refugee Resettlement, which became the primary government agency through which these funds were distributed to the state governments, which administered the money. A later piece of legislation, the Refugee Extension Act of 1986, established that the amount of financial support to the MAAs of each state would be based on the states' refugee populations during the three years preceding the year of funding.

California and Texas, with the largest refugee populations in the United States, have therefore received the largest amounts of federal money for MAAs. Associations have also received money from a variety of other sources, including private donations.

From the early 1980's to the mid-1990's Southeast Asians created more than a thousand MAAs throughout the United States. Some of these have become major community organizations, with annual budgets exceeding a million dollars. Some of the largest and best-known MAAs are the United Cambodian Community in Long Beach, California; the Indochinese Mutual Assistance Association in San Diego, California; the Lao Family Community in Stockton, California; the Vietnamese Community of Orange County, California; the Vietnamese American Civic Association of Boston, Massachusetts; and the Hmong Council in Fresno, California.

Nature and Services of MAAs. In order to be recognized by the U.S. government and to be eligible for grants, MAAs must be incorporated as nonprofit organizations, and at least 51 percent of the members of their boards of directors must themselves be former refugees. Moreover, the primary goal of the associations must be to promote economic self-sufficiency among refugees so that they can eventually live in the United States without public assistance.

Among the services that MAAs have most often offered to their communities have been help in finding employment; ENGLISH AS A SECOND LANGUAGE PROGRAMS, training in everyday skills, such as driving cars; programs to pass their native cultures and languages along to their American-born children; legal help; interpretation and translation; services for seniors; and family reunification assistance. As leaders of the associations have become naturalized American citizens and learned about American political processes, the MAAs have also become increasingly active politically, lobbying elected officials on issues of interest to Southeast Asians and forming advocacy and political action groups.

The associations have also maintained a nationwide network in order to support one another and to exchange information. The SOUTHEAST ASIA RESOURCE ACTION CENTER in Washington, D.C. (formerly known as the Indochinese Refugee Action Center) has coordinated activities among them. In 1991, MAA leaders from around the country gathered in Washington, D.C., at the invitation of the Office of Refugee Resettlement, to meet with representatives from voluntary agencies and state governments and to discuss improving the coordination of activities at the national level.

SUGGESTED READINGS. *Self-help in Urban America* (1980), edited by Scott Cummings, offers general information on mutual aid societies. *The Vietnamese Experience in America* (1992), by Paul James Rutledge, is a short but thorough and well-written overview of Vietnamese settlement in the United States containing useful information on the role of MAAs. Another book by Rutledge, *The Role of Religion in Ethnic Self-Identity: A Vietnamese Community* (1985), examines Vietnamese religion and religious organizations, some of which are MAAs. *Growing Up American: The Adaptation of Vietnamese Children to American Society* (1998), by Min Zhou and Carl L. Bankston III, looks at how Vietnamese communities and community organizations such as MAAs have affected the lives of young Vietnamese Americans. *Southeast Asian-American Communities* (1992), edited by Kali Tal, offers views of refugee communities and their organizations around the United States. Readers interested in modern Hmong communities and self-help among Hmong in the United States will find an introduction in Spencer Sherman's illustrated article, "The Hmong in America: Laotian Refugees in the 'Land of the Giants,'" *National Geographic Magazine* (Oct., 1988).—*Carl L. Bankston III*

N

Natchez Revolt (1729): Uprising of the Natchez people against the French government in colonial Louisiana. The last remnants of the Mississippi valley's Temple Mound Building Culture, the Natchez people revolted against the French after Louisiana governor Sieur Chepart ordered them to leave their main settlement in order to make room for a plantation site. In the autumn of 1729 the Natchez attacked the French at Fort Rosalie and other sites along the Mississippi River. They killed about 250 French soldiers and took about three hundred others prisoner. The prisoners included Governor Chepart, who was clubbed to death by a person of the lowest caste—known as Stinkards—because Natchez warriors refused to defile their weapons with his blood. The Yazoos joined the Natchez, killing a French missionary and an entire French garrison.

The French retaliated by sending two invasion forces from New Orleans into Natchez territory. After shattering the tribe, The French sold many Natchez into slavery and resettled others among neighboring tribes. A few Natchez warriors remained in hiding and continued fighting against the French.—*Karan Ann Berryman*

National Abortion and Reproductive Rights Action League (NARAL): REPRODUCTIVE RIGHTS advocacy organization started in 1969. Also known as the National Association for the Repeal of Abortion Laws, NARAL has worked for pro-choice political candidates and pro-choice legislation in order to ensure full reproductive rights for women. With more than 500,000 members across the United States, the organization ranked as one of the three most effective lobbying groups in Washington, D.C., in 1993. NARAL has also worked to promote responsible attitudes among men and women regarding contraception, pregnancy, childbirth, and ABORTION.

The league comprises three organizations: NARAL, Inc., NARAL-PAC, and the NARAL Foundation. NARAL, Inc., is a nonprofit organization that works through the political system to secure reproductive health policies and reproductive choice for all Americans. NARAL-PAC is a political action committee that mounts campaigns to elect pro-choice political candidates, oppose anti-choice candidates, and encourage voter registration and participation. The NARAL Foundation, founded in 1977, is a charitable organization that supports research and legal work and provides leadership training for activists across the United States.—*Mark Miller*

National Alliance of Spanish-Speaking People for Equality (NASSPE): Organization for professional journalists and others of Hispanic descent working in mass media. Founded in 1970, the NASSPE operates only in the United States. One of its main tasks has been to gather and distribute information on topics of interest to the Hispanic community, such as housing, health, education, IMMIGRATION LEGISLATION, and U.S. foreign policy in Central America. The NASSPE has also worked as an advocacy organization by publicizing the views of Hispanic communities through a network that it has built linking Hispanic organizations with government officials. Other tasks of this organization have included conducting lectures and maintaining a speakers' bureau.

The NASSPE is affiliated with the CONGRESSIONAL HISPANIC CAUCUS, the Consortium of National Hispanic Organizations, and the NATIONAL COUNCIL OF LA RAZA. Its headquarters are located in Washington, D.C.—*Margaret L. Morris*

National Asian American Telecommunications Association (NAATA): Media organization founded in 1980. Formed with the aid of a grant from the Corporation for Public Broadcasting, the NAATA is a nonprofit, tax-exempt body within the National Minority Public Broadcasting Consortia. The consortia was created to provide the Public Broadcasting System (PBS) with culturally sensitive programming; as its Asian American component, the NAATA acquires, packages, and distributes television and radio programs reflecting the Asian American experience.

The NAATA has helped to develop such PBS television programs as *Who Killed Vincent Chin?* (1989) and the Academy Award-winning *Days of Waiting* (1989). From 1983 to 1987 the NAATA produced the PBS series *Silk Screen*. The organization has also produced radio programs aired by National Public Radio and community-based radio stations; these have included *Bamboo Radio* and *CrossCurrent*. CrossCurrent Media, the NAATA's nonbroadcast distribution service, distributes Asian American films, videos, and audio cassettes to libraries and schools. Its quarterly publication, *Network*, covers the Asian American media.—*Christopher E. Kent*

National Association for the Advancement of Colored People (NAACP): Civil rights organization founded in 1910. During the 1950's and 1960's the NAACP was one of the most influential organizations struggling against racial segregation and discrimination. After the CIVIL RIGHTS MOVEMENT had crested with the end of legal SEGREGATION in the United States, however, questions were raised about the future relevance of the NAACP. From the 1970's through the 1990's, the organization saw a gradual decrease in its membership.

Myrlie Evers-Williams talks to the media after her election to the chairpersonship of the NAACP in early 1995. (AP/Wide World Photos)

Decreasing membership—which also meant decreasing funds—became more complicated during the 1990's when the leadership of the NAACP was beset by a series of organizational conflicts and scandals. The problems began in 1992, when Benjamin L. Hooks announced his resignation as the organization's executive director. A battle for leadership followed. The Reverend Jesse JACKSON was one of the persons most frequently named as a possible successor to Hooks, but Jackson also faced such strong opposition from within the NAACP that he withdrew his candidacy in April, 1993. That same month, the organization named the Reverend Benjamin CHAVIS its new executive director.

A scandal broke out in 1994, when it was revealed that Chavis, without the knowledge of the NAACP's board of directors, had committed the NAACP to paying more than $332,000 to a former employee who had threatened to sue him for SEXUAL HARASSMENT. In August, 1994, the NAACP's board voted to dismiss Chavis. Chavis, in turn, filed a legal suit for reinstatement. Examination of the NAACP's financial records at this time showed that the association was in a dangerous situation. It had already been operating at a loss when Hooks resigned, and afterward its finances had deteriorated even more. By the end of 1994 the organization was having trouble paying its staff and obtaining credit.

Journalist Carl Rowan and other persons concerned about the survival of the NAACP accused William F. Gibson, the chairman of the NAACP board, of mismanaging funds and of misusing money to pay for his own travel and other personal expenses. Although Gibson denied any wrong-doing, the association ended the year 1994 in serious difficulty, with insufficient funds, two public scandals, no executive director, and a board chairman under attack.

The NAACP's fortunes began improving in 1995. In February the board of directors voted to replace Gibson as its chairperson with Myrlie EVERS-WILLIAMS, widow of civil rights martyr Medgar EVERS. Ten months later, the board elected Kweisi MFUME, a respected Democratic congressman from Maryland, as its new director. Mfume issued calls for unity within the NAACP, for membership and donation drives, and for renewing the organization's commitment to improving the lives of African Americans. At an annual meeting held in New York City, NAACP members expressed optimism about the future of the association, and Mfume promised delegates that the organization would never again find itself near financial ruin.

SUGGESTED READINGS. Jack Greenberg's *Crusaders in the Courts: How a Dedicated Band of Lawyers Fought for the Civil Rights Revolution* (1994) tells the story of NAACP lawyers in the Civil Rights movement era. Kweisi Mfume's *No Free Ride: From the Mean Streets to the Mainstream* (1996) is the autobiography of the statesman who became head of the NAACP. Richette L. Haywood's article, "Can Kweisi Mfume Turn the NAACP Around?," in *Ebony* (Jan. 1, 1997) examines the problems facing the NAACP when Mfume became executive director.—*Carl L. Bankston III*
(updates original entry; vol. 5, p. 1231)

National Association of Female Executives (NAFE): The largest business women's association in the United States, NAFE has provided the resources and services—through education, networking, and public advocacy—to empower its members to achieve career success and financial security. Since its founding in 1972, NAFE has served as a leading authority on issues and trends affecting women in business. By the mid-1990's NAFE claimed nearly 200,000 members in the United States and abroad.

Arguing that the strongest marketplace is one in which all participants compete on an equal basis for the rewards of the system, NAFE has promoted what it has called the seven Principles of Workplace Equity to guarantee maximum opportunity for all working

While images of multiethnic businessmen have begun to proliferate, images of women executives have not kept pace—a situation that NAFE has worked to change. (Unicorn Stock Photos/Tom McCarthy)

women. NAFE also publishes a bimonthly magazine, *Executive Female*, with more than 600,000 readers. In 1986 NAFE established the NAFE's Women's Foundation, a nonprofit division created to enhance the lives, career aspirations, and self-esteem of American women and girls.—*Bryan Aubrey*

National Association of Hispanic Journalists (NAHJ): Professional journalism organization. Established in April, 1984, NAHJ is dedicated to the recognition and professional advancement of Hispanics in the news industry. NAHJ is a nonprofit organization governed by a sixteen-member board of directors consisting of executive officers and regional directors who represent geographic areas of the United States and the Caribbean. The national office is located in Washington, D.C. The organization has helped create a national voice and unified vision for all Hispanic journalists.

By the mid-1990's NAHJ had approximately 1,700 members, including working journalists, journalism students, other media-related professionals, and academic scholars. NAHJ's annual convention features a job fair and several workshops and panel discussions regarding Hispanic issues and the image of Hispanics in the media. NAHJ has helped advance employment opportunities and career development for Hispanics in the news media by providing a job exchange program that matches members with internship opportunities, professional fellowships, teaching positions, and other print, broadcast, and radio opportunities.—*Lorenzo Chavez*

National Association of Hispanic Publications (NAHP): Nonprofit industry organization. Since its founding in 1982, the NAHP's mission has been to promote the professional development of Hispanic print media. The association's membership comprises daily, weekly, biweekly, and monthly newspapers and magazines. Most NAHP members have published only in Spanish; some have published in bilingual publications. The NAHP has helped its members attain professional standards by providing technical assistance in areas such as writing and editing, circulation methods, advertising, financing, design, layout, and printing, as well as in meeting the public service role of the newspaper industry.

In 1989 the NAHP conducted, through the support of Philip Morris Companies, the first voter registration campaign expressly designed for Spanish language media. This campaign was carried in Hispanic newspapers and magazines and reached more than seven million readers. In 1990 the NAHP had two ongoing programs: the Census Awareness Campaign, "Hagase Contar," sponsored by Philip Morris Companies, and the Dropout Prevention Program, "Tu Educacion: Nuestra Esperanza," sponsored by the Coca-Cola Company.—*Bryan Aubrey*

National Association of Latino Elected and Appointed Officials Education Fund (NALEO): Hispanic advocacy group. Established in 1981, the NALEO Educational Fund is a nonprofit organization governed by a seven-member board of directors. The fund has promoted the participation of Latinos in American civic life by developing and implementing programs that integrate Latino immigrants into American society, develop future leaders among Latino youth, provide assistance and training to Latino elected officials, and conduct research on issues important to the Latino population.

The fund's civic action activities have included the organization's flagship U.S. Citizenship Program, Youth Leadership Initiative, and Training and Technical Assistance Program. NALEO has published a national directory of Latino elected officials and a statistical guide, which provides both historical and current data on the numbers of Latino elected officials

Evidence of the growing electoral clout of Latinos came in 1991, when Gloria Molina became the first Hispanic elected a supervisor in Los Angeles County in more than a century. (AP/Wide World Photos)

by state, level of government, and gender and an analysis of political and social trends affecting Latino electoral gains.—*Lorenzo Chavez*

National Association of Media Women (NAMW): Professional media organization founded in 1965. Formed during the early years of the modern WOMEN'S RIGHTS MOVEMENT, the NAMW set its mission as promoting employment and advancement opportunities for women in the mass media. The organization has provided a forum for the exchange of ideas and experiences among its members, it has funded research and conferences focusing on issues concerning women in the media, and it has sought to create professional opportunities for its members. The NAMW has also awarded scholarships to women pursuing schooling or specialized training in mass communications and has presented Media Women of the Year awards at its annual conferences. In 1995 fourteen local groups were affiliated with the national organization. The NAMW also publishes an annual journal, *Media Women.*—*Alexander Scott*

National Black Women's Political Leadership Caucus (NBWPLC): African American women's organization. Founded in 1971, the NBWPLC has had as its primary goal advancing black women in the political and economic system of the United States by helping them work toward equality and increase their understanding of political processes. The caucus helps women to learn the functions of city, state, and federal government. It has also been involved in research, particularly in the areas of African American families, politics, and economics.

Other services provided by the organization have included public speaking training; legislative federal, state, and local workshops; children's services; charitable programs; awards for humanitarianism; and placement services. The organization publishes a semiannual newsletter and has published election tabloids. The NBWPLC is based in Washington, D.C., with branches in thirty-three states. Its auxiliary membership includes men, OLDER AMERICANS, and youths.
—*Alexander Scott*

National Center for Lesbian Rights (NCLR): National resource center and civil rights and advocacy group

Although the National Center for Lesbian Rights was founded to help protect the civil rights of lesbians, the organization has also worked to safeguard the rights of gay men and bisexuals. (James L. Shaffer)

founded in 1977 and based in SAN FRANCISCO, California. Originally known as the Lesbian Rights Project, the NCLR has worked to end discrimination and ensure civil rights for LESBIANS through litigation, policy advocacy, education, and resource and referral services. Family law, the rights of lesbians of color, lesbian immigration rights, and lesbian, gay, bisexual, and transgender youth rights are areas of particular concern to the organization.

A controversial issue concerning lesbians that has stirred significant national debate has been their CHILD CUSTODY AND VISITATION RIGHTS after divorce. Because of their sexual orientation, lesbian mothers have often risked losing custody of their own children when their cases have been taken to court. The NCLR has been involved in litigation and judicial education in this area. NCLR has fought to protect the custody rights of lesbian mothers through representation in court, and has provided legal referrals of attorneys across the country who would assist in these and other civil rights cases.—*Stephanie Brzuzy*

National Chicano Health Organization (NCHO): Professional development and training organization. Founded in the early 1970's by Chicano medical students, the NCHO has sought to increase Chicano representation in medical school enrollments and in the health care professions. The group has asserted a linkage between a lack of Chicano health-care workers and the poor health standards and high levels of INFANT MORTALITY in Chicano BARRIOS. The organization has sponsored recruitment and preparatory programs for high school and college students and has provided financial assistance to needy students.—*Christopher E. Kent*

National Chicano Moratorium on Vietnam: Series of militant Mexican American protests against the VIETNAM WAR around 1970. Angered by the fact that 20 percent of U.S. battlefield deaths during the Vietnam War were Mexican American troops, the BROWN BERETS, in association with other Chicano activists, formed the National Chicano Moratorium Committee. Their organized protests throughout the Southwest drew thousands of demonstrators. The short-lived movement reached its climax in a national moratorium march organized in LOS ANGELES on August 29, 1970.

On that day more than 20,000 marchers assembled in EAST LOS ANGELES, while sheriff's deputies lined the demonstration route. After the march concluded, the activists prepared to relax in nearby Laguna Park.

On the pretext of a minor incident at a liquor store, five hundred police stormed the park, trampling spectators and clubbing those who got in their way. Four hundred people were arrested, including Corky GONZÁLES, and a prominent journalist, Rubén Salazar, was killed by a tear gas canister after police occupied the park. Three additional marches undertaken through early 1971 were crushed by police repression. —*Douglas W. Richmond*

National Chinese Welfare Council: Coalition of CHINESE AMERICAN organizations working for immigration reform that was formed in 1957. After much discussion and negotiation among the Chinese Consolidated Benevolent Associations of major American cities, the council became an official nonprofit organization in March, 1958. The council has ten district chapters and maintains its headquarters in New York City. Every two years the chapters hold a national conference in a different city.

The council's purpose has been to unite and foster cooperation among people of Chinese descent living in the United States. Members strive to improve the political condition of Chinese Americans, to achieve political equality, and to increase federal government immigration quotas for Chinese. They also seek to work together to solve their own problems and to maintain Chinese traditions and ethics while being loyal American citizens. The organization has also advocated continued American support for the Nationalist Chinese regime on Taiwan.—*George C. Y. Wang*

National Civil Rights Museum: Memphis, Tennessee, memorial. Opened in September, 1991, this institution is located at Memphis' Lorraine Motel, where Martin Luther KING, Jr., was assassinated on April 4, 1968. The museum contains the oldest and most comprehensive overview of the CIVIL RIGHTS MOVEMENT in exhibit form. Its purpose has been to instill in its visitors an appreciation of the history of the U.S. civil rights struggle and its important events and personalities. In addition to its exhibits, the museum has housed an auditorium, a courtyard for dramatic presentations, a changing gallery, a gift shop, and administrative offices. Throughout the year, the museum has offered such ongoing special projects as the Conference on Freedom, an annual two-day symposium held in September; Youth-in-Unity, a Fourth of July event featuring activities, entertainment, and educational seminars for children; live interpretations; and educational seminars.—*Bryan Aubrey*

Jesse Jackson and Rosa Parks converse at the dedication of the National Civil Rights Museum in 1991. Jackson was with Martin Luther King, Jr., when the latter was assassinated at the site twenty-three years earlier. (AP/Wide World Photos)

National Coalition Against Domestic Violence (NCADV): Nonprofit antiviolence organization established in 1978 and based in Denver, Colorado. Dedicated to ending DOMESTIC VIOLENCE directed against women and children, the NCADV has provided a national network for state and local programs helping BATTERED WOMEN and their children. The organization has also provided community awareness campaigns and published literature on the issue of domestic violence. In addition to providing general information and referrals, the NCADV has sponsored national conferences for battered women and their supporters every two years.

The month of October is Domestic Violence Awareness Month and the NCADV has developed a national registry of women killed by domestic violence. Every year the organization releases a new poster listing the names of victims gathered from the previous year. —*Mark Miller*

National Coalition for Haitian Rights (NCHR): HAITIAN AMERICAN rights organization. Founded in 1982 as the National Coalition for Haitian Refugees, the NCHR has worked to promote the rights of Haitian REFUGEES and Haitian Americans under U.S. and international law. Its work has contributed to passage of reforms in IMMIGRATION LEGISLATION that allowed more than 40,000 Haitians to secure legal residency. The NCHR also assisted in the release of nearly three hundred Haitians seeking asylum in the United States after they had been held at the U.S. naval station at Guantánamo Bay, Cuba, for almost twenty months.

The NCHR has also advocated human rights reforms and development of democracy in Haiti. Toward this end, it has focused on strengthening Haitian civil society, training and deploying the Haitian National Police, and reforming Haiti's corrupt judicial system.

In 1995 the NCHR established a community action program that led to formation of the Haitian American Community Action Network. The network's goals have included development of a national movement that will incorporate civil rights promotion and education, as well as gaining a stronger voice in public

Haitians who had hoped to find refuge in the United States are returned to their impoverished homeland in 1992 in a U.S. government effort to repatriate more than twelve thousand detained at the government's Guantanamo Naval Base in Cuba. (AP/Wide World Photos)

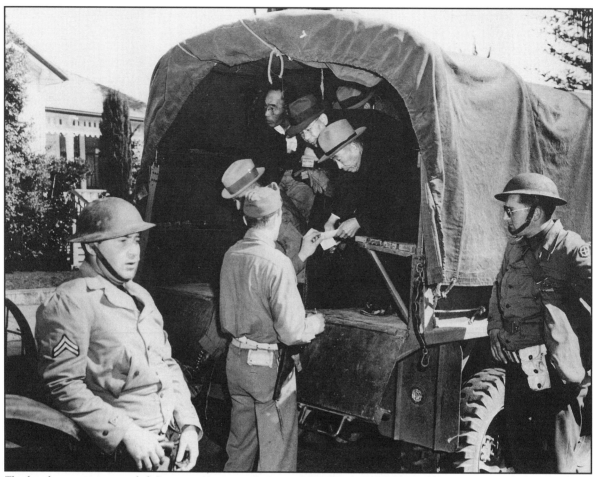

The harsh treatment accorded Japanese Americans living on the West Coast when the U.S. government rounded them up for internment in 1942 is among the grievances for which they later sought redress. (AP/Wide World Photos)

policy-making in the United States. In October, 1996, the NCHR held a national meeting to find a means of building up this network. During the following February, the network itself held a town meeting in Brooklyn, New York, that was aired on a local radio station, reaching thousands in the New York City area. —*Andrea E. Miller*

National Coalition for Redress/Reparations (NCRR): Advocacy group founded in 1980. The NCRR was one of three principal organizations that fought for U.S. government recognition of the injustices of its JAPANESE AMERICAN INTERNMENT policy during World War II. Formed in LOS ANGELES from a variety of Japanese American community groups, the NCRR sought to prod the JAPANESE AMERICAN CITIZENS LEAGUE (JACL) into taking action on the redress issue. NCRR leaders attempted to form a united front with leaders of the JACL and the NATIONAL COUNCIL FOR JAPANESE AMERICAN REDRESS (NCJAR), but organizational differences hindered cooperation among the groups.

In 1987 the NCRR mobilized a delegation to lobby the U.S. Congress for passage of a redress bill. The House of Representatives passed the bill in September, 1987, and the Senate on April 20, 1988. On August 10, 1988, President Ronald Reagan signed the bill into law. The NCRR subsequently continued to work to ensure payment of redress appropriations. In 1990 the organization was renamed Nikkei for Civil Rights and Redress.—*Christopher E. Kent*

National Conference of Puerto Rican Women (NCPRW): Puerto Rican advocacy group founded in 1972. Headquartered in WASHINGTON, D.C., the NCPRW has seventeen state affiliates and a membership of more than three thousand persons. The organization has worked to promote participation of Puerto Rican and other Latina women in U.S. and Puerto Rican political, economic, and social life; it has also lobbied for equal rights for women in concert with other civil rights organizations. NCPRW publications have included books, speeches, and articles, as well as *Ecos Nacionales*, a triennial newsletter devoted to the concerns of Puerto Rican and other Latina women.—*Glenn Canyon*

National Congress for Puerto Rican Rights (NCPRR): Civil Rights organization founded in New York City's Bronx borough in 1981. The largest volunteer organization of its kind in the United States, the NCPRR has been dedicated to ending discrimination and securing equality for PUERTO RICANS. It has been best known for its local and national campaigns against ENVIRONMENTAL RACISM and racially motivated violence. The group has educated both its own members and the public at large on conditions affecting the Puerto Rican and Latino communities and has offered suggestions for improving

the communities. The NCPRR's four main chapters are located in New York City, Boston, Philadelphia, and San Francisco.

The organization has focused particularly on developing new leadership, concentrating its efforts on women and youths. As with many civil rights organizations, the NCPRR has also worked with elected officials, informing them about the problems within communities and holding the officials accountable to their constituencies. As well as publishing national and local newsletters, the NCPRR has published a status report on Puerto Ricans in the United States every two years.—*Mark Miller*

National Congress of American Indians (NCAI): Pan-tribal American Indian political organization founded in 1944. The NCAI has been committed to protecting the rights of sovereign American Indian nations, while ensuring the individual rights and benefits to which Indians are entitled as U.S. citizens. It was founded in 1944,

President Harry S Truman meets with representatives of the National Congress of American Indians at the signing of the Indian Claims Commission bill in 1946. (Library of Congress)

when members of fifty tribes met in Denver, Colorado, to plan a strategy that would give them a united voice and lobbying power when addressing the U.S. Congress about legislation affecting AMERICAN INDIANS. The organization's initial priorities were to improve Indian education, preserve traditional cultural values, and monitor NATIVE AMERICAN LAND CLAIMS settlements. The organization opposed federal policies that sought to end the Indian RESERVATION system in the 1950's. The NCAI has sought to protect Indian resources, encourage economic development, and preserve Indian religious rights and native languages, all issues deemed crucial to Indian self-determination. NCAI has occasionally been criticized by Indian activists for being too moderate because it has generally worked with Congress to frame Indian legislation. The NCAI has, nevertheless, remained an important national advocacy group for preserving Indian rights and tribal sovereignty.—*Carole A. Barrett*

National Council for Japanese American Redress (NCJAR): Japanese American advocacy organization founded in 1979. The Seattle-based NCJAR was formed to seek official redress by the U.S. government for injustices perpetrated on persons confined in relocation camps during World War II in the government's JAPANESE AMERICAN INTERNMENT program. NCJAR members lobbied aggressively for federal legislation authorizing the payment of reparations to internees. In 1983 the NCJAR filed a class-action suit demanding the payment of some $24 billion in damages to Japanese Americans by the U.S. government. The NCJAR's efforts helped to speed passage of a 1988 federal redress bill that awarded $20,000 to each camp survivor. After the U.S. Supreme Court dismissed the NCJAR's suit in October, 1988, the organization was disbanded.
—*Alexander Scott*

National Council of American Indians (NCAI): National AMERICAN INDIAN rights organization created in 1926. Led by well-educated and successful Indians, the NCAI was founded in 1926 by Gertrude Bonnin, a Sioux musician and writer who was a leader in the SOCIETY OF AMERICAN INDIANS and a Peyotist crusader. The NCAI was important as a "Red Progressive" movement; it was concerned primarily with encouraging Indian VOTING RIGHTS after the passage of the INDIAN CITIZENSHIP ACT OF 1924, assimilation of American lifestyle, and supporting the "Indian New Deal" reforms of John Collier, the commissioner of the BUREAU OF INDIAN AFFAIRS. The NCAI slogan was "Help the Indians Help Themselves

in Protecting Their Rights and Properties." The council was also concerned with banning the distribution and use of PEYOTE, the sacrament of the NATIVE AMERICAN CHURCH. The NCAI continued to promote participation and voting. The organization, closely associated with the GENERAL FEDERATION OF WOMEN'S CLUBS, was torn apart by factionalism in 1941.—*John Alan Ross*

National Council of Churches of Christ in the U.S.A. (NCC): Christian religious organization founded in 1950. An umbrella organization, the NCC is composed of thirty-two Protestant and Orthodox denominations representing about forty million church members. Major denominations represented in the NCC have included the United Methodist Church, the Presbyterian Church USA, the Episcopal Church, and the United Church of Christ. The Roman Catholic Church is not a member. The Islamic Society of North America, the American Jewish Committee, the Synagogue Council of America, and the Unitarian Universalist Association, all non-Christian groups, have observer status within the NCC.

Since its formation, the NCC has had a decidedly liberal focus and has come under frequent attack from religious FUNDAMENTALISM and conservative groups for its often controversial public stands on such issues as the arms race, the Civil Rights movement, human rights around the world, and other social, economic, and political issues including crime, welfare, and the environment.—*Glenn Canyon*

National Council of Hispanic Women (NCHW): Nationwide group committed to strengthening the public role of Hispanic women in the United States. The council has comprised Hispanic men and women, universities, corporations, and government delegates, with its members numbering nearly two thousand. The NCHW has had several goals. Through participation in public policy debates, conferences, and television interviews, it has voiced the problems and interests of concern to Hispanic women. It has also been dedicated to enhancing the financial and social status of the nation's Hispanic people. The group has promoted the exchange of ideas with other groups to help bring Hispanics, primarily women, into mainstream society. The NCHW has sponsored a scholarship fund, held annual conferences, and published a quarterly newsletter.—*Andrea E. Miller*

National Council of Senior Citizens (NCSC): Advocacy group for OLDER AMERICANS formed in 1961. NCSC members have worked for legislation at state and federal levels that benefits senior citizens. The organization has also worked to support the interests of senior citizens within their local communities across the United States.

Part of the reason that the NCSC was founded was to lobby in support of legislation that created the federal Medicare program during the early 1960's. The NCSC has also worked to increase benefits under the SOCIAL SECURITY ACT, to improve low-income housing for older people, and to create senior citizen community centers and nutrition sites. The NCSC Housing Management Corporation has been a major advocate of affordable and safe housing for older people and has itself managed residential buildings for seniors and persons with disabilities across the country.

The organization has also provided part-time employment for people over fifty-five years of age by operating the Senior AIDES Program for the U.S. Department of Labor.—*Mark Miller*

National Democratic Council of Asian and Pacific Americans (NDCAPA): Advocacy group founded in 1986. A membership-supported political organization based in Washington, D.C., the NDCAPA has worked to promote representation of Asian American members of the DEMOCRATIC PARTY at all levels of government. The group has addressed legislative issues that have included immigration, BILINGUAL EDUCATION, racial violence, and redress for victims of the government's JAPANESE AMERICAN INTERNMENT program during World War II. Lobbying by NDCAPA members helped to defeat two bills in the Maryland legislature that sought to make English that state's official language. During the early 1990's the NDCAPA was disbanded.—*Alexander Scott*

National Gay and Lesbian Task Force (NGLTF): Progressive gay and lesbian civil rights organization founded in 1973. Formerly known as the National Gay Task Force, the NGLTF is an organization that utilizes grassroots organizing, advocacy, research, education, lobbying, and dissemination of public information to promote equal rights for lesbian, gay, bisexual, and transgender people throughout the United States. It is based in Washington, D.C., and has field organizers throughout the country.

The NGLTF's creation in 1973 grew out of the modern GAY AND LESBIAN RIGHTS MOVEMENT. The movement began with the STONEWALL INN RIOTS of June, 1969, when New York City police raided a gay bar called the Stonewall Inn, sparking five days of vio-

lence. The event expanded awareness of antigay repression, mobilized GAY AND LESBIAN ACTIVISM, and led to formation of new organizations. The NGLTF was one of several groups formed out of this new groundswell of activism.

During the 1970's the NGLTF involved itself in such activities as working to create awareness and pressure on the White House and Congress for change. It worked to introduce the first gay and lesbian civil rights bill in Congress in 1975—and to reintroduce the bill every year since then—and to end discrimination against homosexuals in the MILITARY.

The NGLTF has actively challenged laws discriminating against people because of their sexual orientation. During the late 1970's and early 1980's, for example, it challenged a state law that prohibited discussion of homosexuality in public schools and banned gay teachers from the classroom. The case went before the Supreme Court, which found the law unconstitutional in 1984.

The NGLTF has concerned itself with many different aspects of discrimination and equality. One notable effort during the 1980's was the NGLTF Anti-Violence Project (AVP). The AVP began in 1982 out of concern with the lack of documentation of how much violence was directed against people because of their sexual orientation. The project published its first of what became annual national reports in 1984. This effort has helped the passage of the FEDERAL HATE CRIMES STATISTIC ACT for documenting crimes against people based on sexual orientation.

NGLTF grassroots projects have included the Workplace Organizing Project, which was launched in the early 1990's. This project has led to gay workplace organizations securing antidiscrimination policies and domestic partnership benefits in corporations across America. These efforts continue today along with the push for national nondiscrimination in employment legislation. The NGLTF has provided technical assistance and support to local and statewide gay rights organizations. It has sponsored the annual Creating Change conference, which has brought together activists to learn and share strategies for political action. In 1995 the NGLTF created the Policy Institute, a national policy research and education think tank.

SUGGESTED READINGS. Martin Duberman's *Stonewall* (1993) documents the events of the Stonewall Inn riots that marked the beginning of the modern gay rights movement. A comprehensive examination of the modern gay rights movement and its future can be

Increasing international AIDS awareness is among the priorities of the National Gay and Lesbian Task Force. (AP/Wide World Photos)

found in *Virtual Equality: The Mainstreaming of Gay and Lesbian Liberation* (1995) by Urvashi Vaid. Sarah Schulman, *My American History: Lesbian and Gay Life During the Reagan/Bush Years* (1994), is a collection of essays reflecting the struggles of gay activism in conservative times.—*Stephanie Brzuzy*

National Hispanic Media Coalition (NHMC): Organization founded in 1986 to improve the image and employment of Latinos in radio, television, and films. In 1997 the organization launched a boycott against the Disney Company to protest the latter's failure to hire Hispanic employees in numbers reflecting their importance in the Southern CALIFORNIA region in which Disney was headquartered. NHMC executive director Alex Nogales pointed out that only 1 percent of Disney's executive employees in the LOS ANGELES area were Latino, although the county had a 46 percent Latino population. The organization's boycott was supported by the MEXICAN AMERICAN LEGAL DEFENSE AND EDUCATION FUND, the Mexican American Bar Association, and other Latino rights organizations.

In 1991 the organization began an annual Hispanic Film Project Competition to encourage new Hispanic talent in the filmmaking industry. The success of this competition moved its backers to alter the format of the competition to produce one 35 mm feature, rather than shorts, in 1997. The NHMC also publishes a free annual newsletter, *Positive Image.*—*Christopher E. Kent*

National Immigration, Refugee, and Citizenship Forum (NIRCF): Washington, D.C.-based advocacy organization formed in 1982. Founded as the National Forum on Immigration and Refugee Policy, the forum is an umbrella organization encompassing approximately 150 refugee and immigrant organizations, state and local governments, churches, and labor and advocacy groups. Its members review immigration, refugee, citizenship, and related policies and issues, conduct periodic regional conferences, and publish a monthly information bulletin, as well as the bimonthly newsletters *Advisor*, *EPIC Events*, and *Forum*.

In 1982 the organization absorbed the American Immigration and Citizenship Conference. The following year it changed its name to National Immigration, Refugee, and Citizenship Forum.—*Alexander Scott*

National Indian Association (NIA): Organization founded in 1879 to develop Protestant missions among AMERICAN INDIANS and to protect Indians' rights. Formed by European American women of various Protestant denominations, the NIA was devoted to the particular challenge of pioneering new Christian missions among groups of Native Americans in the South, and particularly in Oklahoma. It was most closely affiliated with the Methodist and Southern Baptist churches. The NIA worked by launching missions among Indian communities that it turned over to denominational boards after they were functioning satisfactorily. For example, in 1883 the NIA turned over missions it had started among the Pawnees and Otoes to a Methodist mission board. The success of NIA efforts is difficult to measure because subsequent closings of missions it started may have had nothing to do with its own work.—*Gretchen L. Green*

National Institute on Aging (NIA): U.S. government agency created by Congress in 1974. Established under the Research on Aging Act, the NIA is one of twenty-three branches of the National Institutes of Health. The institute has overseen government-wide research on aging. Through the Interagency Committee on Research on Aging (IACRA), it has been the chief source of information for research on aging in the United States. It has conducted and supported biomedical, social, and behavioral research. It has also disseminated health information and dealt with other special problems and needs of the aged.

The NIA is organized into four extramural programs and two intramural programs. Alzheimer's disease has been a particular NIA focus, and the institute's research has highlighted the importance of genetic risk factors in the disease. NIA studies have also demonstrated the benefits of exercise and other interventions for maintaining independent function in older people, and that age-related loss of immune function and in-

Studies undertaken by the National Institute on Aging have emphasized the importance of physical exercise for older persons. (AP/Wide World Photos)

creased vulnerability to infectious diseases may be preventable.—*Bryan Aubrey*

National Newspaper Publishers Association (NNPA): African American trade association founded in 1940 and based in Washington, D.C. Originally called the National Negro Publishers Association, the NNPA was established to bring together the publishers of African American-owned newspapers in order to advance their mutual economic and professional interests. The group's mission has been to promote the interest of the black press in all matters concerning JOURNALISTS AND JOURNALISM.

Highly involved in public service responsibilities, the association has advanced the African American press through improved content and a national wire service. Through its National News Wire, National Black News Survey, and National News Feature, the NNPA Wire Service reached ten million readers a week in 210 member publications in 1996. The NNPA Intern Fund has provided summer internships each year for member newspapers. These internships have given black college students hands-on newspaper experience. The organization's scholarship fund has provided financial assistance to students interested in journalism.—*Mark Miller*

National Puerto Rican Coalition (NPRC): Puerto Rican advocacy and political organization founded in 1977. Formed by a group of community leaders invited by the U.S. COMMISSION ON CIVIL RIGHTS to meet in Washington, D.C., to discuss issues concerning PUERTO RICANS, the NPRC has become the leading national organization in Puerto Rican advocacy and policy making. The primary mission of the NPRC has been to further the economic, political, and social well-being of Puerto Ricans in the United States and Puerto Rico. Two programs have been set up to achieve these goals: Public Policy and Research, and Community Development and Training. The main activities of the Public Policy and Research Department have been to analyze and address issues of concern to Puerto Ricans and to act as a liaison to various federal agencies on behalf of the Puerto Rican community. The Community Development and Training Department has provided the leadership skills and training necessary to promote the growth of successful and effective Puerto Rican communities and community leaders.—*Mark Miller*

National Right to Life Committee (NRLC): Largest national grassroots pro-life organization in the United States. Founded in 1973, the NRLC has become well known for its commitment to the preservation of human life from ABORTION. It has also opposed euthanasia and INFANTICIDE. The NRLC contends that unborn fetuses are persons deserving of the full rights of all living human beings. This position contrasts sharply with that of the pro-choice movement, which advocates legalized abortion, claiming that fetuses are not persons since they do not display human characteristics until they are three months old; moreover, the mothers of the fetuses have higher rights over the fetus and therefore should have the freedom to make their own decisions on abortion. Along with the Roman Catholic Church and Christian FUNDAMENTALISTS, the NRLC has remained a bulwark of abortion opponents who support the idea that human life begins at the moment of conception. In June, 1997, the NRLC announced that it does not oppose cloning but strongly "opposes the destruction of living human beings, including human clones."

During the 1960's and 1970's the WOMEN'S RIGHTS MOVEMENT demanded full REPRODUCTIVE RIGHTS, including the right to abortion. In 1973 the U.S. Supreme Court legalized most abortions in its ROE V. WADE decision. This decision gave rise to a countermovement—in which the NRLC has played a large part—to demand restoration of strict control over abortion. Later in the twentieth century, a new method of induced abortion was discovered in the form of RU-486, an artificial steroid closely related to a contraceptive hormone that blocks progesterone, which is necessary to support a fertilized egg. Although the drug was initially legal only in some European countries, the NRLC opposed testing of it by the Federal Drug Administration.

The NRLC claims fifty state branches and three thousand local groups. It has maintained a speakers' bureau and has published a newspaper, *National Right to Life News*. It has also distributed information on alternatives to abortion, including ADOPTION. —*M. Casey Diana*

National Women's Studies Association (NWSA): Organization founded in 1977 to promote WOMEN'S STUDIES PROGRAMS and feminist education. The organization has had three focuses: the curriculum and classroom, scholarship and research, and public programming and student services. Since its creation it has held annual conferences; published a scholarly journal, newsletters, guides, and reports of projects and studies; and offered scholarships, workshops, and legal help. It has also supported a number of task forces on such concerns as discrimination in ACADEMICS, feminist scholarship, science and technology, peace, eco-feminism, and international issues.

Based at the University of Maryland, the NWSA is headed by a governing council elected by mail ballot through proportional representation. Its membership is divided into twelve regions, and it has separate caucuses for African American women, older women, women with disabilities, Jewish women, lesbians, poor and working-class women, elementary school educators, program administrators, students, women's centers, and women of color.

In striving to avoid the use of hierarchical structures and methods and to be true to its commitment to celebrate differences of sex, race, class, sexual identity, physical ability, age, ethnicity, religion, and nationality, it has suffered through internal organizational upheavals.—*Erika E. Pilver*

Native American land claims: After the arrival of Europeans on North American soil, lands occupied by Native Americans were gradually encroached upon and expropriated for European use. Although treaties between American Indians and whites were signed through the late nineteenth centuries, both the U.S. and Canadian governments consistently broke these treaties by seizing Indian lands.

Early Claims. In 1855 the U.S. Congress established the U.S. Court of Claims to handle lawsuits, including land claims, against the government. Although federal courts had recognized the legitimacy of native land claims as early as 1823, an amendment to federal law in 1863 made it impossible for Native Americans to use the courts to reclaim land or money. Tribes were allowed to sue the government only by special act of Congress—a nearly impossible feat for tribes to achieve without financial, legal, or political resources. As a result, few settlements were made and no land was returned to Indians.

In 1946 Congress created the INDIAN CLAIMS COMMISSION (ICC) and passed the Indian Claims Commission Act to handle Native American claims. This legislation enabled tribes to file their own claims without special acts of Congress. The federal government hoped to judge all claims within the following ten years—which was the period within which the tribes had to act. The government's vision in this regard proved shallow. From its inception, the ICC was overwhelmed with cases, and tribal rivalries surfaced as competing Indian groups argued over who the original occupants of certain land areas had been. In addition, the government sought to protect its own land interests and discouraged Indian groups from filing by deliberately delaying its processing of claims. Not surprisingly, the government could not solve a century and a half of land struggles in ten years. As a result, the ICC was authorized to continue its mission until 1978, at which time unsettled cases were turned over to the U.S. Court of Claims. Meanwhile, the ICC heard more than three hundred cases and awarded more than $800 million in claims.

The ICC did not, however, return any land to Indians because it was prohibited from offering any form of compensation other than money. The commission was originally part of the TERMINATION plan, which directed that when tribal land claims were settled with cash payments, the federal government could terminate all its obligations toward the compensated tribes.

Many tribes regarded the government's money-for-land transactions as unfair because land reclamation was their goal. To most American Indians, the European American practice of buying and selling land was an alien concept. Within the traditional cultures of most tribes ownership of land was virtually nonexistent. Ancestral lands were regarded as having religious and cultural meanings; such lands were so integrally linked to tribal life that money alone could not compensate for their loss. Furthermore, the cash values that the government assigned to the expropriated lands were based on their market values prices at the times treaties were signed and did not allow for interest payments. As a result, the cash settlements that the tribes received were well below the lands' current market values. Tribes that accepted the cash settlements also faced the challenge of deciding whether to distribute the money among their members or to use it for overall tribal development.

Return of Native Land. Some tribes refused cash settlements and kept fighting to regain their native lands. Before the 1960's government restoration of native land to tribes was practically nonexistent. During the 1960's public attitudes on this subject began to change because of the influence of the CIVIL RIGHTS MOVEMENT, student radicalism, and government programs such as the WAR ON POVERTY. Moreover, increasing numbers of Native Americans had become directly involved in legal affairs as lawyers, scholars, and citizen activists. As a result of these changes, several high-profile land claims were awarded during this era.

In 1969 pantribal American Indian activists began an occupation of Alcatraz Island in San Francisco Bay that lasted a year and a half, claiming the former prison territory as abandoned federal territory that legally reverted to Indian ownership. (AP/Wide World Photos)

In one famous case, the Taos PUEBLOS of New Mexico claimed 48,000 acres of land, including Blue Lake, which was sacred to them as a resting site for spirits of the dead. The federal government offered them ten million dollars and about three thousand acres near the lake, but they refused to accept the offer. Saying that without the lake itself the settlement was meaningless, the Taos people continued to demand return of their land until 1970, when they were finally awarded the full 48,000 acres, including Blue Lake.

In 1971 Congress passed the ALASKA NATIVE CLAIMS SETTLEMENT ACT, which granted 44 million acres and one billion dollars to Native Alaskans. Although this huge land settlement granted cash as well as land, it has been criticized for returning the land in the form of tribal land-holding corporations instead of placing it under direct control of Native Alaskans. In 1980 Congress passed the Maine Indian Claims Settlement Act, which combined a monetary settlement with a fund for federal land acquisition.

After the early 1980's unsettled land claims continued to be a national issue. In some cases, the federal government acknowledged its treaty violations and that it had illegally seized lands, but it refused to offer tribes anything other than monetary settlements. One such example involved the Sioux of South Dakota's Black Hills. In 1876 the federal government broke its 1868 treaty with the Sioux by seizing part of their lands after a gold rush had brought in a flood of American prospectors. After many years of litigation during the 1980's, the government offered a cash settlement of $122 million for 7.3 million acres. To some of the eight Sioux groups awarded the settlement, cash was an unacceptable exchange for their sacred land. In the absence of agreement among the eight Sioux tribes, the case remains unsettled.

Land claims have also been made against nongovernmental parties residing on land taken from American Indians. These claims have met with some success for lands in which the federal government never held title and which had never been claimed prior to the Indian Claims Commission.

Land Claims in Canada. In 1973 the Canadian supreme court decided the Calder case, in which Indians of the province of British Columbia claimed native land. Their claim was not granted, but it spurred the federal government to create a native claims office within the DEPARTMENT OF INDIAN AFFAIRS. In 1974

In 1971 Indian rights activists attempted to occupy an abandoned government missile base in California's Contra Costa County, citing the same legal principle that was the basis for occupying Alcatraz two years earlier. (AP/Wide World Photos)

the office established a framework for land claims. Individual claims fell under one of two headings: comprehensive or specific claims. Comprehensive land claims involve groups who never signed land surrender treaties with the Canadian government and can prove traditional occupation of the area they claim. Cases that are settled favorably result in cash or land titles, in return for which the claimants must relinquish all their aboriginal rights to the land. Specific land claims are made in cases in which specific treaty rights have been broached. The number of cases adjudicated since the office's creation has been small. This is due to the Canadian government's handling of only a few claims at a time, its reluctance to grant land claims in non-native settled areas, and its failure to provide a clear judicial mandate for establishing native rights. As in the United States, some Canadian tribes have refused to relinquish their rights to lands they traditionally occupied in return for money.

Most comprehensive claims in Canada have been in British Columbia, Yukon Territory, the Northwest Territories, and the Arctic. They have involved four major native groups: the Council of Yukon Indians, Inuit groups of the James Bay, Mackenzie Bay, and Northwest Territories, the Gwi'shin, and the Dene/Metis. One settlement with the Inuit resulted in the creation of Nunavut, a new territory of the Arctic populated almost exclusively by native groups.

SUGGESTED READINGS. A thorough discussion of Native American political and cultural history can be found in Carl Waldman's *Atlas of the North American Indian* (1985). For a detailed treatment of Native American land claims and legal history, see *The Cambridge History of the Native Peoples of the Americas*, vol. 1, part 2 (1996), edited by Bruce G. Trigger and Wilcomb E. Washburn. *The Native American Almanac: A Portrait of Native America Today* (1993), by Arlene Hirschfelder and Martha Kreipe de Montano, offers hard-to-find information and statistics on land, treaties, and court decisions. *American Indians: Answers to Today's Questions* (1993), by Jack Utter, dispels myths about Native Americans with solidly documented answers to common questions, including those dealing with land issues.—*Michelle C. K. McKowen*

Native American Programs Act of 1974: U.S. federal legislation intended to increase Native American self-determination and economic self-sufficiency. During the early 1970's the U.S. Congress passed a number of laws designed to increase Native American participation in the creation and management of programs and policies that influenced their lives. The Native American Programs Act of 1974, which amended the Economic Opportunity Act of 1964, encouraged private nonprofit and public organizations, especially tribal governments, to submit proposals for programs which would benefit Native Americans. Under the terms of that act, the federal government pledged to assist in the creation of project proposals and fund 80 percent of the total costs of approved projects. The act encouraged the founding and operation of the urban community centers, on which many Native Americans living in the nation's cities relied for information and assistance. It also permitted Native Hawaiians and their communities to take part in the programs.—*Thomas Clarkin*

Native Hawaiian Health Care Act (1988): U.S. federal legislation designed to improve the health of Native Hawaiians by promoting health care delivery and education and disease prevention. Due to the illegal overthrow in 1893 of the sovereign government of the kingdom of HAWAII for reasons of self-interest by a group of white American businessmen, the U.S. government has acknowledged a unique historical obligation to the indigenous people of Hawaii. Moreover, Native Hawaiians have suffered a high incidence of health problems and have needed extra assistance.

Administered by the U.S. Department of Health and Human Services, with input from Hawaiian health experts, the comprehensive Native Hawaiian Health Care Act has promoted health education, immunizations, PRENATAL and infant care, mental health, nutrition, physical fitness, and family planning. It also has sought to prevent tobacco and alcohol abuse and combat high blood pressure among Native Hawaiians. Federal monies have encouraged the delivery of health services by Native Hawaiian health centers and providers.—*Robert P. Watson*

Native Hawaiians Study Commission (1983): U.S. federal government investigatory body created by legislation passed in 1980 to study the culture and special needs of Native Hawaiians. Appointment of the commission was motivated, in part, by acknowledgment on the part of the federal government that recognition of the wrongful overthrow of the kingdom of HAWAII in 1893 by exploitative American businessmen was long overdue, and that questions of compensation for Native Hawaiians remained largely unresolved.

The commission found that Hawaiians experienced

higher levels of poverty, unemployment, health problems, substance abuse, and other problems than members of non-Hawaiian groups. The three Hawaiian members of the nine-member commission dissented with the "main" report's findings and issued a separate report of their own. They charged that the six non-Hawaiians appointed to the commission by President Ronald Reagan had failed fully to appreciate the unique history and culture of the people of Hawaii, and that their proposed recommendations were inadequate to remedy past wrongdoing.—*Robert P. Watson*

Nativism: Expression of cultural and ethnic chauvinism that is manifested by extreme opposition to foreign influences, particularly foreign immigrants. During the late nineteenth and early twentieth centuries nativism was widespread in the United States among Anglo-Americans, who expressed often violent disdain for Chinese, Irish, and other non-Anglo immigrants. American nativists have historically targeted foreign ideologies—particularly communism—fearing that they threatened native-born Americans' independence. Na-

tivists have resented having to compete with immigrants for jobs, particularly during periods of economic hardships, and they have blamed the "peril of America" on immigration and what they have perceived as misguided federal spending policies that have given foreign-born members of minorities advantages over native-born American citizens. Even after the COLD WAR ended during the early 1990's, many American nativists continued to fear the menace of communism; however, their focus readjusted to direct their fear against the danger of the United States joining a "New World Order," or a one-world government.

American nativists of the 1990's have tended to oppose the U.S. government's "tyrannical" behavior, lash out against nonwhite Americans, or both. Far-right movements, including MILITIA groups, the John Birch Society, and the Posse Comitatus, have advocated closing U.S. borders to immigrants, adhering literally to what they have called the "Organic Constitution" (the original Constitution with the first ten amendments), and making the U.S. government work *for* the American people, instead of controlling them.

Much of the impetus for modern revivals of the Ku Klux Klan lies in white nativist ideologies. (James L. Shaffer)

Nativists have also charged that the U.S. government has been too greatly involved in international affairs, and that by complying with directives of the United Nations, Americans have been forced to become more dependent on government, forfeiting their freedoms. Nativists have blamed the FOURTEENTH AMENDMENT for lowering the standards of U.S. citizenship. Antigovernment nativists have perpetrated HATE CRIMES by sending government officials and judges threats. Timothy McVeigh, who was convicted of carrying out the worst act of domestic terrorism in U.S. history—bombing a federal building in Oklahoma City, Oklahoma, in April, 1995, killing 168 people—expressed nativistic views.

The nativistic agendas of regional and national WHITE SUPREMACIST MOVEMENTS have called for the preservation the so-called Aryan race. Members of groups such as the KU KLUX KLAN, Nazi SKINHEADS, Aryan Nations, and the Order, have displayed their nativism and hate violence toward nonwhite American citizens and others whom they have considered inferior, through various crimes that have included threatening letters, vandalism, starting African American CHURCH FIRES, burning crosses, destroying property, and committing violent assaults on people.

SUGGESTED READINGS. *The Party of Fear: The American Far Right from Nativism to the Militia Movement* (1995), by David H. Bennett, provides a history of nativism among ultra right-wing Americans and shows the commonalities that exist among the various far-right movements. James Ridgeway details the history of nativist movements, focusing on the mid-1980's through the mid-1990's, in *Blood in the Face: The Ku Klux Klan, Aryan Nations, Nazi Skinheads, and the Rise of a New White Culture* (1995). Lyman Tower Sargent examines the beliefs of what he calls "infamous political radical groups" and lesser-known movements' beliefs in *Extremism in America: A Reader* (1995).—*Gina R. Terinoni*
(updates original entry; vol. 5, p. 1247)

Many of the views expressed by Timothy McVeigh, who was charged with bombing the Oklahoma City federal building in 1995, reflect nativist sentiments. (AP/Wide World Photos)

The members of Congress who drafted the first Naturalization Act in 1790 could not have imagined scenes such as this, in which nearly ten thousand persons from all parts of the world took the oath of citizenship in Miami, Florida, in 1984. (AP/Wide World Photos)

Naturalization Act of 1790: U.S. federal legislation enacted by Congress on March 27, 1790. The Naturalization Act was the first federal law to provide a mechanism permitting aliens to become American citizens. Its basis may have been one of the naturalization laws previously used by one of seven states with similar laws when they were colonies; the most likely model was that of 1779 in Virginia.

Under the 1790 federal law immigrants wishing to become U.S. citizens first had to be residents of the country for two years and residents of their states for at least one year. They also had to be of good moral character and were required to swear oaths in support of the Constitution. An application for citizenship could be filed in any common law court of record. Wives and children of petitioners residing within the United States also became citizens along with the petitioners.

After remaining in effect for almost five years the Naturalization Act of 1790 was replaced by a new law in January, 1795.—*Peter E. Carr*

Navajo Rehabilitation Act (1951): U.S. federal legislation passed in 1951 that ended a land dispute between the NAVAJOS and HOPIS. The dispute's origins went back to the 1860's, when Navajos released from federal detention were returned to their traditional homelands in northeastern Arizona, where a RESERVATION was established for them. During the 1940's, Congress set aside lands for Hopis within the Navajo reservation. As a result, lands that had been held jointly were now being disputed. Several hundred Navajo families were relocated by 1986, but some Navajo continued to live in areas that the Hopi considered sacred. In 1992 the TRIBAL COUNCILS of both groups voted to accept a solution that would involve ceding approximately 500,000 acres of private and public land to the Hopi to compensate for their loss of land to the Navajo. Afterward, the Hopi leased plots to Navajos who remained on the ceded lands.—*John Alan Ross*

Navajo War (1863-1866): Conflict that forced the temporary relocation of the NAVAJOS from northeastern

Frontiersman Kit Carson played a leading role in the U.S. war against the Navajo. (Library of Congress)

Arizona to Bosque Redondo, New Mexico.

The U.S. government's establishment of Fort Defiance in 1851 led to a decade-long conflict between U.S. soldiers who wanted to pasture their horses and Navajo farmers and medicine men who had used the land for centuries for their own livestock and to gather herbs. In 1859-1860 the homesteads of Navajo leaders Manuelito and Barboncito were targeted by army troops; this conflict turned violent, but what has come to be known as the Navajo War began in September, 1863, when Colonel Kit Carson began to lead military forays into Navajo lands.

In January, 1864, Carson and Colonel Albert Pfeiffer took separate scouting parties on parallel routes through Canyon de Chelly, where intransigent Navajo protected themselves from the army by living in crevices in the red sandstone walls and ancient ANASAZI ruins. In the fighting that ensued, twenty-three Navajos were killed, and the army troops destroyed Navajo crops and peach orchards along the canyon floor, beginning a scorched-earth policy that eventually led to eight thousand Navajos taking the LONG WALK to Bosque Redondo. Barboncito did not surrender his band until 1866, but military hostilities were effectively over by the middle of 1864. The Navajo Treaty of 1868 allowed the Navajos to return to their ancestral homeland in what later became the state of Arizona; it also stipulated that no one could enter Canyon de Chelly (later a National Monument) without permission from the Navajo tribe.—*Richard Sax*

Negro League Baseball Museum: Historical museum that opened in Kansas City, Missouri, in 1991. Kansas City was a logical location for the museum for several reasons. The Negro National League was formed there in 1920, and one of the league's best teams, the Monarchs, played there. Moreover, the Monarchs were the pride of a thriving local African American community, whose cultural and commercial achievements were remarkable during the first half of the twentieth century. The museum itself has become the cornerstone of the redevelopment of one of the oldest and best-known black neighborhoods of the Midwest.

The museum features black contributions to baseball from the mid-nineteenth century through the 1950's. Its exhibits have featured original uniforms and equipment, historical photographs, and transcripts

Perhaps the greatest pitcher in baseball history, Satchel Paige did not enter the major leagues until after spending two decades in Negro League baseball. (National Baseball Library, Cooperstown, New York)

of oral histories. During the late 1990's plans were begun to move the museum to a nearby location that would triple exhibition space and make room for interactive video displays.—*Michael John Polley*

Net Noir: Online computer service serving the interests of African Americans. Created for America Online (AOL) subscribers, Net Noir was launched on June 19, 1995, a date of special significance to African Americans as "Juneteenth," the oldest African American holiday. The service was founded in San Francisco by E. David Ellington, a lawyer, and Malcolm CasSelle, a publishing executive, to promote and celebrate the culture of AFRO-CENTRISM. The service has welcomed not only African Americans, but all persons interested in Afrocentric culture.

Net Noir's debut week featured a question-and-answer session with exiled Haitian president Jean-Bertrand Aristide. The service started with four departments: business, education, music, and sports. It has also featured chat rooms, message boards, and online shopping services. Departments added later have included arts and entertainment, lifestyles and special interests, politics, news, and women's issues. —*Andrea E. Miller*

New Age movement: Loosely organized mystical, but world-affirming, cultural, spiritual, and human-potential movement. Highly eclectic and made up of a wide variety of ideas and practices, the New Age movement has influenced a broad spectrum of life, ranging from ecology and personal psychology to religion, education, business, and politics. The movement has no distinct boundaries and cannot even be defined as a movement in the strict sense of the term. While one observer has called it a network of networks, another has seen it as an alternative to atheism, or Christian theism.

Although the New Age movement began flourishing in the early 1970's, when Baba Ram Dass emerged as its first national prophet in the United States, it grew out of an older Western occult-metaphysical tradition and borrowed many ideas and teachings from Judeo-Christian and Eastern religions. It has also been strongly influenced by other metaphysical movements that flourished during the nineteenth century, such as Swedenborgianism, Transcendentalism, Spiritualism, and especially Theosophy.

New Agers believe in the signs of the zodiac, that humanity evolves from the Piscean Age into the Aquarian Age, and that occult worldviews will replace Christianity and occupy a prominent place in the year 2000, when humanity enters into the Age of Aquarius. Monism, pantheism, religious syncretism, deification of humanity, reincarnation, karma, gnosis knowledge, holism, and relativism are all core philosophies of the New Age. With the notions that "all is one" and "all is God," humanity becomes god and sacred in nature. Personal transformation awakening the sacredness within and attaining mystical consciousness is the goal of salvation for New Agers. Social and even planetary transformations are brought about by a "critical mass" of radical personal transformations of humankind.

New Age practices are too varied for inclusive definitions. They include tarot, ACUPUNCTURE, hypotherapy, meditation, yoga, channeling, energy healing, natural farming, and human potential seminars. A generic principle for all these practices is an emphasis on intuition and experience rather than doctrines or logical reasoning.

The New Age movement has become most pervasive in North America, northern Europe, and Australia, but it is also visible in southern Europe, Asia, and Africa.

Emphasis on intuition over logical reasoning has given practices such as tarot card reading a place in the New Age movement. (Yasmine A. Cordoba)

Estimates of the number of followers of New Age beliefs have run as high as twelve million Americans who can be considered active participants and another thirty million who are interested. Most New Agers come from the well-educated urban middle class. After the early 1990's many serious New Age participants tried to shy away from the label "New Age," while continuing to uphold New Age beliefs and practices.

SUGGESTED READINGS. For a detailed account of the movement, see Richard Kyle's *The New Age Movement in American Culture* (1995). *Not Necessarily the New Age* (1988), edited by Robert Basil, focuses on the movement's ideas, while *Perspectives on the New Age* (1992), edited by Gordon Melton, provides a sociological perspective. Ron Rhodes gives a concise description of its essential elements in *New Age Movement* (1995).—*Cheris Shun-Ching Chan*

No-no boys: Nickname given to several thousand young men held during the JAPANESE AMERICAN INTERNMENT of WORLD WAR II who refused to sign loyalty oaths to the United States government and declined to serve in the U.S. armed forces. In 1942 more than 110,000 persons of Japanese ancestry, most American citizens, were confined to internment camps for the duration of the war. Initially, the Selective Service System classified most Japanese American males as enemy aliens (4-C), exempting linguists who were needed as translators. This policy changed after February, 1943, when President Franklin D. Roosevelt declared that no loyal American should be denied the right to serve in the armed forces.

In order to qualify for military service internees were required to swear allegiance to the United States, and male internees were asked if they were willing to be drafted. Of the 22,000 eligible males, about one quarter either responded with a "no," qualified their response, or gave no response. Most of the "no-no boys"—those who responded negatively to the key questions—were separated from other internees and sent to Tule Lake, the harshest internment camp. There was considerable disagreement between the "no-no boys" and the "yes-yes boys" over whether it was appropriate for incarcerated Japanese Americans to demonstrate their loyalty by serving in the military.

The term "no-no boy" appears to have entered the general popular vernacular—at least in the Asian American community—after John Okada published his novel *No-No Boy* in 1957. Okada was a NISEI internee who had served in the U.S. Army during World War II.—*James Stanlaw*

Passage of the Nontraditional Employment for Women Act has made it easier for American women to work in occupations that traditionally excluded them. (James L. Shaffer)

Nontraditional Employment for Women Act of 1992 (NEWA): U.S. federal legislation designed to increase the employment of women in skilled trades. Also known as the Women in Apprenticeship and Nontraditional Occupations Act, the act was passed on October 27, 1992. Its passage demonstrated congressional recognition that significant barriers to women's EMPLOYMENT continued to exist in many skilled trades. The act established two new functions for the Department of Labor: Employers and labor unions were to be informed of the availability of technical assistance to help prepare for the employment of women in nontraditional occupations, and a program of grants for community organizations was created to provide technical assistance to employers and skills training for women.—*Glenn Canyon*

North American Black Historical Museum and Cultural Center: Historical museum that opened to the public in Amherstburg in Ontario, Canada, in 1981. A historic site on the African Canadian Heritage Tour, the museum's purpose is to display the history of the 30,000 to 50,000 African Americans who escaped from SLAVERY in the United States and came to southwestern Ontario—many by way of the UNDERGROUND RAILROAD. The museum depicts their contributions to the development of the area.

As funding has been available, the museum has conducted an antiracism program geared toward local area schoolchildren. The purpose of the program is to educate the children on the existence of racism and its negative impact on society. The program also instructs how to recognize and counteract racism. This program has proven valuable not only to schoolchildren, but to teachers and employment counseling personnel as well.—*Mark Miller*

North American Free Trade Agreement (NAFTA): Regional trade pact among Canada, the United States, and Mexico whose intent was to create a single market for producers and consumers of North America. On December 17, 1992, leaders of the three North American nations signed the NAFTA, which went into effect on January 1, 1994. NAFTA is a multilateral trade accord that eliminates most trade and tariff barriers on goods produced and sold among the three nations. The pact immediately abolished some trade restrictions in 1994 and began to phase out others over ten-to-fifteen-year periods.

NAFTA represents an extended version of the 1989 Canadian-American Free Trade Agreement. The terms of the pact established rights and obligations regarding trading practices and protection for foreign investors. Dispute-settlement procedures were instituted, as well as safeguards for discrepancies in laws regarding intellectual property (such as publishing copyrights). The benefits of this agreement have included moderate job growth and market expansions in the automobile, textile, apparel, agriculture, financial services, transportation, and telecommunications industries. Despite the increase in open markets, the energy sector in Mexico remained closed to foreign influence.

Ratification of NAFTA sparked major controversy. While Canadians exhibited minimal resistance to the pact, the impact of the agreement in the United States

Truckers protesting NAFTA in Arizona in late 1995 emphasized safety issues, charging that allowing Mexican truckers free access to U.S. highways would pose a serious threat to American motorists. (AP/Wide World Photos)

and Mexico was heavily criticized. Opponents to the agreement in the United States argued that it would encourage American-based businesses to relocate their plants to Mexico in search of low-wage workers, resulting in massive job loss in the United States. Many Americans also feared that increased importation of inexpensive Mexican goods would contribute to job losses in the United States. Others were concerned about the possible negative effects of Mexico's lax labor and environmental laws and Mexico's record of human rights abuses. Environmental groups argued that NAFTA would reduce enforcement standards of U.S. food safety laws and increase air and water pollution.

In response to opposition to the agreement, Canada, Mexico, and the United States renegotiated the original terms of the pact to include supplements to NAFTA. Three side agreements were developed to address labor concerns, environmental issues, and the impact of increases in imports.

SUGGESTED READINGS. The benefits and challenges of the agreement are thoroughly discussed by Khosrow Fatemi in *North American Free Trade Agreement: Opportunities and Challenges* (1993). Roy Green's *The Enterprise for the American Initiative: Issues and Prospects for a Free Trade Agreement in the Western Hemisphere* (1993) provides detailed information on possible outcomes of trade agreements. *NAFTA: Here's a Look at What It Is and Isn't* (1993), by Gene Marlowe, offers a brief analysis of NAFTA's controversial points. Gary Hufbauer and Jeffrey Schott examine the advantageous features of NAFTA in *North American Free Trade Agreement: Everybody Wins* (1994). In *North American Free Trade Agreement: What Are We Really Getting* (1993), John LaFalce analyzes the merits and risks associated with NAFTA.
—*Phyllis M. Jones-Shuler*

Nuns and priests: Since its very beginning the ROMAN CATHOLIC Church has been multicultural, and especially since the seventeenth century it has strenuously worked to promote indigenous leadership of its local followers throughout the world. After World War I, Pope Benedict XV set a goal of building up as quickly as practicable the church's indigenous clergy and hierarchy, indicating that the government of the church in the mission lands should be turned over to native leaders without delay. The first bishop of Asian origin was confirmed in 1923, and the first apostolic vicars of African origin were named in 1939. By the time of the church's VATICAN II

council during the early 1960's the church counted ninety Asian and fifty-eight African bishops. This development has been one of the most significant in the modern church.

The church's insistence on native church leadership caused theology as a whole to take a new turn. Rather than being something done merely in the relative calm of the seminary or monastery, it became increasingly sensitive to social and political events and situations. African Americans under SLAVERY, for example, found in the biblical story of Exodus, affirmation for their struggle for freedom. "Let My People Go" was a song that expressed their deep yearning. So called LIBERATION THEOLOGY originated in Latin America in response to the growing realization of priests and nuns of the unjust social and political conditions under which people lived. Latin American church leaders began to interpret the idea of "salvation" from a social perspective, as well as a spiritual one. Under the new view, the concept of sin was applied not only to what individual persons do, but also to what society as a whole does to oppress its peoples.

Nuns were among the first Catholic women to protest their subordinate position in the church and society. They have protested wholeheartedly against injustices in many parts of the world, despite the risks of being tortured, imprisoned, and even murdered for their work among the poor. Many nuns and priests were involved with the SANCTUARY MOVEMENT that challenged U.S. government policies in Central America. In 1985 sixteen Sanctuary workers, including three nuns and two priests, were indicted on charges of smuggling ILLEGAL ALIENS into the United States. This movement was a response to people who were suffering from torture and murder in their own Central American countries.

This move toward CULTURAL PLURALISM has not been accepted wholeheartedly by all parts of the Catholic Church. Pope John Paul II and his supporters have at times seemed to believe that pluralism threatens the church and have called for the return to Roman law and order. However, many believe that pluralism is the unfinished business of Vatican II, and that a collegial or pluralistic church cannot be silenced by heavy-handed discipline. The spirit of Vatican II is a pluralistic, lay-oriented church, which respects religious freedom and cultural diversity.

SUGGESTED READINGS. Penny Lernoux's *People of God: The Struggle for World Catholicism* (1989) explains how the Catholic Church has changed radically

A Roman Catholic priest explains Holy Communion in a classroom of a church school. (James L. Shaffer)

in favor of multiculturalism since Vatican II. *Cry of the People* (1980), also by Penny Lernoux, discusses the struggle of the Catholic Church against military dictatorships, especially in Latin America.—*Winifred Whelan*

Nuyoricans: Persons of Puerto Rican descent born in NEW YORK. During the 1970's second-generation PUERTO RICANS living in New York began identifying themselves as "Nuyoricans," instead of Puerto Ricans. They claimed pride in being Puerto Ricans but also acknowledged their New York spirit.

Puerto Ricans first immigrated to the United States in great numbers after World War II. Most of these immigrants experienced the trauma of being uprooted and the shock of cultural change, cultural conflict, and having to adjust to new ways of life. In literature on

immigrant experience, second-generation "Nuyoricans" have often been called persons in the middle: They have grown up in homes reflecting the native culture of their parents, while socializing in a new American environment. Their experiences have been described in the writings of modern Nuyorican writers.

Nuyorican literature grew significantly between the 1970's and 1990's. Books such as Nicholasa Mohr's *Nilda* (1973), Piri Thomas' *Down These Mean Streets* (1967), and Pedro Pietri's *Puerto Rican Obituary* (1973) have depicted the complexities of Puerto Ricans' growing up in New York. Thomas' classic book portrays his ambiguity about color, his experiences confronting prejudice, his involvement with street gangs, and his eventual conversion. Mohr's novels and short stories speak of the people of the BARRIOS—the Puerto Rican community in which she grew up in New

Children in one of New York City's predominantly Puerto Rican neighborhoods during the 1950's. (Library of Congress)

Puerto Ricans living in New York stage an open-air passion play to celebrate Easter. (Martha Cooper)

York that became known as Spanish Harlem. Pietri's *Puerto Rican Obituary* depicts lost hopes and dreams of better lives in New York.

Recurrent themes for other Nuyorican poets have included the issue of color, the drug scene, poverty and discrimination, and a profound nostalgia for a beautiful culture submerged by American consumerism. Other themes expressed in Nuyorican literature are problems with identity and self-esteem, anxiety and assimilation, and the retelling of past stories. Nuyorican literature is written mostly in English, but many Nuyoricans write in both Spanish and English, often reverting to a mixture known as SPANGLISH.

In 1974 the Nuyorican Poets Cafe was opened on the Lower East Side in New York City by Nuyorican writers Miguel Algarín and

Miguel Piñero. As popular two decades later as it was when it began, it has offered Poetry Slams and other types of poetry readings expressing both the Nuyorican and the American experience. Both professional and amateur poets have participated in these readings.

SUGGESTED READINGS. Miguel Algarín and Bob Holman's *Aloud: Voices from the Nuyorican Poets Cafe* (1994) and *Boricuas: Influential Puerto Rican Writings—An Anthology* (1995), edited by Roberto Santiago, are poetry anthologies whose introductions provide extensive histories of Puerto Ricans growing up in New York. (Boricuas is an alternative name for Puerto Ricans adapted from the pre-Columbian Taino Indian name for the island Puerto Rico.) Joseph P. Fitzpatrick's *Puerto Rican Americans: The Meaning of Migration to the Mainland* (1987) surveys the history of Puerto Rican migration to the United States, as well as Puerto Ricans living in New York. *The Puerto Rican Struggle: Essays on Survival in the U.S.A.* (1990), by Clara E. Rodriguez, discusses aspects of culture of second-generation Puerto Ricans in the United States.—*Jose A. Carmona*

O

Office of Hawaiian Affairs (OHA): State government agency added to HAWAII's state constitution in 1979. The OHA was created as a self-governing body dedicated to the betterment of life and opportunities for all Hawaiians. Its mission covers all areas of the Hawaiian community, from education and housing to health and political concerns. Since its creation the agency has strived for increased awareness of Hawaiian culture and tradition, increased recognition within government, and the enhancement of service-oriented activities.

The OHA was formed to be governed by a board of trustees whose nine members are residents of the islands. There are five members from Oahu, Maui, Kauai/Niihau, and Molokai/Lanai, and four at-large members. The trustees develop and oversee programs in housing, education, and grants as well as coordinate their efforts with other Hawaiian agencies and organizations for maximum coverage with minimum duplication of effort.—*Mark Miller*

Office of Research on Women's Health (ORWH): Branch of the U.S. National Institutes of Health (NIH) established in 1990. The ORWH was formed to promote and expand the development of research on diseases and conditions that affect women. The ORWH has also developed opportunities for recruitment and advancement of women in biomedical careers, and has monitored the participation of women in clinical research trials. In 1991 the ORWH helped launch the Women's Health Initiative, of which it became codirector. The Women's Health Initiative was a fifteen-year study of about 160,000 women to determine how diet, hormone replacement therapy, calcium, and vitamin D might help prevent heart disease, cancer, and osteoporosis. The study took a new approach to women's health care by emphasizing the health of postmenopausal women and by recognizing heart disease as a leading cause of death in women. The federal NIH Revitalization Act of 1993 provided a legislative mandate for the ORWH.—*Karen Lindell*

Ohio v. Akron Center for Reproductive Health (1990): U.S. Supreme Court case concerning ABORTION rights. By a 5-3 margin, the Court voted to uphold an Ohio law that required physicians to notify parents or other adult family members at least twenty-four hours before performing abortions on minors. The law also provided that young women who were unwilling to notify parent or approved substitutes could seek approval for their abortions from juvenile courts. Justices Harry Blackmun, William Brennan, Jr., and Thurgood Marshall dissented from the majority's decision. Arguments developed in this case were later used in the crucial 1992 abortion case, *Planned Parenthood of Southeastern Pennsylvania v. Casey.*—*Christopher E. Kent*

Oklahoma Indian Welfare Act (1936): U.S. federal legislation which extended the benefits of the 1934 INDIAN REORGANIZATION ACT (IRA) to Native Americans in Oklahoma, who previously had been specifically excluded from many IRA provisions. Also known as the Thomas-Rogers Bill after its sponsors, Oklahoma senator Elmer Thomas and representative Will Ro-

Health concerns of special interest to women have inspired a great deal of feminist activism. (Betty Lane)

The increased political clout of minority voters has forced politicians who might otherwise have joined old boys' networks to broaden their political bases. (International Daily News)

gers, the Oklahoma Indian Welfare Act permitted Native Americans in that state to organize tribal governments, own land communally, and create cooperatives that could borrow money from a two-million-dollar fund. In addition, the act empowered the U.S. secretary of the interior to acquire additional land to expand RESERVATIONS. However, the act included no provisions regarding education or medical services, and it permitted the state of Oklahoma to levy a production tax on oil and gas leases located on reservations. Although some tribes organized governments, most Native Americans in Oklahoma chose not to participate in the programs detailed within the act.—*Thomas Clarkin*

Old boys' network: Informal relationships among male—and primarily white—members of alumni, business, political, or social organizations. The network refers to an "insider" status accorded those who participate in this unofficial system. Such status usually comes with certain privileges, such as access to important persons or material rewards. However, membership in an old boys' network carries with it acknowledgment of a *quid pro quo*, whereby members are expected to help each other.

These loose power structures often imply violation of equal opportunity principles, thus making it difficult for outsiders, particularly women and people of color, to break in. Old boys' networks are sometimes credited with facilitating a GLASS CEILING that prevents women and members of minority groups from rising to the highest ranks within organizations. Exclusive clubs, political parties, labor union management, municipal governments and corporate boards are among the organizations that have historically been accused of operating under the informal rules of old boys' networks.—*Maurice Hamington*

Older Women's League (OWL): Women's rights organization founded by social and political activists Tish Sommers and Laurie Shields in October, 1980. With chapters throughout the United States, OWL has worked to improve the economic and social status of middle-aged and older American women by distributing information about health, economic, employment, and retire-

One of the goals of the Older Women's League has been to remove age discrimination—especially against women—in the workplace. (Betty Lane)

ment issues. These issues have included menopause, osteoporosis, heart disease, Medicare benefits, AGE DISCRIMINATION in employment, equal pay for equal work, and retirement and SOCIAL SECURITY benefits. OWL has educated persons working in BATTERED WOMEN shelters, focusing on the unique concerns that abused women from different cultures and ethnic backgrounds may have. OWL has also worked to influence public policy at the grassroots level, informing its membership of impending legislation that may affect the status of mid-life and older women, and encouraging them to contact their legislators as advocates for older women's well-being and economic security.—*Maureen J. Puffer*

Olympic Games: After the 1992 winter and summer games the International Olympic Committee changed the games' format so that the summer and winter competitions would no longer be held during the same years. While the summer games—which were first to begin, in 1896—continued on their original schedule, the winter games began a new quadrennial cycle in 1994.

The 1994 Winter Olympics were held in Lillehammer, Norway. Prior to the start of competition, American figure skater Nancy Kerrigan was deliberately injured by associates of fellow American skater Tonya Harding. It was uncertain whether the injured Kerrigan or discredited Harding would be able to compete in Norway, but both skaters did, with Kerrigan winning a silver medal and Harding finishing out of medal competition. Kerrigan was the only member of the American figure skating team to win a medal.

In women's alpine skiing events, Diann Roffe-Steinrotter won a gold medal in the super G for the American team, while Picabo Street won a silver medal in the downhill for the team. Speed skater Bonnie Blair won gold medals in the women's 500 and 1,000 meter speed skating events and became the all-time leader among American women with five gold medals in Winter Olympics competition. The U.S. to-

tal of thirteen medals in Norway was the best American Winter Olympics performance in history. American women won eight of the thirteen medals offered.

At the 1996 Summer Olympics in Atlanta, Georgia, the United States won a total of 101 medals. As they had done in most previous summer games, African American athletes contributed a disproportionate share of the total. Thirty-five-year-old Carl Lewis surprised the experts by taking the gold medal in the long jump; it was his fourth gold medal in that event and his ninth gold medal overall. Sprinter Michael Johnson made Olympic history by winning gold medals in both the 200 and 400 meter sprints. In women's track and field, Gail Devers won the 100 meter race in dramatic fashion by edging Merlene Ottey from Jamaica. Jamaican-born Canadian sprinter Donovan Bailey set a new world record in the 100-meter race when he won the event in 9.84 seconds. With his victory, he became known as the world's fastest man. Bailey also was a member of the Canadian 4×100 meter relay team that won the gold medal. As expected, both the men's and women's U.S. basketball teams—which were dominated by African American players—came away with gold medals.

Before the 1996 Summer Olympics, astronauts representing the United States, Canada, and France carried the Olympic torch into space with them aboard the space shuttle Columbia. *(AP/Wide World Photos)*

In women's gymnastics, the American team of Amanda Borden, Amy Chow, Dominique Dawes, Shannon Miller, Dominique Moceanu, Jaycie Phelps, and Kerri Strug won the team gold medal in combined exercises. Despite having a badly sprained ankle, Strug made a courageous vault to help the team. American men and women also did well in the swimming events, including Amy Van Dyken who won four gold medals. In women's tennis competition, Lindsay Davenport won the gold medal in singles, and Gigi Fernandez and Mary Joe Fernandez took the gold in doubles. Armenian American Andre Agassi won the gold medal in men's singles. American athletes from various ethnic and racial backgrounds triumphed at the summer games in Atlanta.

SUGGESTED READINGS. Innumerable magazine articles explore different angles of Olympic competition, but only a select number of books give detailed overviews of what transpired at the 1994 and 1996 Olympic Games. These include David Wallechinsky's *Sports Illustrated Presents the Complete Book of the Summer Olympics* (1996), *Chronicle of the Olympics, 1896-1996* (1996), and the U.S. Olympic Committee's official publication *Atlanta 1996* (1996). Martha Ward Plowden has written a stimulating volume titled *Olympic Black Women* (1996).—*Jeffry Jensen*
(updates original entry; vol. 5, p. 1276)

Operation Bootstrap: Economic industrialization plan promoted by Puerto Rico Senate leader Luis Muñoz Marín in PUERTO RICO during the 1940's. Under the plan, U.S. companies were offered tax incentives to develop industry on the island. In addition, industries held by the Puerto Rican government were sold to private investors and the capital invested in infrastructure. During the 1940's and 1950's the program focused on electronics and textile industries; during the 1960's it turned more toward heavy industry, such as petroleum products. In later decades it focused on high-tech industries, pharmaceuticals, banking, and scientific businesses.

Operation Bootstrap has been praised by many for diversifying and greatly expanding Puerto Rico's economy and increasing per capita income. However, it has also drawn some criticism for making Puerto Rico even more financially dependent on the United States. Producing little food or oil for its own consumption, Puerto Rico has relied greatly on imports. Grants-in-aid and FOOD STAMPS from the United States have also increased as many businesses have moved from the island to other countries with cheaper labor

forces and better tax incentives.—*Michelle C. K. McKowen*

Operation Gatekeeper: U.S. federal program to control ILLEGAL IMMIGRATION from Mexico. On October 1, 1994, Attorney General Janet RENO announced the start of a new federal initiative to control the flow of undocumented aliens crossing into the United States from northern Mexico. Through the cooperative efforts of the IMMIGRATION AND NATURALIZATION SERVICE (INS), the Office for the U.S. Attorney for the Southern District of California, and the Executive Office for Immigration Review, increased resources and new strategies were joined in order to secure the San Diego, CALIFORNIA, area border.

Phase I of Operation Gatekeeper concentrated its efforts on the Imperial Beach area, which had historically been the entry point for almost 25 percent of the total of illegal border crossings in the southwestern region. Before Operation Gatekeeper was instituted, the San Diego sector was patrolled by fewer than 1,000 border agents. By the end of 1996, that number had increased to 1,600. The entire San Diego sector is sixty-six miles long.

During the fiscal year of 1994 the Imperial Beach Patrol station apprehended more than 185,000 persons attempting to enter the country illegally. During the fiscal year of 1996, the number of persons apprehended dropped to less than 75,000. Government authorities suggested that the decreased number of apprehensions was a direct result of a high fence built along the border and the new tactical methods used by agents of the BORDER PATROL.

Phase II of Operation Gatekeeper began on June 23, 1995. As it became more difficult to cross the border in the western part of the San Diego sector, the number of apprehensions increased at the East County stations.—*Jeffry Jensen*

Operation Rescue: ANTIABORTION organization founded in 1988. The most conservative right-to-life group in the United States during the 1990's, Operation Rescue traces its roots to Christian FUNDAMENTALISM. The group has comprised both evangelical Protestants and conservative ROMAN CATHOLICS, and has relied upon the methods of civil disobedience and confrontation to protest ABORTION in the United States and Canada. Its tactics have attracted significant media attention, as well as several lawsuits against the organization and its founder, Randall Terry.

Even this wall erected by the U.S. federal government near Tijuana, Mexico, does not deter many Mexicans seeking employment from entering the United States. (Reuters/John Gibbins/Archive Photos)

A born-again Christian and graduate of the Elim Bible Institute, Terry began protesting against abortion rights in 1983, when he picketed an abortion clinic in Binghamton, New York, and tried to persuade women entering the clinic that abortion was morally wrong. In 1986 he and other activists "rescued" the clinic, disrupting its activities by locking themselves inside its building and destroying its telephones. Arrested and later convicted of criminal trespass, Terry served a brief jail sentence. Rather than deterring him, this experience convinced him that direct action and confrontation were effective protest methods. In 1987 he led three hundred followers in blockading another abortion clinic, in Cherry Hill, New Jersey. The following year he announced formal creation of Operation Rescue as a national organization committed to ending abortion.

In 1988 the group garnered national attention at the Democratic National Convention in Atlanta, Georgia, where nearly thirteen hundred antiabortion protesters were jailed. The press coverage resulted in condemnation from both pro-choice organizations and some moderate right-to-life groups, but it also attracted new members and increased financial contributions to Operation Rescue.

Later that year the group held a "National Day of Rescue." It staged a "Holy Week of Rescue" in Los Angeles in 1989, a months-long "Summer of Mercy" in Kansas City in 1991, and a "Cities in Refuge" campaign in 1993. These protests were marked by abortion clinic blockades, thousands of arrests, and intensive media coverage. However, Operation Rescue's success was mixed. The group met with numerous legal challenges, including charges of trespassing and illegally blocking access to clinics. In several cases protesters received jail sentences, and Operation Rescue was subjected to fines and financial penalties. Despite such setbacks, Operation Rescue remained at the forefront of the right-to-life movement.

In the tradition of Christian Fundamentalism, Terry and his followers have contended that abortion constitutes murder. They maintain that confrontational tactics and violations of the law are necessary in order to end the crime of abortion, which they believe has contributed to a decline of morality in the United States. Opponents have charged that Terry and other Operation Rescue members have created a hostile and emotionally charged environment that has led some pro-life supporters to resort to violent acts, such as the murders of physicians who perform abortions and the bombing of abortion clinics.

SUGGESTED READINGS. Faye Ginsburg's "Saving America's Souls: Operation Rescue's Crusade Against Abortion," in *Fundamentalisms and the State Remaking Politics, Economies, and Militance* (1993), places the group's activities in the context of religious fundamentalist movements. Terry himself discusses his views in *Operation Rescue* (1988).—*Thomas Clarkin*

Order Sons of Italy in America (OSIA): ITALIAN AMERICAN fraternal society founded in 1905. OSIA is an umbrella organization with 38 state affiliates, 1,400 local affiliates, and an estimated 100,000 members. Open to both men and women, the group has worked to preserve and disseminate the Italian cultural heritage through charitable, social, civic, educational, and philanthropic activities. It has acted as the antidefamation arm of the Italian American community, awarded scholarships, maintained the Garibaldi-Meucci Museum, and bestowed the Marconi and National Sports awards. Its publications include a periodic national directory and the monthly *OSIA News*.—*Glenn Canyon*

These Italian immigrants were processed at Ellis Island in 1905—the same year that the Order Sons of Italy was founded in the United States. (AP/Wide World Photos)

Organic Act of Guam of 1950: U.S. law defining the relationship of Guam to the United States. Signed into law by President Harry S Truman on August 1, 1950, this act declared Guam an unincorporated territory of the United States and granted U.S. citizenship to all native Guam residents and their children who were born on Guam after April 11, 1899. The organic act also established a civilian government for Guam that mirrored the U.S. government's legislative, executive, and judicial branches.

Before 1950 all of Guam's governors were U.S. naval officers appointed by the presidents of the United States. From 1950 until 1970 its governors were civilians appointed by the presidents. In 1970 Guam began electing its own governors. Guamanians cannot vote in U.S. presidential elections but they do send nonvoting delegates to the U.S. Congress.

Although the organic act has been amended several times and there have been many discussions about Guam's future political status, the Organic Act of Guam was expected, in the mid-1990's, to remain in effect for many more years.—*William Matta*

Organization of Chinese American Women (OCAW): Nonpartisan international organization established in 1977 to lobby for the interests of CHINESE AMERICAN women. Focusing on leadership and community services, it has conducted numerous training conferences for professional women. The organization has helped more than a thousand Asian American women find positions and has provided a national network for both working women and college students. Its community service activities have included conducting English classes and job training programs for nonprofessional women immigrants and providing food and housing assistance for the elderly.

OCAW is headquartered in Washington, D.C. Its board of directors includes nationally known women in government and business, and the organization's prominence has led to White House briefings and presentations of position papers at congressional forums.

OCAW has annually awarded fellowships to outstanding young musicians and has introduced world-class artists from China, Taiwan, and Hong Kong at Kennedy Center concerts that have raised money for scholarships. The organization publishes a quarterly newsletter, *OCAW Speaks.*—*George C. Y. Wang*

Organization of Chinese Americans (OCA): National civil rights group for CHINESE AMERICAN and ASIAN AMERICAN peoples that was founded in 1973. Based in Washington, D.C., the OCA is a nonpartisan and nonprofit body representing nearly ten thousand people. It has promoted political and legislative activities through forty-one chapters in the United States and Hong Kong. Its focus has been to secure the rights of Chinese and Asian American citizens and permanent residents for the purposes of promoting cultural heritage, combating stereotypes and prejudice, achieving equal opportunity and treatment, and advocating for active participation in civic and national matters. Recognizing the importance of working with other political coalitions, OCA's advocacy areas, written in the 1996 platform statement, were immigration, civil rights, health care, public benefits, political participation, and economic growth. OCA sponsors several types of public internships (national, congressional, and government) that have provided opportunities for college-or graduate-level Asian Americans to be involved in political processes.—*Rowena Fong*

Organization of Pan Asian American Women (PANASIA): Washington, D.C.-based nonprofit public-policy organization founded in 1976. Created to help promote the attainment of equal opportunity for Asian American women, PANASIA has sought to eradicate anti-Asian discrimination and ensure that the concerns of its constituents are addressed at the national level. The group has also striven to promote accurate media portrayals of Asian and Pacific Islander American women, lobbied for the elimination of employment barriers, and offered support to women in policy-making positions. —*Alexander Scott*

P

PARC v. Commonwealth of Pennsylvania (1971): U.S. federal court case debating the rights of children with mental disabilities. In this decision, a federal court endorsed the assertion of the Pennsylvania Association of Retarded Children (PARC) that children with mental disabilities were entitled to free public education. The ruling ensured broad protection of the principle of equal access to education. Advocates of the rights of persons with mental disabilities praised the decision as a major victory for the DISABILITY RIGHTS MOVEMENT.
—*Alexander Scott*

Patterson v. McLean Credit Union (1989): U.S. Supreme Court decision limiting redress for claims of racial harassment under the Civil Rights Act of 1966. An African American woman named Patterson brought suit against her employer claiming she had been racially harassed on the job. A previous Supreme Court case, *Runyon v. McCrary* (1976), had outlawed all racial DISCRIMINATION in contractual and property transactions, both public and private. After Patterson argued her case, the justices ordered reargument addressing the issue of whether its earlier *Runyon* decision should be

The Parc v. Commonwealth of Pennsylvania *decision was a major step in public recognition of the right of children with learning disabilities to have a free public education.* (Don Franklin)

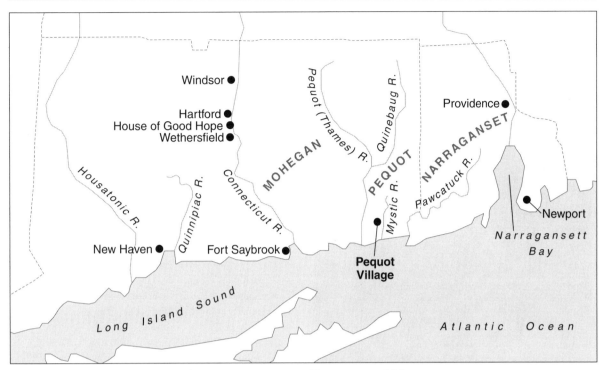

AREA OF THE PEQUOT WAR

overruled. The reargument order provoked considerable outrage, as did the decision that the Court passed down on June 15, 1989. Although the justices did not overturn this precedent, they did find that the statute under which Patterson had brought her claim only protected against racial discrimination in the formation of contracts and did not extend to an employer's post-contractual behavior. In response, Congress passed the CIVIL RIGHTS ACT OF 1991, whose provisions superseded the *Patterson* court decision—*Lisa Paddock*

Pequot War (1637): War in which the Pequot Indians were nearly exterminated by English colonists of Massachusetts and Connecticut and their Indian allies, the Narragensetts. The underlying conflict was over Pequot control of the fertile Thames River Valley and the coastal area trade in beads for wampum, a seventeenth century trade and currency innovation. The Pequots also had trading ties with Dutch settlers living west of Connecticut, whom the English and Narragensetts envied.

The English used a supposed murder of an Englishman by Pequots as their reason for declaring war on the tribe. Under Captain John Mason white raiders destroyed a Pequot village inhabited by women, children, and the elderly, rather than one inhabited mostly by warriors. The English burned all of the dwellings in the Mystic River village and shot those who tried to flee. Few Pequots escaped alive and those who were not killed were sold into slavery. Even the Narragensett allies of the English were horrified at the brutality of the English attack.—*Gretchen L. Green*

Perkins Act (Carl D. Perkins Vocational and Applied Technology Education Act of 1990): U.S. federal government legislation. Passed on September 25, 1990, the Perkins Act attempted to make the United States more competitive in the world economy by developing occupational as well as academic skills of its citizens. After the 1960's the federal vocational education budget declined greatly. The Perkins Act addressed this problem by providing $1.6 billion in federal funds for vocational education at the state and local levels. It required that 10.5 percent of basic state grants go to programs for single parents, single pregnant women, and displaced homemakers, and to programs promoting sex equity by assisting men and women to enter occupations traditionally reserved for the opposite sex. It also required states to ensure that special populations (for example, persons with disabilities or those with limited English proficiency) have equal access to recruitment, enrollment,

Representative Carl D. Perkins in 1965. (AP/Wide World Photos)

and placement in programs. It gave educational agencies more flexibility in designing programs but also mandated accountability and citizen participation.—*Irene Struthers*

Phillips v. Martin Marietta Corporation (1971): First U.S. Supreme Court decision affirming Title VII of the CIVIL RIGHTS ACT OF 1964. This case began when a woman named Ida Phillips filed suit against the Martin Marietta Corporation for having violated the Civil Rights Act of 1964 by refusing to hire her because she had pre-school-age children. The case eventually reached the U.S. Supreme Court. On January 25, 1971, the Court reversed a lower court decision and sent the case back for a hearing to determine whether mothers should have more responsibility than fathers for caring for their children and whether the family obligations of mothers might have a detrimental effect on their job performance. This decision rejected without further proof the stereotype of women as the primary caretakers of young children. In a separate opinion that strengthened the Court's decision, Associate Justice Thurgood MARSHALL argued that while employers may require "parents, both mother and father, to provide for their children's care," the "ancient canard about the proper role of women" cannot "be the basis for discrimination." —*David L. Sterling*

Planned Parenthood of Central Missouri v. Danforth (1976): U.S. Supreme Court decision concerning ABORTION rights. In 1974 the Missouri state legislature passed a series of regulations limiting the right of women to terminate pregnancy. The most controversial of these provisions was the requirement that married women wishing to have abortions obtain the permission of their husbands and that unmarried minors wishing abortions have the consent of one or both parents during the first trimester of their pregnancies. On July 1, 1976, the U.S. Supreme Court, by a 6-3 margin, struck down both provisions of the Missouri law as violations of the due process clause of the FOURTEENTH AMENDMENT to the U.S. Constitution. Justice Henry Blackmun, writing for the majority, noted, in part, that "it is the woman who physically bears the child and who is more directly and immediately affected by the pregnancy, as between the two [spouses], the balance weighs in her favor." The Court's decision was a major affirmation of a woman's right to have an abortion.—*David L. Sterling*

Supreme Court justice Harry Blackmun wrote the opinion in Planned Parenthood *affirming that the decisions of pregnant mothers should be paramount.* (AP/Wide World Photos)

Planned Parenthood v. Ashcroft (1983): U.S. Supreme Court case relating to ABORTION rights. In *Planned Parenthood v. Ashcroft*, the Court ruled on the legality of a Missouri statute requiring hospital stays for all women undergoing second-trimester abortions. By a 6-3 margin the Court ruled that the requirement was an unreasonable infringement on a woman's right to seek an abortion. However, the Court voted to uphold other portions of the Missouri statute; these included requirements that second physicians be present when abortions were performed after fetuses reached viability, that minors seeking abortions either have parental consent or receive judicial determinations that the procedure would be in their interest, and that pathology reports be filed for every abortion performed.—*Glenn Canyon*

Plastic surgery: Branch of medical practice devoted to physical reconstruction of patients' appearances. The two major types of plastic surgery are reconstructive and augmentative.

Reconstructive surgery has been relatively free from controversy because its purpose is to recreate patients' original appearances after they have been disfigured by physical trauma or disease. An example of reconstructive surgery is grafting of skin to repair damage from severe burns. Reconstructive plastic surgery dates back to World War I, when disfiguring injuries and dismemberments occurred in great numbers.

Knowledge gained from reconstructive surgery led to the emergence of elective surgery to enhance the physical attractiveness of patients. Known as augmentative plastic surgery and sometimes called cosmetic surgery, this form of plastic surgery has raised a variety of controversial gender issues.

Standards of female beauty in North America have involved considerable effort and expense including fashion trends, cosmetics, hair styling, and in the twentieth century the potential to improve biology

This Canadian advertisement offers all the major varieties of cosmetic surgery. (Dick Hemingway)

through plastic surgery. In the 1990's plastic surgery became the fastest-growing medical specialty. The fastest growing subcategory of plastic surgery was liposuction, which uses mechanical suction to remove unwanted fat from bodies. The safety and long-term effectiveness of liposuction was a source of concern. Plastic surgery has also included minor procedures to improve defects in facial features such as nose jobs and collagen injections to create fuller lips. Plastic surgery has frequently been employed to counteract the physical signs of aging through such procedures as face lifts, which reduce excess skin and wrinkling. However, none of these procedures achieved the level of controversy of BREAST IMPLANTS.

Augmentation of female breast size has had a long

history. The first women who tried to have their breasts surgically enlarged were apparently Japanese prostitutes, who had silicone in liquid form injected directly into their breasts during the 1940's. This procedure was used in the United States in the 1950's but was eventually halted because of the number of complications and deaths with which it was credited. Silicone gel contained in silicone-rubber envelopes became popular in the United States during the 1970's. By the mid-1980's medical evidence began to circulate that silicone breast implants posed potential health risks. However, implant manufacturers and plastic surgeons denied that were was enough medical evidence to demonstrate a causal link between implants and health problems.

Controversy surrounding plastic surgery has centered on the expense, effort, and risks that women have been willing to take in order to enhance their beauty. Although plastic surgery has been dominated by female clientele, beginning in the 1980's major metropolitan newspapers began to run advertisements for penile implants as greater attention was focused upon male physical appearance.

SUGGESTED READINGS. *Beauty Secrets: Women and the Politics of Appearance* (1986), by Wendy Chapkis, provides commentary and portraits of women and their struggles with notions of beauty in popular culture. Frank B. Vasey and Josh Feldstein examine the public debate over the safety of silicone breast implants, including the roles of cosmetic surgeons, the Federal Drug Administration, and recipients in *The Silicone Breast Implant Controversy: What Women Need to Know* (1993). Naomi Wolfe's *The Beauty Myth: How Images of Beauty Are Used Against Women* (1991) is a comprehensive feminist analysis of the impact and forces in the modern cultural definition of female beauty.—*Maurice Hamington*

Police-community relations: For many people in the United States, the beating of Rodney KING in early 1991 by officers of the Los Angeles Police Department represented the worst example of relations between police and members of minority communities. The riots that followed the acquittal of the officers charged with responsibility for King's beating were evidence of the frustration with the criminal justice system felt by many African Americans and Latinos. Racial prejudice has often merged with economically disadvantaged conditions to create potentially explosive situations between police and inner-city residents. Perhaps paradoxically, members of minority communities in the United States often feel overpoliced and underprotected.

Public Opinion. Surveys of public attitudes have indicated that race and ethnicity, as well as age and income, correlate closely with levels of confidence in the police of members of the public. Young, low-income males, for example, have the most negative attitudes toward the police. Surveys of police attitudes provide seemingly inconsistent results. On the one hand, police attitudes toward race seem to mirror those of the general population. Yet those who have worked primarily in high-crime, poor, or minority neighborhoods have tended to report less respect from the public than those in other areas. This perceived lack of respect may be related to the "cues" that police officers typically use to identify possible perpetrators of criminal activity, such as dress, demeanor,

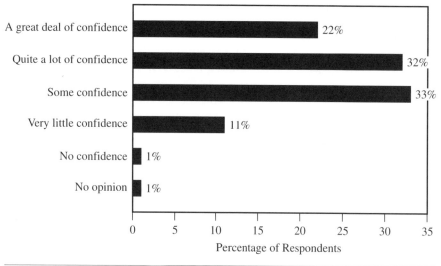

Public Confidence in the Police: 1994 Opinion Poll

A great deal of confidence — 22%
Quite a lot of confidence — 32%
Some confidence — 33%
Very little confidence — 11%
No confidence — 1%
No opinion — 1%

Percentage of Respondents

Source: George Gallup, Jr., ed., *The Gallup Poll: Public Opinion, 1994* (Wilmington, Del.: Scholarly Resources, 1995).

Intense publicity relating to the beating of undocumented Mexican immigrants by California police officers in Riverside County in early 1996 provoked this anti-police brutality demonstration in Seattle, Washington. (AP/Wide World Photos)

gender, age, and race. Thus the mutually suspicious attitudes on the part of police and minority youths create the potential for conflict and misunderstanding.

Although the people with whom police officers are most likely to have direct contact are persons living in low-income and minority neighborhoods, many residents of those same areas believe that law enforcement agencies do not protect their communities from crime. There is, in fact, ample historical evidence indicating that police have paid less attention to crime victims in poor inner-city neighborhoods, and that this neglect has been related to both racial discrimination and inadequate resources.

The most traditional law enforcement agencies are likely to place their officers in areas that generate the most reported crimes and most calls for service, ac-

counting for their disproportionate presence in minority areas. Young males in public places who are likely to be stopped by the police complain about harassment. Other residents who call the police for noncrime services, such as medical emergencies, family problems, DOMESTIC VIOLENCE, or public order violations, may find the police unhelpful.

Police Use of Force. After the mid-1980's most U.S. police departments began tightening the rules governing when officers could use deadly force. Earlier procedures had followed the "fleeing felon" rule, which permitted police to shoot to kill anyone suspected of running away from scenes of suspected felonies. Research has indicated that the fleeing-felon rule was used against African Americans about seven times more often than against whites. In 1984 the U.S. Su-

This San Francisco police booth in the city's Chinatown is an example of community policing. (International Daily News)

Brutality on the part of law enforcement officers has been a long-standing problem in the United States, as acknowledged in the Wickersham Commission report in 1931, which described the use of physical coercion against criminal suspects. Later studies have indicated that police use of excessive force is most likely in arrest situations, when suspects challenge officers' authority, and when suspects offend the moral values of the arresting officers. Typical victims of police brutality are low-income males.

Most examples of police use of excessive force occur in high-crime neighborhoods. Again, the intersection of race and economic status means that many such episodes occur in minority neighborhoods, adding to the perception that police brutality is typically directed against black and Hispanic youths. A 1993 report commissioned by the National Association for the Advancement of Colored People on six cities found that verbal abuse, unjustified searches, excessive force, vicious police dogs, and shootings were far more likely to be directed against African Americans than against whites.

Corruption. Police corruption is another issue that interferes with effective police relationships with their communities. Although the majority of police officers practice their profession with integrity, the culture within some departments fosters theft, protection rackets, evidence-planting, and record-falsification. Whether individual police officers become involved in illegal activities because of personal greed or to justify their own negligence or mistakes, most police adhere to a strong code requiring them above all else to be loyal to their fellow officers—a fact that makes addressing corruption difficult. In addition, alienation and hostility between police and the communities in which they work increase the potential for corruption. Supervisors may cover up

preme Court declared the fleeing-felon rule unconstitutional in *Tennessee v. Garner*. Afterward most law enforcement agencies began following the "defense of life" rule, which permits use of deadly force only when the lives of officers or other persons are threatened. In addition, agencies have adopted mandatory reporting rules requiring officers to account for each time they discharge their firearms. These procedures have led to decreases in disparities in the frequency of police shootings of minority and nonminority suspects, but some discrepancies have remained.

departmental corruption out of fear that bad publicity will damage the standing of the police with the public even more than the illegal activities themselves.

Community Policing. The most hopeful prescription for improving relationships between police and civilians, especially in high risk neighborhoods, has been community policing. It is a strategy whereby law enforcement officers work not as adversaries but in partnership with citizens to identify and address community concerns. It may include community meetings to define neighborhood problems, foot patrols by police officers to build rapport with residents, and cleanup and recreational projects. Instead of merely responding after crimes have been reported, community police are expected to work with the public to prevent crimes from taking place. Many agencies have increased the racial, gender, and ethnic diversity of their officer corps; however, expanding recruitment has proven to be most effective in improving the likelihood of successful community policing.

SUGGESTED READINGS. *The Real War on Crime: The Report of the National Criminal Justice Commission* (1996), edited by Steven R. Donziger, summarizes some of the best current research and analyses. Andrew Hacker's *Two Nations: Black and White, Separate, Hostile, Unequal* (1992) examines a broad spectrum of race relations. *Search and Destroy* (1996), by Jerome G. Miller, focuses on the experience of young black men. In *The Color of Justice* (1996), Samuel Walker, Cassia Spohn, and Miriam DeLone examine racism in all aspects of the criminal justice system. *—Mary Welek Atwell*

Polish Falcons of America (PFA): POLISH AMERICAN fraternal organization founded in Chicago in 1887 by Felix L. Pietrowicz. This national nonprofit organization, headquartered in Pittsburgh, Pennsylvania, numbered thirty thousand members in 1997, with representation from each state in the union. Its primary purpose has been to promote and preserve Polish culture in the United States and to document Polish and Polish American achievements. Physical education and sporting events have been constant parts of PFA activities. Officer-training programs existed prior to World War I, helping PFA recruits to serve with distinction in the U.S. armed forces during both world wars. Among the organization's most recent activities have been local and national golf, bowling, and folk dancing tournaments, as well as a national convention. The PFA has offered its members annuities, insurance coverage, and mortuary

benefits, and it has published the bilingual newspaper *Sokol Polski* (Polish Falcon) since 1896.—*Beau David Case*

Polish National Alliance of the United States of North America (PNA): POLISH AMERICAN fraternal organization founded in Philadelphia in 1880. Later headquartered in Chicago, the PNA set as its purpose protecting the interests of Polish immigrants. By the late twentieth century it ranked as the largest ethnically based BENEVOLENT AND FRATERNAL ORGANIZATION in the United States with more than 300,000 members and assets of more than $300 million. The PNA has offered annuities and insurance to it members; donated millions of dollars for scholarships, libraries, and subsidies for Polish-language classes; and published *Zgoda* (Unity). The oldest Polish or Polish American newspaper in the United States, *Zgoda* began publication in 1881. Individual PNA lodges have worked to preserve and promote Polish culture through such activities as Saturday morning Polish-language schools for children, public dinners, festivals, folk dances, and sporting events. Internationally, the PNA has offered political and economic support to Poland, such as creating joint Polish-United States business ventures in Poland.—*Beau David Case*

Postfeminism: Late twentieth century responses of women to FEMINISM who have been disillusioned by the application of feminist ideals in their lives. American women who grew up in the 1960's and 1970's, when feminism had a revolutionary aura, have been more likely to describe themselves as feminists than younger women of the 1980's and 1990's. Despite feminists' involvement in the EQUAL RIGHTS AMENDMENT movement, AFFIRMATIVE ACTION, and laws outlining and prohibiting SEXUAL HARASSMENT, postfeminists have emphasized individual determination as the only real necessity for women to succeed. They may desire a sense of unity with other women, but grow disappointed with the apparent lack of progress that feminism has made in a time when SEXUAL DISCRIMINATION has persisted and society has continued to expect women to fulfill their roles as wives and mothers, while at the same time maintaining careers.—*Holly L. Norton*

Poverty, feminization of: The incidence of poverty in the United States has varied substantially across gender and ethnic lines, but women have always constituted the majority of adults living in POVERTY and receiving public assistance. Families headed by females have emerged as one of the major American poverty groups, and one with particular relevance to welfare reform and social delinquency.

Estimates of the numbers of Americans in poverty are published by the U.S. BUREAU OF THE CENSUS. In 1992 a family of four was considered to be in poverty if its annual income was under $14,463. The official poverty line varies with family size and is adjusted upward each year to match inflationary increases in price levels. Between 1959 and 1973 the proportion of American families living in poverty declined from 22 percent to 11 percent. From then to the mid-1990's the proportion did not show any significant downward trend.

Female-headed Families. In 1992 only 6.2 percent of families headed by married couples were living in poverty. In contrast, 34.9 percent of SINGLE MOTHER families (with no husband present) were poor. Among African Americans and Hispanics, nearly half of all female-headed families were in poverty. The propor-

tion of female-headed households has been much higher for African Americans (47 percent in 1992) than for whites (14 percent) or Hispanics (23 percent). However, the proportion of households which were headed by women increased for both white and black Americans, from around 10 percent of all families during the 1960's to 17.5 percent in 1992.

Female-headed families traditionally were created because of divorces or deaths of husbands. However, increasing numbers of such families have reflected a growing trend of women having babies who have never been married. Between 1960 and 1990 the numbers of births out of wedlock increased from 255,000 to more than one million despite the fact that access to birth control and ABORTION became far easier. By the mid-1990's, more than one fourth of all American births were occurring out of wedlock.

The median income for families headed by divorced women was $15,762 in 1990, but families headed by never-married women averaged only $8,337. These income disparities did not differ greatly across ethnic

Three quarters of older Americans living below the poverty line are women, a growing number of whom are homeless. (James L. Shaffer)

By the early 1990's nearly half of all female-headed Hispanic and African American families were living in poverty. (Lester Sloane)

lines. The never-married women were typically poorly educated, not regularly in the work force, and prone to alcohol or drug abuse. In 1991 only 42 percent of poverty-level female heads of households worked at all during the year, and only 10 percent worked full time for the entire year. About three-fourths of unwed teenage mothers went on welfare within five years of giving birth.

One reason given for the declining attractiveness of marriage in the United States has been the poor wage and employment status of many unmarried young men. Children born into households without fathers are less likely than others to become well educated, productive, and crime- and drug-free members of the community. The highest risks involve fatherless boys.

Older People. The incidence of poverty among OLDER AMERICANS—those over the age of sixty-five, has actually been below the average for all age groups. This is true partly because of the effectiveness of older Americans' political lobbying efforts, which have con-

tributed to the creation of generous Social Security and Medicare programs. However, the proportion of the American population over the age of sixty-five has increased steadily. Of older persons living below the poverty line, three-fourths are women, predominantly widows. In 1992, 29 percent of unrelated women over the age of seventy-five were living in poverty. Women tend to outlive men by several years. Many of these women did not work and they received substantially smaller pensions after their husbands died. Those who worked received lower wages than men and spent less time in the labor force. In 1996 only 9 percent of women over the age of forty expected to receive retirement benefits from their employers.

Welfare. During the early 1990's only about 55 percent of persons officially classified as poor received welfare assistance—mostly through AID TO FAMILIES WITH DEPENDENT CHILDREN (AFDC), FOOD STAMPS, and Medicaid. The vast majority of welfare families were headed by nonworking females with young children. In 1992 about thirteen million Americans were on welfare, including about one-fourth of the country's children. About 43 percent of welfare recipients were white, 40 percent black, and 17 percent Hispanic.

The relationships among poverty, welfare, and lifestyle patterns came in for heavy discussion in connection with the so-called WELFARE REFORM enacted by Congress in 1996. The new legislation abolished AFDC and relegated much of welfare policy-making decisions to individual states. Emphasis was placed on limiting the duration of eligibility for benefit recipients and requiring claimants to work or pursue further education and training.

Remedies. If poverty were simply equated with low incomes, it could easily be relieved by giving the poor more income—provided that the nonpoor cooperate. Most Americans accept this principle when poverty reflects infirmity or misfortune. By the 1990's, however, much poverty was perceived as arising from poor lifestyle choices, especially childbearing by young, poorly educated, unwed mothers. The welfare system was criticized for subsidizing such behavior, encouraging dependency and lack of personal responsibility, and helping to foster home environments that would be very damaging to the children raised in them.

Numerous policy experiments have demonstrated that there are no easy ways of reducing problem pregnancies. Avenues offering some hope of improvement have included improving the schools (particularly in inner cities), reducing exposure to drugs and alcohol, and increasing awareness of BIRTH CONTROL AND FAMILY PLANNING opportunities. Although moving young, poorly educated mothers from welfare to jobs is not likely to improve their incomes, advocates hoped it would increase their sense of personal responsibility and self-respect. Efforts to increase male responsibility have involved stronger measures to enforce child-support payments by fathers, aided by DNA testing to establish paternity. There appears to be no easy way to improve the life situations of the children in poor female-headed households

SUGGESTED READINGS. These issues are admirably surveyed by Harrell R. Rodgers Jr., in *Poor Women, Poor Children: American Poverty in the 1990s* (3d ed., 1996). Diana DiNitto's *Social Welfare: Politics and Public Policy* (4th ed. 1995) gives a comprehensive overview of poverty problems and policies and is sensitive to women's issues. *Reducing Poverty in America* (1996), edited by Michael Darby presents a wide variety of viewpoints.—*Paul B. Trescott*

Powell, Colin Luther (b. Apr. 5, 1937, New York, N.Y.): Chairman of the Joint Chiefs of Staff of the U.S. MILITARY. Powell became the first African American to hold the position of chairman of the Joint Chiefs of Staff when President George Bush appointed him to the U.S. military's highest-ranking office in 1989. Powell had previously served two tours of combat duty in the VIETNAM WAR, risen to the status of four-star general, and served as national security adviser to President Ronald Reagan. With the assistance of President Bush and General H. Norman Schwarzkopf, Powell was widely credited with engineering the U.S.-led alliance's overwhelming victory in the 1991 Persian Gulf War.

The son of first-generation JAMAICAN AMERICAN immigrants, Powell has been a Harlem-born version of the classic American success story. After working his way through school, he graduated from the City College of New York in 1958 and later earned a master's degree from George Washington University. Throughout his career Powell stressed the importance of hard work, education, and the calling of public service to audiences within and without the armed forces. Following his success in directing allied efforts in the Gulf War and his retirement from the Joint Chiefs of Staff in 1993, Powell's popularity reached a peak in 1995, when his tour to promote his memoirs, *My American Journey,* brought him unprecedented publicity, as well as rumors that he might seek the U.S. presidency.

In the prelude to the 1996 presidential election, both major political parties courted Powell, who had never held elective office or even publicly announced his po- litical affiliation—just as both parties had courted General Dwight D. Eisenhower after World War II. Many Democrats and Republicans hoped that a Powell candidacy, for either the presidency or the vice-presidency, would lend their respective parties instant credibility at a time when record numbers of Americans claimed to be disillusioned with government. At that time public opinion polls indicated that Americans regarded the armed forces as the part of the federal government that worked best, and Powell was largely credited with the military's high repute. Many commentators thought that what Powell's army had learned from the lessons of the Vietnam War was used to win the Gulf War. Under Powell's guidance the armed forces became the one sector of American life in which the policy of AFFIRMATIVE ACTION appeared to have been an unquestioned success.

Not since the draft-Eisenhower movement of the

After Colin Powell became the first African American to achieve the highest rank in the U.S. military, many political observers thought he might also become the first African American to run for president on a major-party ticket. (Reuters/Archive Photos)

early 1950's had the nation been so interested in the political opinions of a war hero. Powell's 1995 book tour was covered extensively, and major media outlets dissected every statement that he made, looking for clues as to his political leanings and ambitions. After announcing that he considered himself a moderate-to-liberal Republican, Powell allowed speculation to build for weeks that he would challenge Senator Robert Dole for the party's nomination, accept the second spot on a Dole ticket, or perhaps serve as secretary of state in a Dole administration.

Pundits of all political persuasions predicted that a Powell candidacy would draw African American voters away from the Democratic Party and challenge conservative dominance of the Republican Party. However, in November, 1995, Powell made all speculation moot when he publicly announced his refusal

to run for the presidency in 1996. However, he left the door open for possible future political campaigns.
—*J. Todd Moye*
(updates original entry; vol. 5, p. 1346)

Pregnancy and employment: The roots of public concern about women working while pregnant date back to the Industrial Revolution of the late nineteenth and early twentieth centuries. At that time many women were employed in factories, laundries, and other workplaces to supplement their family incomes or, in some cases, to provide entire family incomes. Working conditions for most workers at that time were hazardous, dirty, and unhealthy. Concern still exists for pregnant women who are employed: While many workplaces do not have the same hazards that existed in the nineteenth century, modern technology has created new hazards that place pregnant women in jeopardy. In addition, increased numbers of women in the workforce have raised concerns about competition for jobs traditionally held by men, fueling debates over whether pregnant women should work at all.

History. Throughout history some women have worked primarily in the home, others outside of the home in industrialized workplaces. The condition of pregnant women who worked outside the home in the late nineteenth century caught the attention of several physicians who began documenting the effects of industrial substances and work practices on pregnant women. One of these physicians, Alice Hamilton, documented the effects of carbon monoxide and benzene exposure on pregnant women. She found that death rates for both infants and mothers during childbirth were 75 percent higher for women working in mills than for women who did not work outside the home.

Findings such as Hamilton's fueled a drive for protective legislation for women in the United States. Advocates of protective legislation focused on the long hours that women worked and the conditions under which they worked. Early protective labor laws limited women's participation in the labor force, cutting the hours they could work and prohibiting them from working night shifts. In the landmark case MULLER v. OREGON (1908), the U.S. Supreme Court upheld a state law limiting working hours for women. This case helped set forth a view of women that has long persisted: that they should be childbearers first and wage earners second.

Federal Legislation. Protective legislation stood its

Reported Incidents of Discrimination Against Pregnant Workers in the United States

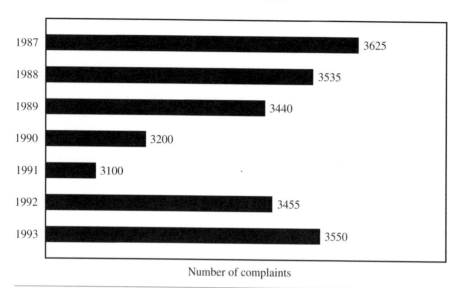

Year	Number of complaints
1987	3625
1988	3535
1989	3440
1990	3200
1991	3100
1992	3455
1993	3550

Number of complaints

Source: Equal Employment Opportunity Commission

drawing attention to the special needs of pregnant workers. Instead, they emphasized similarities between men and women and compared pregnancy with medical conditions that temporarily disabled workers. A serious problem with this approach was that many companies did not cover their workers with disability insurance, without which pregnant workers were left with no protection at all. Most disability policies provide for six weeks of paid leave for natural births and eight weeks of paid leave for CESAREAN SECTION births. Women who take disability leave for pregnancy return to their same positions when they resume work, assuming that no other disability prevents them from performing their same tasks.

ground for generations. It was not until passage of Title VII of the CIVIL RIGHTS ACT OF 1964 that the validity of state protective laws came into question. The civil rights law prohibited DISCRIMINATION in employment on the basis of race, religion, national origin, and sex. After its enactment, state laws that sought to single out women for protection were challenged. Such laws could only be defended only when it could be proven that sex was a BONA FIDE OCCUPATIONAL QUALIFICATION.

The EQUAL EMPLOYMENT OPPORTUNITY COMMISSION (EEOC) was created to administer Title VII of the Civil Rights Act of 1964. In 1972 the commission issued guidelines stating that pregnancy should not be grounds for treating a woman differently from male workers. However, these guidelines did not deter employers from developing policies that distinguished between pregnant and nonpregnant workers.

In 1978 Congress passed the PREGNANCY DISCRIMINATION ACT, which amended Title VII to classify all exclusions based on pregnancy, childbirth, or related medical conditions as sexual discrimination. Pregnancy was then considered to be a "disability" that could be covered under disability insurance. This act represented an attempt to deny the gender-specificity of pregnancy. Many women who were pushing for pregnancy benefits legislation were concerned about

By the 1990's the United States was the only industrialized country that did not have a national maternity or paternal leave policy. Nevertheless, the government and many employers began to change their attitudes and policies toward pregnant workers and working parents. Women's paid employment was increasingly recognized as vital to the American economy. Several major corporations began adopting policies regarding pregnant workers, parental leave, child care, and flexible work schedules to meet the needs of working parents. The passage of the FAMILY AND MEDICAL LEAVE ACT of 1993 represented a major step in family care policy in the United States. Under this legislation, both male and female employees can request up to twelve weeks of unpaid leave for the births or adoptions of children or the serious medical needs of immediate family members.

SUGGESTED READINGS. *Double Exposure: Women's Health Hazards on the Job and at Home* (1984), edited by Wendy Chavkin, is the only book dedicated to describing women's job hazards. *Maternity: Letters from Working Women* (1978), edited by Margaret Llewelyn Davies, collects letters from women about working conditions in factories during the early twentieth century. Regina Kenen's *Reproductive Hazards in the Workplace: Mending Jobs, Managing Pregnancies* (1993) examines the impact of pregnancy and work. *The Politics of Pregnancy: Policy Dilemmas in the Maternal-Fetal Relationship* (1993), edited by Janna Merrick and Robert Blank, examines specific policy issues relating to pregnancy, including abortion, drug testing, fetal protection policies, and reproductive hazards.—*Robin Sakina Mama*

Pregnancy Discrimination Act (PDA): U.S. federal legislation targeting DISCRIMINATION against pregnant women in the workplace. A 1978 amendment to Title VII of the CIVIL RIGHTS ACT OF 1964, this law categorized PREGNANCY discrimination as a form of sex discrimination in the workplace. It required that private employers treat pregnancy, CHILDBIRTH, and related medical conditions in the same ways they do other medical disabilities. The PDA was promoted by women's groups because pregnant women were often demoted, fired, or deprived of their seniority. A 1990 study by the Institute for Women's Policy Research found that the PDA had successfully safeguarded pregnant women's rights to keep working with equal employment conditions, terms, and benefits. The PDA does not cover small businesses and federal agencies, and many women, fired illegally, may not know their rights or may be unable to afford to retain a lawyer. In 1992 the hotline of the women's group 9 TO 5 NATIONAL ASSOCIATION OF WORKING WOMEN received more than 15,000 calls claiming pregnancy discrimination.—*Glenn Ellen Starr*

Premenstrual syndrome (PMS): Term characterizing a variety of symptoms resulting from chemical changes produced in women's bodies as a result of their menstruation cycles. Symptoms of PMS typically begin ten to fourteen days prior to menstruation and continue until the first days of menstruation. Symptoms can occur at puberty, after pregnancies, or after hysterectomies.

Researchers have estimated that millions of women suffer from PMS, but some women never experience any symptoms of PMS at all. More than 150 symptoms have been linked with PMS. The most common are tension, mood swings, irritability, depression, cramps, sugar-craving, acne, joint pain, water-retention, fatigue, headache, backache, swollen or tender breasts, and constipation. Women frequently experience combinations of these symptoms, with their severity varying among individual. Some women have reported that PMS disrupts their ability to perform daily functions,

while others describe it as merely an annoying inconvenience.

An important aspect of PMS diagnoses is the fact that symptoms regularly occur prior to menstruation and disappear once menstruation begins. Research has indicated that imbalances of estrogen and progesterone hormone levels are the likely cause of PMS. The hypothalamus, a gland located in the brain, releases hormones that act upon the pituitary gland, which in turn releases the follicle-stimulating hormone (FSH) and the luteinizing hormone (LH), which stimulate follicles to produce eggs. During this stage, estrogen and progesterone are produced to aid in the development of eggs and thicken the lining of the uterus in the event of fertilization. Imbalances in these hormones produce chain reactions of symptoms resulting in PMS.

Although PMS once received little recognition, doctors and researchers have come to acknowledge it as an authentic and treatable medical disorder. Despite increased awareness and attention from the medical community, some people have remained skeptical that PMS is a real disorder; they tend to attribute its numerous symptoms to sufferers' imaginations. Such skepticism likely results from the numerous and vague symptoms commonly linked to PMS.

Women suffering from mild PMS symptoms find relief through nonprescription pain relievers or medications specifically designed to alleviate PMS symptoms. For some women, simple alteration of diets relieves their discomfort. Many women with severe effects of PMS seek advice from doctors who evaluate their individual condition and prescribe appropriate medications to correct the hormonal imbalance.

SUGGESTED READINGS. Katharina Dalton's *Once a Month: The Original Premenstrual Syndrome Handbook* (1995) provides a thorough analysis of the causes and treatment of PMS. *PMS Premenstrual Self-Help Book* (1995), by Susan Lark, offers a variety of suggestions to relieve PMS symptoms, from altering diet to reducing stress. Sharon Sneed and Joe McIllhaney define PMS and illustrate solutions in *PMS: What Is It and What You Can Do About It* (1988). *Premenstrual Syndrome: Index of Modern Information* (1990), by Jacob Liehaus, lists recently published sources on the subject.—*Sandra Leigh Walton*

Prenatal care: Practices and education designed to promote the well-being of unborn children. The germinal period of human life begins with the meeting of a

Modern technology has made it possible for physicians to examine unborn fetuses on television monitors using ultrasound imaging. (American Institute of Ultrasound Medicine)

male's sperm with an egg in a woman's fallopian tube. The cells divide and multiply as the fertilized egg, the zygote, begins its journey to the uterus. After about two weeks, tiny threadlike structures called villi are produced that penetrate the uterine wall. Then the embryonic stage begins. The embryo is about one-quarter inch in length, has a heart that beats, and an umbilical cord that functions through a placenta, and is encased in a protective amniotic sac. Differentiation of major body systems and organs begins occurring during this period.

Developmental birth defects during this period range from cleft palate, missing or small limbs, blindness, and deafness. After six weeks, the embryo is called a fetus.

The fetal period is characterized by rapid growth of all parts of the body and brain. Monthly visits by the mother to an obstetrician typically begin at this stage. Mothers are encouraged to eat healthy, well-balanced diets, supplement their diets with vitamins, exercise regularly, and refrain from exposing themselves to external forces that might harm their babies.

African American babies are twice as likely as white babies to die during the first year of life. Very young mothers are more likely to have premature babies, as are women who are poor. This can be explained by undernourishment of young mothers and poor mothers, lack of prenatal care, and complications during pregnancy and delivery.

External forces can effect unborn babies in many harmful ways. It is thus important that pregnant mothers avoid contact with people with infections. Pregnant women exposed to German measles, for example, have produced babies with mental retardation and deafness. Other damaging agents are airborne chemicals, such as paint or gas fumes. Pregnant women are also advised to avoid drinking caffeinated beverages such as coffee, tea, and colas. Smoking by pregnant women has been shown to retard the growth of their babies. Mothers-to-be are encouraged to avoid drugs, both prescription and nonprescription. Research has clearly described the devastating effects of mothers' alcohol consumption on their unborn babies. The damage drinking does to unborn babies is irreversible. Fetal alcohol syndrome, the condition suffered by babies exposed to alcohol prenatally, has became the leading cause of mental retardation in the United States.

SUGGESTED READINGS. The most informative book on fetal alcohol syndrome is Michael Dorris' *The Broken Cord* (1989). In *Life Before Birth and a Time to Be Born* (1992), Peter Nathanielsz describes medical aspects of prenatal life. Thomas Verny raises questions and describes what prenatal babies know and feel in *The Secret Life of the Unborn Child* (1981). The photographs in Lennart Nilsson's *A Child Is Born* (1990) present a visual essay on the development of the unborn baby.—*Betsy L. Nichols*

Prenuptial agreements: Legal documents signed by couples before MARRIAGE specifying the terms of their relationships, particularly what will happen in the event of DIVORCE. Also called antenuptial contracts, prenuptial agreements have been legally recognized in all fifty states of the United States. They became increasingly commonplace during the 1980's and 1990's, especially among wealthy persons and those who had been previously married. In 1994 prenuptial agreements were signed by approximately 5 percent of American couples whose partners were marrying for the first time and by 20 percent of couples, at least one of whose partners was remarrying.

Most prenuptial agreements have a primarily finan-

cial focus, specifying how couples' assets will be divided if a divorce occurs. Couples with children from previous marriages are typically concerned with preserving their children's inheritance rights. Some contracts, however, have addressed other issues which became more significant in the latter half of the twentieth century. For example, with an increase in INTERMARRIAGE among couples of different races and religious faiths, prenuptial agreements have sometimes addressed which religious or cultural training children born to the newly marrying couples will receive. In addition, as more families have included two working adults instead of one, prenuptial agreements have included provisions specifying the numbers of children couples will have, or under what circumstances spouses should be willing to relocate for the sake of their partners' careers.

Opponents of prenuptial agreements have argued that such contracts are symptoms of the deterioration of the traditional family, indicating lack of trust, as well as pessimism about the chances of marriages enduring. Some people have charged that the unromantic nature of negotiating prenuptial agreements may, in itself, discourage people from marrying. Supporters of prenuptial agreements, however, have countered that people have simply become more realistic in their outlook, since it is well-known that divorce rates in the United States have been higher than 50 percent or higher for several decades. Negotiating contracts, they say, forces couples to communicate in advance about their expectations of marriage, thereby strengthening their relationships. Moreover, when marriages do end in divorce, prenuptial agreements—which can cost from $500 to $50,000 in legal fees, depending on their complexity—can save both the divorcing couples and the courts a great deal of time and money.

Although one might think that such contracts would be legally binding under any circumstances, there have been cases in which judges have nullified prenuptial agreements. Judges may overrule them for such reasons as their being unfairly biased in favor of one partner, the changed circumstances resulting from the birth of children, or evidence indicating that a person has signed an agreement under duress. However, the vast majority of prenuptial agreements have been upheld by courts when challenged.

SUGGESTED READINGS. An overview of the rising popularity of prenuptial agreements is given in "What Price Love? Read Carefully," by Jill Smolowe in *Time* (Oct., 1990). Karen Davis' *The M Word: Pre-*

nuptial Agreements (1991) and David Saltman's *Don't Get Married Until You Read This: A Layman's Guide to Prenuptial Agreements* (1989) offer advice and guidelines to those considering prenuptial agreements. —Amy Sisson

President's Commission on the Status of Women: U.S. federal advisory panel established by the executive order of President John F. Kennedy in December, 1961. Kennedy charged the commission with recommending changes that would end the "prejudices and outmoded customs that act as a barrier to full realization of women's basic rights." Chaired by former FIRST LADY Eleanor ROOSEVELT, the commission made a number of policy recommendations, most specifically concerning employment and labor standards. Provisions of the EQUAL PAY ACT OF 1963 and the CIVIL RIGHTS ACT OF 1964 followed from its recommendations. This legislative legacy did much to promote greater participation by women in business and politics. In addition, some of the female members of the commission went on to become leaders in the WOMEN'S RIGHTS MOVEMENT of subsequent years.—Steve D. Boilard

Proposition 187 (1994): California voter initiative whose passage made ILLEGAL ALIENS ineligible for publicly financed social services, education, and non-emergency health care. California voters approved the initiative in a state-wide referendum held on November 8, 1994. Dubbed the "Save Our State" proposition, it passed by a margin of 59 percent to 41 percent.

Specifically, the proposition was designed to deny public education, all but emergency publicly funded health care, and public social services in California to immigrants living illegally in the United States. Such health care and social services programs as medical vaccinations, PRENATAL CARE for expectant mothers, services for neglected and abused children, as well as

Immediately after California voters endorsed Proposition 187 in the November, 1994, elections, protests against the provisions of the initiative erupted throughout the state. It was not until November, 1997, that a federal court ruled the proposition unconstitutional. (AP/Wide World Photos)

services and rest homes for older persons were all to be prohibited. The initiative also required that all government agencies involved in providing these services—such as school and health officials—report persons even suspected of being in the country illegally to the U.S. IMMIGRATION AND NATIONALIZATION SERVICE and to the state attorney general.

Shortly after the proposition's passage at least eight law suits, both federal and state, were filed in Los Angeles, San Francisco, and Sacramento, the state capital, to block its implementation. A temporary restraining order was given in a federal district court in Los Angeles. Two cases were filed on behalf of undocumented children, charging that Proposition 187 violated both federal law and a 1982 U.S. Supreme Court decision, PLYLER V. DOE, that had originated in Texas.

The initiative was also challenged on EQUAL PROTECTION grounds. The AMERICAN CIVIL LIBERTIES UNION filed a suit challenging the proposition on a variety of legal grounds, including the supremacy clause of the U.S. Constitution. The most broadly encompassing case, *Gregorio T. v. Wilson*, was filed in November, 1994, by several civil rights organizations, including the MEXICAN AMERICAN LEGAL DEFENSE AND EDUCATION FUND, the Asian Pacific American Legal Center, and the Center for Human Rights and Constitutional Law. Filed as a class action suit by five families, the case represented the interests of an estimated 300,000 children and their families.

In addition to the lawsuits, several mass protests took place throughout the United States. The largest involved about seventy thousand persons in Los Angeles. School walkouts by predominantly Latino high school students were also staged to dramatize opposition to Proposition 187. Masses of commentaries supporting and opposing the proposition appeared in the news media.

In November, 1997—three years after Proposition 187 passed—U.S. District Judge Marianna R. Pfaelzer ruled that it was unconstitutional. Among her objections to the California law was its attempted intrusion on immigration matters, which she declared to be solely federal responsibilities. Backers of Proposition 187 still hoped to carry their case to the U.S. Supreme Court, but Pfaelzer's ruling appeared to settle the issue for the time being.—*Sonia R. Garcia*

Protective legislation for women: Laws designed to safeguard what are perceived to be the special needs of women. Protective legislation has its roots in the early twentieth century, when social reformers focused their attention to the conditions and long hours that women worked. Early protective labor laws limited women's participation in the labor force, restricting the numbers of hours they could work in a day and prohibiting them from working night shifts. Such legislation also restricted their occupational choices; for example, many states made it illegal for women to be barkeepers. The laws were viewed as a means of relieving some of the worst aspects of industrialization—overwork and exploitation—at a time when most forms of labor legislation were likely to be struck down by U.S. courts as unconstitutional. A major focus of protective legislation was to emphasize the childbearing function of women and to minimize their participation the workplace, thereby limiting their competition with men for jobs.

In the landmark case MULLER V. OREGON (1908), the U.S. Supreme Court upheld a maximum-hours law for women. The Court's majority opinion in this case articulated a view of women that persisted throughout the twentieth century: that women are childbearers first and wage earners second. Justice David Josiah Brewer's opinion upholding the Oregon law stated that

woman's physical structure and the performance of maternal functions place her at a disadvantage in the struggle for subsistence is obvious. This is especially true when the burdens of motherhood are upon her. Even when they are not, by abundant testimony of the medical fraternity, continuance for a long time on her feet at work, repeating this from day to day, tends to injurious effects upon the body, and, as healthy mothers are essential to vigorous offspring, the physical well-being of women becomes an object of public interest and care in order to preserve the strength and vigor of the race.

After this ruling protective legislation stood its ground for generations. It was not until the passage of Title VII of the CIVIL RIGHTS ACT OF 1964 that the validity of state protective laws came into question. State laws that sought to single out women for "protection" were challenged. The EQUAL EMPLOYMENT OPPORTUNITY COMMISSION, which was created to administer Title VII, issued guidelines on PREGNANCY AND EMPLOYMENT in 1972 stating that pregnancy should not be grounds for treating women differently from male workers. These guidelines did not, however, deter employers from developing policies that distinguished between pregnant and nonpregnant workers.

In 1978 Congress passed the PREGNANCY DISCRIMI-NATION ACT, which amended Title VII to incorporate all exclusions based on pregnancy. During the same year, several companies began to implement policies barring fertile women from jobs involving substances known to be, or suspected of being, harmful to fetuses, such as lead. Fetal protection policies were designed to protect employers from lawsuits for workplace-induced harm to unborn children. Several companies' fetal protection policies have, however, been challenged in court. It was not until 1990 that the U.S. Supreme Court ruled that the Civil Rights Act of 1964 prohibited fetal protection policies. Despite the Court's ruling, some employers continued to try to justify their exclusionary protective policies.

SUGGESTED READINGS. *Fetal Protection in the Workplace: Women's Rights, Business Interests, and the Unborn* (1993), by Robert Blank, discusses issues relating to protective legislation and women's rights, from sex discrimination to protective legislation. *Workplace/ Women's Place: An Anthology* (1997), edited by Dana Dunn, is a comprehensive collection of essays on women and work, working conditions, effects on families, and other social issues affecting women.—*Robin Sakina Mama*
(updates original entry; vol. 5, p. 1354)

Puerto Rican nationalism: Expressions of nationalism among PUERTO RICANS are rooted in the complex colonial experiences of their Caribbean island, which was colonized first by Spain and later by the United States. Puerto Rican national consciousness began coalescing in the nineteenth century, when Puerto Ricans began demanding their political independence from Spain. Spain responded in 1897 by granting the colony broader powers for self-government. However, the movement toward independence suffered a major setback the following year, when the United States invaded the island during the SPANISH-AMERICAN WAR. The postwar treaty signed by the U.S. and Spain stipulated that the future political status of Puerto Rico would be determined by the U.S. Congress. The island eventually became a largely self-governing territory, with an elected governor and a legislature; however, all three branches of the U.S. federal government have retained authority over its internal and external affairs.

In 1917 the U.S. government granted Puerto Ricans U.S. citizenship; however, it did not grant them full representation in the U.S. Congress or give them the vote in national elections. As a result, the burden of

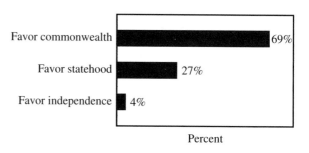

Opinions of Puerto Ricans Living in the United States on the Status of Puerto Rico

Favor commonwealth — 69%
Favor statehood — 27%
Favor independence — 4%

Percent

Source: Data are from the Latino National Political Survey, which polled a representative sample of 589 Puerto Ricans in forty metropolitan areas in 1989-1990. See Rodolfo O. de la Garza et al., *Latino Voices: Mexican, Puerto Rican, and Cuban Perspectives on American Politics* (Boulder, Colo.: Westview Press, 1992), Table 7.28.

being saddled with the responsibilities of U.S. citizenship—except paying federal taxes—without having direct and full representation in the U.S. government has made Puerto Ricans see themselves as second-class citizens. Meanwhile, Puerto Rico's historical goal of political independence has remained unfulfilled. As has been the case in other world colonies, Puerto Rico's ongoing independence struggle has occasionally taken violent turns. For example, it has included an assassination attempt on President Harry S Truman in 1950, a shoot-out in a session of the U.S. Congress in 1954, and an attempt to commandeer the Statue of Liberty.

Puerto Ricans have been concerned about the Americanization of their culture and language. Shortly after the end of the Spanish-American War, English replaced the SPANISH LANGUAGE as the medium of instruction in public schools. Puerto Ricans reacted to this change by starting an anti-English movement culminating in 1949, when Spanish was reinstated as the official medium of instruction in public schools. Puerto Ricans have wanted not only to preserve Spanish as their common language but to have it established as the official language at all levels of government, including offices of the federal government in Puerto Rico. However, their heavy economic dependence on the United States has forced them to communicate mainly in English. Furthermore, as large numbers of Puerto Ricans have traveled back and forth between Puerto Rico and mainland United States in a cyclical pattern of migration in search of employment, they have had little choice but to master English. For

Puerto Ricans living in the United States, language has been a barrier that has caused them problems in assimilating to a society in which they are often regarded as foreigners.

An estimated two million Puerto Ricans were living in the United States by the mid-1990's. These people have been among the poorest ethnic groups in the country and they have experienced discrimination because of both their language and their skin color. Most Puerto Ricans living in the United States have not participated in politics or other forms of public life; many have not considered themselves to be Americans.

Puerto Rico's future political status has frequently arisen as a topic of discussion in the United Nations. The United States has consistently attempted to block U.N. action on the issue, claiming that it is in an internal matter to be determined by the people of Puerto Rico. By the mid-1990's it appeared that a majority of Puerto Ricans favored statehood over independence. If statehood were to be granted, Puerto Ricans would want assurances that their ethnic identity and cultural and artistic heritages would be preserved, and that Spanish would remain the island's official language.

SUGGESTED READINGS. *A Political and Cultural History of Puerto Rico* (1983), by Arturo Carrison and others, views Puerto Rico as having a distinctively Caribbean culture and examines the history of its special relationship with the United States. *Puerto Rico: A Socio-Historic Interpretation* (1972), by Manuel Maldonado-Denis, translated by Elena Vialo, sees Puerto Rican history as a struggle between supporters of colonialism and those who seek independence. *The Political Status of Puerto Rico* (1986), edited by Pamela S. Falk, collects highly readable essays examining contradictions in Puerto Rican politics. For a discussion of language issues, see Edith Algren de Gutierrez's *The Movement Against Teaching English in Schools of Puerto Rico* (1987).—*Mathew J. Kanjirathinkal*

Purple Heart Battalion: JAPANESE AMERICAN army unit during WORLD WAR II. Nicknamed the Purple Heart Battalion because of its heavy combat losses during the war, the 100th Infantry Battalion was composed almost exclusively of Americans of Japanese ancestry from Hawaii. After serving in North Africa, the battalion was sent, in September, 1943, to Salerno, Italy. There its members became the first U.S. combat troops in Italy to capture German prisoners, the first to destroy German tanks, and the first to take a German gun emplacement by bayonet charge.

The following year the unit landed at Anzio, where it was joined by the 442ND REGIMENTAL COMBAT TEAM, another distinguished Japanese American unit. Together they fought in Europe until war's end, gaining fame with the motto, "Go for broke!" In ironic counterpoint to the JAPANESE AMERICAN INTERNMENT on the West Coast of the United States, the men of the 100th Battalion became the most decorated soldiers in U.S. Army history. Their courage and sacrifices greatly advanced the political and social causes of all Japanese Americans after the war.—*William Matta*

Quinto Sol Publications: First Chicano publishing house in the United States. Founded in Berkeley, California, in 1967, Quinto Sol was an independent book-publishing company dedicated to publishing contemporary Chicano literature. Its name, Quinto Sol, meaning "fifth sun" in Spanish, reflected its Mexican/Aztec identity. The founders of the company, Octavio I. Romano-V. and Hermínio Ríos, recognized the linguistic diversity of their readers by using bilingual texts in their quarterly journal *El Grito: A Journal of Contemporary Mexican-American Thought* and other publications.

In 1970 Quinto Sol instituted a national award for Chicano literature, Premio Quinto Sol, offering thousand-dollar awards and book publication as prizes for new manuscripts. Awards went to some of the most significant modern Chicano fiction, such as Rudolfo A. Anaya's *Bless Me, Ultima* (1972) and Estela Portillo Trambley's short story collection *Rain of Scorpions* (1975).

By the late 1970's most Chicano book publishers had disappeared. Quinto Sol itself stopped publishing in 1974. Two years later Romano-V. established Tonatiuh International and started a new journal, *Grito del Sol*. Romano-V. then merged Tonatiuh and Quinto Sol to form Tonatiuh-Quinto Sol International, Inc., which continued to publish Chicano works into the 1990's. —*Maria L. Alonzo*

R

Rabbis, women as: The issue of ordaining women as rabbis has provoked intense controversy throughout Jewish communities around the world and especially among JEWISH AMERICANS. In the United States the question of ordaining women as rabbis has received considerable media attention partly because of the news coverage given to debates over ordination of women in Christian churches and the role of women in American society generally.

JEWISH AMERICAN WOMEN have been ordained as rabbis in American rabbinical schools since 1972; however, Judaism was historically a religion in which men filled all leadership roles, including that of the rabbi, or religious teacher and leader. The Hebrew Bible and Talmud—which contain commentaries on biblical law—do not expressly forbid women rabbis; however, other Hebrew texts restricting the religious roles of women were long used to support male dominance in leadership roles. Jewish religious traditions and certain biblical passages were long interpreted to emphasize the primary roles of the Jewish woman as wife, mother, and household manager. Judaism has traditionally ascribed authorship of the Bible to men, traced genealogies through the male line, and recognized—with rare exceptions—males as priests, prophets, and civil leaders such as kings and magistrates. In one ancient prayer, rabbis thanked God that they were not created as females.

In traditional Jewish culture, boys received lessons in Hebrew, biblical studies, and Jewish traditions, while girls were given rudimentary education and groomed for household duties. Thus the primary qualification for becoming a rabbi—extensive biblical knowledge—was not available to women. After being firmly in place for several thousand years, these traditions began to change during the early twentieth century. A woman named Regina Jonas was ordained privately (as opposed to formal ordination by a rabbinical college) in Germany in the early 1920's. She served as a rabbi in a home for the aged and in hospitals until she died in the Nazis' Auschwitz concentration camp during the HOLOCAUST. The first American woman to be ordained privately, in 1976, was Lynn Gottleib. She did significant work as a rabbi to a deaf congregation and as a creator of Hebrew sign language.

Judaism has four major branches or divisions in the

A woman rabbi discusses traditional symbols for the Twelve Tribes of Israel. (James L. Shaffer)

United States: Orthodox, Conservative, Reform, and Reconstructionist. Of these, both the Reconstructionist and Reform branches began offering biblical schooling for girls in the early 1900's. This development paved the way for the first Bas Mitzvah (the female equivalent of the Bar Mitzvah) in America in 1922. The Bar Mitzvah—the ceremonious entry into full Jewish community membership—had until then been for boys only.

The Reform Hebrew Union College began accepting female students in 1922, and the Reconstructionist Rabbinical College opened its doors to women in 1968. In 1972 the Reform branch ordained Sally Preisand as its first woman rabbi. Later that same year the Reconstructionist movement ordained Sandy Eisenberg Sasso. In 1985 Amy Eilberg became the first Conservative woman rabbi.

Despite have successfully overcome barriers to college degrees and ordination, women rabbis have faced severe challenges in finding employment in synagogues. Most traditional congregations have preferred to employ male rabbis.

SUGGESTED READINGS. An overview of women and Judaism from a feminist viewpoint can be found in Roslyn Lacks's *Women and Judaism* (1980). For an activist stance that includes addresses of Jewish colleges and women's networks, see *Jewish and Female* by Susan Weidman Schneider (1984).—*Keith Atwater*

Race—scientific theories: RACE has long been a controversial category for classifying human beings. Since the mid-eighteenth century, when Louis LeClerc, Comte de Buffon, introduced the term into scientific discourse, it has been used to label ethnic, linguistic, cultural, religious, national, and geographical groupings of human beings.

Twentieth century scientists have argued over the meaning and usefulness of the term. Because of the concern that the science of race can be imprecise and can potentially degenerate into scientific RACISM—in which racial classification is used to justify the inferiority or superiority of certain groups—some scientists have argued that human traits and variations can be discussed without invoking the term "race." Others have argued that race is in fact a useful designation for groups, defining categories of people united by common origins and sharing at least some physical traits that are transmitted genetically. Nevertheless, because racial classifications have been used to justify such practices as SLAVERY and GENOCIDE, some have

argued that using "race" as a scientific category can be not only imprecise, but morally suspect.

History of the Concept. The increasing interest of Europeans concerning race coincided with European IMPERIALISM and colonization, as they confronted the question of knowing how to regard the human status of colonized peoples. They asked whether all human beings were descended from Adam—a theory known as monogenesis (one origin)—or whether human beings originated from different groups—the theory of polygenesis (many origins).

François Bernier was perhaps the first person to classify human races, in the late seventeenth century; however, Carolus Linnaeus, the founder of scientific taxonomy, devised the first version of a vast classification scheme in *Systemae Naturae* (1735). His book classified all living things according to "genus" and "species." Regarding human beings as members of the same species—descended from a common ancestor and mutually able to mix and produce fertile offspring—Linnaeus divided human beings into four ba-

British naturalist Charles Darwin, whose theories of evolution have been used to support modern theories of race. (National Archives)

sic groups: *Europaeus, Americanus, Asiaticus,* and *Africanus.* His descriptions of these groups mixed physical features (such as skin color) with behavioral and psychological traits (such as tendencies toward indolence, inventiveness, or civilization). This system reflected the proclivity of scientists to make ideological assumptions about observed human variations. The system of classification suggested that human differences were fixed and hierarchical. For racial theorists, such as the late eighteenth century English surgeon Charles White, fair-skinned Europeans stood at the top of the racial hierarchy, while dark-skinned Africans stood at the bottom.

Nineteenth century developments in geology, paleontology, and comparative anatomy moved many scientists to suppose that living organisms existed on an evolutionary and progressive scale. Scientists such as Alfred Russel Wallace and Charles Darwin struggled with how to endorse an evolutionary view of humankind—in which the strongest species survive the evolutionary process—without espousing a hierarchical view of human races. Others, however, such as the pro-slavery physician Samuel Morton, who argued that whites had larger cranial capacities than blacks; Count Arturo de Gobineau, who wrote the influential *Essay on the Inequality of the Human Races* (1853-1855); and Francis Galton, the founder of the EUGENICS movement, all drew upon scientific discourses to justify their beliefs in the superiority of the white race and the notion that mixed races undermine superior racial stock.

Twentieth Century Transformations. At the turn of the twentieth century, the earlier views of race as an essential biological category came under attack. Cultural anthropologists, such as Franz Boas, exposed the racial misconceptions of physical and cultural anthropology, rejecting schemes in which cultural groups were labeled as "superior" or "inferior." Moreover, genetic scientists began to question the science of human heredity which served as the foundation of eugenics. Even scientists who agreed that three basic races—Negroids, Mongoloids, and Caucasoids—existed also acknowledged that general physical traits, such as skin color, eye shape, and stature, vary greatly within populations, and that measurable differences within populations can be even greater than those among different populations.

Scientists also wondered how persons of mixed racial ancestry should be classified. Furthermore, some geneticists introduced a dynamic model of heredity, exploring the ways that processes such as natural selection and environmental adaptation modified hereditary traits. Despite these new challenges to racial determinism, eugenicists, whose influence grew during the first third of the century, argued for the selective breeding of innately "superior races." During WORLD WAR II, the world witnessed the terrible results of the eugenics-based racist German Nazi ideology in the HOLOCAUST.

Post-World War II Science. Even before the world war, many scientists, because of new genetic discoveries, believed that old paradigms of racial typologies were fast becoming outdated by new studies in genetics, ecology, and evolution. In 1941 Ashley Montagu argued that race itself was a myth—an obsolete and arbitrary concept.

In 1950 and 1952 scientists working in an international forum sponsored by the UNITED NATIONS EDUCATIONAL, SCIENTIFIC, AND CULTURAL ORGANIZATION, issued two statements on the nature of race. Both statements rejected the doctrine of pure races and racial hierarchies. They espoused a new science for human diversity, replacing racial classifications with the concept of genetic populations—groups of people sharing characteristic distributions of genes (such as similar blood types)—which can form populations statistically distinct from one another.

Despite these changes in scientific thinking, some people have continued to believe that race is a credible category for scientific inquiry. Using racial classifications in the late sixties, scholars such as Arthur Jensen argued that intelligence is hereditary and that whites have higher average intelligences, as measured by INTELLIGENCE TESTS, than blacks. In *The Bell Curve* (1994), R. J. Hernstein and C. Murray resurrected this controversy by again comparing intelligence quotient (IQ) measurements of black and white subjects. Scientists such as L. L. Cavalli-Sforza have dismissed such findings by raising questions concerning the validity of IQ measurements and noting the importance of environment in shaping intelligence.

Although discredited in many scientific arenas, race has continued to be a powerful social concept, one that will continue to influence scientists even as they find other terms to measure human variations and differences.

SUGGESTED READINGS. Nancy Stepan's *The Idea of Race in Science: Great Britain, 1800-1960* (1982) provides a British overview of the history of race and science. Audrey Smedley's *Race in North America:*

Origin and Evolution of a Worldview (1993) focuses on the impact of scientific theories of race on U.S. social history. Thomas Sowell's *Race and Culture* (1994) discusses the impact of culture on race, while Ethel Tobach and Betty Rosoff's *Challenging Racism and Sexism: Alternatives to Genetic Explanations* (1994) challenges biological determinist arguments. *The Great Human Diasporas: The History of Diversity and Evolution* (1995), by Luigi Luca Cavalli-Sforza and Francesco Cavalli-Sforza, provides a broad view of human development, including the topic of race.—*Sandra K. Stanley*

(updates original entry; vol. 5, p. 1377)

Rape trauma syndrome (RTS): Post-traumatic stress disorder (PTSD) common among victims of RAPE. This syndrome has three phases. During its acute phase—immediately after rape—victims may seem shocked, angry or upset, or even surprisingly unconcerned. They also feel anxiety, fear, guilt, and denial, and have difficulty sleeping. The disorientation phase includes problems interacting with others and avoidance of situations in which they fear another rape may occur. The reorganization phase, in which victims come to terms with their assaults, is not reached by all victims. One-fourth of rape victims experience negative effects (such as drug or alcohol abuse and major depression) years after their assaults.

PTSD is more likely to result from rape than from robbery, physical assault, combat service, or natural disaster. Thirteen percent of reported rape victims have attempted suicide. Courts have admitted evidence on RTS when it is offered to explain victims' seemingly bizarre behavior—but not to prove that the incidents were rape.—*Glenn Ellen Starr*

Rastafarianism: Black religious movement that arose in Jamaica as an outgrowth of ethnic pride and early black nationalist ideologies. A controversial and revolutionary black-consciousness movement, Rastafarianism has no organized structure or hierarchy. It has, however, achieved official recognition, of sorts, as a religion, thanks to a 1990 U.S. Supreme Court decision upholding the right of prisoners to have their Rastafarian beliefs respected as a religion. The ruling specifically allowed Rastafarian prisoners to leave their hair uncut in "dreadlocks—the long matted, uncombed tresses they wear in accordance with the Bible's Nazarite code (Numbers 6:5). Although some whites belong to the Rastafarian movement, most adherents are persons of African descent. The early leaders of Rastafarianism were black Christian ministers. Reverend Leonard Howell, for example, made significant contributions to the movement from 1930 to 1960, before he was imprisoned.

Six basic beliefs underlie Rastafarianism: that Haile Selassie is God, that people of African descent are reincarnations of ancient Israel, that whites are inferior to blacks, that Jamaica is a hopeless place and Ethiopia is heaven, that the emperor of Ethiopia will help persons of African origin to return to Ethiopia, and that one day blacks will rule the world.

Some Rastafarians reject Western medicine and legal marriages. Others place taboos on funerals, secondhand clothing, physical contact with white people, the eating of pork, and any magic or witchcraft. A particularly controversial aspect of Rastafarian practices is the smoking of ganja (marijuana) for medicinal purposes and as a sacrament for creating communion with god while in trance-like states.

After World War I the Jamaican leader Marcus GARVEY, founder of the UNIVERSAL NEGRO IMPROVEMENT ASSOCIATION (UNIA) and one of the founders of black nationalist thought in the United States, called for the redemption of Africa and repatriation of all African peoples to their natural homeland, Africa. Although Garvey himself had no direct ties with Rastafarianism, his name is closely associated with the movement because he predicted the emergence of

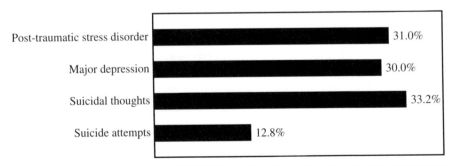

Mental Health Problems Experienced by U.S. Rape Victims

Post-traumatic stress disorder	31.0%
Major depression	30.0%
Suicidal thoughts	33.2%
Suicide attempts	12.8%

Source: National Victim Center

Although Emperor Haile Selassie (wearing cape) enjoyed a near-divine status in his native Ethiopia, he never acknowledged the divinity attributed to his person by Rastafarians, most of whom were West Indians. (AP/Wide World Photos)

a powerful black king in Africa by calling attention to a passage in the Bible: "Princes shall come out of Egypt; Ethiopia shall soon stretch out her hands unto God" (Psalms 68:31).

The initial impetus for Rastafarianism was the crowning of Ethiopia's prince regent Ras Tafari as Emperor Haile Selassie I, the King of Kings, Lord of Lords, and Conquering Lion of Judah, in 1930. Also known as Abyssinia, Ethiopia had a long history and was consolidated as a modern state in the late nineteenth century. At a time when all but a handful of the world's peoples of African descent were under white rule, the sovereign Ethiopia empire stood as a powerful icon of black pride throughout the world. The oppressed, poor, and working-class blacks in Jamaica and other West Indian colonies proclaimed Haile Selassie—who claimed direct ancestry from Solomon and Sheba—a living god of the black race. Selassie's courageous opposition to Italy's brutal invasion of Ethiopia in 1935 further enhanced his prestige. So strongly did many people believe in his divinity that they continued to revere him as a god after his death in 1975. By then Rastafarianism had spread from Jamaica and the Caribbean to Great Britain, Canada, and the United States. Major Rastafarian communities have developed in NEW YORK CITY, MIAMI, and CHICAGO, as well as in several British cities, and throughout the Caribbean.

SUGGESTED READINGS. Basic overviews of Rastafarianism can be found in Leonard E. Barrett, *The Rastafarians: Sounds of Cultural Dissonance* (Rev. ed., 1988); Horace Campbell, *Rasta and Resistance: From Marcus Garvey to Walter Rodney* (1987); and William F. Lewis, *Soul Rebels: The Rastafari* (1993). *Black Religions in the New World* (1978), by George Eaton Simpson, examines Rastafarianism from the broader perspective of black religion generally.—*Adolph Dupree*

Raza Unida Party, La: Third-party movement founded in Texas in January, 1970. The party was part of the larger MEXICAN AMERICAN civil rights activism that was then developing nationwide. One of its leaders was José Ángel Gutiérrez, who launched the party in a South Texas town, Crystal City, in order to support Latino candidates for the city council and school. Afterward the party established chapters throughout the western states.

The party began because neither the Republican nor the Democratic Party had been responsive to the needs of Mexican Americans. The primary goal of La Raza Unida was to register voters and win local and school board elections. The party also held its first state nominating convention in Texas, slating a candidate for governor. The party enjoyed some early success, particularly in Texas, but did not last because of regional and ideological differences among its members. By the late 1970's it ceased to be an active political force. —*Sonia R. Garcia*
(updates original entry; vol. 5, p. 1298)

Red River War (1874-1875): Confrontation that ended serious resistance to U.S. authority among Southern Plains Indians. In 1867 representatives of Arapaho, Cheyenne, Comanche, and Kiowa Indian tribes signed the Treaty of Medicine Lodge Creek, by which their peoples agreed to be resettled onto RESERVATIONS located in the western INDIAN TERRITORY (later the western part of the state of Oklahoma). The treaty stipulated that the tribes would have the right to hunt in the Staked Plains region of the Texas Panhandle. Because white settlers in the region had wiped out most of its buffalo herds, some Indians began raiding white settlements and wagon trains.

On June 27, 1874, several hundred Cheyenne, Comanche, and Kiowa men, under the leadership of Quanah Parker and Lone Wolf, attacked a white trading post near Adobe Wells. The ensuing battle lasted for five days before the Indians withdrew. As a result of this battle, General William Tecumseh Sherman, commander of the army, decided that it was time to crush Indian resistance in the area and force the renegades back to their reservations. Sherman ordered Lieutenant General Philip Sheridan, commander of the Department of the Missouri, to send three thousand soldiers to deal with the situation.

In the resulting confrontation, known as the Red River War, Indians and federal troops fought fourteen pitched battles. Half the battles might be considered no more than skirmishes; however, seven of them were major battles, including those at Palo Duro Canyon, the Upper Washita, and Buffalo Wallow. Eventually the Indians were starved into submission; by the summer of 1875 all remaining warriors had surrendered. Most of the Indians returned to the reservations, but some were sent to prison in Florida.

The Red River War ended Indian resistance on the Southern Plains and persuaded Sherman that in the future he would have to deal more harshly with other Indian tribes.—*Jeffry Jensen*

Redistricting: Legislation designed to change the boundaries of voting districts used for U.S. congressional, state legislative, and local governing body elections. Federal law requires district lines to be redrawn whenever the results of the U.S. Census, which is taken every ten years, show population shifts that create imbalances in the numbers of registered voters in districts within states.

Although the constitution of the United States and most states require redistricting after every census, these requirements historically were rarely honored. During the first 180 years of America's history as a nation, federal courts refused to examine the subject of redistricting, calling it a question best left to legislative discretion. Without judicial oversight or legal penalties for failing to comply, legislators who benefited from existing district arrangements simply stopped complying with the redistricting provisions, and there was no way to force them to comply.

Courts Mandate Redistricting. By the 1950's numerous legislative districts at all levels in the United States had become substantially unequal in size, usually favoring rural areas over more densely populated urban areas. Legislators representing rural areas tended to outnumber urban legislators in many state legislatures, and they were also overrepresented in the U.S. Congress, thereby favoring rural interests at the expense of big cities.

During the 1960's the U.S. Supreme Court decided in several cases that courts could judge such matters and that voting districts had to be substantially equal in population size. However, the Court did not establish criteria, such as compactness or physical contiguity, to be used in redistricting decisions. After legislative bodies in the various states began drawing district lines, new districts were mathematically equal in population, but often oddly contorted and sometimes only barely contiguous. These distortions were typically drawn into district lines for the political benefit of the politicians responsible for drawing them.

New Redistricting Rules. The federal VOTING RIGHTS ACT OF 1982 amended earlier voting rights laws by requiring state legislatures to draw district lines to favor election of recognizable racial or ethnic groups, such as African Americans, Latinos, and American Indians wherever possible. The 1982 amendment was intended to increase the numbers of elected ethnic representatives but had the unexpected and ironic effect of *reducing* their overall political influence.

To create voting districts meeting the new federal requirements, small ethnic neighborhoods were often strung together into oddly shaped districts with overall majorities of members of specified ethnic groups. Their purpose was to give members of the minority groups better opportunities to elect members of their own groups to representative offices. However, redistricting undertaken to meet ethnic criteria overlooked the fact that many ethnic voters had been strong supporters of the Democratic Party since the 1950's, and that they were being removed from adjacent districts in which they had allied with white Democrats to form Democratic majorities. In many cases removing ethnic Democratic voters from majority Democratic districts caused the Democrats who remained to lose their majority status to Republicans. Thus, at the same time that new ethnic Democratic districts were created, the overall number of Democratic majority districts declined.

In 1994 the number of Democrats elected to the U.S. House of Representatives so declined that the Republican Party won control. Most of the redistricting required by the CENSUS OF 1990 had been completed by the time of the 1992 elections, in which the Republicans might have taken control of the House, had it not been for the strong Democratic tide that Democratic candidate Bill Clinton's presidential campaign brought with it, pulling a number of Democratic representatives into office from districts expected to favor Republicans.

In the midterm elections of 1994, however, Clinton did not lead the ticket and his party's popularity had slipped enough to allow the Republicans to gain control of the House of Representatives for the first time in forty-two years. A popular perception of this electoral result was that the Republicans had created a revolutionary "change of mind" among a majority of Americans, and that the Republicans would become the new national majority party and easily defeat Clinton's bid for reelection in 1996. This view overestimated Republican popularity, however, and underestimated the effect that racial districting (or gerrymandering) had had on the congressional elections. Clinton was reelected in 1996 and Democrats recaptured some, but not all, of the districts they had lost to the Republicans in 1994.

U.S. Supreme Court Revisions. After 1992 lawsuits challenging the 1982 redistricting changes began reaching the Supreme Court. In the case of *Shaw v. Reno* (1993) the Court voted 5-4 to reject a particularly contorted congressional district that had been created for African American voters in North Carolina. The Court sent the case back to the lower courts for further deliberation, warning that creation of districts drawing together widely separated voters of the same race who might have little in common beyond the color of their skin was an unacceptable form of "political APARTHEID."

Other federal courts then ordered adjustments in similarly distorted districts in Florida, Louisiana, Georgia, and Texas. These adjustments were so small that they had little effect on the overall pattern of ethnic and Republican gains. All six African American congresspersons affected by redistricting adjustments were reelected, and only one Texas Republican from

Effect of Redistricting on Southern Congressional Districts

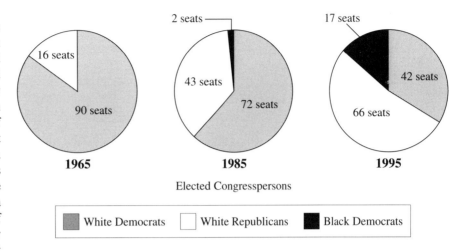

Elected Congresspersons

White Democrats   White Republicans   Black Democrats

Source: Congressional Quarterly
Note: Illustrates shift in representation in eleven states of the Old South: Alabama, Arkansas, Florida, Georgia, Louisiana, Mississippi, North Carolina, South Carolina, Tennessee, Texas, Virginia. Two African American representatives in 1985 were Tennessee's Harold E. Ford, and Texas' George "Mickey" Leland. In addition to Ford, the African American representatives in 1995 included Alabama's Earl F. Hilliard; Florida's Corrine Brown, Alcee L. Hastings, and Carrie P. Meek; Georgia's Sanford Bishop, John Lewis, and Cynthia McKinney; Louisiana's Cleo Fields and William J. Jefferson; Mississippi's Bennie G. Thompson; North Carolina's Eva M. Clayton and Melvin Watt; South Carolina's James E. Clyburn; Texas' Eddie Bernice Johnson and Sheila Jackson Lee; and Virginia's Robert C. "Bobby" Scott.

an adjacent district into which ethnic Democrats were reinserted was defeated.

Racially motivated district line drawing has had the effect of increasing minority ethnic legislators directly while diminishing the overall strength of the party to which most of them have given allegiance. The best proof this assertion comes from the fact that President Clinton was reelected in 1996, while his party failed to regain control of the House of Representatives.

SUGGESTED READINGS. Issues of redistricting are set in their broadest political context in *Losing to Win: The 1996 Elections and American Politics* (1997), by James W. Ceaser and Andrew E. Busch. A comprehensive review of the modern House of Representatives districts can be found in the two volumes of *CQ's Guide to 1990 Congressional Redistricting* (1993). Mark E. Rush has raised questions about the partisan effects of redistricting in *Does Redistricting Make a Difference?* (1993). For the condition of the districts and redistricting immediately before the 1990 census, see Leroy Hardy, Alan Heslop, and George S. Blair's *Redistricting in the Nineteen Eighties: A Fifty-State Survey* (1993).—*Richard L. Wilson*

Reed v. Reed (1971): U.S. Supreme Court decision relating to SEX DISCRIMINATION. *Reed v. Reed* was one of the first court cases to bring down a ruling against discrimination on the basis of sex as a violation of the equal protection clause of the FOURTEENTH AMENDMENT. An Idaho woman named Sally Reed sued her former husband for the right to administer the estate of their dead son. Owing to an Idaho law that favored males over females as executors of wills, she lost her case in a state court. She appealed her case to the U.S. Supreme Court. On November 22, 1971, the Court overturned the state court's decision, thereby invalidating the Idaho statute that Reed was challenging. Noting that this law was "the very kind of arbitrary legislative choice forbidden by the equal protection clause," the justices set a precedent that was later used to strike down numerous other laws supporting sex discrimination. In *Reed*, the Court ignored such earlier decisions such as *Bradwell v. Illinois* (1873), in which it had upheld state bans on women in legal practice.—*Lisa Paddock*

Religious Freedom Restoration Act (RFRA): U.S. federal government legislation enacted in 1993 to overturn Supreme Court decisions restricting certain religious freedoms. In 1978 the U.S. Congress passed the AMERICAN INDIAN RELIGIOUS FREEDOM ACT (AIRFA), recognizing its obligation to protect traditional Native American religions. The act was soon seen to lack teeth, as government agencies routinely ignored it. The Supreme Court in *Lyng v. Northwest Indian Cemetery Protective Association* (1988) allowed the U.S. Forest Service to build a logging road through land sacred to Northern California Indians in Six Rivers National Forest. In EMPLOYMENT DIVISION V. SMITH (1990), the Court denied members of the NATIVE AMERICAN CHURCH their right to use PEYOTE, a recognized legitimate religious sacrament. These Court decisions moved members of Congress to restore American Indian religious rights by passing the RFRA, which required proof of a "compelling government interest" before further encroachments on Indian religious freedoms could be undertaken. This move to restore respect for cultural diversity was followed by AIRFA Amendments of 1994, which specifically addressed the peyote issue.—*Gary A. Olson*

Religious Right: Political interest group arising in the United States during the 1980's and 1990's that encompassed Christian conservatives who denounced ABORTION, homosexuality, DIVORCE, liberalism, and FEMINISM. With formal and informal links to religious institutions, the coalition included evangelical congregations, parachurch organizations, media networks, and political activists.

History. The Religious Right has continued a long tradition of Christian activism in American political culture. By engaging moral issues in the public sphere, abolitionists, prohibitionists, and other crusaders influenced several periods in American history. In the modern period, religious organizations became active in politics during the 1920's in order to challenge the secularization of American life, particularly the teaching of evolution in the public schools. During the 1930's some Fundamentalist ministers, such as Gerald Winrod and Gerald L. K. Smith, espoused fascist ideas, though such reactionaries were only a vocal minority. The American Council of Christian Churches, Christian Crusade, Church League of America, and the Defenders of the Christian Faith represented fiery anticommunist organizations during the 1950's. Most significantly, the social upheavals of the 1960's inspired a religious crusade as a reaction against what was perceived as the erosion of certain traditional values.

The 1970's and 1980's marked a period in which the United States experienced a major religious revival. In 1977 more than seventy million Americans described themselves as "born-again" Christians, that is, people who claimed a direct relationship with Jesus. While support for Fundamentalist religion was strong in the South, particularly among Southern Baptists congregations, the appeal extended across the country to others with conservative sensibilities. This kind of religiosity appealed not simply to the dispossessed, but rather to the so-called "guppies"—God-fearing urban professionals. Private Christian academies surged as parents chose to keep their children out of public schools, and they demanded tax credits from the government. At the same time, suburban communities built huge new churches, while capital from successful entrepreneurs launched Christian radio stations, publishing houses, and gift stores.

Media and the Message. With the extraordinary renaissance of evangelicalism, ministers used the mass media to become a significant force supporting conservative gospel and the political success of President Ronald Reagan. Broadcasting his message across more than five hundred radio stations, the Reverend Jerry Falwell of Virginia organized the self-proclaimed Moral Majority. Furthermore, Christian Voice was established to distribute the literature of extensive antigay and antipornography campaigns through direct mail. The messages of the Religious Right railed against liberal views on the Bible, communism, and the state, thereby emerging as a powerful obstacle to social change.

Another conservative messenger using the media was Pat Robertson, founder of the Christian Broadcasting Corporation, which underscored a peculiar mixture of programs about individual moral triumphs, unrestrained free enterprise, idealized family values, and a strong American posture around the world. Indeed, Robertson even sought the Republican nomination for president of the United States during 1988. Personal scandals and financial excess weakened the appeal of the televangelists, however, particularly after Jim Bakker, who with his wife, Tammy Faye Bakker, had personally profited from his *Praise the Lord* radio and television shows, was sentenced to prison for fraud and conspiracy in 1987.

Culture Wars. With a broadening of the evangelical base, the agenda of the Religious Right moved beyond the issues of personal piety to engage in culture wars.

Paramilitary "Christian patriots" with a penchant for violence appeared, though such groups were located far to the right of the Moral Majority or grassroots activists. When Congress approved the EQUAL RIGHTS AMENDMENT in 1972, religious conservatives—both males and females—mobilized such strong resistance to the amendment that its period for ratification expired in 1980 before it was approved by the necessary three-fourths of the states. The Religious Right also fought against prohibitions upon SCHOOL PRAYER, demanded the right to teach "CREATIONISM" as an alternative to evolution, decried the educational influence of "secular humanism," and resisted redefinitions of sexuality and sex roles.

Whatever the cultural issue, the Religious Right battled the judicial activism of the U.S. Supreme Court. In particular, the movement activists supported a "right to life" or fought against legalizing ABORTION because they opposed the right of women to terminate pregnancy on moral grounds. Therefore, they denounced the U.S. Supreme Court's 1973 ROE V. WADE decision legalizing abortion. They decried the decision as sup-

Jerry Falwell, the leader of the Moral Majority, leading an "I Love America" rally in Kansas in 1981. (AP/Wide World Photos)

porting murder of the unborn, spurring sexual promiscuity, and attacking the male-dominated family. During the 1980's right-to-life activists such as OPERATION RESCUE called for more drastic, even militant, tactics, including civil disobedience measures and decidedly uncivil demonstrations at abortion clinics around the nation.

Conservative evangelical leaders attacked homosexuality as blasphemous and an abomination, while a number of parent groups feared that openness about sexual orientation might influence children through public schools. While activists organized against the extension of civil rights protections to homosexuals, cohorts participated in movements to repeal gay and lesbian rights laws in Florida, Minnesota, Kansas, and Oregon from 1981 to 1982. Indeed, the Religious Right's hostility toward homosexuals intensified when the deadly ACQUIRED IMMUNE DEFICIENCY SYNDROME (AIDS) began to ravage gay men in particular. Extremists claimed that the disease represented divine judgment against immoral lifestyles, and a wave of homophobia—including a sharp increase in GAY BASHING—spread across the nation.

As the Religious Right engendered a cultural war to claim the soul of America, the Republican Party came to represent a critically significant force for the crusade to shape public policy. Ostensibly a profamily organization, the Religious Right built bridges with a diverse constituency that included evangelical Christians, conservative politicians, and ROMAN CATHOLICS. Under the leadership of Ralph Reed, membership of the Christian Coalition rose to more than 1.7 million persons by 1993, and they mobilized as many as 4 million voters sympathetic to their values and positions. Ironically, the organization assumed leadership of the Religious Right by demanding traditional religious ends through modern political means. The pious soldiers on the front lines of the culture wars shared a desire to make America a "Christian Nation" in spirit, if not in law.

SUGGESTED READINGS. Well-written examinations of the Religious Right can be found in William Martin,

The Religious Right movement has also found expression in Canada, where these born-again Christians demonstrate against gay rights. (Dick Hemingway)

With God on Our Side: The Rise of the Religious Right in America (1996) and Clyde Wilcox, *God's Warriors: The Christian Right in Twentieth Century America* (1992). Leo Ribuffo explores the antecedents of the Religious Right in *The Old Christian Right: The Protestant Far Right from the Great Depression to the Cold War* (1983). *The New Christian Right* (1983), edited by Robert C. Liebman and Robert Wuthnow, and *Under God: Religion and American Politics* (1990), by Garry Wills, analyze the complicated relationships between religion and American politics during the 1980's.—*Brad D. Lookingbill*

Religious Roundtable: U.S. Christian political organization founded in 1980 by Ed McAteer, a Southern Baptist organizer for the Conservative Caucus. The organization was created for the purpose of attracting mainstream members of Baptist, Presbyterian, and other Protestant denominations who did not fully support RELIGIOUS RIGHT organizations, such as the Moral Majority and the Christian Voice. McAteer recruited popular television evangelist James Robison to serve as the organization's vice president and worked to attract prominent conservative politicians to the group. After the 1992 Republican National Convention, the Religious Roundtable sponsored a widely publicized convocation of conservative luminaries demonstrating their support for President George Bush and the REPUBLICAN PARTY.—*Christopher E. Kent*

Reproductive rights: Legal rights relating to the choices that individual women make about procreation, contraception, ABORTION, and sterilization in order to control their own reproductive status.

History. Abortion is one of the oldest forms of human birth control. One of the earliest references to it has been found in the Chinese royal archives going back to the year 3,000 B.C.E. References to abortion have also been found in ancient Greek and Roman societies as well. Throughout time, methods for the procedure have differed, but they have often included use of herbs and other natural substances. During the 1700's women used parsley as well as ergot, a substance derived from rotten rye and wheat as an abortive stimulant. Women using these substantially occasionally overdosed, with fatal results.

Although abortions have always posed physical risks, there were few legal obstacles to abortion in Western societies before 1820. On the other hand, no laws existed that supported a right to abortion; how-

ever, rulings by Massachusetts courts in 1812 and 1845 did confirm this right. The Massachusetts court required only that abortions be performed before the fetus had "quickened," that is, began to move inside the womb.

Robert Owen attempted to educate the public about how to prevent pregnancy by publishing *Moral Physiology* in 1830; his was the first book containing contraceptive advice that was printed in the United States. Similar books by other authors followed. By the 1860's information on birth control was easily available throughout the United States. Coincidentally, American abortion rates increased between 1820 and 1850. The American Medical Association (AMA) responded by declaring its opposition to the practice. The AMA opposed abortion for several reasons. Its members primarily claimed moral reasons, believing that abortion betrayed the maternal role of women. They also cited the need to stop the problems caused by unlicensed abortion practitioners, usually midwives, who handled most aspects of female health at that time. A stronger motivating factor may have been the need to legitimize the medical profession by focusing on criminalizing abortion because medical doctors were not the only authorities in the medical field. Whatever its reasons, however, the AMA successfully initiated a movement that helped change state laws against abortion.

One law that particularly helped to set the foundation for restrictions on reproductive freedom was the Comstock Act of 1873. (This law was named after Anthony Comstock, head of the New York Society for the Suppression of Vice, who fought against anything that encouraged immoral behavior.) The law included restrictions on mailing any type of written material dealing with BIRTH CONTROL AND FAMILY PLANNING or abortion because it was considered obscene. Soon after, state restrictions on abortions were introduced. By 1900 almost every state had banned abortion, with some exceptions for those pregnancies that endangered the mothers' lives. These laws left American women with few reproductive options.

Margaret Sanger. In reaction to the increasingly restrictive laws, a nurse who had witnessed their negative effect started a campaign that influenced a reversal in those laws. In 1916 Margaret Sanger, with her sister, Ethel Byrne, opened a birth control clinic in Brooklyn, New York. Ten days later they were arrested for violating the Comstock Act and their clinic was closed down. Nevertheless, about five hundred women

In her pioneering efforts to disseminate birth control information Margaret Sanger had to fight against antipornography laws. (AP/Wide World Photos)

had approached the clinic for information, evidence of the need for such services.

Thereafter, Sanger gathered contributions from the wealthy which she used to establish the American Birth Control League, later known as the PLANNED PARENTHOOD FEDERATION OF AMERICA. Due largely to Sanger's efforts, legal restrictions were changed. In 1936 a federal court ruled that birth control was not obscene, as had been asserted in the Comstock Act. Sanger herself helped file a suit to test the law by mailing contraceptive material that led to the Supreme Court's 1936 *United States v. One Package* decision. The court confirmed its earlier ruling and the distribution of birth control information became legal again.

The 1920's and 1930's. Through most of the twentieth century, the American birth rate has declined. Between the 1880's and 1900 the average number of children per woman fell by half—from seven children per woman to 3.5. By 1929 the rate decreased to 2.4 children per woman. One probable reason for this decline was the increased availability of birth control. Although birth control was still formally banned in many states, there was some liberalization in a few. In 1924, for example, a Chicago court found that birth control clinics should be granted licenses because the state could not support religious dictates. Such liberalization led to increasing numbers of clinics. By 1930 there were fifty-five birth control clinics throughout the country; only eight years later the number increased to three hundred. Middle-class women had always had access to birth control devices through their physicians and now working-class women could seek help from the clinics.

Unfortunately, the support for birth control legalization also attracted some racist supporters. For instance, white southern state officials feared large increases in their states' African American populations. To curb this growth, the Birth Control Federation of America created "The Negro Project" in 1939; its purpose was to distribute birth control information to African American women.

The 1940's and 1950's. An important exception to the declining birthrate began after the World War II—a period that produced a "baby boom" lasting for about twenty years. During the latter part of the era, progress occurred in the development of birth control. Most legal restrictions on contraceptives disappeared by the 1950's, and condoms, diaphragms, and other devices were becoming more readily available. Research continued on intrauterine devices (IUDs) and oral contraceptives. Meanwhile, many women continued to undergo illegal abortions—a subject that received attention from professionals in relevant fields who wrote journal articles and held conferences on the topic.

After most contraceptives were legalized, they gained public acceptance. Some 81 percent of married women of childbearing age used some form of contraception during the 1950's. Moreover, abortion—despite its illegal status—remained a birth-control option for many women. According to a report issued by Alfred C. Kinsey in 1953, one in four married women above the age of forty admitted having had abortions. Kinsey's report also found that about 90 percent of American pregnancies outside of marriage were being aborted. Unfortunately, abortion was the cause of an estimated 40 percent of deaths of pregnant women.

The 1960's. The liberalized political climate of the

1960's helped to broaden reproductive options. In 1960 the federal Food and Drug Administration (FDA) approved oral contraceptives. A year later, the National Council of Churches of Christ endorsed birth control for family planning. In addition, the Supreme Court explicitly gave physicians the right to prescribe birth control in its 1965 GRISWOLD V. STATE OF CONNECTICUT decision. By the end of the decade, only two U.S. states continued to restrict contraception: Wisconsin and Massachusetts.

Legalizing Abortion. Legalization of abortion occurred incrementally, gaining momentum in the 1960's and culminating in the Supreme Court's landmark *Roe v. Wade* decision in 1973. The impetus for change came from the American Law Institute, which created a Model Law in 1959 that became the prototype for the reform of abortion. Essentially, the code stated that licensed physicians should be allowed to end pregnancies if they endangered the health of mothers, if fetuses had birth defects, or if fetuses were produced by rape, incest, or statutory rape

This code was adopted by groups who began campaigning for reform or repeal of abortion laws. Lawrence Laderk was author of one of the earliest books to discuss abortion: *Abortion* (1966). In 1967 the NATIONAL ORGANIZATION FOR WOMEN (NOW) adopted the goal of legalizing abortion as part of a larger campaign for women's rights, and the National Association for Repeal of Abortion Laws (NARAL) formed specifically for that purpose.

In 1967 Colorado altered its state abortion laws. The same year, CALIFORNIA passed the Beilenson Bill, based upon the model law, excluding only the section on fetal deformity. Over the next three years, another fifteen states revised their laws. Broad reforms took place in New York, Hawaii, Alaska, and Washington. Both Alaska and Hawaii permitted abortions for any reason, so long as they were performed by licensed doctors in accredited hospital on fetuses that were nonviable (unable to survive outside the womb). Moreover, almost every state allowed abortion when birth might threaten a mother's life or a pregnancy resulted from rape or incest. Nine states also allowed for termination for fetal deformity. During this period, the only losses for abortion reform occurred in Arizona, Vermont, and Maryland.

The fight for reproductive rights gained momentum as women's issues captured attention. During this period, some groups focused exclusively on reproductive issues. For example, the Boston Women's Health Collective formed in an attempt to educate members on topics such as birth control and pregnancy with information later collected in *Our Bodies, Ourselves* (1971). Additionally, *Everywoman's Guide to Abortion* (1971) listed referrals to doctors performing safe, affordable although illegal abortions.

Despite growing support for abortion, opposition to it remained strong. Some African Americans, for example, opposed abortion because of their Christian beliefs, fear of GENOCIDE, or other considerations. Despite such dissent, American childbirth rates dropped throughout the decade for all population groups after the peak birthrate years of the late 1950's.

The Roe v. Wade Decision. The case of ROE V. WADE was a collective suit filed by a group known as "Jane Roe" to protect their privacy at the time of the suit. The group's members—who later came forth publicly—were Norma McCorvey, a twenty-one-year-old SINGLE MOTHER; a married couple; and a medical doctor. Attorneys Linda Coffee and Sarah Weddington filed the suit against Henry Wade, the district attorney of Dallas, Texas, to contest Texas state laws that allowed abortions only in cases in which giving birth might pose a threat to a mother's life. Although the state court ruled in their favor, it did not require Texas to stop enforcing its antiabortion law. For this reason, the Jane Roe attorneys filed an appeal. On January 22, 1973, the U.S. Supreme Court ruled that state laws against abortion were unconstitutional based on the FOURTEENTH AMENDMENT, which included the right to privacy. The issue of abortion was declared to be a private matter of mothers before their fetuses became viable; the ruling allowed for unrestricted abortions during the first trimester of pregnancy.

The *Roe* ruling changed laws that had been in place for almost a century. Inevitably, there were challenges that sought to repeal, reform, or circumvent it. Restrictive laws included bans on physicians advising mothers to have abortions or referring their clients to abortion providers. Some laws required women seeking abortions to notify their husbands or parents or to undergo mandatory waiting periods. Some legislation included prohibitions on the use of public facilities, employees, or public funding for abortions.

During the 1970's the U.S. Supreme Court continued to uphold *Roe* in decisions such as DOE V. BOLTON (1973), which overturned a Georgia law requiring that abortions be performed in hospitals. The Court also ruled against spousal and parental consent requirements, among other things, in PLANNED PARENT-

HOOD OF CENTRAL MISSOURI V. DANFORTH in 1976.

One avenue to restricting abortions involved prohibiting the use of federal funds. For example, in 1976 the U.S. Congress passed the HYDE AMENDMENT, which was designed to limit the use of federal funds for abortion. However, the amendment was defeated in the Senate because it made no provision for funding abortions in cases in which a mother's life might be endangered. In 1978 Congress allowed the Department of Defense to pay only for abortions that fell in accordance with the Hyde Amendment. The following year the Supreme Court determined, in *Bellotti v. Baird*, that abortion funding through Medicaid was not mandated under the SOCIAL SECURITY ACT. That same year it also ruled that the U.S. Constitution's EQUAL PROTECTION clause did not mandate abortion funding through Medicaid either in *Maher v. Roe*.

Attempts at repealing *Roe* continued. In the Su-

preme Court's 1979 *Colautti v. Franklin* decision, the Court overturned a Pennsylvania law requiring doctors to save fetuses even if they were nonviable. That same year, the Court found that parental or judicial consent for minors presented an unnecessary burden in *Bellotti v. Baird*.

After Ronald Reagan was elected president of the United States in 1980, his administration sought to undermine *Roe*. In 1980 the Supreme Court declared the Hyde Amendment constitutional in *Harris v. McRae*. Other major cases that followed reversed previous precedents favoring *Roe*. For example, in *H. L. v. Matheson*, the court upheld a Utah law requiring parental notification for minors in 1981. The only exceptions to the reversal rule occurred in 1983. That year, the court found several laws unconstitutional. In its AKRON V. AKRON CENTER FOR REPRODUCTIVE HEALTH, INC. decision, for example, the twenty-four-hour wait-

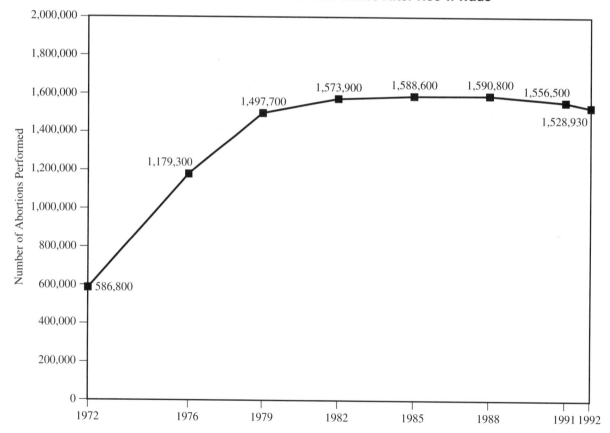

Abortions Performed in the United States After Roe v. Wade

Source: Data are from the *Statistical Abstract of the United States, 1992* (Washington, D.C.: U.S. Government Printing Office, 1992) and *Information Please Almanac*, 1995 (Boston: Houghton Mifflin, 1995).

ing requirement and the requirement that abortions after the first trimester be performed in a hospital in addition to other requirements were overturned. Also, in PLANNED PARENTHOOD V. ASHCROFT (1983), the Court overturned a similar hospital requirement but allowed the required pathology reports for abortions to stand, as well as two other stipulations.

The politics of abortion even extended into international relations. In 1984 the Reagan administration stopped providing funds to the Planned Parenthood Federation. That same year Reagan also declared the "the Mexico City policy" requiring foreign nongovernment organizations to prohibit any abortion-related services in order to receive financial support from the United States. The policy went a step further in 1985, when the Reagan administration withheld $10 million from the United Nations Fund for Population Activities.

In 1987 Reagan directed Surgeon General C. Everett Koop to study the effect of abortion on women. The resulting report was never released to the public, although Koop wrote a letter to Reagan explaining that he was unsatisfied with the quality of the research.

In 1989 *Roe* was further undermined by the Supreme Court's WEBSTER V. REPRODUCTIVE HEALTH SERVICES decision, which upheld a Missouri law requiring doctors to conduct viability tests on fetuses at least twenty weeks old. Other stipulations that were upheld included forbidding public employees from performing abortions, except in cases in which mothers' lives were endangered. Yet another reversal of a precedent occurred in *Hodgson v. Minnesota* (1990), when the Supreme Court allowed a parental notification law to stand. In 1991 the Court's RUST V. SULLIVAN decision went even further, stopping clinics from using money from the federal Title X program to present abortion as an option to clients or to give referrals if prompted. This became known as the gag rule.

In 1990 Guam, a U.S. Pacific island territory, enacted the most restrictive American law on abortion,

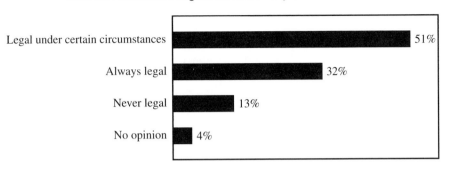

U.S. Opinion on Legalizing Abortion

In 1993 the Gallup Poll asked a cross section of Americans whether abortion should be legalized under any circumstances.

Legal under certain circumstances — 51%
Always legal — 32%
Never legal — 13%
No opinion — 4%

Source: U.S. Department of Justice, Bureau of Justice Statistics, *Sourcebook of Criminal Justice Statistics—1993.* Washington D.C.: U.S. Government Printing Office, 1994. Primary source, *The Gallup Poll Monthly,* April, 1993.

allowing abortions only in cases in which women's lives were threatened. In June, 1991, Louisiana adopted a similar law, allowing abortions only in cases of rape or endangerment. For doctors performing abortions, penalties ranged as high as ten years of imprisonment and fines of $100,000.

Later in 1991 Congress passed legislation prohibiting funding foreign-aid programs that supported abortions or related programs. In addition, an amendment to another bill passed that forbade individuals and institutions from receiving federal monies or requiring employees to perform abortions if the procedure violated their beliefs. A further blow to *Roe* occurred in the *Planned Parenthood of Southeastern Pennsylvania v. Casey* (1992) case, in which the U.S. Supreme Court upheld a twenty-four-hour waiting period and parental consent among other requirements. In fact, the only requirement that the Court overturned was spousal consent.

American abortion rates increased dramatically immediately after the *Roe* decisions, climbing steadily and then leveling off. In 1989 abortion rates began to decline. Reasons for this decline were not clear: More pregnant women may have decided to have their babies, or the decline may have been due to the reduction of accessible abortion services or even a combination of factors.

Meanwhile, abortion legislation continued to be an important political issue. By 1993 nearly three hundred measures relating to abortion had been introduced in the legislatures of forty-seven states; half of these bills sought to restrict abortion; a third validated abortion rights, eliminated restrictions, or protected abortion clinic access. The rest dealt with minor issues. Maine was the only state that enacted a law favoring abortion rights, in 1993.

Although the antiabortion movement has not succeeded in overturning *Roe*, its actions have seriously undermined it. Due to the legal allowances given to states, states such as Pennsylvania have made it more difficult for women to obtain abortions. In addition, the violence, protests, and harassment at abortion clinics has reduced the numbers of doctors willing to perform abortions. Moreover, the number of abortion training programs nationwide that are sponsored by hospitals has itself decreased. For women at the poverty level, these problems are even more pronounced.

Roe Under Bill Clinton. The Clinton administration did not reverse the damage to *Roe* completely. Some victories occurred but many issues remained unresolved. Individual states continued to pass strong laws intended to overturn *Roe*. In 1996, for example, Mississippi passed a law imposing stringent restrictions on physicians who advertise abortions or perform more than ten abortions per month. There has been progress, however. Federal policy under Clinton mandated that states finance Medicaid abortion in cases of rape or incest after previous administrations had left such funding decisions to the individual states. Further, in 1993 President Clinton eliminated prohibitions against privately paid abortions in military hospitals and stopped Reagan's "Mexico City" policy.

Other Medical Issues. Human tissue obtained from aborted fetuses has a special importance in scientific research because it lacks the immunities of adult tissue; it has been used in research yielding promising results in the treatment of Parkinson's disease and other brain disorders. However, the legality of using human fetal tissue for such research has been another area of controversy since the *Roe* decision. In 1993 President Clinton eliminated federal prohibitions on fetal tissue research and mandated that the FDA reconsider its reason for banning import of the abortion drug RU-486.

Tbe drug RU-486 is an abortive stimulant developed in France during the early 1980's. It is an alternative to surgical abortions and works by blocking hormones that encourage fertilized eggs to develop. The FDA banned its importation, possibly because of pressure from pro-life groups, based upon a federal policy that allows blocking import of unapproved drugs. In 1996, however, the agency announced a plan to approve the drug.

SUGGESTED READINGS. *The Information Series on Current Topics: Abortion, an Eternal Social and Moral Issue* (1980), edited by Alison Landes, Mark A. Siegel, and Carol D. Foster. Provides comprehensive coverage of abortion including generous use of graphs, charts, and other visual aids. *American Women in the 1960's: Changing the Future* (1993), by Blanche Lindon Ward and Carol Hurd Green, contains a detailed history of the events leading up to *Roe v. Wade*. A book written for young adults, *The Abortion Battle: Looking at Both Sides* (1996), by Felicia Lowenstein, covers the history and the controversy of reproductive rights.—*Dolores Lopez*

Resegregation: Period of apparently increased racial SEGREGATION, especially in schools, that followed efforts to achieve racial integration during the 1960's and 1970's.

The Civil Rights Era and Desegregation. From the end of RECONSTRUCTION in 1877 until the middle of the twentieth century, the lives of black and white Americans were largely separated. Demands of African Americans for an end to racial discrimination during the CIVIL RIGHTS MOVEMENT era of the mid-1950's until the late 1960's, resulted in movements toward racial integration in a number of areas. The school desegregation was a central goal of the Civil Rights movement and legal segregation was outlawed by the U.S. Supreme Court's ruling in BROWN V. BOARD OF EDUCATION in 1954. Ten years later the federal CIVIL RIGHTS ACT OF 1964 banned discrimination in most areas of public life, and it contained specific provisions to enforce educational integration. The Civil Rights Act of 1968 contained the Fair Housing Law, which was intended to end discrimination in housing.

After the early 1970's desegregation came to be seen as a matter of increasing the actual numbers of African Americans in schools, jobs, and neighborhoods. and not simply a matter of outlawing discrimination. In the 1971 case of SWANN V. CHARLOTTE-MECKLENBURG BOARD OF EDUCATION, the Supreme Court recognized that de facto segregation in public schools was linked to residential segregation since children attended schools in the areas in which they lived. The Court's ruling in this case launched the practice of BUSING students to desegregate schools.

After the early 1970's, movement toward desegregation slowed substantially and sometimes even reversed. The level of segregation in the nation's schools generally remained constant or increased. Black isolation in racially segregated urban neighborhoods also generally remained at the same level or intensified, contributing to school *re*segregation.

Resegregation in the Schools. The desegregation of public schools at the end of the Civil Rights movement era was especially notable in education in the South, home to a majority of black Americans. In 1964 fewer than 2 percent of southern black schoolchildren attended white-majority schools. By 1968, 19 percent of southern black students attended schools that were at least one-half white. By 1972, 45 percent of students attended schools that were at least one-half white. From the early to mid-1970's onward, however, the percentages of black students attending white-majority schools remained stable or declined.

While the percentage of black students attending black-majority schools in the United States decreased by 13.7 percent from 1968 to 1980, it actually increased slightly, by 0.5 percent from 1976 to 1980. This trend was particularly marked in the Northeast, where the percentage of black students attending black-majority schools increased by 13.1 percent over the period 1976 to 1980, with most of this increase occurring during the late 1970's. Moreover, the percentage of black students in the Northeast attending schools that were 90 to 100 percent black increased 6.0 percent overall between 1968 and 1980. Desegregation continued to slow or reverse in most parts of the country throughout the 1980's; in 1989 the National School Boards Association estimated that 63.3 percent of black school children in the United States were attending segregated black schools.

Resegregation also occurred within schools. In many school districts ability grouping, or "tracking," tended to place black and white students in different classrooms, sometimes even within otherwise desegregated schools. Although black students made up 16 percent of all public school students in the United States during the early 1990's, they constituted 40 percent of those who qualified for special education classes. In most school districts, black students were underrepresented in both college preparatory programs and programs for gifted and talented students.

Sources of Resegregation. At least five possible sources of resegregation following the civil rights era may be identified. First, white Americans became an increasingly suburban population, while blacks increasingly concentrated in urban areas. According to

the U.S. BUREAU OF THE CENSUS, 57.2 percent of African Americans lived in central parts of cities in 1990, compared to 25.8 percent of whites. In many American cities the residential separation of blacks and whites remained so pronounced in the early 1990's that some sociologists called the situation "hypersegregation."

Some investigators, such as sociologist David Armor, have argued that busing actually contributed to both school and residential resegregation, by provoking whites to move out of school districts in which their children were likely to be bused in court-ordered desegregation plans. Efforts to keep middle-class whites in public school systems by offering them special programs may have helped promote tracking.

Meanwhile, some African Americans began questioning the value of desegregation itself. In the mid-1990's, for example, Sharon Sayles Belton, the black mayor of Minneapolis, sought to end court-ordered busing in her city, arguing that black school children would be better served by spending government money on improving the quality of their schools instead of efforts to achieve racial balance. Other black leaders and intellectuals, such as educator Felix Boateng, maintained that taking black children out of neighborhood black schools removed them from their cultural roots and undermined the power of black communities. Finally, presidents Ronald Reagan and George Bush both appointed federal judges who tended to be opposed to judicial activism, and who were therefore less likely than earlier judges to make decisions promoting active desegregation.

SUGGESTED READINGS. Gary Orfield, one of the best-known academic experts on school segregation in the United States, offers a thorough discussion of educational resegregation in *Dismantling Desegregation: The Quiet Reversal of Brown v. Board of Education* (1996). *The New American Dilemma: Liberal Democracy and School Desegregation* (1984), by Jennifer Hochschild, describes the retreat from desegregation and argues that a return to it is vital to America's survival as a democratic society. Andrew Hacker's *Two Nations: Black and White, Separate, Hostile, Unequal* (1992) discusses the racial divisions that have continued to cut across most areas of American society. *American Apartheid: Segregation and the Making of the Underclass* (1993), by Douglas Massey and Nancy Denton, argues that residential segregation has increased in the United States and that it has isolated the black poor in cities.—*Carl L. Bankston III*

Retirement Equity Act (1984): U.S. federal legislation mandating reform of many pension plans. President Ronald Reagan signed the Retirement Equity Act, which reduced the age at which employees must be allowed to participate in employer-sponsored pension plans from twenty-five to twenty-one, on August 23, 1984. A number of the act's provisions were designed to benefit female employees in particular. For example, it required pension plans to provide survivor benefits to spouses of vested employees, even if the employees died before reaching retirement age. The law also required pension plans to allow employees to leave and return to their jobs without sacrificing their pension benefit accumulations in certain circumstances. In addition, the act prohibited pension plans from counting one-year maternity or paternity leaves as breaks in service for purposes of determining pension eligibility.—*Alexander Scott*

Return migration: Process by which migrants return to their countries of origin. Throughout recorded history people have emigrated from their homelands later to return. Reasons for both emigration and return migration have included economic, social, cultural, political, and family considerations.

Perhaps the most important reason people migrate to new lands is the search for economic opportunity and jobs. A great many people throughout the world have engaged in seasonal migrations as agricultural jobs have shifted with harvests, or as the demand for labor in service and tourist industries has changed with the seasons and business cycles. Apart from seasonal migration, many people seek jobs in foreign countries when they are plentiful, returning to their homes when work becomes less plentiful, such as during recessions. In some cases, young men go abroad for periods of five or ten years to earn enough money to return to their homelands, purchase property, and establish families. Economic causes of return migration vary with the circumstances, however, and many people who migrate abroad with the intention of returning home stay abroad and even take on new citizenship.

Return migration is often also inhibited by the countries of origin when they enjoy substantial benefits from the money their overseas migrants send home. However, when economic times are hard in host nations, their governments may force foreign workers to return home. Deportation of economic migrants is permitted under international law and the domestic laws of most countries.

Migrants often return to their homelands after they

German artist and writer Georg Grosz aboard the ship carrying him home to Germany in 1959—twenty-six years after he fled his homeland to escape Nazi persecution. (AP/Wide World Photos)

have accumulated enough money to meet their goals at home, where they may be able to live more cheaply than in the countries where they have earned their money. Also, they may return because they miss their families and friends and the hospitable cultural environments in which they have been raised. This motivation is likely to be greater if they have experienced discrimination in their host countries.

Return migration is sometimes stimulated by political factors, especially in the case of REFUGEES, who may have fled their native homes under fear of persecution. If the governments that have caused their flight are overthrown, they will often voluntarily return home in the hope of reestablishing their lives as they had been earlier. Occasionally seekers of political asylum and refugees are forced to return to their homelands by unsympathetic host governments, but such actions are contrary to international law and often provoke international outcries of protest.

Most return migration is spontaneous; however, it occasionally is actively promoted through incentives offered by the governments of the host countries and countries of return. The International Organization for

Migration, for example, funds a Return of Talent Program designed to promote the return of professionals and skilled laborers to developing countries where their services are often desperately needed.

SUGGESTED READINGS. Myron Weiner's *The Global Migration Crisis* (1995) is a comprehensive and balanced treatment of modern migration issues, including return migration. *The Politics of Return* (1981), edited by Daniel Kubat, is an excellent collection of articles on European return migration. *Immigrant America: A Portrait* (1990), by Alejandro Portes and Rubén G. Rumbaut, provides insights into American migration patterns.—*Robert F. Gorman*

Richmond v. J. A. Croson Co. (1989): U.S. Supreme Court decision that tightened restrictions on race-conscious AFFIRMATIVE ACTION programs in munici-palities. In 1983 the city council of Richmond, Virginia, adopted a minority set-aside program for city contracting. After the city rejected the low bid of the J. A. Croson Company on a city construction project, the contracting company sued the city because it accepted a higher bid submitted by a minority-owned firm. The case eventually reached the Supreme Court, which decided in favor of Croson on January 23, 1989. The Court held that race-conscious affirmative action programs were only valid in situations in which it could be shown that there had been a history of past racial DISCRIMINATION by the government itself.

Dissenters on the Court argued that there had, in fact, been systematic discrimination, which could be only be remedied in practice by a set-aside or QUOTA program. *Richmond v. Croson* cast doubt on the future of race-conscious programs designed to remedy past discrimination. At the least it appeared to mean that racial quotas, however well meant, were likely to be held unconstitutional by the Supreme Court.—*Robert Jacobs*

Rivera, Diego (Dec. 8, 1886, Guanajuato, Mexico— Nov. 25, 1959, Mexico City, Mexico): Mexican muralist. A child prodigy, Rivera studied art in Mexico and several European countries then applied his background in pre-Columbian art and use of color to paint monumental murals of Mexican history and folklore. He was also fascinated by industrial and architectural technology as themes for murals. His need to incorporate aspects of his own life in his work sometimes hindered his career. An avowed activist who allied with such revolutionary figures as Russian revolutionist Leon Trotsky, Rivera believed art to be a tool of political change. Working for as long as thirty-six hours at a stretch, he painted more than three thousand square meters of surfaces in Mexico in seventeen major murals and in the United States, where some of his work was destroyed because of political opposition.

Rivera was twice married to another noted Mexican

Mexican muralist Diego Rivera at work. (Archive Photos)

painter, Frida Kahlo. Since his death, Rivera's work has been officially designated a national treasure of Mexico.—*Debra D. Andrist*

Royal Commission on Aboriginal Peoples (RCAP): Canadian federal government commission established to study the role of Indians in 1991. In 1990 the town of Oka, Quebec, announced plans to expand its public golf course into land containing a Mohawk burial ground. Local Mohawks (members of the SIX NATIONS) resisted the plan by occupying the land and erecting barricades to protect it from development. The Mohawks held their ground for three months in the face of government efforts to remove them by force. After this incident, the federal government promised to address Indian leaders' concerns about the place of Native Canadians in the country by establishing the RCAP on August 27, 1991.

The commission produced the most extensive study ever conducted on the lives of Native Canadians. Headed by Canada's former chief justice Brian Dickson, the seven-member commission sought input from Indian leaders and organizations, academics, and government officials. The RCAP proposed four principles: recognition that Indians are Canada's original inhabitants and have distinctive rights and responsibilities because of this; that Canadians must work to create a climate of respect and positive mutual regard for Native Canadians; that there must be a principle of real equity among all Canadian peoples; and that everyone must recognize past wrongdoing and take responsibility for developing practices both the government and Canadian Indians agree are appropriate in the future. —*Patricia L. Gibbs*

RU-486 (mifepristone): Drug that induces spontaneous ABORTION when taken during the early stages of PREGNANCY. Developed in France, RU-486 works by preventing the essential natural hormone progesterone from sustaining pregnancy by maintaining the uterine lining.

The drug was first synthesized by the French pharmaceutical firm Roussel-Uclaf in 1980 but was not approved for use in France until September, 1988. In response to protests of antiabortion groups in France, the United States, and West Germany, Roussel-Uclaf stopped distributing RU-486 a month later. However, the French minister of health, citing public health interests, ordered the firm to resume distribution of the drug. RU-486 was approved for use in Great Britain in 1991 and in Sweden in 1992. Officials of Roussel-Uclaf were pleased that other countries approved dis-

Dr. Etienne Baulieu, inventor of RU-486, at a press conference in 1995. (AP/Wide World Photos)

tribution of its drug but it was not anxious to market it in countries where public opposition was strong, such as the United States. By 1997 more than 200,000 women in Great Britain and France were estimated to have used RU-486 to terminate pregnancies, but the fight to legalize the drug in the United States still continued.

Because RU-486 can be used as a medical alternative to surgical abortion, the drug's proponents have argued that it is a woman's right to use the drug as a less invasive and less expensive alternative to surgical abortion. Those opposed to abortion have contended that RU-486 poses the danger of making abortion so easy that it will become much more frequent.

In addition to the drug's use as an "abortion pill," it has been proven effective as a "MORNING-AFTER PILL," or postcoital contraceptive, when taken within seventy-two hours of sexual intercourse.—*Jeffry Jensen*

Rust v. Sullivan (1991): U.S. Supreme Court case that significantly limited the reach of the landmark ROE V. WADE (1973) decision, which upheld a woman's right to ABORTION. In 1988 Congress passed regulations imposing a gag order prohibiting federally funded BIRTH CONTROL AND FAMILY PLANNING clinics not only from performing abortions, but from even providing information on abortion. Family planning services protested the new rules as violations of both *Roe v. Wade* and their right of free speech. The Supreme Court brushed aside these First Amendment arguments, upholding the right of government to ensure that federal funds are spent only for allocated purposes. Because the 1970 law allocating funds to family planning clinics stated that these funds could not be spent on programs performing abortions, the Court found the new rules a permissible exercise of what has come to be known as the doctrine of unconstitutional conditions or conditional spending.—*Lisa Paddock*

S

St. Francis College v. Al-Khazraji (1987): U.S. Supreme Court case concerning racial DISCRIMINATION. The case originated in a tenure suit filed by an Arab American college teacher who claimed his college had discriminated against him because of his race. The Court faced the problem of sorting out racial discrimination charges in a case in which both plaintiff and defendants were considered to be whites. Nevertheless, writing for a unanimous Court, Justice Byron White ruled that the Civil Rights Act of 1866, a RECONSTRUCTION-era measure designed to protect newly freed slaves, also protected Arab Americans because they clearly had been regarded as a distinct "race" at the time that law had been written.

On the same day, in *Shaare Tefila Congregation v. Cobb*, Justice White expressed an opinion ruling that the Civil Rights Act of 1866 also protected JEWISH AMERICANS from racial discrimination.—*Brian G. Tobin*

Samoan Civic Association: Ethnic-oriented social organization for Samoans and people of Samoan heritage living in the United States. The Samoan Civic Association was formed in 1960 by a group of several hundred ethnic Samoans, who created the organization to promote service programs in Samoan communities. The group's principal activities center on the Pacific Coast, where tens of thousands of Samoans had settled by the latter decades of the twentieth century.—*Glenn Canyon*

San Jacinto, Battle of (1836): Decisive battle in the TEXAS REVOLT. After the Texan fight for independence from Mexico suffered a defeat at the Battle of the ALAMO and 340 Texans were executed by General Antonio López de Santa Anna at Goliad, the Texas army under the command of General Sam Houston launched a surprise attack on Santa Anna's army near the San Jacinto River. In the ensuing battle the Mexicans panicked and were quickly and soundly defeated. The Texans lost only two men, against 1,568 Mexicans killed, wounded, or captured.

Among those captured was Santa Anna himself. While he was imprisoned he signed the Treaty of Velasco, granting independence to Texas. Mexico's congress immediately renounced the treaty as having been negotiated under duress and refused to ratify its pro-

General Antonio López de Santa Anna, commander of the Mexican force at the Battle of San Jacinto. (Library of Congress)

visions. Nevertheless, Texas operated as an independent republic for nine years until it was annexed by the United States. American recognition of Texas' independence and its later annexation helped provoke the MEXICAN-AMERICAN WAR.—*Leslie Ann Stricker*

San Pascual, Battle of (Dec. 6, 1846): Fiercest battle of the MEXICAN-AMERICAN WAR, fought in California about forty miles from San Diego. Under the command of Andrés Pico, 160 Mexican lancers defeated the advance group of the U.S. Army of the West, commanded by Colonel Stephen Kearny. When the confident U.S. troops sighted the Mexican force, they charged without realizing in what great danger they were. An excellent cavalryman, Pico had prepared a clever ambush. In fifteen minutes, his lancers killed eighteen of Kearny's troops. Kearny's troops retreated and anxiously awaited reinforcements. Kearny himself received a lance wound in the groin that forced him to turn over command to his deputy, Captain Henry S. Turner. Both sides agreed to an exchange of prisoners as a standoff ensued.

The Battle of San Pascual proved to be the most significant victory that Mexico won during the war. However, the final resolution of the battle occurred after 160 fresh U.S. troops relieved Kearny and forced Pico to retreat.—*Douglas W. Richmond*

Saybrook, Battle of (1636): Military conflict between British settlers and the Pequot people of colonial New England. Actually a nine-month-long siege of a fort during the PEQUOT WAR, this conflict contributed to the demise of the Pequot tribe as a significant power in colonial Connecticut. A 1634 treaty between the Pequot tribe and the Massachusetts Bay Colony guaranteed peace, but the Pequots apparently did not understand that its terms covered Pequot-British relations as far as Connecticut River Valley settlements that lay beyond the geographical boundaries of the Massachusetts Bay Colony's royal charter.

Establishment of Fort Saybrook at the mouth of the Connecticut River increased tensions between the English and the Pequots, whom the settlers often blamed for depredations actually committed by Western Niantic and Narragansett Indians. By September, 1636, the Pequot had effectively surrounded Fort Saybrook, which was cut off from outside help because of internal strife in the Massachusetts Bay Colony. The Pequots expected help from the Narragansett Indians in the spring of 1637, but Roger Williams forged a Narragansett-Massachusetts Bay agreement that doomed the Pequot to defeat and obliteration in a culminating battle at Mystic in early May, 1637. The Treaty of Hartford (1638) included a provision that disbanded the Pequot tribe as a political entity.—*Richard Sax*

School prayer: Formally organized or directed prayers conducted in public schools. In 1962 the U.S. Supreme Court ruled that prayer ceremonies in the public schools were unconstitutional because of the establishment clause of the First Amendment's freedom of religion protections. Because Americans have enjoyed the freedom to practice their religious beliefs without government hindrance, no court has ever challenged the right of students to pray or meditate as individuals. However, the Court has interpreted the First Amendment as prohibiting public institutions from either supporting or opposing religious practices, or from giving preference to one religion over another.

Historical Background. During the nineteenth century many school districts began allowing—and in some cases requiring—their schools to schedule times for short prayer ceremonies. These usually conformed to the practices of the dominant local churches, which were typically Protestant sects. Because the protections of the First Amendment were not interpreted as restricting state and local government actions for many years, federal courts were not called upon to decide on the constitutionality of school prayers, and the matter was left to state courts to decide, following the provisions of their state constitutions.

In 1947 the U.S. Supreme Court ruled, in *Everson v. Board of Education*, that the establishment clause was binding on the states by way of the FOURTEENTH AMENDMENT. The decision also held that the First Amendment required a "wall of separation" between church and state. How high that wall had to be was not, however, clearly defined.

In 1951 the New York Board of Regents recommended that public schools should begin the day by reciting a prayer of twenty-two words:

> Almighty God, we acknowledge our dependence upon Thee, and we beg Thy blessings upon us, our parents, our teachers, and our country.

Shortly afterward, the AMERICAN CIVIL LIBERTIES UNION joined with Steven Engel and other parents of students in a legal suit charging that the state-authored prayer was an unconstitutional establishment of religion. These litigants argued that public institutions were prohibited from giving either direct or indirect support to religion. They relied heavily on the writings of Thomas Jefferson and James Madison, primarily in the context of the debates about the ending of an established religion in eighteenth century Virginia. The Board of Regents answered that the school prayers involved no expenditures of tax money, that such exercises were entirely in keeping with American traditions, that participation by students was voluntary, and that the endorsement of prayers did not amount to an unconstitutional establishment of religion.

After the case reached the U.S. Supreme Court, its members voted 7-1, in *Engel v. Vitale* (1962), to support the opponents of oral prayers. Writing for the majority, Justice Hugo Black declared that it was "inconsistent" with the establishment clause for public schools to sponsor or to encourage religious prayers, even when they were voluntary and nondenominational.

Attempts to Restore School Prayer. Many American citizens, church leaders and members of Congress were shocked and angered by the Supreme Court's

Engel decision; Gallup polls revealed that about 75 percent of the public disagreed with the decision. Numerous attempts were made to pass constitutional amendments to readmit school prayers. In 1963, after the Supreme Court disallowed devotional Bible readings in schools, hundreds of school districts, especially in the South, simply ignored its rulings and continued to have both oral prayer and Bible readings. During the 1980's a conservative majority of the Supreme Court began showing a tendency to allow accommodation of religious practices. Proponents of accommodation on this issue were encouraged when the Court voted 6-3, in *Marsh v. Chambers* (1983), to permit legislative bodies to begin each session with prayers delivered by paid chaplains.

By the early 1980's nearly half of the states had passed "moment-of-silence" laws, which allowed schools to set aside periods of time for individual reflection or meditation. Alabama, for example, passed a law allowing a brief period of silence "for meditation or voluntary prayer." Ismael Jaffree, the father of three school children, objected to the Alabama law and filed a suit that led to a new Supreme Court decision. In *Wallace v. Jaffree* (1985), the majority of the Court held that Alabama's law was unconstitutional because it consisted of a governmental endorsement of a religious practice. Drawing a subtle distinction, Justice Sandra Day O'CONNOR explained that the establishment clause did not prohibit the states from allowing children to pray silently during a moment of silence, but that laws must have a secular purpose and not be based on a desire to "advance" religion. In a strong dissent, Chief Justice William Rehnquist argued that the establishment clause requires only that the government not favor one religious sect over another, and that it does not require neutrality between religion and "irreligion."

Prayers at Graduation Ceremonies. Meanwhile, it remained common for public school officials to schedule invocations and benedictions at promotional and graduation ceremonies. In Providence, Rhode Island, for example, school officials regularly invited mem-

In contrast to public schools, Roman Catholic and other parochial schools encourage prayer in the classroom. (Don Franklin)

bers of the clergy from various Christian and Jewish groups to offer invocations and benedictions at their school graduation ceremonies. The invited clergy were given guidelines that encouraged "inclusiveness and sensitivity," and attendance at the ceremonies was "voluntary." One graduating student, Deborah Weisman, went to court, charging that oral prayers advanced the cause of religion. She also noted that such rituals caused persons holding minority views on religion to feel like outsiders. In *Lee v. Weisman* (1992), the majority of the Supreme Court agreed with Weisman and ruled that Rhode Island's school officials had unconstitutionally created "a state-sponsored and state-directed religious exercise in a public school." The majority also insisted that because prayer exercises carry the risk of "indirect coercion," public schools must be careful in "protecting freedom of conscience from subtle coercive pressure."

After the *Weisman* decision, it appeared clear that public schools were prohibited from giving any direct or indirect encouragement of religious activities; however, it was uncertain to what extent students acting independently of school officials could legally organize such activities at school-sponsored events. Although Supreme Court justices often disagreed among themselves about how they should interpret the establishment clause, most of them were consistent in upholding the principle that the public schools themselves should neither promote nor oppose the cause of religion.

SUGGESTED READINGS. On the *Engel* decision and its impact, see William Muir's *Prayer in the Public Schools: Law and Attitude Change* (1967) and Kenneth Dolbeare and Phillip Hammond's *The School Prayer Decision* (1971). For the pro-separationist perspective, see Leonard Levy's *The Establishment Clause* (1986) and Leo Pfeffer's *Church, State, and Freedom* (1967). For the pro-accommodationist point of view, see Robert Cord's *Separation of Church and State: Historical Fact and Current Fiction* (1982) and Rodney Smith's *Public Prayer and the Constitution: A Case Study in Constitutional Interpretation* (1987). Peter Irons examines the *Jaffree* decision in *The Courage of Their Convictions* (1988).—*Thomas T. Lewis*

School vouchers: Type of educational finance reform in which the government gives families vouchers with which they can enroll their children at the public or private schools of their choice.

Proposals to use public tax money to pay student tuition at the schools of their own choosing were made as early as the eighteenth century by both Adam Smith and Thomas Paine. In 1955 American economist Milton Friedman advocated using vouchers to create a "free market." Common goals in modern school-choice programs have included racial desegregation; expanded opportunities for minority, ethnic, and poor families; and promotion of multicultural diversity and understanding—a concept also known as pluralism.

In 1969 Christopher Jencks, president of the Center of the Study for Public Policy, proposed establishing an Educational Voucher Agency (EVA) to issue vouchers to parents of elementary school children that would be payable to any public or private schools meeting eligibility requirements, such as setting tuition limits and maintaining racial balance. Opponents raised two concerns: that school choice would tend to increase racial and economic segregation, and that the plan would subsidize PAROCHIAL SCHOOLS.

The state of Connecticut passed school voucher legislation in April, 1972; however, the Alum Rock School District in San Jose, California, was the first school system actually to implement an Education Voucher Project, for the 1972-1973 school year. Providing for "only secular" education, the San Jose program disallowed discrimination on the basis of race, color, national origin, economic status, or political affiliation. It was funded by the Office of Economic Opportunity and continued for five years, but it achieved limited success.

By the early 1980's school vouchers were part of the conservative political agenda. The Reagan administration submitted legislation to Congress for federal tax credits to parents paying private school tuition. Modified proposals included vouchers for low-income youth to purchase remedial education through school choice.

By 1991 twenty-nine states had authorized some type of school-choice provision, including plans for programs within single districts, across districts, and among specific populations. The school systems of St. Louis, Louisville, and other cities developed school-choice programs, sometimes without vouchers attached. Milwaukee's voucher program, begun in 1990, was considered a model; it was initiated by Polly Williams, an African American state representative and former state chair of Jesse JACKSON's presidential campaign. Milwaukee's program allowed a maximum of 1 percent of children of low-income families to attend nonsectarian private schools. Only 341 students participated in the program initially, however, making its success difficult to measure. Through the late 1990's other school systems continued to explore the use of vouchers to expand school choice.

Gallup polls have indicated that educators and members of school boards generally oppose vouchers, while parents of schoolchildren—both white and non-white—support them. In polls taken in 1986 and 1989 higher proportions of nonwhite parents supported the idea of vouchers than did white parents.

SUGGESTED READINGS. *Education Vouchers: From Theory to Alum Rock* (1972), edited by James A. Mecklenburger and Richard W. Hostrop, presents the background of the first Education Voucher Project in the United States. *The Choice Controversy* (1992), edited by Peter W. Cookson, Jr., surveys types of school-choice programs, including vouchers. David W. Kirkpatrick presents a case for tuition vouchers in *Choice in Schooling* (1990).—*Beverly L. White*

Seabrook Farms: New Jersey agricultural operation largely staffed by JAPANESE AMERICANS. Seabrook Farms was created by Charles F. Seabrook on a sixty-acre family farm. By the 1930's it had grown to become one of the leading producers of canned and frozen vegetables in the United States. To alleviate labor shortages during WORLD WAR II, the operation's management recruited many Japanese American laborers, including many sent by the federal government relocation camps under its wartime JAPANESE AMERICAN INTERNMENT program. By 1947 more than 2,300 Japanese Americans were employed at Seabrook.

During the 1950's Seabrook Farms was eclipsed by larger food-processing facilities, and the plant was eventually closed. A small Japanese American community remains in the area, and construction of a local Japanese American museum has been proposed. —*Alexander Scott*

Self-Help for the Elderly: Nonprofit social-service organization established in 1966. Formed in SAN FRANCISCO, California, Self-Help for the Elderly was a project of President Lyndon B. Johnson's WAR ON POVERTY programs and was created primarily to serve the needs of the San Francisco area's large CHINESE AMERICAN community. The organization has provided assistance to more than twenty-five thousand OLDER AMERICANS annually. Its services have included home delivery of meals; in-home support and home health care, including day care for sufferers of Alzheimer's disease; voca-tional training; residential repairs and construction; and other educational, recreational, and social activities. —*Christopher E. Kent*

Self-Realization Fellowship (SRF): International religious organization founded in 1920. Seeking to create a better understanding of diverse cultures and people around the world, the Self-Realization Fellowship has been dedicated to maintaining the humanitarian and spiritual work of Paramahansa Yogananda. Yogananda created the fellowship to share the teachings of kriya yoga, a sacred spiritual science originated in India.

With its international headquarters in Los Angeles, California, the fellowship has 470 meditation centers located in fifty-four countries. These centers have provided places for students to gather for spiritual fellowship and meditation. Meetings have typically included healing prayer services, readings from the teachings of Yogananda, and devotional chanting. Retreats and lectures have been conducted in cities across the United States and in many other countries, offering classes in the meditation techniques of Yogananda. At its annual convocations held in Los Angeles, the fellowship has conducted week-long programs of classes, presentations, and tours of the ashram centers in which Paramahansa Yogananda lived and worked. The convocations have attracted about six thousand participants from around the world.—*Mark Miller*

Self-segregation: Situation occurring when persons from the same ethnic group or of the same gender draw together and try to insulate themselves from outsiders. Self-segregation is often considered to be an example of the lingering effects of de jure SEGREGATION, by which separation of racial or other groups occurs even though such separation is no longer sanctioned under the law. However, such behavior is often more reflective of the persistence of class segregation than it is of patterns of racial discrimination traditionally associated with the concept of segregation. Housing patterns, educational opportunities, and social standing have continued to be determined, to a large extent, by the size of family incomes. Despite more than two decades of court rulings that have ordered school desegregation throughout the United States, Americans have been slow to discover satisfactory methods of teaching tolerance and respect for cultural differences. As whites have become a decreasing portion of the total U.S. population, more Americans have come to realize that new solutions are necessary.

During the 1980's and 1990's examples of self-segregation were commonly found on college campuses, where "ethnic-themed" dormitories and ethnic student associations flourished. Critics of ethnic dormitories claimed that such programs tend to encourage ethnic STEREOTYPES and to undermine the role that higher education should play in exposing students to a broad range of life experiences. On many campuses, students from the same ethnic minorities have drawn together in efforts to provide each other with mutual assistance and emotional support in pursuing their academic goals in what for many of them are unfamiliar and more competitive environments. Others have drawn together because they feel more comfortable in the company of persons who share their cultural heritage and values, allowing them to assert their identity and resist pressure to assimilate to the majority culture.

Some observers have even pointed to the efforts to preserve all-women's colleges and HISTORICALLY BLACK COLLEGES as part of a larger trend toward tolerating or even encouraging self-segregation. Forging a sense of identity and offering mutual assistance are compelling factors that have accounted for the creation of support groups based on gender, sexual orientation, disabilities, age, and other nonethnic criteria. While allowing such groups to establish a sense of community, many college administrations are concerned that such groups might encourage minority students to withdraw and reject others who want to associate with them. Many colleges and universities have launched freshman orientation seminars and other programs that encourage students to reach out to people who are unlike themselves without sacrificing their own cultural identities.

SUGGESTED READINGS. For general background on the legacy of segregation in the United States, see Douglas S. Massey and Nancy A. Denton's *American Apartheid: Segregation and the Making of the Underclass* (1993). For insight into the psychological aspects of various forms of segregation with regard to ethnic relations, see *Groups in Contact: The Psychology of Desegregation* (1984), edited by Norman Miller and Marilynn B. Brewer. For perspective on the controversies surrounding self-segregation in academia, consult Mary Jo Hill's article "Do Theme Dorms Sanction Self-Segregation?," *Christian Science Monitor* (July 15, 1996).—*Wendy Sacket*

Selph v. Council of the City of Los Angeles (1975): U.S. District Court case relating to the rights of persons with disabilities. Jacqueline Selph, a woman confined to a wheelchair, found it impossible to enter her neighborhood polling place on her own to vote because of the steps at its entrance. The polling place officers offered to carry her over the steps, but she refused because she thought it would be embarrassing and was concerned about the danger of being dropped. Supported by several organizations, she sued in federal court arguing that the "architectural barriers" were a violation of her constitutional right to vote. The plaintiffs wanted all 3,800 polling places in the city of Los Angeles to be made accessible to persons in wheelchairs. However, the district court rejected the idea that persons with disabilities had the right to insist on modifying all polling places in the city. The court suggested that there were reasonable alternatives, such as using absentee ballots or designating a limited number of polling places as accessible to wheelchairs.—*Thomas T. Lewis*

Sentencing Project Report (1995): Study of racial effects on the U.S. criminal justice system. Released in October, 1995, by the Washington, D.C.-based Sentencing Project, the report represented an expanded and updated version of an earlier series of reports entitled *Dilemma of Black Male Youth* (1955). The new report found that one in three young African American males was under some form of criminal justice jurisdiction. Its authors asserted that public policies developed to control crime and drug abuse had contributed to a growing racial disparity in the administration of criminal justice, while at the same time having little actual impact on the problems they were designed to address. The authors also called for expanded drug-treatment and other programs and for a renewed national dialogue concerning drug policy, with special attention to be paid to the racial inequities resulting from so-called "three-strikes" laws and other mandatory-sentencing measures.—*Glenn Canyon*

Serpent mounds: Earthworks built by MOUND BUILDERS. Among many thousands of diverse earthen mounds scattered across North America between the northern Appalachians, Great Plains, Gulf of Mexico, and Great Lakes, serpent mounds represent one type of mound. As many as ten thousand such mounds were reported to have been found in Ohio alone during the early 1800's. By then midwestern American Indian tribes did not build mounds and appeared—to Europeans—incapable of doing so. Moreover, local tribes knew neither who had built the mounds nor the fate of their builders. Europeans thus assumed that a mysterious, highly civilized early people—identified simply as the mound builders—had built the mounds. Speculation ascribed the mounds to such unlikely peoples as ancient Phoenicians, the Lost Tribes of Israel, Vikings, or the pyramid builders of Mexico and Central America. By the early twentieth century, however, most scholars believed that the mounds had been built by indigenous North American peoples, who either moved away or had been exterminated.

Archaeologists have distinguished several sequences of mound-building cultures, ranging in dates from 2200 B.C.E. to the 1500's, when Hernando de Soto found active mound-building tribes in Florida and elsewhere. The Adena culture, which was centered in the southern Ohio region from c. 500 B.C.E.-c. 800 C.E., is thought to have been responsible for the serpent mounds. A site known as Great Serpent Mound,

located about eight miles east of Cincinnati, Ohio, is the best preserved of about a half dozen similar mounds in the Ohio region. A rounded embankment, 1,245 feet long, three to five feet high, and about thirty feet wide, Great Serpent Mound has the shape of a partially coiled, idealized snake. Its tail, arranged in three spiral coils, connects with a body thrown into four broad undulations. The head is outlined as a nearly equilateral triangle, with its mouth portion curved inward. The rear part of a large oval within the jaws projects forward. This oval, which has been variously interpreted as representing an egg or a frog, contains a small circle of stones within its unfilled center.

Although the Great Serpent Mound site was extensively excavated before 1896, when it was purchased for preservation, no artifacts or burials were found in

Located near modern Cincinnati, Ohio, the impressive site known as Great Serpent Mound is merely the best preserved of about a half dozen similar mounds in the region. (Courtesy Department Library Services, American Museum of Natural History/D. M. Reeves)

it. A small conical mound located about four hundred feet south of the serpent's tail contains Adena burials and artifacts and is the principal evidence for assigning the serpent itself to the Adena culture.

Only five or six poorly preserved, similar serpent mounds of presumed Adena origin occur elsewhere. However, thousands of conical burial grounds and mounds outlining other geometric shapes belonging to the Adena culture have been identified. Other mound-building cultures did not construct similar serpent mounds. Because the serpent mounds are not burial mounds, building platforms, or fortifications, they are assumed to have been created for ceremonial or religious purposes. Similar serpentiform images associated with globes or eggs have been part of many religious traditions, including those of Mexico's Aztec and Maya peoples.

SUGGESTED READINGS. Two books by Robert Silverberg, *Mound Builders of Ancient America: The Archaeology of a Myth* (1968) and *Mound Builders* (1986) are histories of mound building peoples and the theories that have been advanced about them. William N. Morgan's *Prehistoric Architecture in the Eastern United States* (1980) concentrates on mound construction and physical forms. Henry Clyde Shetrone's *The Mound Builders* (1930) describes the mounds and their significance.—*Ralph L. Langenheim, Jr.*

Serra, Junípero (Nov. 24, 1713, Petra, Majorca, Spain—Aug. 28, 1784, Carmel, Calif.): Franciscan monk who oversaw the founding of California's SPANISH MISSIONS. Born Miguel José Serra, Serra entered the Roman Catholic Church's Franciscan order in 1731, taking the name Junípero from a companion of Saint Francis. During the late eighteenth century he worked in California, where he personally founded missions at San Diego, Carmel, San Antonio de Padua, San Gabriel, San Luis Obispo, San Francisco, San Juan Capistrano, Santa Clara, and San Buenaventura (now Ventura).

Serra's modern legacy has become controversial. Critics have denounced him as a representative of Spanish imperialism who helped to enslave and mistreat American Indians. Others have praised him as a man who made great personal sacrifices to bring Christianity to an unenlightened land. During the 1980's a campaign was launched to have Serra canonized—a process that normally goes through several stages. In 1985 the Vatican proclaimed Serra "venerable"; three years later it proclaimed him "blessed." The Roman Catholic Church requires two proven

This early painting of the Franciscan monk Junípero Serra anticipated the modern movement to have him canonized as a saint. (Library of Congress)

"miracles" before it elevates candidates to sainthood. It has accepted one miracle connected with Serra—the case of a nun who suddenly recovered from an apparently terminal case of lupus after praying to Serra in the mid-1980's.—*Maria L. Alonzo*

Sex-change operations: Surgical procedures performed to switch the sexes of human patients. Called sexual reassignment surgery (SRS) by physicians, sex-change operations are generally performed on persons suffering from gender dysphoria, or gender identity disorder. Relatively few such persons, who are commonly known as TRANSSEXUALS, have sex-change surgery, which is extremely expensive and is rarely covered by health insurance.

Surgery for male-to-female transsexuals (MTFs) includes breast augmentation and construction of vaginas—often using the skin of the penis. Surgery for female-to-male transsexuals (FTMs) is more complex, requiring removal of breasts, uteruses, ovaries, tubes and vaginas, as well as construction of penises and scrota and extension of the urethras so that FTMs may urinate standing up. Between 1966 and 1988 fewer than 10,000 persons in the United States underwent these procedures.

To understand gender identity disorders, it is important to distinguish between the words "sex," a biological classification that is usually based on physical appearance of genitals, and "gender," which applies to traits associated with being male or female with society. A transsexual has the genital appearance of one sex, but strongly identifies with the gender of the other, often feeling "trapped" in the wrong body from a young age. MTF cases appear to have been more numerous than those of FTMs. Transsexuals are not transvestites, homosexuals, female impersonators, or others whose sexuality differs from heterosexual norms.

Americans became widely aware of transsexualism in 1952, when a young American soldier named George Jorgensen had a sex-change operation in Denmark and returned to the United States as a woman named Christine Jorgensen—a name that for a generation became almost synonymous with transsexual. Years later, another highly publicized case was that of a male physician who became famous as a female tennis player Renée Richards. Despite the media attention that these cases attracted, transsexualism remained poorly understood by the public at large and even by many health professionals.

In 1966 Harry Benjamin, a pioneer in the study of gender dysphoria, published *The Transsexual Phenomenon*, one of the most important works yet published on the topic. The Harry Benjamin International Gender Dysphoria Association (HBIGDA), named in Benjamin's honor, later became the leading professional organization for gender specialists.

Because changing one's gender is a life-altering decision, specialists have followed a treatment code known as Standards of Care, which was first codified in 1979. This code has provided guidelines for choosing to undertake hormone treatment and surgery. Persons with gender dysphoria may locate specialists through HBIGDA, online services, information hotlines, or national referral sources, such as the American Educational Gender Information Service.

The code requires therapists to make accurate diagnoses of gender identity disorder, counsel on specific gender issues, and discuss the pros and cons of various treatments with their patients. Many transsexuals have elected simply to "cross-live" as persons of the opposite sex without undergoing surgical change. Others have chosen hormone therapy with estrogen (MTFs) or testosterone (FTMs). In addition, they may undergo cosmetic treatments to provide physical appearances more consistent with their chosen genders. Before undergoing sexual reassignment surgery, most transsexuals are required to spend a year living as persons of the other gender.

SUGGESTED READING. *True Selves: Understanding Transsexualism—For Families, Friends, Coworkers, and Helping Professionals* (1996), by Mildred Brown and Chloe Ann Rounsley, provides a thorough discussion of transsexualism from its origins to its treatment. In addition the book provides a list of resources for transsexuals and those who love them.—*Rebecca Lovell Scott*

Sexist language: Words and grammar practices that reinforce or reflect MISOGYNY.

Linguists, psychologists, and communication theorists have agreed that language affects how people understand and respond to the social world. They argue that perceptions of any society are shaped by the particular language its members use, and that people cannot see, hear, or even think of things unless they have the words to express them. In simple terms, this means that the limits of one's language are the limits of one's world. It also means that the more people can and do talk about certain experiences, the more "real" they become. This explains what scholars mean when they discuss "social construction of reality." Therefore, language is seen as a politically charged system of expression that leads to better realities for some people than for others, and changes to this system are usually initiated by the less powerful groups.

During the late 1960's and early 1970's advocates of FEMINISM began exposing the previously unrecognized male biases of traditional American English, arguing that these biases were fundamentally linked to the subordination of women in American society. Though there has been disagreement over whether male-biased language actually "causes" sexist attitudes in society or merely reflects their existence, there has been widespread agreement that the problem of sexist language should be addressed. The cause was slow to take root among the general population. It did, however, win support from newspaper and book publishers that led to creation of guidelines designed to correct what the National Institute of Education termed "the impression embedded in the English language that people in general are male." By the mid-1980's words such as "chairperson," "worker's compensation," and "congresswoman" were being commonly used in place of words such as "chairman," "workman's compensation," and "congressman."

Presuming Maleness. Despite these changes, the problem of eliminating sexism from the English language was far from resolved. Among the remaining challenges was society's persistent attachment to the so-called "generic masculine," which uses words such

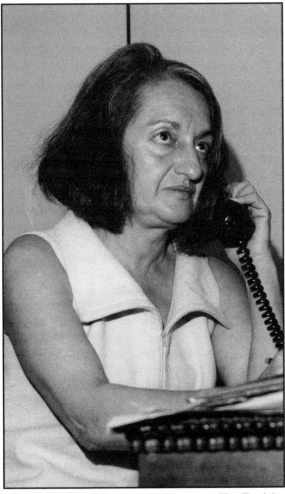

When feminist author Betty Friedan wrote The Feminine Mystique *in 1963 she faced the subtle problem of the inadequacy of English vocabulary to describe experiences unique to women.* (AP/Wide World Photos)

as "man" to refer to all of humanity, and the pronoun "he" to refer to all otherwise unspecified persons. Proponents of these old forms have claimed their use shows respect for tradition and grammatical integrity by asserting that "woman" is a derivative of the word "man." However, linguists and historians have shown that this is not true. In fact, the word "man" came to refer to both men and women not through any natural process of linguistic modification, but through a British act of Parliament in 1850. Similarly, use of "he" to refer to both sexes was also arbitrarily adopted and enforced by early grammarians, who were males themselves, and whose students were also exclusively male.

A strong body of evidence has indicated that the generic masculine is awkward and difficult at best, misleading and exclusionary at worst. Further, it has been well established that neither "man" nor "he" is truly generic. Because the terms are decidedly masculine, their use for all persons makes "maleness" the normal and standard condition. In addition, because "man" and "he" are used generically only occasionally, they are inherently ambiguous. This ambiguity prompted one linguist to observe that the terms would have naturally died out long ago, had they not been so closely linked to the sensitive issue of male dominance.

Other Problems. In addition to presuming "maleness" as the normal condition of human beings, sexist language also perpetuates sexual STEREOTYPES and social roles. For example, women employed outside of their homes have long been referred to as "working women" or "working mothers." Use of the adjective "working" in this way suggests that women are defined primarily in terms of their domestic roles, and that whatever labor and energy they expend in the domestic realm does not count as real work. The same connotations are suggested by the popularity of the term "housewife" and the awkwardness of the term "househusband."

Other ways of speaking about men and women ensure that men have continued to be seen as strong, virile, and effective, while women have continued to be regarded as submissive, small, and silly. For example, adjectives used to describe males and females differ considerably. Behaviors that in men might be labeled "assertive" are typically labeled "aggressive" when observed in women. What makes a man "decisive" would be considered "domineering" in a woman. Verbs also differ according to the sex of the subject.

For example, women are said to "bicker," while men are said to "disagree." Similarly, women "gossip," "nag," and "whine," while men "talk shop," "insist," and "object."

Subordination by Omission. Yet another way in which sexist language contributes to female inequality is through missing vocabulary—the inadequacy of terminology to describe female experience. Because traditional American English has been developed and regulated mostly by men, women have found it difficult to express and share certain aspects of their lives and to bring these issues and concerns into the public arena. Betty FRIEDAN encountered this difficulty as she wrote *The Feminine Mystique* in 1963, when she found it necessary to describe the discontent experienced by middle-class homemakers as "the problem with no name." Having vocabulary adequately to describe one's experience is essential to both self-expression and social change. For example, it was only after feminists coined terms such as "sexism," "male chauvinism," and "consciousness raising" that the WOMEN'S LIBERATION MOVEMENT developed significant popular support.

By the late 1990's the campaign to eradicate sexist language was still not expected to end soon. Institutional support for the movement was widespread; it included gender-sensitive textbooks, fresh biblical translations, and training manuals. Nevertheless, many subtle manifestations of sexist bias persisted.

SUGGESTED READINGS. For specific guidelines about avoiding sexist language, see Casey Miller and Kate Swift's *The Handbook of Nonsexist Writing* (1981). Francine Frank and Frank Anshen have written a book that is both thorough and easy to understand: *Language and the Sexes* (1983). A more advanced work that is useful for both its articles and its bibliography is *Women and Language in Literature and Society* (1980), edited by Sally McConnell-Ginet, Ruth Borker, and Nelly Furman.—*Regina Howard Yaroch*

Shakur, Tupac Amaru (June, 16, 1971, New York, N.Y.—Sept. 13, 1996, Las Vegas, Nev.): RAP MUSIC artist and film actor. The son of a SINGLE MOTHER who had been a member of the BLACK PANTHER PARTY during the 1960's, Shakur was surrounded by controversy during his brief life. After dropping out of high school, he began to sell drugs. When he was nineteen his life seemed about to turn around when he was hired as a dancer and road manager for the rap group Digital

Underground. The following year he himself released a rap music album, *2pacalypse Now*, which went gold. Shakur also began to develop an acting career, with leading roles in such films as *Juice* (1992), *Poetic Justice* (1993), and *Above the Rim* (1994).

Despite these major successes, trouble continued to haunt Shakur. He experienced a string of arrests on charges ranging from jaywalking and resisting arrest in 1991 to shooting two off-duty police officers in Atlanta, Georgia in 1994. In 1995, he was sentenced to eighteen to fifty-four months in prison on a sexual abuse conviction. After Shakur was released from prison, he released his fourth album, *All Eyez on Me*, which passed beyond racial and class lines to sell more than five million copies.

Meanwhile, Shakur resumed his acting career, but his success was not to last. After driving away from a boxing match he had attended in Las Vegas, Nevada, Shakur and his entourage were hit by a barrage of gunfire from a passing car. Shakur died from his

Tupac Shakur and Janet Jackson in Poetic Justice, *a film written and directed by the young African American filmmaker John Singleton.* (Museum of Modern Art, Stills Archive)

wounds six days later. His assailant—thought to be a black male—was never apprehended.—*Andrea E. Miller*

Sickle-cell anemia: Hereditary blood disorder. An inherited, noncontagious disease, sickle-cell anemia is most commonly contracted by persons tracing their ancestry to Africa—especially West Africa—or to the southern Mediterranean area. In the United States more than fifty thousand African Americans had the disease in the 1990's. Persons afflicted with the disease inherit two sickled genes, one from each parent. Persons with sickle-cell trait never contract the disease, since they only inherit one damaged gene. However, if a man and a woman, each of whom has the sickle-cell trait, have children, it is possible that their offspring will have the sickle-cell disease.

Sickle-cell anemia is caused by abnormal hemoglobin, the oxygen-carrying molecule of red blood cells. Hemoglobin normally carries oxygen from the lungs to other parts of the body. Sickle-cell hemoglobin cannot reach other parts of the body because it crystallizes, making it impossible for red blood cells to fit through the tiny passageways meant as routes to the rest of the body. The condition causes organs to become damaged because they cannot receive the oxygen they require to function properly. The red cell membrane becomes damaged from the crystallized hemoglobin, signalling the body to destroy these cells. The result is chronic anemia.

Sickle-cell disease sufferers become weak and prone to bacterial infections, particularly in early childhood. They commonly develop chronic skin ulcers on the legs. Sickle-cell anemia also affects growth, although most sufferers eventually reach average size and maturation in their late teen years. Life expectancy is generally shortened, but it can vary greatly, according to the severity and conditions of the disease and the quality of treatment that patients receive.

Medical advances of the late twentieth century have significantly extended the life spans of sufferers of sickle-cell anemia. Life expectancy for persons with the disease rose from an average of fourteen years in 1973 to forty-two years for men and forty-eight years for women by 1995. The increase has been attributed to better treatment and earlier diagnosis (it can now be diagnosed in fetuses). These medical improvements have also improved the quality of life for those suffering from the disease.

Although it is not known precisely how sickle-cell disease began, it is known that it once existed only in tropical and subtropical areas of the world, and that it afflicted black and white peoples alike. It has been hypothesized that those with the sickle-cell trait had some advantage that helped them to survive malaria, as the malaria parasite does not multiply well in sickled cells of human beings. Hence, the trait persisted in part because it allowed those who had it to survive malaria.

By the late 1990's there was still no known cure for sickle-cell anemia. The best medical strategy for helping patients involved treating the symptoms. It also included managing pain and infections and providing careful nutritional guidance to combat chronic anemia. Scientists have continued to search for cures through gene therapy, the development of antisickling agents, and bone-marrow transplants. With the advice of family planning experts, especially genetic counselors, it has become possible for at-risk couples to have families without the worry of conceiving sickle-cell afflicted children.

SUGGESTED READINGS. For overviews of the disease, see Miriam Bloom, *Understanding Sickle Cell Disease* (1995); Stuart J. Edelstein, *The Sickled Cell: From Myths to Molecules* (1985); Anita Landau Hurtig and Carol Therese Viera, eds. *Sickle-Cell Disease: Psychological and Psychosocial Issues* (1986); and Graham R. Serjeant, *Sickle Cell Disease* (1985). For information on treating the disease, see the National Institutes of Health's *Management and Therapy of Sickle Cell Disease* (1995).—*Roberta Fiske-Rusciano*

Sikhism: Indian religion. Developed in India during the fifteenth century, Sikhism represents a mixture of HINDU and MUSLIM religious ideas and practices. The founder of Sikhism, Guru Nanak (1469-1539), was born to Hindu parents in a village that later became part of predominantly Muslim Pakistan. One day, after taking a ritual bath in a river, Nanak experienced an enlightenment that moved him to declare that God is neither Hindu nor Muslim. At that moment he is said to have uttered the Mool Mantra, the basic text with which the sacred Sikh canon, the *Adi Granth*, opens. Devout Sikhs have silently repeated that mantra as a devotional rite into modern times.

Nanak's teachings proclaimed monotheism with an emphasis on bhakti (meditation). He called his god the true name, the eternal, sovereign, and the omnipotent who is at the same time the creator, sustainer, and

Sikh men, such as this Canadian, characteristically wear turbans and beards. (Photo Search Ltd.)

destroyer. Nanak believed that god dwells within the world and in humankind's heart. He wrote that religion's social mission is to improve the lot of all men and believed that a good person is pure in motive and in act, seeks brotherhood, and craves for divine knowledge. His followers became known as Sikhs, after the Sanskrit word for disciple, and called Nanak their guru (teacher).

After Nanak's death, leadership of the Sikhs passed through nine other gurus. The fifth, Arjan, compiled Nanak's writings, which became the *Granth*, the holy scriptures of the Sikhs. Under the sixth guru, Har Govind, the Sikhs began becoming militant. The tenth guru, Govind Singh transformed them into a fraternity of believers, the Khalsa (the Pure). He initiated them into this new order of life by requiring them to drink out of the same basin, to change their last names to Singh (lion), and charged them to wear long hair and

beards, short drawers, and steel bracelets, and to carry steel combs and swords. Modern Sikh men are easily recognized by their distinctive turbans, beards, and steel bracelets on their right wrists.

Large Sikh communities can be found outside of India, especially in Great Britain and the United States. The arrival of Sikhs on the West Coast of the United States during the early 1900's was a by-product of their migration to Canada. Overcoming the anti-Asian sentiments, today the Sikhs have successfully distinguished themselves in the fields of business, medicine, science, technology, and farming. Sikh temples (gurudwaras) have served religious, social, cultural, and political functions. The Sikhs in the United States continue the struggle for political independence and the demand for a separate Punjabi-speaking state in India.

SUGGESTED READINGS. W. H. McLeod's *The Sikhs: History, Religion and Society* (1989) is an expert analysis by an eminent scholar, while Khushwant Singh's *A History of the Sikhs* (1966) is a journalistic interpretation of Sikhism. In *Sikh History and Religion in the Twentieth Century* (1988), J. O'Connell, M. Israel, and W. Oxtoby present a collection of essays exploring the stable and the changing nature of the Sikh community.—*R. Ashok Shankar*

Simpson, O. J., case: The arrest and criminal and civil trials of former football star Orenthal James Simpson, who was charged with brutally slaying his former wife and a friend who was with her. In the early morning hours of June 13, 1994, LOS ANGELES police officers found the butchered bodies of Nicole Brown Simpson and her friend Ronald Goldman outside of Brown's Brentwood condominium. Five days later, Brown's former husband, O. J. Simpson, was arrested and charged with both murders.

The Issues. By the time a Los Angeles jury acquitted Simpson on criminal murder charges more than fifteen months later, news coverage of the case had so dominated the print and broadcast media that the problem of balancing the constitutional right to a fair trial with the constitutional right to freedom of the press had itself become a major national issue. The Simpson case also focused national attention on the issue of DOMESTIC VIOLENCE and exposed deep racial divisions in public perceptions of the American justice system. Moreover, after Simpson was acquitted on criminal charges, he lost a second, civil, trial in which he was sued by relatives of the murder victims for wrongful death; the contrast between the verdicts of the two trials raised additional questions about flaws in the criminal justice system.

Because of Simpson's celebrity and the unusual circumstances surrounding his arrest, media coverage of the murders revealed incriminating details long before the case came to trial. Immediately before Simpson surrendered to police, several days after the murders took place, he was a fugitive in a two-hour police pursuit seen by tens of millions of Americans on national television. Print and broadcast media also released details from the transcript of an emergency telephone call made by his former wife several months before her death, when a man identified as Simpson shouted obscenities in the background. That call was part of an apparent pattern of domestic disputes that had gone on both before and after the couple were divorced.

Details of Simpson's no-contest plea after his arrest on misdemeanor domestic abuse charges in 1989 were made public.

The Criminal Trial. When Simpson's criminal trial began in October, 1994, television cameras were allowed to record the court proceedings for broadcasting over television stations around the world. In addition, reports on courtroom proceedings were updated regularly on both local and national news broadcasts, and tabloid magazines seized every opportunity to run stories about anyone and everyone remotely connected with Simpson or his trial. Along with Simpson himself and Judge Lance Ito, Los Angeles County prosecutors Marcia CLARK and Christopher A. DARDEN and Simpson's so-called "dream team" defense attorneys, F. Lee Bailey, Johnnie L. COCHRAN, and Robert L. Shapiro, became household names, as did controversial wit-

Prosecutor Christopher Darden (left) and defense attorney Johnnie Cochran during an early stage of O. J. Simpson's criminal murder trial. (Reuters/Sam Mircovich/Archive Photos)

nesses, such as Los Angeles police detective Mark Fuhrman and Simpson's onetime houseguest Kato Kaelin.

In the absence of an eyewitness to the murders and the knife presumed to have been used to commit them, Simpson's prosecutors relied heavily on other physical evidence and circumstantial factors to construct their case. Extensive deoxyribonucleic acid (DNA) analysis was used to bolster the prosecution's case that blood traces found at the crime scene came from Simpson and that blood from the victims had been found in his vehicle and home. Los Angeles Police detective Mark Fuhrman testified that he found a bloody glove, a blue knit cap, and bloody shoe prints at the crime scene that allegedly belonged to Simpson, along with a second and similar bloody glove at Simpson's estate. A

Murder defendant O. J. Simpson (center) listens to testimony while seated between defense attorneys Carl Douglas (left) and Johnnie Cochran (right). (AP/Wide World Photos)

limousine driver hired to take Simpson to the airport the night of the crime testified that a white Ford Bronco was not outside the house when he arrived and that Simpson did not answer the door for more than fifteen minutes. The prosecution also showed that Simpson had a past record of assaulting his former wife.

To counteract such evidence, Simpson's legal defense team worked to establish a secure alibi for Simpson's whereabouts at the time of the murders. His attorneys also suggested that police officers assigned to the case had planted evidence against Simpson as part of a racist conspiracy. Forensic experts questioned the validity of the DNA evidence, indicating that the police department's sloppy procedures were likely to have tainted the blood samples. When Simpson, at the prosecution's request, attempted to try on the bloody gloves, they seemed too small for his hands. Later testimony revealed that Fuhrman, in previously taped interviews with an aspiring screenwriter, had recounted stories in which he planted evidence used against African American defendants and—contrary to his earlier sworn testimony—Fuhrman did, indeed, use racial epithets.

After hearing the closing arguments in a trial that lasted a full year, the jury deliberated a mere four hours before coming to a unanimous verdict. On October 3, 1995, millions of people listened as that verdict was read: The jury acquitted Simpson on all charges. Many observers were surprised by the swiftness of the jury's decision. With its racial overtones, the trial had served to polarize the opinions of blacks and whites concerning Simpson's guilt or innocence and the conduct of the trial itself. African Americans were more likely to believe that members of the Los Angeles police department had conspired to frame Simpson, whereas many white Americans were convinced that the preponderance of physical evidence left little doubt of Simpson's involvement.

Although Simpson vehemently maintained his innocence throughout the trial proceedings and was acquitted, the murder charges cost him lucrative product endorsements and his dual career as a sports broadcasting and film star. Nearly a year after his arrest, Simpson published his own account of his marriage, the divorce, and the abuse allegations, along with an emphatic denial of his involvement in the murders in a book entitled *I Want to Tell You: My Response to Your Letters, Messages, and Your Questions* (1995).

The Civil Trial. In 1996 lawyers for the families of Nicole Brown Simpson and Ronald Goldman began taking depositions for a wrongful death civil lawsuit filed against Simpson. After testimony in the civil trial got underway in November that year, Simpson seemed to undermine his own credibility. His performance on the stand during the civil trial was often inconsistent and contradictory, and he repeatedly denied having ever hit, struck, slapped, or kicked his wife. However, it was physical evidence that proved most damaging against Simpson. During the criminal trial, prosecutors revealed that footprints found at the murder scene matched the distinctive tread of Bruno Magli shoes, an expensive brand of footwear favored by many celebrities. As part of his testimony in the civil trial, Simpson repeatedly denied ever owning such shoes. Lawyer Daniel Petrocelli secured photographs of Simpson wearing Bruno Magli shoes at a football game before the murders occurred. Additional pictures came to light after another photojournalist searched his files. Although Simpson's lawyer, Robert Baker, hoped to rehabilitate Simpson as a credible witness, he was hampered in his attempts construct an effective defense.

In February, 1995, the civil jury rendered its verdict. It found Simpson guilty on all counts and awarded the Goldman family $8.5 million in compensatory damages and another $25 million in punitive damages to be split with the Brown family. Simpson's attorneys filed an appeal, seeking a reduction of the award. Ultimately, however, Simpson was forced to sell much of his personal property to cover his court fees in both trials and to make payments against the civil trial damage awards. Creditors foreclosed on his Brentwood estate, which was sold for $2.6 million at auction in July of 1997.

SUGGESTED READINGS. Because participation in Simpson's case made them instant celebrities, many of the leading figures associated with his criminal trial wrote books about their experiences. These books include Christopher A. Darden's *In Contempt* (1996), Marcia Clark's *Without a Doubt* (1997), Robert L. Shapiro's *The Search for Justice: A Defense Attorney's Brief on the O. J. Simpson Case* (1996), and Alan M. Dershowitz's *Reasonable Doubts: The Criminal Justice System and the O. J. Simpson Case* (1997). Los Angeles police investigators Tom Lange and Philip Vannatter tell their side of the case in *Evidence Dismissed: The Inside Story of the Police Investigation of O. J. Simpson* (1997). Grand jury witness Faye Resnick provided her perspective on the life of her friend

Nicole Brown Simpson and the trial itself in two books: *Nicole Brown Simpson: The Private Diary of a Life Interrupted* (1994) and *Shattered: In the Eye of the Storm* (1996). For an informed outsider's legal perspective on the case, see Vincent Bugliosi's *Outrage: The Five Reasons O. J. Simpson Got Away with Murder* (New York: W. W. Norton, 1996).—*Ellyn West*

Single mothers: Women who raise children on their own because of DIVORCE, death of their spouses, ADOPTION, voluntary in-vitro insemination, or involuntary pregnancy due to RAPE. From the 1970's through the 1990's, traditional American nuclear family units were increasingly replaced by single-parent families—most of which were headed by women. Through those years, rises in American divorce rates, the deterioration of nuclear family units, and the increasing freedom of choice that women won to have children without ongoing involvement of biological partners combined to increase the incidence of single motherhood.

Demographics. Single mothers can be classified in several groups. The most common are divorced women, who have generally been more likely than divorced men to win legal custody of their children. Women also become single mothers by individual choice or fate. Some are LESBIANS who prefer to parent children with female partners. Many other women become single mothers because of the deaths of their spouses or partners.

Among ethnic groups, the incidence of single motherhood is highest among African American women, particularly unwed teenagers. The 1980's and 1990's saw a significant increase in the number of female-headed homes, especially in black families. During the 1980's alone there was a 73 percent increase in the number of families headed by single black women; much of this increase was due to higher rates of teenage pregnancy among African Americans. U.S. Bureau of Census statistics for 1991 indicated that there were almost three times as many black single mothers as

The high correlation of poverty and single motherhood has made single-mother families among the heaviest users of government services. (Don Franklin)

American Single Mothers by Race and Age

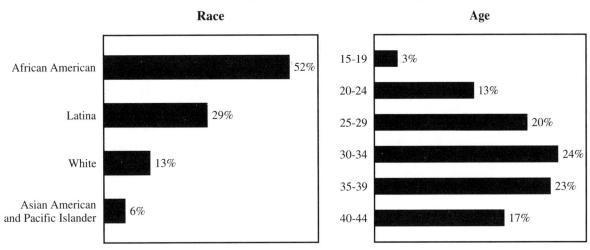

Source: Margaret McFadden, ed., *Women's Issues* (Pasadena, Calif.: Salem Press, 1997).

Hispanic single mothers and almost eighteen times as many black single mothers as Asian and Pacific Islander single mothers. Part of these discrepancies may be attributed to the insufficient social and economic reforms for educational and occupational opportunities for young black women. The feminization of poverty has also been a special problem for black single mothers, as well as single mothers from other ethnic groups.

Single Mothers and Stress. POVERTY, unemployment or DISCRIMINATION in hiring practices, poor job skills and career preparation, inadequate parenting supports, and the lack of emotional and psychological support are some of the special problems that plague single mothers. Many single mothers live below the poverty line because their financial support and incomes have been drastically reduced as a result of divorce or abandonment by the fathers of their children.

Other stresses that single mothers confront center on their relationships with their children. They face special challenges in maintaining consistent discipline techniques, trying to serve as dual role models in the absence of fathers, and maintaining respect as authority figures. Moreover, their children face special problems in their own struggles with issues of identity, intimacy, and peer affiliation.

Multicultural Dimensions. Single mothers who are members of ethnic minorities face additional problems arising from conflicts between their traditional cultural norms and values and acculturation patterns they face in adjusting to new environments. This is especially true of single mothers who are unfamiliar with American norms, such as those from Asian and Pacific Islander cultures. Many Asian cultures are grounded in CONFUCIAN TRADITION, whose family norms require mothers to raise their children to respect parents and elders. In some cases of divorce, single mothers have to deal with trying to teach their children to respect their deserting parents, while refraining from expressing their own anger overtly. In some ethnic cultures public displays of emotion are not acceptable. In contrast, American culture tends to encourage the expression of emotion in order to prevent people from internalizing their stress and endangering their own physical and emotional health.

Cultural Ramifications. Single mothers from multicultural backgrounds may carry the additional burdens of coping with stigmatized behaviors of failure within their own cultures. They may be perceived as having failed to be dutiful wives, daughters-in-law, or mothers. On the other hand, cultural norms favoring large extended families can add protective layers to ease the burden of individual women. For example, in some cultures sisters-in-law become surrogate mothers and thereby help to support single mothers. Among Filipinos godparents become surrogate parents to children, and single mothers are embraced in large extended families.

SUGGESTED READINGS. For an overview of the special problems faced by African American single mothers, see Bette Dickerson's *African American Single Mothers: Understanding Their Lives and Families* (1995) and Ann Nichols-Casebolt's article "Black Families Headed by Single Mothers Growing Numbers and Increasing Poverty" in *Social Work* (July-Aug., 1988). Broader treatments of the subject can be found in Dennis Hogan, Ling-Xin Hao, and William Parish, "Race, Kin Networks, and Assistance to Mother-Headed Families," *Social Forces* 68, no. 3 (1990); K. Kissman, "Feminist-based Social Work with Single Parent Families," *Families in Societies* 72, no. 1 (1991); and Marsha Leslie, *The Single Mother's Companion: Essays and Stories by Women* (1994). —*Rowena Fong*

Sixty-fifth Infantry Regiment: Puerto Rican unit that served in the U.S. Army throughout most of the twentieth century. The Sixty-fifth Infantry Regiment was formed in San Juan, Puerto Rico, as a constabulary force in March, 1899. Made up largely of Spanish-speaking soldiers, it was never a National Guard or reserve unit. It was integrated officially into the U.S. army in 1920 and was activated during WORLD WAR II. It served first at the Panama Canal, then trained at New Orleans and Virginia before being sent to North Africa in early April, 1944. One of its five battalions served in Sardinia and became officially attached to the Army Air Force—making it the only unit to earn such a distinction. It was also the sole outfit to receive a maritime streamer for its service in Sardinia. The regiment's other battalions were incorporated into the Army's Third Infantry Division. Most of these soldiers fought in France until they were shipped back to Puerto Rico in November, 1944. From there they went to Trinidad until 1947. The regiment was nationalized to serve in the KOREAN WAR. It was officially disbanded in 1957.—*Douglas W. Richmond*

Skateboarding: Recreational activity and competitive sport of the American youth culture. The first skateboards can be traced back to the early twentieth century, but it was not until the early 1960's that skateboarding became a popular recreational activity. Skateboarding became popular among Southern California surfers. When they had trouble finding waves to ride, they often hopped onto their skateboards and rode the streets instead of the surf. It was thus no coincidence that skateboards were made of surfboard-shaped pieces of wood with clay wheels. As the popularity of skateboarding

Skateboarding expert Tony Hawk performing in Toronto, Canada. (Reuters/Mike Blake/Archive Photos)

grew, millions of skateboards were sold across North America.

While skateboard technology remained primitive, it was common for riders to injure themselves while attempting difficult tricks. Medical authorities soon spoke out, warning of the hazards of skateboarding. By the late 1960's the popularity of skateboarding had waned, and the pastime was little more than a cult activity. During the 1970's, however, skateboarding again grew popular. The introduction of urethane wheels allowed the sport to become both more adventuresome and safer. Moreover, skateboarding was no longer restricted to the United States. Its popularity spread worldwide and skateboard parks were built.

Although skateboarding has attracted participants of all ages, a large majority of skateboarders have been teenagers. The physical challenges presented by skateboarding have made it popular among all racial groups and both sexes. By the mid-1980's skateboarding had become a significant commercial industry, and many amateur and professional competitions were being regularly held. Since safety has remained a major concern, helmets, goggles, and knee and elbow pads have been specially designed for skateboarding. The National Skateboard Association and the Professional Skateboard League are only two of the many skateboarding organizations that exist. Some of the other countries where the sport has grown include Brazil, Canada, Mexico, South Africa, and Spain.—*Jeffry Jensen*

Skinheads: Loosely formed WHITE SUPREMACIST MOVEMENT associated with modern NATIVISM and HATE CRIMES. The original movement whose members identified themselves as "skinheads" peaked in Great Britain during the 1970's. At that time "skinhead" was applied more to a style statement than a racial stance. British

groups such as the Fourth Reich Skins were essentially gangs devoted to bullying immigrants and honoring Adolf Hitler's birthday.

During the late 1980's the NEO-NAZI versions of the skinheads began to appear in the cultural crossroads of the United States, such as SAN FRANCISCO's Haight-Ashbury District. The skinheads attracted immediate attention for their shaved heads, dedication to British Oi! music, black Doc Martens boots and their violence against African Americans, gays, and Jews. Their behavior was so outrageous that they gained notoriety, with some of their members appearing as guests on popular television talk shows.

Skinheads also captured the attention of former KU KLUX KLAN member Tom Metzger, head of the White Aryan Resistance, CALIFORNIA's best-known hate group. Metzger expounded a philosophy advocating

Skinhead members of the Aryan Nations Church gathered at Hayden Lake, Idaho, in April, 1989, to celebrate the centennial of Adolf Hitler's birthday. (AP/Wide World Photos)

expulsion of Latinos and Asians from the United States and creation of separate black and white states. His organization recruited successfully among skinhead groups in the West and Midwest. In 1988 skinheads spurred by Metzger's message of hate beat an Ethiopian student to death in Portland, Oregon. The case drew national attention to the dangers that the organization posed to members of minority groups. The Southern Poverty Law Center in Alabama sued Metzger, winning $12.5 million in damages for the victim's family. Although Metzger withdrew his vocal support of the skinheads, his example encouraged members of other established hate groups, such as the Ku Klux Klan and Idaho's Aryan Nations. These organizations began using skinheads to recruit new members and commit violent crimes.

Religious beliefs of skinheads have varied, encompassing ideas from calling blacks God's "mud people" to Odinism, a worship of the ancient Norse gods. They have also adopted the white supremacist credo: a belief in a "territorial imperative" to be fulfilled by setting aside parts of the continent as all-white strongholds with the hopeful expectation of an Armageddon-like racial holy war—which they often abbreviate to the battle cry "RaHoWa!"

The total skinhead population appears to be small but widespread. However, a new generation of members aged thirteen and up has become active. They attend boot parties and wear caps bearing the number 88—a symbol for "Heil Hitler!" derived from the fact that the letter *H* holds the eighth position in the English alphabet.

Skinheads wear Doc Martens boots with shoelaces in various colors. White stands for racial purity, red for the blood they are willing to shed, and yellow for the blood of others that they have shed. Their modes of dress have begun to vary among groups. Offshoots of the skinheads have included groups with names such as the Confederate Hammerskins, the Atlantic City Skins, and the Army of Israel. Skinheads have been traditionally identified by their shaved heads, but many members of the movement have allowed their hair to grow out so they can meld into society undetected. The ANTI-DEFAMATION LEAGUE has labeled them as a dangerous threat to minority groups and warned that what began as disorganized violence has increasingly become organized violence with skinhead meetings being held throughout the United States.

SUGGESTED READINGS. A sociological examination of skinheads can be found in *American Skinheads: The*

Criminology and Control of Hate Crime (1993), by Mark S. Hamm. James Ridgeway's *Blood in the Face: The Ku Klux Klan, Aryan Nations, Nazi Skinheads, and the Rise of a New White Culture* (1990), describes the various right-wing racist groups and offers many illustrations. Insightful magazine articles on the skinheads include "Confessions of a Skinhead," by J. Willwerth, in *Time* (Aug. 19, 1996); and "Young, White and Surrounded," by J. Allen in *Rolling Stone* (June 30, 1994).—*Lela Phillips*

Skirball Museum and Cultural Center: JEWISH AMERICAN cultural center in Los Angeles, California. Founded by a group of three hundred individual and foundation donors in 1996, after fifteen years of planning, development, and construction, the Skirball Cultural Center has set its mission as interpreting the American Jewish experience, nurturing American Jewish identity, and helping to strengthen American society at large. The center presents a range of cultural programs including temporary exhibitions, lectures, concerts, performances, symposia, readings, film and video screenings, and educational offerings for adults and children, inspired by the American Jewish experience, and addressed to people of all ages and backgrounds. The center's components include the Skirball Museum, the Discovery Center, a Grand Plaza, auditorium, conference, banquet, and classroom facilities, museum store, restaurant, and study gallery. The 125,000-square-foot complex designed by architect Moshe Safdie and built at a cost of $65 million, stands on a fifteen-acre site adjacent to the San Diego Freeway in the Santa Monica Mountains.—*Patricia Jessup-Woodlin*

Sleepy Lagoon case (1942-1944): LOS ANGELES murder case that generated strong anti-Mexican American publicity. In August, 1942, the fatally injured body of a young man named José Díaz was found on a south-central Los Angeles city road. Police heard that a scuffle had occurred at a nearby ranch the night before; though lacking proof that there was a connection between that disturbance and Díaz's death, they arrested about six hundred suspected Mexican American gang members, whom they questioned on suspicion of having murdered Díaz, who died of a head injury without recovering consciousness. The alleged crime had occurred near a swimming hole dubbed Sleepy Lagoon by Mexican American adolescents, who were not allowed to use local swimming pools.

No murder weapon or proof that Díaz's fatal injury was inflicted by another person was ever found. Nevertheless, twenty-two Mexican American youths and one Anglo youth were tried for his murder. They were all charged with murder in the first degree because of the prosecution's charge that their alleged crime had been a conspiracy. The chief counsel for eight of the defendants argued that such a charge could only be leveled if the court believed that the "conspiracy to crash a party" was proof of felonious intent. However, the judge did allow this charge. On January 12, 1943, three of the defendants were convicted of murder in the first degree. Nine were convicted of second-degree murder and five of assault; the rest were found not guilty.

Legal critics later agreed that the trial was a travesty of justice, and an appellate court later proved that the presiding judge was biased. Among the unfair advantages he granted the prosecution was refusing to allow the defendants haircuts or clean clothes, thus permitting prosecution to cite the shabby appearance of the defendants as an indication of their guilt. Moreover, the trial was conducted in an atmosphere of intense community-wide prejudice which had been manufactured and sustained by the entire press of Los Angeles in which daily headlines declared that a Mexican crime-wave was underway, particularly after the so-called ZOOT-SUIT RIOTS erupted.

The trial was filled with prejudicial testimony. An officer of the sheriff's department, for example, went so far as to give a lecture on the genetic disposition toward violence of Mexicans. He argued that Mexican American men were naturally violent and had inherited an "utter disregard for the value of life" from their Aztec ancestry.

The conviction of the Sleepy Lagoon defendants brought about the formation of the Sleepy Lagoon Defense Committee, which successfully organized the support of labor unions, religious groups, popular film stars, and artists in a highly publicized effort that won the release of the defendants in late 1944. Although the integrity of the judicial system was restored with the reversal of the Sleepy Lagoon convictions, STEREOTYPES of delinquent Mexican Americans remained widespread and ingrained in the popular imagination of many Americans.

SUGGESTED READINGS. Mauricio Mazon's *The Zoot Suit Riots* (1984) provides an in-depth look at racism in California during the 1940's. Rodolfo Acuna's *Occupied America* (2d ed., 1981) gives a broad historical analysis of the case. See also Carey McWilliams' *North from Mexico* (1949) for an account written by

a leader of the Sleepy Lagoon Defense Committee. See also *The Government Riots of Los Angeles, June, 1943* (1973) by Solomon J. Jones.—*Manuel Luis Martinez*

Society of American Indians: National AMERICAN INDIAN rights and improvement organization founded in 1911. The first Pan-Indian movement commenced with the establishment of the Society of American Indians on October 12, 1911. It was founded by Fayette McKenzie, a former reservation schoolteacher who had earned a doctorate in sociology by studying the subject of AMERICAN INDIAN ASSIMILATION. The major goals of the society were to help promote assimilation of Indians into mainstream American culture through improved education, land allotments, and enforcement of the unresolved matter of native citizenship. Many of the society's early leaders and participants were concerned with promoting Indian social progress through assimilation, but not under what they regarded as the paternalistic policies of the BUREAU OF INDIAN AFFAIRS. They rejected the notion of "tribalism," feeling that, as citizens, Indians should fully participate in making social, economic, and

Carlisle Indian School, in Carlisle, Pennsylvania, was founded to help acculturate Indians to Western ways—one of the goals of the Society of American Indians. (National Archives)

political decisions and policies. Until the society disbanded in 1923 (the year before passage of the INDIAN CITIZENSHIP ACT OF 1924), it was the only Indian lobby to raise questions regarding Indian health, education, self-determination, and civil rights.—*John Alan Ross*

Society of Hispanic Professional Engineers (SHPE): Latino professional organization established in Los Angeles, California, in 1974. Founded to increase the number of Hispanic engineers, the SHPE has been geared toward engineers, students, and scientists by providing motivation, guidance, and support to students through sponsorship of professional chapters and student chapters. Student chapters have organized speakers (such as representatives from area companies or Latin American countries), tutored high school students in related subjects, and sought funding from professionals.

The organization has expanded to have more than eight thousand members. It has sponsored competitions, internships, scholarships, and educational programs to promote the career of engineering. It has also maintained a placement service and speakers' bureau and has compiled statistics on where Hispanics stand in engineering, science, and technology fields. The society's publications include *SHPE Magazine* and the *SHPE National Newsletter*, which discuss current issues in the field and upcoming events. Its annual career conference, held in February, includes résumé-writing workshops, interviews, and exhibits from companies. —*Maria L. Alonzo*

Sokol: International organization for physical fitness and moral strength founded in 1862. During the early nineteen century, a German named Friedrich Ludwig Jahn invented many of the exercises and apparatuses later used in the sport of gymnastics. His inventions led to the Sokol movement, which originated in Prague and spread throughout Bohemia—the core of what later became the modern Czech Republic—during the 1860's. The Sokol organization was originally founded to help promote social and community unity.

The American Sokol Organization was founded in St. Louis, Missouri, in 1865. Various forms of physical exercise and apparatus events were conducted in Sokol societies throughout the United States during the early part of the twentieth century. By the 1990's there were about sixty Sokol chapters in the United States, with the organization's national headquarters based in Berwyn, Illinois. Sokol has no political or religious connections, and people of any age may join. In addition to the United States, chapters of Sokol exist in Australia, Canada, South America, and Europe.—*Alvin K. Benson*

Southeast Asia Resource Action Center: Advocacy organization founded in 1979. Originally called the Indochinese Refugee Action Center and later the Indochina Resource Action Center, the Southeast Asia Resource Action Center is a Washington, D.C.-based organization formed to promote economic advancement and community development among Southeast Asian REFUGEES living in the United States. It accomplishes much of its work by coordinating a network of MUTUAL ASSISTANCE ASSOCIATIONS throughout the United States. With a staff of eight and approximately 150 local affiliates, the center has conducted research, produced reports, sponsored training workshops, and maintained a library of international and domestic refugee documents. It has also developed a computer lettering system for Southeast Asian languages. Its publications include the quarterly *The Bridge*, business directories, and bibliographies.—*Alexander Scott*

Spanglish: Colloquial, sometimes derogatory, portmanteau word for language varieties emerging in situations in which English and Spanish are spoken alternately, sometimes in the same sentence. Although narrower definitions have been put forward, the term "Spanglish" can be taken to encompass any mixture of English and Spanish.

The emotional connotations carried by the word "Spanglish" derive from the history of the relations between the United States and its Spanish-speaking neighbors. Because the English-speaking United States has often imposed its will on its Spanish-speaking neighbors—most notably in the MEXICAN-AMERICAN WAR of 1848—English-speaking North Americans have tended to regard Spanish as an inferior language. Moreover, English-speaking Americans have regarded any mixture of the two languages with contempt. At the same time, many LATINOS who wish to exert their independence from Anglo culture have also tended to view any English influence upon the SPANISH LANGUAGE as a corruption.

Although printed references to Spanglish are rare, a general consensus holds that Spanglish is more than a simple mixture of two languages. It is instead a form of Spanish whose vocabulary reflects a significant English influence. This is especially evident in Puerto Rico, a Spanish-speaking territory of the United States whose consumer products derive almost exclusively from the United States. Puerto Rican Spanglish displays three variations. In one, unaltered English words appear within Spanish sentences. Aside from scientific terms, these English words include words used so frequently that they replace their Spanish equivalents. For example, *Estaba en el army hace tres anos* (I was in the army for three years) substitutes the English word *army* for Spanish *ejercito.*

Other English words that have appeared in Puerto Rican Spanglish include slang terms that have no Spanish equivalents, For example: *Quiero llevar mi T-shirt* (I want to wear my T-shirt). Still other examples are *calques*, that is, close translations from English expressions. For example, *hacer sentido*, a word-for-word translation of the English phrase "makes sense," occurs in Puerto Rican Spanish, replacing standard Spanish's *si tener sentido.*

English-influenced Spanish (or, for that matter, Spanish-influenced English) is not at all unusual. Spanish and English have been in close contact in the Western Hemisphere for centuries. Standard American English has borrowed many words from Spanish, such as *canyon, rodeo*, and *lariat*. There must be few speakers of Mexican Spanish who do not know—or use—such popular English expressions as "okay." If Spanglish in a broad sense refers to any influence between one language and another, almost anyone living in the United States, Mexico, or the Spanish Caribbean speaks a form of "Spanglish" to some extent.

SUGGESTED READINGS. An analysis of Puerto Rican Spanglish can be found in Rose Nash's "Spanglish: Language Contact in Puerto Rico," in *American Speech* 1, no. 5 (1970). A good example of English dialogue with Spanish influence appears in the conversation of Chicano street gang members in Luis J. Rodriquez's autobiographical *Always Running: La Vida Loca, Gang Days in L.A.* (1993), a memoir of a former gang member. More detailed examples of English and Spanish contact in the southwestern United States appear in Rosaura Sanchez, *Chicano Discourse: Socio-Historic Perspectives* (1983).—*Timothy C. Frazer*

Spingarn Medal and medal winners: Annual achievement award given by the NATIONAL ASSOCIATION FOR THE ADVANCEMENT OF COLORED PEOPLE (NAACP) to outstanding African Americans. The award was initiated in 1914 by Joel E. Spingarn, then chairman of the NAACP's board of directors and president of the organi-

Spingarn Medal Winners

1915	Ernest E. Just	1957	Martin Luther King Jr.
1916	Charles Young	1958	Mrs. Daisy Bates and
1917	Harry T. Burleigh		the Little Rock Nine
1918	William S. Braithwaite	1959	Duke Ellington
1919	Archibald H. Grimké	1960	Langston Hughes
1920	W. E. B. Du Bois	1961	Kenneth B. Clark
1921	Charles S. Gilpin	1962	Robert C. Weaver
1922	Mary B. Talbert	1963	Medgar W. Evers
1923	George W. Carver	1964	Roy Wilkins
1924	Roland Hayes	1965	Leontyne Price
1925	James W. Johnson	1966	John H. Johnson
1926	Carter G. Woodson	1967	Edward W. Brooke
1927	Anthony Overton	1968	Sammy Davis Jr.
1928	Charles W. Chesnutt	1969	Clarence M. Mitchell Jr.
1929	Mordecai W. Johnson	1970	Jacob Lawrence
1930	Henry A. Hunt	1971	Leon H. Sullivan
1931	Richard B. Harrison	1972	Gordon Parks
1932	Robert R. Moton	1973	Wilson C. Riles
1933	Max Yergan	1974	Damon Keith
1934	William T. B. Williams	1975	Henry (Hank) Aaron
1935	Mary McLeod Bethune	1976	Alvin Ailey
1936	John Hope	1977	Alex Haley
1937	Walter White	1978	Andrew Young
1938	no award	1979	Mrs. Rosa L. Parks
1939	Marian Anderson	1980	Dr. Rayford W. Logan
1940	Louis T. Wright	1981	Coleman Young
1941	Richard Wright	1982	Dr. Benjamin E. Mays
1942	A. Philip Randolph	1983	Lena Horne
1943	William H. Hastie	1984	Thomas Bradley
1944	Charles Drew	1985	Bill Cosby
1945	Paul Robeson	1986	Dr. Benjamin L. Hooks
1946	Thurgood Marshall	1987	Percy E. Sutton
1947	Dr. Percy L. Julian	1988	Frederick D. Patterson
1948	Channing H. Tobias	1989	Jesse Jackson
1949	Ralph J. Bunche	1990	L. Douglas Wilder
1950	Charles H. Houston	1991	Gen. Colin L. Powell
1951	Mabel K. Staupers	1992	Barbara Jordan
1952	Harry T. Moore	1993	Dorothy I. Height
1953	Paul R. Williams	1994	Maya Angelou
1954	Theodore K. Lawless	1995	John Hope Franklin
1955	Carl Murphy	1996	Carl T. Rowan
1956	Jack R. Robinson	1997	A. Leon Higginbotham

Source: World Almanac

zation. The purpose of the awards is to highlight distinguished achievements, while providing models for young African Americans. Recipients of the award have demonstrated excellence in fields as varied as science, literature, education, entertainment, politics, journalism, and law. Recent award winners have included Virginia governor Douglas Wilder, the Reverend Jesse JACKSON, comedian Bill COSBY, Los Angeles mayor Tom BRADLEY, singer Lena HORNE, U.S. chief of staff Colin POWELL, Congresswoman Barbara JORDAN, historian John Hope FRANKLIN, and federal judge A. Leon Higginbotham.—*Timothy L. Hall*

Steel Strike of 1919: Massive union-led strike by steelworkers. After twenty striking steelworkers were killed in the Homestead strike of 1892, union activity in the steel industry was subdued until a renewed organizational campaign was launched in 1918. Working conditions in the industry were oppressive. To keep the blast furnaces operating continuously, many workers put in twelve-hour shifts, seven days a week. In 1918 the AMERICAN FEDERATION OF LABOR created a Steel Workers Organizing Committee (SWOC), which was led by William Z. Foster. In July, 1919, this committee presented demands to the giant United States Steel Corporation that included wage increases and eight-hour workdays. After Judge Elbert H. Gary, the corporation's chief executive, refused to bargain, SWOC leaders called for a strike that began in September.

Some 280,000 steelworkers walked off their jobs. The companies used all their resources to defeat the strike, which was called off early in the following January. The industry hired nonunion workers, and police broke up picket lines. An extensive investigation of the strike in 1922 by the Interchurch World Movement denounced management abuses.—*Paul B. Trescott*

Sterilization of women: Surgical procedures on women's reproductive organs that make PREGNANCY impossible. The most common sterilizing operation is tubal ligation, a virtually 100-percent effective procedure that involves cutting and or blocking the Fallopian tubes so that eggs and sperm cannot make contact with each other. The early 1970's saw a sharp increase in this procedure in the United States; by the 1990's it was the most frequently used method of contraception among married couples. At the same time, however, this surgical procedure was coming under scrutiny because of its possible inappropriate use in a significant number of

cases in which patients were not sufficiently informed about what the procedure involves. In some instances, patients were not even told that the procedure had been performed on them.

Voluntary Sterilization. Some women regard the decision to undergo sterilization as an active measure in avoiding pregnancy permanently. They may already have as many children as they want or simply choose never to have children. For these women, sterilization may be the most practical and sensible BIRTH CONTROL option. Nearly a third of American women who have chosen to be sterilized have later come to regret their decisions; those who have chosen sterilization as a permanent method of birth control represent a small fraction of that number. Most women who make active, informed choices to be sterilized are at least thirty years old; most of sterilized women who have considered having their procedures reversed made their original decisions at less mature ages.

Some women choose sterilization because of their husbands' or partners' unwillingness to take responsibility for birth control, or because of their desire to be unencumbered with the inconvenient measures and planning that other contraceptive methods, such as birth control pills and diaphragms require. Women in this group may also lean toward Norplant, which is in the form of six silicone capsules inserted into the upper arm that secrete the hormone progestin, blocking ovulation and preventing pregnancy for periods of five years.

A number of women have chosen sterilization for religious reasons. In fact, after 1970, the number of sterilizations performed on ROMAN CATHOLIC women increased markedly, due mainly to the fact that the Catholic Church, while disapproving of contraception generally and vehemently opposed to ABORTION, has taken a relatively muted position on sterilization.

By 1993 more than a quarter of married women in the United States were sterilized. Many feminists have charged that the rate of female sterilization in the United States is excessive, particularly since a significant number of these operations involve unnecessary HYSTERECTOMIES and may be linked to the increased number of CESAREAN SECTIONS—during which sterilization can be performed more inconspicuously. Women with histories of delivering babies by cesarean section are also able to claim medical grounds for sterilization. Hysterectomy is unnecessary for sterilization alone, and the risk of death or complication from hysterectomies is ten to a hundred times greater than from tubal ligations. Feminists also emphasize the lack of real choice to women when sterilization is easily available and abortion is not.

Involuntary Sterilization. Since 1974 many cases of sterilization abuse have been documented. These cases have included instances of sterilization without the patients' knowledge. Possibly the most infamous of these cases involves the young Relf sisters. In June, 1973, twelve-year-old Mary Alice and fourteen-year-old Minnie were sterilized in a Montgomery, Alabama, hospital under the auspices of a project funded by the Office of Economic Opportunity, a federal agency commissioned to fight poverty. Unable to read or write, the girls' mother signed a form with an *X*, unknowingly consenting to having her daughters sterilized after a nurse told her the girls were simply to get shots. Without even talking with Mary Alice, Minnie, or their mother, a physician sterilized both girls the next morning. Afterward, welfare officials explained that the girls had been sought out for surgery because boys had been "hanging around" them; the officials believed that the girls lacked the "mental talents" to take birth control pills. According to a U.S. Senate subcommittee report in 1973, a third, older Relf daughter, Katie, locked herself in her room and refused to go when the family-planning nurse returned for her the same day.

Some women have chosen sterilization at the urging of population-control advocates in the United States and developing or overcrowded countries who consider sterilization to be the most cost-effective and reliable measure to prevent pregnancy. These advocates have offered economic incentives to women to undergo the operation; in some case, they have imposed penalties on those who decide against it. In many cases, women have chosen to have this procedure performed without being adequately educated about it or without fully considering other options. The targets of these population-control policies have tended to be low-income, young, and nonwhite women. They may not be sufficiently informed about the possible risks and consequences of this surgery, such as infection or the difficulty of reversal. While these women must legally consent to the operation, they may agree to it under coercion

Legal Measures. Feminists, health activists, and others have worked together to expose sterilization abuse and have organized against it in hospitals, communities, courts, and legislatures. As a result, in 1975 New York City became the first city in the United States

to produce guidelines for conditions under which sterilization may ethically be performed. In March, 1979, federal regulations concerning sterilization went into effect. These requirements included securing voluntary and informed consent, using standardized forms written in the patients' own preferred languages; prohibition of overt or implicit threats of loss of welfare or Medicaid benefits for refusing to consent; explaining—orally and in writing—to women alternative methods of birth control, as well as the risks, side effects, and irreversibility of sterilization; thirty-day waiting periods; prohibition of consent while patients are in labor, or when they have just had—or are about to have—abortions, or when they are under the influence of alcohol or drugs; and prohibition of hysterectomies for sterilization in federally funded programs.

SUGGESTED READINGS. *The New Our Bodies, Ourselves: A Book by and for Women* (1984), by the Boston Women's Health Book Collective, is an indispensable resource for information about women's issues. Ruth Dixon-Mueller's *Population Policy and Women's Rights: Transforming Reproductive Choice* (1993) provides a thorough discussion of the sociopolitical history of birth control practices and laws. *Population Control Politics: Women, Sterilization, and Reproductive Choice* (1985), by Thomas M. Shapiro, illuminates the ways in which sterilization has been used in discriminatory and exploitative manners.—*Holly L. Norton*

Supplemental Food Program for Women, Infants, and Children (WIC): U.S. federal program administered by the states that provides supplemental foods, nutrition counseling, and health-care referrals to low-income pregnant women and new mothers, and to infants and children at nutritional risk. WIC began in 1972 as a pilot program to combat malnutrition among low-income women; it became a permanent program in 1974. During that same year the program served eighty thousand women, children, and infants. By 1996 the program had served more than seven million persons. The program cost the federal government $10.4 million to administer in 1974 and $3.7 billion in 1996.

The Food and Consumer Service of the U.S. Department of Agriculture has administered WIC at the federal level. Unlike the FOOD STAMP program, WIC has not been an ENTITLEMENT PROGRAM. It thus must compete with other federal agencies for funds, which the federal government passes along to the states as grants.

The ideas behind WIC are simple. Inadequate nutrition and health care among low-income women, infants, and children make them vulnerable to adverse long-term health effects. Pregnant women must eat properly or risk having children with low birth weights that can lead to increased INFANT MORTALITY, mental retardation, cerebral palsy, and blindness. Pregnant women, new mothers, infants, and children up to age five are eligible for WIC assistance. They must meet income guidelines, a state residency requirement, and be at "nutritional risk." People receiving food stamps, Medicaid, and AID TO FAMILIES WITH DEPENDENT CHILDREN are considered income-eligible for WIC, in which they enroll for specified periods. Children, for example, enroll for six months, then must be recertified for continued eligibility.

Most state WIC programs provide WIC beneficiaries vouchers with which to purchase monthly food packages at authorized stores. The packages contain foods high in protein, calcium, iron, and vitamins A and C—the nutrients most frequently lacking in the diets of the program's target population. WIC foods include iron-fortified infant formula and cereal, iron-fortified adult cereal, vitamin C-rich fruit or vegetable juice, eggs, milk, cheese, and peanut butter or dried beans or peas.

By combining nutrition and health education with food vouchers, WIC has helped to reduce infant mortality in the United States. Its programs have also helped increase birth weights and gestation rates, improve intellectual development, and lower health care costs. Studies have found the birth weights of infants born to women participating in WIC to be higher than those of babies of mothers who did not participate. Moreover, participating women have been found to be more likely to be healthy during and immediately after their pregnancies. WIC participation during pregnancy has thus reduced medical costs for both mothers and children. One study found that every dollar spent on a pregnant woman's participation in WIC saved between $1.77 and $3.13 in Medicaid costs.

SUGGESTED READINGS. Charles R. King provides a historical overview in *Children's Health in America* (1993). Federal health and nutrition policy are explained in William Shonick's *Government and Health Services: Government's Role in the Development of U.S. Health Services, 1930-1980* (1995) and Ardith L. Maney's *Still Hungry After All These Years: Food Assistance Policy from Kennedy to Reagan* (1989). Graham Riches writes about hunger in *First World Hunger: Food Security and Welfare Policy* (1997).—*Fred Buchstein*

Supreme Court rulings—discrimination and minority status: During the early to mid-1990's the U.S. Supreme Court made significant rulings concerning discrimination and minority status in three broad areas: AFFIRMATIVE ACTION, jury selection, and VOTING RIGHTS.

Shortly after becoming president in 1993, Bill Clinton appointed to the Supreme Court Ruth Bader GINSBURG, a judge on the Court of Appeals for the District of Columbia, to replace retiring justice Byron White. The following year Clinton appointed Stephen Breyer of the Court of Appeals for the First Circuit to replace Justice Harry Blackmun (Breyer had previously been considered as the replacement for White). After taking their seats on the Court, both Ginsburg and Breyer exhibited generally moderate views. With closely aligned voting records, they often joined President George Bush's appointee, Justice David Souter, in a three-person bloc.

Affirmative Action. Originally instituted to end racial DISCRIMINATION by changing the institutional environment in which it had historically flourished, affirmative action did not always achieve the outcomes sought. New preferences deliberately favoring formerly oppressed minorities were introduced under the same rubric. "Goals" were established setting out numbers of African Americans, Hispanics, and Native Americans to be enrolled, hired, or promoted. Although racial QUOTAS were forbidden, "goals" or "set-asides" functioned much like quotas, and minority hiring and admissions practices were often pervaded by dishonesty. Consequently, affirmative action came to be understood by many as a euphemism for favoritism. What was once the name for the active pursuit of equal treatment, regardless of race, became the name for deliberate preference on the basis of race, essentially turning the original philosophy on its head.

A major Supreme Court case in the affirmative action area was ADARAND CONSTRUCTORS V. PEÑA (1995), in which Justice Sandra Day O'CONNOR, speaking for the 5-4 majority, held that federal affirmative action programs, like state programs, must meet a test of strict scrutiny narrowly tailored to further a compelling interest. That standard requires the highest level of justification and applies to all racial classifications: state, local, or federal. Strict scrutiny is required to ensure that the government adopts race-based measures only after careful deliberation and only when truly necessary because other less restrictive measures are unavailable or would be ineffective. Prior to the *Adarand* decision, the Supreme Court's 1980 *Fullilove v. Klutznick* decision had authorized a lower standard for federal government than for the states. Another decision, *Metro Broadcasting v. Federal Communications Commission* (1990), had allowed the FCC to favor racial minorities in awarding broadcast licenses. The rulings coming out of both of these cases were overturned by *Adarand*, which required the federal government to meet the same strict test required by the states.

As a consequence of these later Supreme Court decisions, it appeared that while properly designed affirmative action programs remained constitutional, something less well designed might not be upheld by the Court. In *Missouri v. Jenkins* (1995) the Court ordered reconsideration of a remedial school DESEGREGATION program in Kansas City, Missouri, that had

been designed to attract nonminority students from the suburbs. The Court held that the goal of attracting white students from other school systems amounted to an impermissible remedy. The state was responsible for lower student achievement levels only to the extent that racial segregation itself caused the underachievement. Minority student achievement could thus be considered only as it related to the effects of past discrimination.

Jury Selection. The earliest Supreme Court case involving racial discrimination in jury selection was *Strauder v. West Virginia* (1880). In that case the Court struck down a West Virginia state law permitting only whites to qualify for jury duty. After that decision the Court struggled for decades with the question of what constituted fair cross-sections of communities on jury panels or jury pools. In 1954 a question relating to Mexican Americans serving on juries was addressed in the Court's *Hernandez v. Texas* decision. In that case the Court held that failure to include repre-

The U.S. Supreme Court in 1993; seated (from left to right): Sandra Day O'Connor, Harry Blackmun, Chief Justice William Rehnquist, John Paul Stevens, and Antonin Scalia; standing: Clarence Thomas, Anthony Kennedy, David Souter, and Ruth Bader Ginsburg. (AP/Wide World Photos)

sentatives of a major portion of the local population in the jury process violated due process. In *Swain v. Alabama* (1965), however, the Court concluded that there was no requirement for perfect proportionality between juries and the racial mixes of the populations in the communities from which jurors were drawn, nor was it a violation of constitutional standards to remove all African Americans from a jury by exercising peremptory challenges.

Peremptory challenges, available to both parties in limited numbers (specific numbers have varied among states), are traditionally used to remove jurors regarded as undesirable by either the prosecution or defense. The reasons may be related to gender, race, or other factors that are not stated. These challenges differ from challenges "for cause," in which potential jurors are not seated because of some bias or prejudice that they might display during their preliminary questioning. The Supreme Court has consistently held that racial, ethnic, or gender discrimination in the selection of grand or petit juries violates defendants' Sixth Amendment right to be judged by juries selected from representative members of their communities.

In *Batson v. Kentucky* (1986) the prosecutor in a burglary case used his peremptory challenges to strike from a jury pool all four African American members, leaving an all-white jury. After the African American plaintiff, Batson, moved for discharge of the jury, claiming discrimination, the Supreme Court upheld his position. This decision prohibited prosecutors from using racial criteria for systematically excluding jurors. In GEORGIA v. McCOLLUM (1992), the same limitation was placed on criminal defense attorneys. The Court extended this limitation on use of peremptory challenges still further in *J.E.B. v. Alabama ex rel. T.B.* (1994) to prohibit systematic exclusion of jurors by gender.

Ostensibly expanding rights under the Fourteenth Amendment's EQUAL PROTECTION clause, the implications of a Court decision made the following year gave trial judges discretion to accept or reject *any* reasons for excluding jurors, including systematic exclusion by race or gender, so long as attorneys do not freely admit the reasons for the exclusions. In *Purkett v. Elem* (1995) a prosecutor explained his decision to exclude two African Americans from the jury pool by pointing out that one of them had unkempt, shoulder-length hair, a mustache, and a goatee; the other also had facial hair that "looked suspicious." Fanciful or implausible justifications for exclusion were, apparently, acceptable.

Voting Rights. In *Shaw v. Reno* (1993) the Supreme Court's decision allowed white voters to challenge on equal protection grounds "racial GERRYMANDERING"—the creation of oddly shaped voting districts apparently designed to classify voters according to race. After *Shaw* litigation challenging congressional districts arose in eight states, as well as numerous suits attacking state and local legislative districts. Congressional districts were upheld in North Carolina and California, but others were invalidated in Georgia, Louisiana, and Texas. The Supreme Court's decision in *Miller v. Johnson* (1995) involved a case challenging Georgia's black-majority Eleventh Congressional District. In that decision the Court's majority, led by Justice Anthony Kennedy, held that where race was a predominant factor in drawing district lines, the district was presumptively unconstitutional and would survive only if the government could demonstrate that its use was narrowly tailored to serve a compelling interest. Critics viewed these decisions as casting doubt on the constitutionality of majority-black and majority-Hispanic districts drawn after the 1990 census.

SUGGESTED READINGS. The *Affirmative Action Debate* (1996), edited by George E. Curry, presents essays arguing all sides of affirmative action and discrimination issues relating to women, Latinos, and Asian Americans. In *Not All Black and White: Affirmative Action, Race, and American Values* (1996), the White House point man on affirmative action, Christopher Edley, Jr., focuses on policy issues. *Naked Racial Preference* (1995), by Carl Cohen, gives a critical account of affirmative action examined in major court cases from 1974 through *Adarand*. Gregory D. Russell, *The Death Penalty and Racial Bias: Overturning Supreme Court Assumptions* (1994), uses social science research in death penalty and jury selection cases, and emphasizes policy implications. —*Marcia J. Weiss*

(updates original entry; vol. 6, p. 1577)

Supreme Court rulings—women's issues: During the 1990's the U.S. Supreme Court continued to advance the cause of women's equality in rulings on issues such as SEXUAL HARASSMENT, jury selection, ABORTION rights, and access to equal EDUCATION.

Sexual Harassment. In 1992, in *Franklin v. Gwinnett County Public Schools*, the Court ruled that Title IX of the federal Educational Amendments Act of 1972 allowed students in schools receiving federal funding to sue for damages because of sexual harassment and other forms of sexual discrimination. In a subsequent ruling, the Court made it easier for women to prove they were victims of an illegal "hostile work environment." In the case of *Harris v. Forklift Systems, Inc.* (1993) a women named Teresa Harris claimed to have been subjected to repeated verbal abuse and sexual insults by the president of the company for which she worked for a period of two years. After the case reached the Supreme Court, the Court ruled that Harris need not prove that she had suffered psychological injury; the fact that the insults created what to a reasonable person would be perceived as an abusive environment "sufficiently severe or pervasive to alter the conditions of the victim's employment" was enough to constitute illegal sexual harassment under Title VII of the Civil Rights Act of 1964. In these two rulings, both unanimous, the Court opted to interpret statutes broadly in favor of women's equality before the law.

Abortion. The Supreme Court has accepted no case threatening to upset its decision in *Planned Parenthood of Southeastern Pennsylvania v. Casey* (1992) reaffirming a woman's constitutional right to terminate a pregnancy before the fetus is viable. Protests at abortion clinics, however, have caught the Court's attention. While turning back challenges to a federal law making it a crime to use threats or force to block access to abortion clinics, the Court decision in *National Organization for Women v. Scheidler* (1994) made it possible for abortion clinics to bring civil damage suits under the federal Racketeer Influenced and Corrupt Organizations Act (1970) against some antiabortion organizations.

In 1994 the Court recognized limited free speech rights of abortion protesters in *Madsen v. Women's Health Center*, in which it struck down a lower court ban on antiabortion picketing within three hundred feet of the homes of doctors and a three-hundred-foot "no approach" zone around an abortion clinic. However, the Supreme Court upheld the lower court's imposition of a thirty-six foot "buffer zone" around clinic entrances in an attempt to balance free speech rights with "the woman's freedom to seek lawful medical counseling" and with the state's concern with public safety.

The Equal Protection Clause. When interpreting the constitutional obligation that government afford persons EQUAL PROTECTION of the law, the Supreme Court has continued to attack laws and policies which discriminate on the basis of gender. In *J.E.B. v. Alabama ex rel. T.B.* (1994), for example, the Court found

Future Supreme Court justice Ruth Bader Ginsburg during her confirmation hearings in the Senate in mid-1993. (AP/Wide World Photos)

that the practice of prosecutors using peremptory strikes to exclude potential jurors solely because of gender was an unconstitutional form of discrimination akin to excluding people from juries solely because of race. This decision continued a long line of Court decisions removing state sponsored barriers to women's equal access to jury service.

Support for women's equal protection claims was given a boost in 1993 when President Bill Clinton named Ruth Bader GINSBURG the second woman justice on the Supreme Court. As director of the Women's Rights Project of the AMERICAN CIVIL LIBERTIES UNION during the 1970's, Ginsburg had led major court battles in which her arguments in such cases as *Frontiero v. Richardson* (1973) and *Craig v. Boren* (1976) greatly influenced constitutional law on gender discrimination. Her rulings as a Supreme Court justice have continued to reflect her lifelong support of women's equality.

In 1996 Justice Ginsburg wrote the majority opinion in one of the Supreme Court's most controversial cases, *United States v. Virginia.* This case concerned the Virginia Military Institute (VMI). Established in 1839 as a state-supported college, VMI admitted only males into its rigorously disciplined educational program. Litigation against the college began in 1991, after a female high school student was refused admission. With the support of the U.S. Department of Justice, the young woman challenged VMI's admissions policy as a violation of the FOURTEENTH AMENDMENT's equal protection guarantee. A U.S. district court judge ruled in favor of VMI, but after a successful appeal by the federal government, the state of Virginia established a separate, but arguably "equal," military-style educational program for women at a private women's college near VMI. This decision was approved by both a district judge and the Fourth Circuit Court of Appeals; however, the federal government appealed the decision to the Supreme Court. The government challenged both the VMI admissions policy and creation of the separate school for women as violations of the Constitution. The Supreme Court agreed.

In a strongly worded defense of women's equality, Justice Ginsburg labeled the separate program a "pale shadow" of the well-established and prestigious male institution. In addition, the state of Virginia did not offer the "exceedingly persuasive justification" necessary to maintain the male-only admissions policy. VMI's argument that the unique military-style education offered at the school would be compromised by the admission of women did not convince the Court's majority. Ginsburg affirmed the rights of "women who want a VMI education and can make the grade," arguing that VMI's admissions policy relied on "overbroad generalizations about the different talents, capacities, or preferences of males and females." Her decision in this case signalled that the Supreme Court would thereafter view with great skepticism any state policy based on gender STEREOTYPES.

In another controversial equal protection ruling with implications for LESBIANS, the Court struck down an amendment to the COLORADO CONSTITUTION BALLOT AMENDMENT 2, which prohibited all governmental action aimed at protecting persons based on their "homosexual, lesbian or bisexual orientation, conduct, practices or relationships." In *Romer v. Evans* (1996) the Court saw this as an attempt to make gays into second-class citizens in violation of the Constitution.

SUGGESTED READINGS. Two comprehensive sources on the legal status of women stand out: *The Law of Sex Discrimination* (2d ed., 1993), by J. Ralph Lindgren and Nadine Taub, and *Law, Gender, and Injustice: A Legal History of U.S. Women* (1991), by Joan Hoff. The broad subject of abortion law and politics is well treated in Karen O'Connor's *No Neutral Ground?: Abortion Politics in an Age of Absolutes* (1996). Written for juvenile readers, Carmen Bredeson's *Ruth Bader Ginsburg, Supreme Court Justice* (1995) is an informative account of Ginsburg's life and legal career.—*Philip R. Zampini*
(updates original entry; vol. 6, p. 1586)

Surrogate mothers: Mothers who substitute for women incapable of normal PREGNANCY by carrying embryos fertilized in vitro from the eggs of the other women, whose natural babies they deliver. The advent of artificial insemination, in vitro fertilization, and embryo transplantation have made it possible for surrogates to bear children for infertile couples—a possibility with the potential of creating various multicultural complications. Two basic types of surrogacy have been developed: biological surrogacy, in which surrogates furnish the eggs and the husbands of adopting couples, or donors, furnish the sperm; and gestational surrogacy, in which both egg and sperm are provided to surrogates, who then give birth to the resulting children.

Profiles of Surrogate Mothers. Women who consent to "renting out" their wombs to allow infertile couples to have children have, according to the best available information, been mostly in their late twenties or early thirties. Most have also been married and have several children of their own; for financial reasons, they have generally not wanted to have more children. The average education of surrogate mothers has been about thirteen years, and most have been in the lower range of the socio-economic scale. Some studies have indicated that as many as 40 percent of surrogate mothers were receiving governmental assistance when they agreed to become surrogates. Approximately 80 percent have been Anglo-Americans, with almost no Jewish, black, or Asian women. Most have been reared in the Christian faith.

Cases in Point. In 1987 the "BABY M" case became major news across the United States. Mary Beth Whitehead contracted to bear a child for William and Elizabeth Stern, in exchange for ten thousand dollars and all medical expenses relating to her pregnancy. William Stern was particularly interested in having a child to whom he was genetically related, so the couple arranged to have Whitehead artificially inseminated with his sperm. All went as planned until near the time when the baby was about to be born, and Whitehead changed her mind about the agreement. When she announced that she wanted to keep the baby and refused to accept the Stern's fee, the Sterns sued her in a New Jersey court.

During the ensuing court battle Whitehead was depicted as being irresponsible, of questionable mental stability, and in other ways unfit to be a mother. By contrast, both Sterns were respected professionals. In early 1987 a judge ruled that the Sterns' contract was legal and ordered the baby to be turned over to them; he did not even award Whitehead visitation rights. After Whitehead appealed that decision, New Jersey's supreme court overruled the lower court judge. However, because the child had by then been living with the Sterns for almost two years, the court decided it was in the child's best interests to remain with the Sterns, with Whitehead allowed visitation rights.

There appear to have been no ethnic dimensions to this battle for Baby M, but there can be little doubt that the difference in socio-economic status between the Sterns and the Whiteheads was a real, if unacknowledged, factor in the outcome of the case.

A case in which multiculturalism came clearly into play was the California case of Anna Johnson versus Mark and Crispina Calvert. Johnson, a black woman, agreed to be a gestational surrogate for a white couple, Mark and Crispina Calvert. Although Crispina Calvert had had a partial hysterectomy, she was able to produce an egg, which was to be fertilized in vitro with her husband's sperm and then implanted in Johnson. Johnson was to receive a fee of ten thousand dollars, plus medical expenses associated with the pregnancy. Toward the end of the pregnancy, however, Johnson sued to have her surrogacy contract voided and for permission to keep the child. During the ensuing trial

While fighting a custody battle for her daughter "Baby M," Mary Beth Whitehead is consoled by Elizabeth Kane, who claimed to have been the first woman to enter a surrogate-mother contract. (AP/Wide World Photos)

her fitness as a mother was questioned. She was already a SINGLE MOTHER, and testimony was brought forward that she had been negligent in caring for the child she already had. Moreover, her financial means were limited, and she had a history of difficulties in keeping jobs. No one can say how much these factors affected the outcome of the trial, but California's supreme court ruled in favor of the Calverts by a vote of 6-1. The judgment was made on the basis of intention. The court declared that the woman who intended to procreate and rear the child was the natural mother under California law.

Possibilities. The multicultural possibilities of surrogacy are almost unlimited. With the advent of sperm banks and the technology for in vitro fertilization and embryo transplanting, prospective parents can choose the genetic makeup, and even the sex, of their children. Among the possibilities is that of widespread exploitation of women. Since surrogates are usually paid ten thousand dollars or more, it is easy to see how agencies that arrange surrogate births might increase their profits by drawing on an almost inexhaustible supply of women from Third World countries willing to serve as surrogate mothers in return for lesser rewards. As long as the laws of most states permit surrogacy, this potential will exist.

SUGGESTED READINGS. For a firsthand account of the intricacies of surrogate motherhood, including a profile of surrogate mothers see Cheryl Saban, *Miracle Child: Genetic Mother, Surrogate Womb* (1993). A thorough analysis of the "Baby M" case and an introduction to the possibilities of new reproductive technologies can be found in Robin Fox's article, "Babies for Sale," in *The Public Interest* 111 (Spring, 1993). *Surrogate Motherhood: A Worldwide View of the Issues* (1994), by Diederika Pretorius, provides a comprehensive and readable discussion of issues concerning surrogacy in the United States and abroad. *Expecting Trouble: Surrogacy, Fetal Abuse, and New Reproductive Technologies* (1995), edited by Patricia Boling, is an anthology of feminist essays on aspects of surrogate motherhood.—*Joseph E. Lunceford*

Swann v. Charlotte-Mecklenburg Board of Education (1971): U.S. Supreme Court decision relating to school DESEGREGATION. This case arose as a result of a federal district judge's efforts to promote racial balance in the school systems of Charlotte, North Carolina, and the surrounding Mecklenburg County by BUSING students. A federal district court found that the Charlotte

and Mecklenburg County schools had remained segregated despite the Supreme Court's decision in *Brown v. Board of Education* (1954). This continuing SEGREGATION was found to be the responsibility of local school authorities, who had not only failed to submit an acceptable plan for desegregation but had also located schools in racially segregated neighborhoods and fixed their size to serve the neighborhoods in question. Based upon this finding of de jure segregation, the lower court applied busing as a remedy for the failure of the two North Carolina districts to fulfill their desegregation plan. The Supreme court upheld the actions of the lower court.—*Jerry A. Murtagh*

Sweatshops: Exploitative workplaces that have been notorious for taking advantage of newly arrived immigrants in the United States. In the late twentieth century the numbers of sweatshops in the United States grew in response to the growing numbers of clothing retailers seeking low-cost suppliers of goods manufactured within the United States. Sweatshop operators are notorious for exploiting ILLEGAL ALIENS, violating wage and tax laws, employing children, and operating oppressive and unhealthful workplaces.

In their ongoing search for cheaper supplies, clothing manufacturers deal with contractors who "squeeze" their workers by paying them as little as possible and by reducing standards for working conditions. This practice of squeezing labor is known as "sweating," hence the term "sweatshop" for the workplace where the sweated workers perform their labor. The system of contracting out work allows both manufacturers and retailers to distance themselves from the unpleasantness of the sweatshops in which their goods are made and to avoid the embarrassment of government raids.

During the 1950's and 1960's many apparel manufacturers avoided dealing with unionized shops in the northern states by moving their operations to the South, which offered a low-wage, nonunion female workforce. As this labor became more expensive during the 1970's, the manufacturers transferred much of the work overseas to places such as Hong Kong, Korea, Singapore, and Taiwan. As U.S. factories shut down, they were replaced by smaller sweatshops, which employed immigrants willing to work for low wages, often under appalling conditions.

As the nation's largest apparel centers, LOS ANGELES and NEW YORK CITY are home to the largest numbers of sweatshops in the United States, followed by SAN FRANCISCO and MIAMI and cities in New Jersey

Early twentieth century sweatshops, such as this New York City shoe factory, often made heavy use of child labor. (Library of Congress)

and Texas. An estimated 800,000 employees worked in contract shops by the mid-1990's; about 80 percent of these workers were women. Latina and Asian women immigrants, both illegal and legal, are believed to be the most heavily represented in the shops.

Sweatshop employees are often required to work as many as fourteen and sixteen hours a day, seven days a week, and overtime pay is unheard of. Workers are paid piece rate—for the work they finish, rather than the time they put in. Piece rates are theoretically paid to provide productivity incentives, not to circumvent MINIMUM WAGE LAWS. In practice, however, they have the effect of forcing employees to work longer and faster so they can earn more money, and no matter how efficiently they work, their pay rarely reaches minimum wage levels.

A government raid on an El Monte, California, sweatshop in August, 1995, discovered seventy-two immigrant Thai workers who were forced to work and live within a barbed wire enclosure, while being paid less than a dollar an hour for their work. After exposure of what became known as the THAI GARMENT WORKERS SLAVERY CASE, U.S. labor secretary Robert Reich promised a tougher government crackdown on the retailers and manufacturers handling garments produced in sweatshops. Similar raids in many other cities throughout the United States increased public concern about the social costs of the clothing they buy. Organizations, such as Sweatshop Watch and Common Threads, have been created to educate consumers about sweatshop conditions and to help eliminate them nationally and globally.

SUGGESTED READINGS. Susan Chandler includes many useful statistics in "Look Who's Sweating Now," *Business Week* (Oct. 16, 1995). "Made in the U.S.A." is an undercover look at the sweatshops in San Francisco that appeared in *Ms.* (Jan.-Feb. 1996).—*Douglas Dixon*

T

Tailhook scandal (1991): SEXUAL HARASS-MENT scandal involving U.S. Navy aviators attending a convention in Las Vegas. An annual event (named after a device that stops airplanes landing on aircraft carriers), the Tailhook Convention began in 1956 and was funded by both the Navy and private sponsors. Its ostensible purpose was to permit private contractors to exhibit products to pilots and other Navy personnel involved in the Navy's aviation program. While a great deal of product information was actually exchanged, the annual convention was viewed by many aviators as primarily a social event. In 1991 four thousand naval aviators, contractors, and related personnel attended the convention at Las Vegas' Hilton Hotel.

During the 1980's the social portion of the Tailhook Convention acquired an increasingly raucous tone, with heavy consumption of alcohol, carousing, exhibitions of pornography, and hiring of prostitutes becoming accepted features of evening activities. In a particularly popular annual ritual dubbed the "gauntlet," naval officers lined the hallways outside their squadron suites and harassed women who were invited or cajoled to pass by them. Their behavior often got out of hand; in 1991 the Hilton Hotel billed the Navy $123,000 for damage to twenty-two squadron suites.

The social festivities of the largely male Tailhook Convention went unreported for many years. That silence ended, however, when Lieutenant Paula Coughlin and four other women claimed to have been fondled and attacked by drunken officers. Dissatisfied with the Navy's initial investigation, Coughlin went public with her charges, prompting a second and more thorough investigation, which included 2,900 interviews and 800 photographs. However, investigators faced a "code of silence" as naval personnel were reluctant to breach loyalties to fellow officers.

Eventually, fifty-one officers were found to have made false statements to officials. When the investigation concluded in 1992, it was determined that one hundred persons had been sexually assaulted at the

After reaching a settlement with the Tailhook Association, former Navy lieutenant Paula Coughlin (left), seen with attorney Nancy Stagg, sued the Las Vegas Hilton Hotel in 1994 for permitting the conditions that allowed her and other women to be sexually abused at the association's convention three years earlier. (Reuters/Steve Marcus/Archive Photos)

Tailhook Convention, and the names of seventy men were reported to their commanding officers for their roles in the improprieties. In June of 1992 U.S. Navy secretary H. Lawrence Garrett III resigned, accepting responsibility for a "leadership failure" in the scandal.

Many critics including Congresswoman Patricia Schroeder, who sat on the Congressional Armed Services Committee, called for demoting Admiral Frank Kelso, alleging that he knew of the misconduct and had attempted a cover-up. However, the Senate voted not to reprimand him. Ultimately, only three junior officers were formally charged with criminal misconduct; all other cases were dismissed by a military court before reaching criminal status. Nevertheless, the negative publicity surrounding the scandal caused cancellation of the 1992 Tailhook Convention. It resumed in 1993 in a much subdued format after the Navy withdrew its official sanction of the event and many sponsors pulled out.

SUGGESTED READINGS. Gregory L. Vistica's *Fall from Glory: The Men Who Sank the U.S. Navy* (1995)

explores the roles and lives of the male commanding officers in the Tailhook scandal. *Tailspin: Women at War in the Wake of Tailhook* (1995), by Jean Zimmerman, is a feminist analysis of the incident. Jean Ebert and Marie-Beth Hall examine the history of naval women in *Crossed Currents: Navy Women from World War I to Tailhook* (1993). The official investigation of the Tailhook scandal, published by the U.S. government, is *Women in the Military: The Tailhook Affair and the Problem of Sexual Harassment* (1992). —*Maurice Hamington*

Teenage pregnancy: Roughly a million American teenagers become pregnant every year. Pregnancy rates for girls between fifteen and nineteen years of age rose from 95 per 1,000 in 1972 to 110 per 1,000 in 1989, and there has also been a significant increase in the numbers of teenagers giving birth who are not married and thus become SINGLE MOTHERS. In 1960 only 15 percent of teenage mothers were unwed, compared to 66 percent in 1988.

A third of American teenagers who become pregnant have ABORTIONS to terminate their pregnancies. For some, this is an easily accessible, low-cost method which does not require parental consent. The remaining two-thirds of pregnant teenagers, however, deliver their babies, and nine out of ten of these girls keep their babies.

Statistics on teenage pregnancy also reflect differences among racial, ethnic, and economic groups. Adolescents from poor urban families have the highest rates of pregnancy. Most of these teenage mothers are black or Hispanic. For example, motherhood for some teenagers, particularly those in the African American community, represents independence and control of their lives—both goals that typically prove elusive. Teenage pregnancy occurs among members of all groups, however. The United States as a whole has had significantly higher rates of teenage pregnancy than all other industrialized nations.

Reasons for Teenage Pregnancy. Some sociologists have suggested that much of teenage pregnancy results

To counter the high incidence of school dropouts among pregnant teenagers, some cities have offered special programs, which often include instruction on childbirth and infant care, to encourage girls to finish high school. (AP/Wide World Photos)

In the face of rapidly rising rates of teenage pregnancy, some communities have taken to public advertising to discourage the trend. (James L. Shaffer)

from the low self-esteem of teenage girls, who think that having children will give them someone who will return their affection. Sociologists have also suggested that many adolescents knowingly become pregnant in the hope of maintaining emotional and legal holds on their boyfriends—another hope that more often than not proves vain.

The fact that a large proportion of pregnant girls come from poor families has much to do with their impoverishment. For example, teenagers whose poverty limits the range of their dating activities tend to spend more time on "dates" within their homes, where they have greater opportunities for sexual activity than they would if they were involved in activities outside their homes. Moreover, many pregnant teenagers have mothers who were pregnant as teenagers themselves, for there appears to be a clearly cyclical nature in teenage pregnancy.

Among other factors credited with producing high rates of teen pregnancy in the United States

States Requiring Parental Consent/Notification or Counseling for Minors Seeking Abortions in 1994

Alabama	Louisiana	Missouri	Tennessee
Arkansas	Maine	Nebraska	Utah
Georgia	Maryland	North Dakota	West Virginia
Idaho	Massachusetts	Ohio	Wisconsin
Indiana	Michigan	Rhode Island	Wyoming
Kansas	Minnesota	South Carolina	

Source: Planned Parenthood of America

has been a significant reduction in the social stigmas historically associated with teen pregnancy. Greater public acceptance of sexual activity among unmarried teenagers has combined with inadequate sex education and the failure of many teenagers to use contraceptives to produce growing numbers of pregnant teenagers.

Some schools have offered sex education as part of health classes, but the information they have provided has tended to pertain mostly to anatomy and the functioning of organs, not to information about intimate relationships, contraception, sexually transmitted diseases, and pregnancy and childbirth.

Consequences of Teenage Pregnancy. Many teenagers who become pregnant drop out of school and condemn themselves to lives without financial security. So many teenage mothers go on welfare that 25 percent of all persons on public assistance are teenagers. Teenagers that do marry two times more likely to divorce than older persons. In addition, teenage mothers and their children face higher risks of both mental and physical health problems. Inadequate PRENATAL CARE and failure to maintain healthy diets during pregnancy place both pregnant teenagers and their unborn infants at risk. The offspring of teenage mothers often require specialized medical care. Many of their babies are born prematurely or have low birth weights—both conditions that contribute to high rates of INFANT MORTALITY.

SUGGESTED READINGS. For broad surveys on this subject, see Judy Berlfein's *Teen Pregnancy* (1992), Gisela Meier's *Teenage Pregnancy* (1994), and *Teenage Pregnancy in the United States: The Scope of the Problem and State Responses* (1989), by Stanley K. Henshaw and others. A world perspective on this subject can be found in *Children Having Children: Global Perspectives on Teenage Pregnancy* (1988), edited by Gary E. McCuen. Janet Bode's *Kids Still Having Kids: People Talk About Teen Pregnancy* (1992), looks at the problem from the viewpoint of teenagers.—*Christopher E. Kent*

Terminal Island: Artificial island in Southern California's Los Angeles Harbor that was the base of an important Japanese American fishing community that was uprooted by the JAPANESE AMERICAN INTERNMENT during World War II.

Known before the 1890's as Rattlesnake Island, the island then belonged to the Dominguez family, which sold it to the Terminal Land Company after which it was renamed. Around the turn of the twentieth century

the southeastern side of the island was settled by a growing number of Japanese immigrants, who developed a thriving community based on a local fishing industry. The men in the community worked at jobs directly related to the fishing, while many of the women worked in affiliated canneries. Most of the families lived in company-owned housing.

The Japanese community reached a peak population of about three thousand persons. Because of its relative isolation from surrounding non-Japanese communities, it maintained an unusually high degree of Japanese cultural identity and provided its residents with most of the cultural amenities and institutions found in larger Japanese American communities.

After Japan's sudden attack on Pearl Harbor brought the United States into WORLD WAR II, the federal government's Japanese American internment made the residents of Terminal Island the first major Japanese American community to be removed to relocation centers. By the end of February, 1942—less than three months after Pearl Harbor—Terminal Island's Japanese community ceased to exist. The residents lost almost everything; after the war none of them returned to the island. Some relocated in the Los Angeles area; many went to New Jersey's SEABROOK FARMS; the rest scattered. The spirit of the original community lived on, however. In 1970 nearly a thousand of its former residents gathered together for a reunion, and similar reunions continued in later years.—*Christopher E. Kent*

Texaco boycott (1996): National boycott of Texaco, Inc., undertaken to protest racist remarks made by top company officials. The boycott helped bring about the most lucrative settlement ever reached in a racial discrimination case.

On Monday, November 4, 1996, *The New York Times* printed transcripts of a 1994 meeting among top Texaco officials that included racially charged remarks within conversations about shredding or changing subpoenaed documents concerning the company's employment practices, keeping two sets of books, and deleting handwritten notes from certain papers. The tapes had been recorded by Richard Lundwall, a former Texaco human resources official whose duties had included keeping the meeting minutes. After he was laid off by Texaco during a downsizing move, he turned the tapes over to the plaintiffs' attorneys in a racial discrimination lawsuit, *Roberts v. Texaco,* that had been filed two years earlier by 1,400 African American Texaco workers.

Jesse Jackson calls for a boycott of Texaco, Inc., outside the company's Wilmington, California, refinery, in November, 1996. (Reuters/Sam Mircovich/Archive Photos)

Shortly after their appearance in *The New York Times*, the tapes were aired on national television and radio, causing an uproar. A week later civil rights leader Jesse JACKSON met with Texaco's chief executive office and chairman, Peter I. Bijur; he then called for a nationwide boycott of Texaco products and asked members of the public to sell their Texaco stock. Leaders of the NATIONAL ASSOCIATION FOR THE ADVANCEMENT OF COLORED PEOPLE (NAACP), including Kansas City mayor Emmanuel Cleaver, discussed the possibility of long-term boycotts, stock divestiture programs, and targeted picketing. The oil company's stock soon dropped a billion dollars in value on the New York Stock Exchange.

In reaction to the growing national boycott and its public embarrassment over the contents of the tapes, Texaco settled its lawsuit with its black employees by agreeing to pay $115 million to about 1,400 current and former African American workers, as well as $26.1 million in pay raises to African American employees over the following five years, and $35 million dollars for diversity-training programs. The settlement also created an independent task force to oversee changes in Texaco's employment policies that was to report twice a year to the company's board of directors.

This settlement did not, however, end the boycott. Jackson and NAACP leaders called for it to continue until Texaco agreed to a specific plan to increase minority ownership of service stations and to do more business with minority-owned companies. On December 18, 1996, the company capitulated; it unveiled a new diversity plan that promised to increase Texaco's minority workforce by about 1,200 employees and to increase its spending with minority-owned businesses from $135 million to $200 million a year. The plan was well received by Jackson and the NAACP who called it a standard for other companies to follow, and the boycott was called off.

SUGGESTED READINGS. Kurt Eichenwald includes a partial transcript of the notorious taped conversations in an article titled "Texaco Executives, on Tape, Discussed Impeding a Bias Suit," in *The New York Times* (Nov. 4, 1996). An article in *Time* magazine (Nov. 25, 1996), "Texaco's High-Octane Racism Problems," by Jack E. White, examines the Texaco lawsuit settlement. Michael Davis discusses the boycott and Texaco's diversity plan in "Texaco Diversity Plan Ends Boycott" in the *Houston Chronicle* (Dec. 19, 1996).—*Douglas Dixon*

Texas Folklife Festival: Annual celebration of Texas culture. The Texas Folklife Festival is held every August in San Antonio on the grounds of the Institute of Texan Cultures in HemisFair Park. Begun in 1970, the festival has attracted more than 100,000 visitors annually to a celebration of the varied cultural heritages of the state's population. Many of the exhibits showcase Mexican and Mexican American culture, and performances of

Young Filipino men perform a traditional rhythmic dance with coconuts at the Texas Folklife Festival. (Diane C. Lyell)

mariachi and *conjunto* musicians are traditionally popular features of the event. Other exhibits focus on local foods, dances, and folk arts and crafts.—*Christopher E. Kent*

Jose Francisco Ruiz, a prominent Tejano who served in the Texas congress and signed the Texas declaration of independence from Mexico. (Institute of Texas Cultures, courtesy of Mrs. Ruby Hermea)

Texas Revolt (1835-1836): Conflict through which American settlers in Texas won their independence from Mexico. The conflict arose because of the settlers' dissatisfaction with the Mexican government of the territory, whose capital was Saltillo. Among the issues that led the settlers to revolt was Mexico's abolition of SLAVERY, an institution that most of the American settlers in Texas wished to perpetuate.

Not long after Americans began settling in Texas in the early 1820's, they outnumbered Texas Mexicans, known as Tejanos, by a wide margin. Nevertheless, many Tejanos shared the Americans' dissatisfaction with the Saltillo government; many of them played prominent roles in the Texas Revolt. Some died inside the Alamo, others died fighting with Sam Houston at San Jacinto, and many provided both food and intelligence to participants in the revolt.

Ethnic animosity did, however, soon become a severe problem. Texas was the portion of the Southwest that drew the bulk of its Anglo population from the Deep South. The southern whites' commitment to slavery was fully developed when they arrived in Texas with five thousand African slaves. It required little effort to transfer their attitudes about skin color to Mexicans.

Texas was the only Mexican province that the United States acquired through warfare on the part of its own inhabitants. The revolt left a legacy of resentment against Mexicans that grew into negative STEREOTYPES fostering an Anglo hatred of Mexicans in Texas unmatched in California, New Mexico, or other territories taken from Mexico after the MEXICAN-AMERICAN WAR.—*Douglas W. Richmond*

Thai garment workers slavery case (1995): Incident involving public exposure of forced labor in Southern CALIFORNIA. Early on August 2, 1995, agents of several state and federal law enforcement bodies raided an apartment complex in El Monte, California, after receiving reports that an illegal SWEATSHOP operation was being run inside. The agents' worst fears were realized when they found seventy-two Thai garment workers laboring and living under conditions of SLAVERY within the complex. Neighbors in the residential area had assumed that the complex's windows had been boarded up and that barbed-wire had been strung around the complex to prevent break-ins. In reality, these security measures had been taken to keep workers from leaving.

Most of the Thai workers were women in their twenties and thirties. During the investigation that followed, they described being forced to work long hours under horrendous conditions, while being paid pitiful wages. Their employers, who brought them into the United States, had told them that they must work to repay their transportation costs; however, even after the workers had repaid those costs in full, their employers kept them in the complex against their will. Those who tried to escape were severely beaten. A few workers did escape, however, and informed authorities of the conditions in the complex.

The IMMIGRATION AND NATURALIZATION SERVICE (INS) was first alerted to the El Monte sweatshop as early as 1992, but no action was taken until another informant talked to state authorities three years later. After exposure of this slavery case, both state and federal agencies stepped up their efforts to monitor the GARMENT INDUSTRY. The operators of the El Monte

factory were prosecuted and sent to federal prison.

In March, 1996, a ceremony was held in nearby Los Angeles to present checks to workers who had been exploited after $1.1 million was collected from those responsible for violating their civil rights. During that same month U.S. secretary of labor Robert Reich issued a statement formally condemning sweatshops and asking the fashion industry to commit itself to never let it happen again by refusing to purchase goods from illegal sweatshops. In October, 1997, five major retailing companies—including Mervyn's and Montgomery Ward—agreed to paying more than $2 million to the exploited workers. Although these companies admitted to no wrongdoing themselves in the case, the settlement was widely expected to have an important positive impact on the retailing industry's influence on apparent industry labor conditions.

SUGGESTED READINGS. The *Los Angeles Times* published a series of articles on this case, starting with a detailed account of the government raid in its August 3, 1995 edition. *The Economist* also had a detailed article on the case titled "The Profits of Sin" (Aug. 12, 1995). David Finnigan wrote a brutally honest article titled "Our Cheap Clothes Are Their Horror Stories: Thais, Other Minorities Abused in Sweatshops That Keep Prices Down," *National Catholic Reporter* (Dec. 29, 1995). For general background on the history of workers in the garment industry, see Susan A. Glenn's *Daughters of Shtel: Life and Labor in the Immigrant Generation* (1990) and Roger D. Waldinger's *Through the Eye of the Needle: Immigrants and Enterprise in New York's Garment Trades* (1986).—*Jeffry Jensen*

Transcendental meditation (TM): Known primarily as a stress reliever, TM is a simple, nearly effortless technique that allows the practitioner's mind to settle down, contact the source of thought, and thereby create stability in the nervous system. Many scientific experiments have proven that the meditative state, also called the fourth state of consciousness, is more restful than the other three states of waking, sleeping, dreaming. It is through the increased rest received by the TM meditator that beneficial effects develop, such as fewer illnesses and mental disturbances.

More than five hundred published studies have documented the wide-ranging physiological, psychological, and sociological benefits of practicing the TM technique. A time-honored Indian technique, TM was brought to the United States in 1959 by Maharishi

Mahesh Yogi and is now widely practiced around the world. Maharishi's explanation of the TM technique is contained in his translation of, and commentary on, the *Bhagavad Gita.—Ann Stewart Balakier*

Transsexuals: Persons whose gender identities are the opposite of their genetic and biological features. For example, transsexuals who are biologically male feel and experience life as women; those who are biologically female feel and experience life as men. Transsexualism has been labeled a gender-identity disorder because it involves problems in the feelings one has about being male or female. Two related conditions are homosexualism and transvestism; however, transsexualism, homosexualism, and transvestism are different from each other.

Distinctions. Homosexual persons, who are gay or lesbian, are normally satisfied with their own anatomy and identify themselves as appropriately male or female. Homosexuals have appropriate gender identity but are sexually attracted to members of their own sex. In contrast, heterosexuals are sexually attracted to members of the opposite sex.

Transvestites also are satisfied with their anatomy and identify themselves as appropriately male or female. Transvestites, too, have an appropriate gender identity. However, they experience a strong need to dress in the clothing of the opposite gender. Most transvestites are married men who engage in sexual relations with their wives. Transsexuals, in contrast, think of themselves as members of the opposite sex— often from their early childhood. They usually have normal genetic instructions and biological (hormonal) factors but view their sexual orientation as heterosexual because they feel trapped in bodies of the wrong sex.

Not all transsexuals feel that the desire to change sex is an illness, and some protest labeling transsexualism as a psychological disorder. They feel that it takes courage to admit their discomfort before the transition, and openness and flexibility to willfully accept the challenge of re-creating themselves.

Reasons. There is currently no clear understanding of why transsexuals reject their biological sex. Since these disorders are often apparent from early childhood, biological factors are suspected (such as prenatal hormonal imbalances). However, family factors and learning cannot be ruled out as causes. Indeed, experts such as John Money believe that most cases of transsexualism result from child-rearing practices that discourage persons from becoming content and confident with their own sexuality. For example, if a child's parents would strongly prefer having a girl but have a boy instead, they might treat the child ambiguously

Christine Jorgensen's surgical transformation into a woman made Americans aware of transsexualism during the early 1950's. (AP/Wide World Photos)

and in an inconsistent manner.

Exactly how many people regard themselves as transsexuals is unknown. Past researchers suggested that transsexualism was more common among men than women, but more recent data have indicated that the incidence of transsexualism is about the same among both men and women.

Sex-Change Surgery. Because transsexuals acquire gender identities that do not match their external sex organs, some male transsexuals go so far as to cut off their own penises. Others undergo sex change operations. Physicians have performed several thousand sex-change operations in the United States.

For males, hormone treatments can enlarge the size of their breasts, reduce their beard growth, reduce the size of their Adam's apples (a distinctive male feature), and make their bodies more rounded overall.

Surgical procedures involve removing the testes and part of the penis and shaping the remaining tissue into a vagina and labia. For women, hormone treatments can increase beard growth, firm their muscles, and deepen their voices. Surgical procedures involve removing the ovaries and uterus, reducing breast tissue, and in some instances constructing penis-like organs. Male-to-female surgery can produce functional and authentic-looking vaginas; however, female-to-male surgery can produce only artificial penises incapable of spontaneously becoming erect. Nonetheless, inflatable penile implants can make artificial erections. Although sex-change operations cannot make reproduction possible, they can produce remarkable changes in physical appearance.

Because sex-change surgery is both drastic and irreversible, it is undertaken only after careful consideration. Individuals are usually given counseling and hormone treatments, and are required to live as members of the opposite sex for a year or more prior to having operations. During the trial period, transsexuals periodically undergo psychological evaluations. If they appear to be stable and have adjusted psychologically to adopting the lifestyles of the desired gender, they are then cleared for the surgery.

Expert opinion has remained divided on whether sex-change surgery actually helps transsexual persons to feel better adjusted to their environments. One survey found that 20 percent of the persons who underwent the surgery regretted their decisions. Another found that more than half of thirteen subjects showed no psychological improvement as a result of surgery. Thus, although some transsexuals have been pleased with their changes, others have had adjustment difficulties.

Some instances of sexual reassignment have been well publicized. In the United States, one case involved a physician named Richard Raskind who became Renée Richards. His sex change led to a court case to deter-

During the late 1970's a male physician underwent sex-change operations and became tennis player Renée Richards, who challenged legal definitions of gender by winning court orders in order to compete in women's tennis tournaments. (AP/Wide World Photos)

mine if Dr. Richards could play in women's tennis matches. A judge ruled that she could because she was legally a woman. In England a well-known journalist, father of four, and mountain climber named James Morris resolved his own identity conflict by undergoing a sex-change operation. Renamed Jan, Morris has written a book describing the transformation.

SUGGESTED READINGS. Two classic works *Man and Woman, Boy and Girl: The Differentiation and Dimorphism of Gender Identity from Conception to Maturity* (1972), by John Money and Anke A. Ehrhardt, and *Sexual Signatures: On Being a Man or a Woman* (1975), by Money and Patricia Tucker, describe Money's work with hermaphrodites and argue that transsexualism occurs as a result of ambiguous rearing, a pattern of social influence that leads people to feel that their sexual physiology must be changed. A more recent work by I. Pauly, "Gender Identity Disorders: Evaluation and Treatment," in *Journal of Sex Education and Therapy* 16 (1990), discusses current thinking on treatment. A fascinating survey titled "Long-term Follow-up of 'Sex Change' in Thirteen Male-to-Female Transsexuals," in *Archives of Sexual Behavior* 15 (1986), by G. Lindemalm, D. Korlin, and N. Uddenberg, presents details of the lives of individuals who have undergone surgery. The definitive text on sexual identity is *Human Sexuality* (5th ed., 1995), by William H. Masters, Virginia E. Johnson, and R. C. Kolodny.—*Lillian M. Range*

Tricksters: Mythic figures in Native American oral and written literature. Also called trickster-transformers, trickster figures regard themselves as superior to all other beings and rely on cunning, deception, and mean tactics to achieve their goals of rebelling against conventional systems and establishing ingenious enterprises. Among many Native American societies myths about the mischievous acts of tricksters have helped to teach proper behavior to children. They have also provided outlets for socially unacceptable feelings and impulses, instructed and inspired adults, entertained through humor, explained how the universe came into being, and presented culture heroes who save the people or otherwise make the world better by their brave acts. Tricksters are usually male and they take different forms, most of which are animals. Coyote tricksters have been common in the Southwest, spiders in the High Plains, hares in the Great Lakes and Southeast, ravens in the Northwest, old men among the Blackfeet people in the Northern Plains, and jays and wolverines in Canada.—*Cassandra Kircher*

Tuskegee Airmen: African American pilots trained at segregated facilities at Alabama's TUSKEGEE INSTITUTE during World War II. Until WORLD WAR II, African Americans were totally excluded from the U.S. Army Air Corps. As it became evident that the United States would enter the war, civil rights leaders began to pressure the U.S. government to end SEGREGATION and DISCRIMINATION in the MILITARY and to expand opportunities for blacks.

In 1939 the government established a flight training school at Tuskegee Institute, a renowned black educational institution in Alabama. Although there was already an airbase in nearby Montgomery, leaders in the War Department believed that training blacks and whites together at a southern base would be too controversial. In January, 1941, the War Department announced that it would form a black flight squadron, to be trained at Tuskegee. This provoked opposition from many civil rights leaders, who felt that this was simply an extension of segregation. The NATIONAL ASSOCIATION FOR THE ADVANCEMENT OF COLORED PEOPLE, in particular, criticized Frederick D. Patterson, head of the Tuskegee Institute, for agreeing to participate in this segregated project. Many African Americans, however, regarded the advantages to be gained through creation of a large number of black officers as outweighing the disadvantages of segregation. The program went ahead.

In April, 1943, the first Tuskegee Airmen went to the Mediterranean theater of the war as the 99th Pursuit Squadron, under the command of Lieutenant Colonel Benjamin O. DAVIS, JR., a 1936 West Point graduate and the son of the first black general in the U.S. Army. The 99th was attached to the 33rd Fighter Group, commanded by Colonel William M. Momeyer, whose initial evaluation of the squadron was so negative that it almost provoked the closing of the Tuskegee program. Davis, however, appeared before the War Department's Committee on Special [Negro] Troops to defend his squadron and a War Department study found that the 99th was, in fact, an effective fighting unit.

In 1944 the 99th was followed by another group of Tuskegee Airmen, the 332nd Fighter Squadron, which also was placed under Davis' command. An African American bomber group, the 477th, was organized in late 1943, but its training was slow because of the limited facilities at the segregated Tuskegee airbase and it was not ready for combat until the combat had ended.

During their service, the Tuskegee Airmen achieved

Members of the first group of African American flyers to train at Tuskegee line up for review in early 1942. (AP/Wide World Photos)

an admirable fighting record. The 926 black pilots who earned their commissions at Tuskegee Army Air Field Base flew a total of 15,553 sorties. They escorted bombers, engaged in combat, and flew on a variety of other missions. They destroyed 111 enemy aircraft in the air and another 150 on the ground.

In 1972 a group of Tuskegee veterans formed Tuskegee Airmen, Inc., which sought to preserve ties among black veterans, to promote minority interests in aviation and aerospace activities, and to provide scholarships to students. This organization also operates the National Museum of Tuskegee Airmen in Historic Fort Wayne, Michigan.

SUGGESTED READINGS. Benjamin O. Davis, Jr., tells his own story in *American: An Autobiography* (1991). Readers can find more information on African American military contributions in *Strength for the Fight: A History of Black Americans in the Military* (1986) by Bernard C. Nalty. Pat McKissack's *Red Tail Angels: The Story of the Tuskegee Airmen in World War II* (1995) is a well-researched account for general readers. *Farewell to Jim Crow: The Rise and Fall of Segregation in America* (1997), a young adult book by R. Kent Rasmussen, discusses the Tuskegee Airmen in the fuller context of segregation in U.S. military history and in U.S. history generally.—*Carl L. Bankston III*

Tyson, Mike (b. Jun. 30, 1966, Brooklyn, N.Y.): African American heavyweight boxer. Tyson began boxing at the age of thirteen and went to the 1984 Olympics as an alternate on the U.S. boxing team. The following year he turned professional. At twenty he became the youngest heavyweight boxing champion in history by winning the World Boxing Council (WBC) title in 1986. A year later he became undisputed heavyweight champion of the world by adding the World Boxing Association (WBA) and International Boxing Federation (IBF) titles. After winning his first thirty-seven professional fights—including thirty-three by knockout—he lost his championship by knockout to James "Buster" Douglas in 1990, in what was then considered one of the greatest upsets in boxing history.

In early 1992 Tyson began serving a six-year prison sentence in Indiana after being convicted of raping a beauty pageant contestant. He was paroled in March, 1995, and returned to the ring. After winning several bouts he suffered his second professional defeat in 1996 to Evander Holyfield. In a rematch held in Las Vegas, Nevada, in mid-1997, Tyson was disqualified for biting off pieces of Holyfield's ears. The Nevada state boxing commission fined him 10 percent of his $30 million purse and revoked his license. The decision effectively made it impossible for Tyson to fight again in the United States until the commission reinstated him.—*Alvin K. Benson*

Former heavyweight champion Mike Tyson (right) throws a punch at reigning champion Evander Holyfield during the first round of their title fight in Las Vegas in November, 1996. (Reuters/Gary Heshorn/Archive Photos)

U

Undocumented persons: Noncitizens of the United States who enter, reside, or work in the United States without possessing the documents that enable them to do so legally. Enabling documents can include birth certificates or naturalization papers, which verify United States citizenship; visas permitting entry for tourism, business, or study; or residency permits—the so-called GREEN CARDS—which give holders the right to reside and be employed in the United States. Moreover, all legal residents need identification numbers—the social security or taxpayer identification numbers assigned by the federal government. Persons in the United States who lack these documents are considered to be violating the laws of the country and are commonly, though incor-rectly, referred to as "ILLEGAL ALIENS." Undocumented persons come from countries all over the world, includ-ing Asia, Europe, the Middle East, Latin America, the Caribbean, and Africa.—*Helen Jaskoski*

United Mine Workers of America (UMWA): Labor union representing coal miners and related workers in the United States and Canada. At a convention in Co-lumbus, Ohio, the Knights of Labor Trade Assembly No. 135 and the National Progressive Union of Miners and Mine Laborers merged to form the UMWA in 1890. The first constitution adopted by the union members stated that DISCRIMINATION based on race, religion, or national origin would not be tolerated. Although mine operators were violently opposed to their workers organizing, the UMWA grew steadily in membership during its early years of existence. In 1898 the union forced the operators to agree that the coal miners should work only eight-hour days.

From 1920 to 1960 the UMWA was led by the leg-endary figure of John L. Lewis. With Lewis at the helm, the union won col-lective bargaining rights in 1933 and health and retire-ment benefits in 1946. Af-ter Lewis' retirement, the UMWA lost focus and was inefficiently run for a number of years. The un-ion's membership reached 500,000 in 1946, but plum-meted to less than 200,000 by the early 1990's. During the 1990's the UMWA re-gained some of its lost glory by redoubling its efforts in the struggle for labor and human rights in North America.—*Jeffry Jensen*

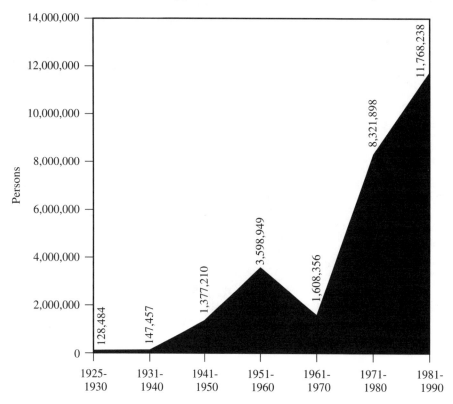

Undocumented Persons Apprehended in the United States, 1925-1990

Source: Allison Landes, ed., *Immigration and Illegal Aliens.* (Wylie, Tex.: Information Plus, 1991); Marlita A. Reddy, ed., *Statistical Record of Hispanic Americans* (Detroit: Gale Research, 1993).

News reporters converge on an informal press conference by a delegation at the United Nations Decade for Women Conference held in Nairobi in 1985. (United Nations Photo)

United Nations Decade for Women: In December, 1975, the General Assembly of the United Nations (U.N.) proclaimed the decade of 1976 to 1985 the United Nations Decade for Women. The objectives of this proclamation included formulation of international and national standards to eliminate discrimination against women, integrating women in economic development, and increasing the involvement of women in political life. In 1976 this declaration was followed by adoption of a program by the U.N. Commission on the Status of Women that provided a political stimulus for a variety of measures supportive of women that would continue well beyond the decade. Notable among U.N. activities were the sponsorship of international conferences on the status of women in Mexico City (1975); Copenhagen, Denmark (1980); and Nairobi, Kenya (1985); as well as the UNITED NATIONS FOURTH WORLD CONFERENCE ON WOMEN in Beijing, China (1995). The U.N. Educational, Scientific and Cultural organization (UNESCO) helped increase the literacy rate among women in the developing world from 36 percent to 55 percent by 1990.—*Joseph L. Nogee*

United Nations Fourth World Conference on Women (1995): Also known as the Beijing Conference because it was held in Beijing, China, this event was the fourth in a series of international meetings to improve the condition of women worldwide. Previous U.N. conferences on women met in Mexico City (1975), Copenhagen, Denmark (1980), and Nairobi, Kenya (1985). Approximately fifty thousand people—more than two thirds of whom were women—attended the Beijing Conference and related events in early September, 1995. They included nearly five thousand official delegates from 189 participating nations. A parallel, unofficial conference met in the city of Huairou, located thirty miles outside of Beijing. The Huairou conference attracted some thirty thousand participants representing nongovernmental organizations (NGOs).

Several aspects of the Beijing Conference were controversial, including its meeting in China, a nation whose record on human rights was widely considered to be poor. China welcomed the conference to boost its international prestige; however, the behavior of its security agents who tailed visitors, photographed gath-

Participants representing the world's different cultures hold up a peace torch at the opening of the U.N. World Conference on Women in Beijing in August, 1995. (AP/Wide World Photos)

erings, searched rooms and personal handbags, confiscated videotapes and documents, and limited peaceful protests proved damaging to its image. Many attending the NGO conference at Huairou were outraged by its inconvenient distance from Beijing and the poor accommodations provided for delegates.

Despite the logistical problems and interference by security officers, delegates to the Beijing Conference completed their work successfully by adopting the Beijing Declaration and Platform for Action. This document identified twelve critical areas that were obstacles to women's advancement and proposed a set of actions to be carried out by governments over a five-year period. These areas encompassed poverty, education, health, violence against women, armed con- flict, economic structures, power sharing and decision-making, mechanisms to promote the advancement of women, human rights, the media, the environment, and the female child.

Among the issues that drew particular attention at the conference was the need to protect women from violence, including the right to say no to sex. African delegates stressed that women should have the right to equal inheritance. Some issues were contentious. For example, a proposal calling for the elimination of DISCRIMINATION based on "sexual orientation" was dropped for lack of support. Among the activities criticized in the conference's platform were RAPE, forced pregnancy, ABORTION as a method of BIRTH CONTROL AND FAMILY PLANNING, religious extremism, ETHNIC CLEANSING, and all forms of discrimination against women.

Language in the platform calling for governments to establish guidelines to stop negative and potential harmful and exploitative MEDIA IMAGES OF WOMEN AND MINORITIES were criticized by some as potential threats to freedom of the press. Although the platform lacked the force of law, it was considered to be a politically important instrument to improve the status of women worldwide.

Famous women, such as First Lady Hillary Rodham CLINTON, Pakistani prime minister Benazir Bhutto, and future U.S. secretary of state Madeleine AL-BRIGHT, galvanized the conference with stirring speeches. Aung San Suu Kyi, the Burmese human rights activist and dissident, appeared at the conference in a specially recorded videotape that was smuggled out of Rangoon.

SUGGESTED READINGS. A concise but authoritative account of the Beijing conference is "Fourth World Conference on Women," *United Nations Chronicle* (Dec., 1995). An account of the conditions of the conference is James Walsh, "Spirit of Sisterhood," *Time* (Sept. 18, 1995). Texts and summaries of important speeches can be found in *U.S. Department of State Dispatch* 6, no. 36 (Sept. 4, 1995).—*Joseph L. Nogee*

United States v. Lopez (1995): U.S. Supreme Court decision restricting congressional authority over interstate commerce.

In 1990 Congress passed the Gun-Free School Zone Act, making carrying firearms near schools a federal crime; forty states already had similar laws. In 1992 Alfonso Lopez, Jr., a San Antonio, Texas, high school senior was arrested for taking a handgun to his school. Lopez was tried under federal law because the penalties were greater than under Texas law.

Lopez's defense team argued that the federal law under which he was charged was outside of the power of Congress over school boards. The federal district court disagreed, however, holding that Congress did have the power to regulate activities that affect interstate commerce. On appeal, the Court of Appeals for the Fifth Circuit reversed the decision and Lopez's conviction, ruling that the 1990 federal statute was unconstitutional. The court called it a "singular incursion by the federal government into territory long occupied by the states." The government then appealed the case to the U.S. Supreme Court, which voted 5-4 to uphold the appeals court decision, agreeing that the Gun-Free School Zone Act was unconstitutional.—*Sonia R. Garcia*

In the face of weak state gun-control laws, the U.S. Congress passed the Gun-Free School Zone Act to make it more difficult for students to acquire firearms they make take to school. (AP/Wide World Photos)

United Steelworkers: Labor union founded in 1936. Before the Great Depression of the 1930's little unionization had taken place in the steel industry of the United States. To take advantage of favorable new federal legislation, the newly formed CONGRESS OF INDUSTRIAL ORGANIZATIONS (CIO) created the Steel Workers Organizing Committee (SWOC) in 1936; six years later this body was the United Steelworkers of America. Meanwhile, membership in the new union reached 300,000 by mid-1937, and the largest steel-producing firm, United States Steel, agreed to recognize the union and bargain collectively. However, the smaller steel companies fought the union fiercely until 1941, when the National Labor Relations Board ordered them to recognize the union.

Under the leadership of Philip Murray, the United Steelworkers of America encouraged membership of African Americans and members of other minorities, and worked to improve benefits to unskilled workers. Not a militant or grassroots union, United Steelworkers encouraged peaceful collective bargaining. By 1980 the union had more than a million members. However, as technological changes and international competition reduced American steel production and employment in the industry, the union's membership fell to 565,000 in 1996.—*Paul B. Trescott*

United Steelworkers v. Weber (1979): U.S. Supreme Court case relating to AFFIRMATIVE ACTION. This case led to the Court's first decision concerning affirmative action programs for minorities in employment. Kaiser Aluminum Company had a training program to promote unskilled workers in craft positions. Although participation was mostly based on seniority, 50 percent of the positions were reserved for African American employees. Kaiser defended the policy as necessary to promote black workers because they generally had less seniority due to prior DISCRIMINATION. After Brian Weber, a white employee who applied to enter the program, was passed over in favor of black applicants with less seniority, he went to court arguing that racial preference was a violation of Title VII of the CIVIL RIGHTS ACT OF 1964. After his case reached the Supreme Court, the Court voted 7-2 to uphold the program, even though it appeared to violate the literal wording of the 1964 law. The Court reasoned that the spirit of the law was to help racial minorities gain equality, and that the program did not excessively trammel on the interests of white employees.—*Thomas T. Lewis*

V

Vatican II (1962-1965): Ecumenical council of the Roman Catholic Church. Regarded by many as the most significant religious event since the Protestant Reformation, this modern council had the largest number of participants and represented the most nations and cultures of any Church council in history. Nearly three thousand church leaders participated in the council and non-Roman Catholic Christian churches and communities sent delegates to observe the sessions and submit comments to the commissions.

Convinced that the Roman Catholic Church needed a "new Pentecost" or "aggionamento" (spiritual renewal), Pope John XXIII announced his plans for an ecumenical council shortly after his election to the papacy in 1958. Unlike previous councils, the council he planned would not be called to combat heresy or to deal with a serious threat to the Church's unity. Rather, this council would help the Church adapt to a new historical situation, revitalize it by redefining its doctrines, and open the way toward reunion with churches of the Eastern rite.

The death of Pope John in June, 1963, caused a suspension of the council, but his successor, Pope Paul VI, promised to continue it. The new pope invited additional non-Catholic Christian observers and even added women auditors to the council. He saw the council as serving to define more fully the role of the Church, to renew the Church, to restore unity among all Christians, and to begin a dialogue with the contemporary human race. In its four sessions the council enacted four constitutions (on the Church, divine revelation, liturgy, and the Church in the modern world), nine decrees (including decrees on ecumenism and the laity) and three declarations (on religious freedom, the Church's attitude toward non-Christian religions, and Christian education).

In his closing address on December 8, 1965, Pope Paul called the council "one of the greatest events in the history of the Church." One of its outstanding successes was in the area of ecumenism. Vatican II initiated a spirit of openness and dialogue without condemnation; indeed, it was the first council in Christian history to issue no condemnations. While admitting its own responsibility for the separation of the Christian Church into different sects, the Roman Catholic Church acknowledged that there were positive elements in all religions, thus advancing the unity of believers of various faiths. Internally, it redefined its hierarchical structure by using the metaphor of the Church as the People of God (including all Christians) and emphasizing the collegial role of its bishops. It also acknowledged that not all teachings of the Church are equally essential to the Catholic faith. One of its most observable results was to give the laity a more active role in the mission of the Church, in part by allowing the Mass to be said in non-Latin languages of parishioners.

SUGGESTED READINGS. The constitutions, decrees, and declarations of the council are collected in *Documents of Vatican II* (1966), edited by William M. Abbot. Bernard Häring, a participant at Vatican II, offers his reflections on the changes made to the Church as a result of the council in *The Road to Renewal* (1966). Christopher Hollis' *The Achievements of Vatican II* (1967) gives a behind-the-scenes look at both the achievements and the failures of each session of the council.—*Mara Kelly-Zukowski*

Vietnam War Memorial: Monument commemorating U.S. military personnel who served in the VIETNAM WAR. U.S. involvement in the Vietnam War lasted from 1961 to 1975, making it the longest war in U.S. history, and it cost 58,000 American lives.

Because the military draft affected minority communities disproportionately, more African Americans died in Vietnam than any other group. The divisive war helped to raise inflation in the United States, it exacerbated the generation gap, and it undermined President Lyndon B. Johnson's GREAT SOCIETY programs. Despite the war's great costs in lives, money, and public trust, the United States failed to achieve its stated political and military goals: to preserve a noncommunist government in South Vietnam. With the capitulation of Saigon to North Vietnamese troops in 1975, the war ended. One of the legacies of the war was an influx of Indochinese refugees into the United States.

Veterans returning to the United States from the war were regarded not as conquering heroes, but as symbols of the trauma and loss that Americans wanted to

The walls of the Vietnam War Memorial list the names of Americans who lost their lives in the war in the order in which they died; guidebooks at the site help visitors find where individual names appear. (James L. Shaffer)

forget. In 1979 Jan Scruggs, a veteran who had been wounded in Vietnam, conceived of the idea of building a national memorial inscribed with the name of every service person who died in Vietnam. He envisioned the memorial as a symbol of national reconciliation, bringing together bipartisan support as the nation would be honoring Vietnam War veterans without necessarily endorsing U.S. policy in the war. Although some initially laughed at his dream, eventually a number of volunteers, media spokespeople, veteran's organizations, and a bipartisan group of Republicans and Democrats worked to make sure that the memorial, financed by private contributions, was built in three and half years.

In 1980 President Jimmy Carter signed legislation designating two acres on Washington's Mall as the site for the memorial. That year the Vietnam Veteran Memorial Fund (VVMF) organized an open design competition; the following year a jury of prominent professionals in art and architecture selected Maya Ying Lin, a Chinese American undergraduate at Yale University, as the winner of the competition.

Lin's plan for the memorial was austere: It consisted of two polished black granite walls forming a V pattern, with one wall pointing toward the Washington Monument and the other toward the Lincoln Memorial. The names of the American soldiers who died in Vietnam were incised on the walls in the order in which they died. On November 13, 1982, the VVMF held an official ceremony to dedicate the wall. Previous to the dedication, the choice of the design excited controversy, some people desiring a grand figural monument, others voicing concern that an Asian American had been selected as the designer of the memorial. As a compromise, in 1984 a bronze flagpole and an eight-foot sculpture of three multiracial infantrymen, designed by Frederick Hart, was added to the site. Some have noted that the infantrymen seem to be searching for the names of their dead comrades inscribed on the walls—reminding Americans of the cost of all wars.

SUGGESTED READINGS. Jan C. Scruggs and Joel L.

Swerdlow's *To Heal a Nation: The Vietnam Veterans Memorial* (1985) provides a personal account of the building of the memorial. For a historical overview of the Vietnam War, see Stanley Karnow's *Vietnam: A History* (1983) and James S. Olson's *The Vietnam War: Handbook of the Literature and Research* (1993), which includes a section on minorities and the war. —*Sandra K. Stanley*

Vietnam Women's Memorial (1993): The first Washington, D.C., memorial paying homage to women who served the United States in wartime, the Vietnam Women's Memorial honors American women in the VIETNAM WAR. The memorial is a six-foot, eight-inch-tall bronze sculpture made by Glenna Goodacre; it portrays three women, one of whom is tending a wounded male soldier. It stands in the Washington Mall, near Maya Ying LIN's VIETNAM WAR MEMORIAL, and is surrounded by eight trees planted to commemorate the eight American servicewomen who died in Vietnam. The memorial was dedicated on November 11, 1993, before a crowd of 25,000 people.

The memorial was authorized and funded by the U.S. Congress in 1988. Government authorization owed much to the tireless efforts of Diane Carlson Evans, a former Army nurse who had launched the Vietnam Women's Memorial Project four years earlier and relentlessly lobbied the government with the help of many volunteers.—*Jeffry Jensen*

Violence Against Women Act (1994): U.S. federal legislation passed to reduce violence against women. Also known as Title IV of the Violent Crime Control and Law Enforcement Act of 1994, this legislation authorized use of federal resources to provide nationwide protection for victims of DOMESTIC VIOLENCE and sexual assault. Stricter enforcement of laws and penalties for domestic abusers at local, state, and national levels were key aspects of the act. The act prohibited possession of firearms by domestic offenders and punished abusers who crossed state lines. Victims of gender-motivated violence were permitted to sue offenders for damages and financial restitution. Provisions for a National Domestic Violence Hotline in various languages, increased

After being wounded in a bomb explosion in a Vietnam hotel, these nurses were the first American women to receive Purple Heart medals in the Vietnam War. (AP/Wide World Photos)

funding for shelters for BATTERED WOMEN, and federal grants for law enforcement training programs were implemented. Federal guidelines were also passed to encourage states to institute registration systems for convicted child molesters and sexual offenders.—*Phyllis M. Jones-Shuler*

Voting Accessibility for the Elderly and Handicapped Act (1984): U.S. federal VOTING RIGHTS legislation designed to improve access to polling places for OLDER AMERICANS and citizens with disabilities. Endorsed by disability-rights and elderly-rights groups and signed into law by President Ronald Reagan on September 28, 1984, the act required states to ensure that all federal polling places are made accessible to older voters and those with disabilities. The law also required states lacking provisions to register voters by mail or by door-to-door registration drives to provide registration sites easily accessible to older persons and those with disabilities.—*Glenn Canyon*

Voting Rights Act of 1970: U.S. federal legislation banning LITERACY TESTING as a qualification for VOTING RIGHTS. The federal VOTING RIGHTS ACT OF 1965 banned voting tests only in states where voter turnout fell below 50 percent of those eligible to vote. Elsewhere, many members of minority groups were still denied the right to vote unless they passed literacy tests, which were often unfairly administered. Accordingly, the Voting Rights Act of 1970 amended the 1965 statute by prohibiting literacy tests for persons wishing to register to vote anywhere in the United States.

The 1970 law had two other notable provisions. It lowered the minimum age for voting from twenty-one to eighteen years and it abolished state residency requirements for voting in federal elections. After Congress passed this law the U.S. Supreme Court ruled, in *Oregon v. Mitchell* (1970), that Congress had no power to lower the voting age for state and local elections, but could do so for federal elections. Within a year Congress and state legislatures responded by ratifying the Twenty-sixth Amendment to the Constitution, which uniformly lowered the voting age to eighteen for all voting districts in the United States. —*Michael Haas*

Voting Rights Act of 1975: U.S. federal legislation expanding provisions of the VOTING RIGHTS ACT OF 1965. Before 1975 most congressional efforts to protect VOTING RIGHTS were designed primarily to address the needs of African Americans. The Voting Rights Act of 1975 continued this trend by extending the scope of federal voting rights law to reach discrimination occurring in more than sixty political subdivisions. The law was also written to address the needs of other minorities, such as American Indians and Spanish-speaking Americans.

Millions of Americans with limited English-speaking ability—whether born in the United States or abroad—remained unable to vote effectively because they could not read their ballots or locate their polling stations. The Voting Rights Act of 1975 expressly banned literacy tests and expanded coverage of the original voting rights act to jurisdictions with significant disadvantaged language minorities. The law provided that voting instructions and materials should be available in all languages spoken by at least 5 percent of the population in a voting district, provided that more than half of the persons speaking the language in that district had completed fewer than six grades of education. —*Michael Haas*

Voting Rights Act of 1982: U.S. federal legislation expanding key provisions of the VOTING RIGHTS ACT OF 1965. Congress passed this legislation largely in response to the U.S. Supreme Court's decision in *City of Mobile v. Bolden* (1980), in which the Court held that an *intent* to discriminate had to be shown in voting rights litigation attempting to overcome attempts to dilute the voting power of minority groups. The 1982 act expanded the provisions of the original act of 1965 by stating that the existence of discriminatory rules was enough to substantiate claims of vote dilution.

The 1982 law also added a new protected class to existing voting rights legislation: citizens who require assistance at polling places because they are illiterate, blind, or impaired by other physical disabilities. The law authorized such citizens to bring into the polls persons to assist them in voting.—*Christopher E. Kent*

Wards Cove Packing Co. v. Atonio (1989): Landmark U.S. Supreme Court decision concerning DISCRIMINATION in EMPLOYMENT. The case originated when Frank Atonio and twenty-one other Native Alaskan and Filipino American seasonal employees of Alaskan salmon canneries owned by Wards Cove Packing Company and Castle and Cooke brought suit charging that they had been illegally "disparately impacted" by the canneries' hiring and promotion policies. They alleged that a large proportion of employees like themselves were assigned to unskilled, low-wage jobs at the canneries and that only a few of their number ever made it into the higher echelons. On June 5, 1989, the Court ruled that the plaintiffs had failed to make a persuasive case of conscious racial discrimination. Moreover, the Court ruled that in future disparate impact cases, plaintiffs, rather than defendants, would have the burden of proof, and that employers could counter with a "business necessity" defense. Congress responded to this Court decision by passing the CIVIL RIGHTS ACT OF 1991, which reversed both of the Court's rulings in *Wards Cove Packing.—Lisa Paddock*

Washington Urban League v. Washington Metropolitan Area Transit (1973): Landmark court decision concerning the right of disabled people to have access to public transportation. The decision in *Washington Urban League* resulted in a prohibition that forbade the District of Columbia's new public transportation system to operate until all its facilities were made accessible to persons with disabilities. The case marked one of the first times in U.S. history that operation of a public facility was delayed because of a lack of provisions for persons with disabilities.—*Alexander Scott*

Webster v. Reproductive Health Services (1989): U.S. Supreme Court decision on ABORTION. This important decision had contradictory implications. While it reaffirmed the ROE V. WADE decision's basic principle that women had a right to abortion, it also expanded the power of the individual states to place restrictions on abortion.

The case originated in Missouri, where a group of health care professionals brought suit against a 1986 state statute that banned the use of state property for abortions and required that physicians test all fetuses at least twenty weeks into gestation in order to determine their viability outside the womb. After their case went through district and appeals courts, it reached the U.S. Supreme Court. On July 3, 1989, the Court handed down a complex decision.

By a 5-4 vote, the Supreme Court upheld Missouri's law. Four of the five justices in the majority thought that their ruling either overturned or fundamentally altered *Roe*. However, the fifth justice, Sandra Day O'CONNOR, disagreed. She voted with the other four justices to uphold *Roe*.

The net result of the complex decision was preservation of *Roe*'s basic right to abortion through the first two trimesters of pregnancy, with recognition that states had new leeway to regulate abortions during the

Norma McCorvey—the "Jane Roe" of the 1973 Roe v. Wade *decision—spoke out in 1989 against court decisions such as* Webster v. Reproductive Health Services *that eroded the abortion rights gains of* Roe. *In later years, however, she regretted her earlier support of abortion.* (AP/Wide World Photos)

third trimester. Afterward other states passed laws similar to Missouri's that included such requirements as parental notification for minors wishing abortions.

In the wake of the *Webster* decision, abortion foes and pro-choice advocates alike viewed *Webster* as a prelude to overturning *Roe*. Afterward, however, new coalitions formed among the justices, and the Court retreated from its aggressive assault on legalized abortion.—*Lisa Paddock*

Weeks v. Southern Bell

Weeks v. Southern Bell (1969): U.S. federal court decision regarding SEXUAL DISCRIMINATION in employment. In 1966, after a woman named Lorena Weeks had been an employee of Southern Bell Telephone for nineteen years, she applied for promotion to a switchman's job but was notified by the company that women were not being considered for the position. She then filed a charge with the federal EQUAL EMPLOYMENT OPPORTUNITY COMMISSION complaining that Southern Bell was discriminating against her because of her sex. When her suit came to trial, the federal district court ruled against her, holding that the job of switchman was "strenuous," requiring the routine lifting of thirty-pound electronic testing equipment that disqualified women from holding the job. However, the U.S. Court of Appeals for the Fifth Circuit reversed the lower court's decision, holding that a generalized finding that a job is "strenuous" may not be used as a pretext to disqualify all women from a particular kind of job. Individual, rather than assumptions about group abilities, had to be the test of employability.—*Robert Jacobs*

Welfare system and reform

Welfare system and reform: The term "welfare" has come to be closely associated with the government's giving monetary assistance to persons in need. The question of who is "in need" has elicited multiple answers. Those in need are most often understood to be persons who are poor enough to be living near or below the POVERTY line. In their cases, welfare simply constitutes a transfer of monetary assistance from those able to pay taxes to those who cannot. Government welfare programs in the United States have included AID TO FAMILIES WITH DEPENDENT CHILDREN, Medicaid, FOOD STAMPS, subsidized housing, and others.

The Intention of Welfare. Government welfare programs generally begin by recognizing that some persons are so poor they cannot purchase the essentials of life. The short-term goal of such programs is to protect beneficiaries from starvation; the long-term goal is enable people permanently to escape from their poverty. The money given to the poor must come from those in society who are not poor. Those who are not poor can either give money to the poor voluntarily through charity, or the government can use its taxing powers to redistribute the money through welfare programs. Welfare options are adopted when it is believed charity will be insufficient.

Welfare Controversies. In the United States modern experiments with government welfare programs began in earnest in 1965, when President Lyndon B. Johnson launched the WAR ON POVERTY. Over the next three decades all levels of government spent increasing amounts of money on various types of welfare programs. Between 1965 and 1993 the total amount of American government spending on welfare was roughly $3.5 trillion. Controversy over welfare spending increased in the mid-1980's and early 1990's as analysts recognized that, despite all the money spent, the problem of poverty was not being solved. In many cases, it seemed, the problem of the poor was even more entrenched. This led to a vigorous discussion of whether the welfare system was indeed failing, and if so whether that was because the welfare system needed to be made more effective or, more radically, because it was a wrongly conceived method of fighting poverty.

A premise of the welfare system was that money could solve the problems of poverty. Accordingly, the more money spent on welfare, the more quickly the problem of poverty should be solved. This reasoning suggests a method of testing the effectiveness of government welfare spending: Comparing the poverty rate before 1965, when relatively little was spent on welfare, to the rate after 1965, when large amounts were spent. Between 1950 and 1965 the poverty rate was declining steadily. In 1950 roughly 45 million people in the United States were regarded as living under the poverty line. By 1965 that number had declined to about 30 million people. Between 1965 and 1980, however, the poverty rate remained essentially unchanged. In 1967 about 25 million people lived under the poverty line; in 1972 the number was about 24 million; in 1977 it was about 26 million. By 1980 the number had crept up to about 29 million. Despite rapid increases in the rate of welfare spending between 1965 and 1980, no apparent progress was made in combating poverty.

These figures suggest two controversial hypotheses that have been at the heart of discussions of welfare reform. First, the money spent on welfare was inef-

An Iowa woman discusses her benefits with a state welfare officer. (James L. Shaffer)

fective in solving the problem of poverty because essentially the same number of people were living below the poverty line in 1980 as in 1965. Second, the money spent on welfare may have made the problem of poverty worse; the downward trend in the poverty rate prior to 1965 was halted after the introduction of increased spending on welfare.

Questions of Welfare Reform. Discussions of welfare reform have focused on rethinking welfare by posing basic questions. The first questions would be about the nature of the problem that the government is trying to solve: Who are the poor and how did they come to be poor? Here the controversy is about whether the poor are poor because of their own behavior or because they are victims of forces beyond their control. Some persons clearly fall into one category or the other: Some poor people are poor because

of bad choices they have made; others are poor because they have had bad luck. Within each category are subcategories. Some people remain in poverty only temporarily; they escape from poverty fairly quickly, either through their own efforts or because of temporary assistance from charity or welfare. Some poor people, however, because of bad choices or bad luck, remain poor chronically. Some of these suffer from severe physical or mental handicaps, while others are chronically poor because of their habits or character.

A second set of questions pertains to who is responsible for solving the problems of poverty: Is it primarily the responsibility of the poor themselves, or is it primarily society's responsibility? To the extent the poor are viewed as in control of their characters and actions, self-help and self-responsibility are seen as solutions. By contrast, the extent to which the condition of the poor is viewed as shaped by forces beyond their control—such as physical disabilities, discrimination, or economic dislocations—the responsibility for improving their condition will fall on others in society. As society's agent, government will then assume control of the destiny of the poor.

A final set of questions relates to what welfare achieves: Does it effectively give to the poor what they need? If the cause of poverty is a lack of money, does the welfare system efficiently redistribute money to those who lack it? If the solution to poverty is self-responsibility, does the welfare system foster self-responsibility? And if the current system seems not to be effective, is the proper direction of reform to expand the system, to make it more efficient, or to abolish it?

Analysts of the modern welfare system fall into three broad categories—conservative, libertarian, and liberal—depending on how they answer the above series of questions.

Conservative Views. Conservatives have argued a two-fold strategy against the modern welfare system. One part of their strategy has been to argue that despite the best of intentions, all welfare programs necessarily have unintended destructive consequences. The other part of the strategy is to argue that welfare programs would be much more efficient if they were administered locally rather than nationally.

Conservatives have argued that the intent of welfare is to help decent people though tough times. Decent people are self-responsible; they accept that they must be financially independent and must work to support themselves and their families. Moreover, decent people cultivate in themselves the habits of hard work and perseverance; if they meet with failure they will reorient themselves and try again. When decent people encounter bad luck and become destitute, the welfare system can provide them with a safety net—a temporary helping hand while they get back on their feet.

However, conservatives have pointed out that the very existence of welfare programs might encourage

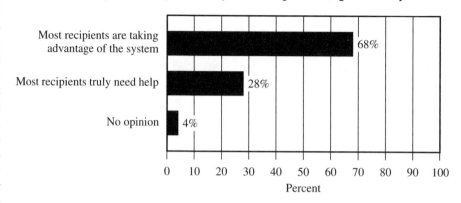

U.S. Public Opinion on Welfare Recipients

In 1994 the Gallup Poll asked a cross section of Americans if most people on welfare truly need help, or if they are taking advantage of the system.

Most recipients are taking advantage of the system: 68%
Most recipients truly need help: 28%
No opinion: 4%

Source: George Gallup, Jr., ed., *The Gallup Poll: Public Opinion, 1994* (Wilmington, Del.: Scholarly Resources, 1995).

otherwise decent people to abandon the habits and attitudes that lead to financial independence and instead encourage habits that lead to chronic dependence. Unskilled workers earning twelve thousand dollars per year may be punctual, hard-working, and accustomed to being self-supporting. However, if they lose their jobs and go on welfare that pays them ten thousand dollars per year for doing nothing, they may naturally wonder if it is worth it to get up in the morning, five days a week, fifty weeks a year, to go to work for an additional two thousand dollars per year. For many such persons the answer will be no. The existence of welfare can, therefore, lower the incentive of individuals to be self-responsible and to cultivate the habits that lead to financial independence. According to conservatives, welfare increases the number of dependent individuals, actually making the problem of poverty worse.

Pregnant, unwed teenage girls are primary targets for welfare programs because their financial position is so difficult. They not only are less likely to have much job experience or marketable skills, they must also support the children they will bear. Their economic plight makes many people wish to help them; however, some conservatives have argued that the existence of welfare programs changes their incentives. Knowing they can collect welfare money will make some young women less careful to avoid pregnancy. Moreover, young men may be less apt to avoid impregnating their girlfriends if they feel less concerned about their own responsibility for supporting the children for whom they are responsible. Thus, the unintended results of welfare for pregnant teenagers will be increases in teen pregnancy and increases in single parenting. Since single parents are less likely to be financially independent, the overall problems of poverty are made worse, not better.

The second part of the conservative analysis is to favor making welfare a local, rather than federal, responsibility. Local welfare programs, they argue, will be much more efficient for a number of reasons. Factors that contribute to poverty differ from community to community, and local officials are more likely than federal officials to understand local problems. Nationally administered programs, by contrast, are more likely to be one-size-fits-all programs that do not take into account local differences.

Conservatives also argue that locally administered welfare programs will generate more experimentation than national programs. Some local experiments will work better than others, but with more experiments going on, what does and does not work will be discovered more quickly than programs designed at the national level. Locally administered programs can be more flexible. If an approach to welfare is not working, local programs will be quicker to abandon it and try another. Finally, if welfare is a local matter, members of local communities are more likely to contribute money, time, and ideas to solving community problems. By contrast, if welfare is administered nationally, people are more likely to see poverty as a more distant problem and be less generous.

Libertarian Views. Libertarians have tended to agree with conservative critiques of the current welfare system, while adding a more radical moral critique of the premise of government welfare. Libertarians argue that individuals should be free to do with their lives and property whatever they want, so long as they respect the rights of others to do the same. Individuals should be self-responsible and self-supporting and not be forced to support other individuals. To libertarians, forcing one person to support another is akin to enslavement. They see the purpose of government as primarily to protect individuals' rights to their own lives, liberty, and property. The government is an institution that uses force to achieve its ends, and libertarians believe that force should only be used against those who violate other individuals' rights. Unless people have violated the rights of others, they should be dealt with peaceably and noncoercively.

Libertarians see welfare programs as government efforts to forcibly redistribute wealth. By levying taxes for welfare, while supported by its police power, the government uses force against individuals who have not violated anyone else's rights. Thus, libertarians conclude, welfare is a fundamentally immoral program. They propose that government welfare be abolished and that helping the poor be solely a function of private charity by individuals and organizations. Private charity, they argue, is not only more moral but more likely to be effective. If government welfare is abolished, taxes will go down, leaving citizens more money to invest and spend. If there is more investment and spending, then the economy will improve and there will be more jobs for poor people. Also, if taxes are lower and the economy improves, people will be more likely to give to charities. Moreover, if they do not feel they are being forced by the government to support the poor, they will be more likely to want to help them.

Liberal Views. The liberal analysis of welfare has differed markedly from both the conservative and libertarian views. Liberals have tended to argue that most of the poor are poor through no fault of their own. They may be victims of severe physical or mental disabilities; they may have been raised in dysfunctional families or have been deprived of educational opportunities; they may have been victims of changing economic circumstances, losing their jobs because their employers have gone bankrupt or their skills have been made obsolete by advances in technology.

Accordingly, liberals argue that expecting the poor to solve their own problems is both naïve and dangerous. Too few of the poor are able to behave in the independent and self-responsible way that conservatives and libertarians expect. The poor need help, and it is society's obligation to provide it, with government leading the way. Rather than scale back or eliminate the welfare system, liberals would like to see the current system become more effective. Welfare systems could be made more effective by doing a better job of identifying the poor and their particular problems—whether they be cyclical employment, changing job skills, drug addiction, teen pregnancy, or physical disabilities.

Liberals have pointed out that in many cases desperately poor people drop through the cracks of welfare systems because they are unaware of their options or because there are not enough social workers to identify those needing help. Accordingly, increasing staffing and education are necessary. In many cases the poor lack up-to-date job skills. Accordingly, more job training programs are necessary. In many cases, the poor are dispirited or have turned to drugs or alcohol for consolation. Accordingly, government programs must step up counseling and rehabilitation efforts. In many cases, employers cannot afford to hire more workers to perform unskilled jobs. Accordingly, the government needs to consider increasing wage subsidies, especially to employers who hire unskilled workers.

Liberals have argued that government welfare must remain at the forefront. Private charity is not a sufficient option, since there is no guarantee that people will voluntarily be generous enough. Nor can the economy be expected to generate enough jobs for all those who want to work. The free market economy is marked by constant change and innovation, and these changes inevitably throw some people out of work with no resources.

Some liberals have agreed with conservatives that making welfare a local rather than national government matter may increase efficiency. However, they have also argued that doing so brings additional risks of inequalities that may end up hurting the poor more. For example, if one state were to abolish welfare while a neighboring state did not, there would likely be a movement of welfare recipients from the first state to the second. This influx of welfare recipients in the second state would increase the strain on its welfare system, bringing yet another set of new problems.

SUGGESTED READINGS. As an examination of poverty in the United States, Michael Harrington's *The Other America* (1971) has become a modern classic. *The Unheavenly City: The Nature and Future of Our Urban Crisis* (1970), by Edward Banfield, examines the special problems of American cities. *The Mean Season: The Attack on the Welfare State* (1987), by Fred Block, Richard A. Cloward, Barbara Ehrenreich, and Frances Fox Piven, examines the welfare controversy from several perspectives.—*Stephen R. C. Hicks*

West, Cornel (b. June 2, 1953, Tulsa, Okla.): American social critic and educator. Born to a middle-class African American family, West was drawn to both intellectual pursuits and political activism at an early age. His parents encouraged his interests, and he was educated at Harvard and Princeton. He later taught at Yale, but moved to Princeton in 1986 to become director of its African American studies department because of Yale's failure to divest itself of South African investments. He has

also been a professor of the philosophy of religion at Harvard and taught and lectured at many leading universities and colleges. His other activities have included honorary co-chairmanship of the Democratic Socialists of America.

West's writings have drawn together many disparate streams of thought, including such seemingly contradictory elements as Christianity and Marxism. The resulting synthesis has been an egalitarian socioeconomic morality informed by intercultural and interracial objectivity. His commentaries on race relations include the best-selling, controversial *Race Matters* (1993). His other books include *Prophesy Deliverance!: An Afro-American Revolutionary Christianity* (1982) and *The Ethical Dimensions of Marxist Thought* (1991).—*Alice Myers*

West Indian culture: Twentieth century West Indian migration to United States and Great Britain might suggest to some that Caribbean immigrants are a unified community because of their common Caribbean heritage and certain outward physical similarities. However, these commonalities mask the great diversity of West Indian communities, the many different customs, ideas and attitudes reflecting geographical differences and origins.

The first American territories settled by Europeans at the end of the fifteenth century were the islands of the Caribbean, which also became known as the West Indies because of Christopher Columbus' mistaken belief that he had reached the Indies of the Far East. Columbus named the Caribbean's largest string of islands the Antilles after a fabled land of the Indies. As Europeans colonized the West Indies, they introduced their own cultures among those of the native Carib and Arawak peoples.

Wars of conquest and Old World diseases—against which native islanders Americans had no natural immunity virtually exterminated the Native Caribbean peoples. To fill their growing labor needs, Europeans began importing Africans to work in SLAVERY on the islands. People of African descent eventually formed majorities on most of the islands. By the mid-nineteenth century, slavery was legally abolished throughout the Caribbean. The loss of their cheap labor supply caused many Europeans to return home, raising the proportion of West Indian residents who were black to about 90 percent; however, indentured Chinese and East Indian workers were brought in, thereby introducing Asian elements to Caribbean culture—particu-

A Jamaican American family poses in the family's Brooklyn shoe repair shop. (Hazel Hankin)

larly in Trinidad. The various ethnic populations of the islands tended to keep their own cultures, adopting both useful improvements and bad habits from a succession of European rulers.

The Greater Antilles island chain, which begins near the tip of Florida, includes the Republic of Cuba. Cuba was under Spanish rule until the SPANISH-AMERICAN WAR of 1898, in which the United States helped it to become independent. Cuba has been under communist rule since 1959, when Fidel Castro led a successful revolution. A U.S. embargo initiated in 1960 depressed Cuban trade and trade. During the 1980's many African Cubans began coming to the United States.

The Commonwealth of Puerto Rico, a U.S. territory since the Spanish-American War, has been influenced by its past political and family ties with Spain and its twentieth centuries ties with the United States, where many Puerto Ricans have resettled. The architecture of Puerto Rico reflects African and Spanish influences, which can be seen in dwellings with wide terraces and enclosed courtyards. By the late twentieth century residents of Puerto Rico were debating whether they should continue their special commonwealth status, or opt for statehood or independence.

The island of Hispaniola is shared by French-influenced Haiti, which became the world's first black republic in 1804 under Toussaint L'Ouverture, and the Dominican Republic, a former Spanish colony that has become the largest Caribbean democracy. Since the Dominican Republica declared its independence from Haiti in the nineteenth century, relations between the two independent countries have ranged from strained to openly hostile.

Haitian folk art was created out of a mix of Native Caribbean and African elements, strongly influenced by the country's great poverty. A particular vivid influence has been surviving figures hand-drawn by ancient cave dwellers. Peasant patois and Creole languages add spice to the country's official language, French, which is spoken by only a minority of Haitians. Haitian Christianity is tempered by infusions of West African Voodoo and Native Caribbean rituals.

Haiti has had a long history of authoritarian governments, which continued after the dictator Jean Claude Baby "Doc" Duvalier was ousted in 1986. Jean-Bertrand Aristide was democratically elected president of Haiti, but he had to flee the country after a military coup in 1991. Three years later pressure from the United States restored him to power.

Jamaica, a former British colony, is the birthplace of Marcus GARVEY, an early proponent of American BLACK NATIONALISM and founder of the UNIVERSAL NEGRO IMPROVEMENT ASSOCIATION (UNIA). Another Jamaican, poet and novelist Claude McKay, made notable contributions to the HARLEM RENAISSANCE. Singer Bob Marley, a Rastafarian and outspoken exponent of freedom, helped to popularize reggae music in the United States.

The Lesser Antilles. The smaller islands that continue the arc of islands begun by the Greater Antilles stretching east to the northern coast of South America are the Lesser Antilles. Just east of Puerto Rico, the British and U.S. Virgin Islands begin the group's Leeward Islands. Sharing the island of St. Martin are the French and Dutch dependencies of St. Martin and Saint Maarten. To the south are Antigua and Barbuda—a former slave-breeding center that has become a parliamentary democracy.

The future of Montserrat, another British territory with a crown-appointed governor, came into question in mid-1997, when the eruption of the island's massive volcano threatened to make the island permanently uninhabitable. St. Christopher (also known as St. Kitts) was first a British Caribbean colony; together with nearby Nevis, it has become totally independent. Guadeloupe, an overseas department of France, is the last of the Leeward Islands.

Beginning at independent Dominica, a former British colony, the Windward Islands continue the chain of the Lesser Antilles. An example of the volatile political and complex cultural history of the Caribbean, the island of St. Lucia changed colonial rulers thirteen times before it became an independent parliamentary democracy. Though the island nation is minuscule, it produced poet and playwright Derek Walcott, who was awarded a Nobel Prize for Literature in 1992.

St. Vincent and the Grenadines islands, whose histories have been disrupted by volcanos, Carib resistance, French and British colonization, and forcible relocation to Belize—have become independent states within the Commonwealth. The French dependency of Martinique was one of the last Carib-occupied islands

Shirley Chisholm, the first African American woman elected to the U.S. Congress, was the child of West Indian immigrants and she spent seven years of early childhood living with her grandmother in Barbados. (Library of Congress)

to resist Europeans. Martinique produced the poet Aimé Cesairé, one the founders of the worldwide NEGRITUDE MOVEMENT, which culturally reunited West Indians and Africans.

Barbados, the most densely populated Caribbean island, produced the Caribbean American novelist Paule Marshall and the first black U.S. congresswoman, Shirley CHISHOLM. The islands of Trinidad and Tobago, which together form an independent republic, are extensions of a submerged South American mountain range. Home to the largest Asian population in the Caribbean, Trinidad and Tobago have a culture noted for its calypso music, limbo dancing, and steel band music featured in colorful carnivals and festivals.

The last islands in the Caribbean circle and part of the Netherlands Antilles off South America's coast, Aruba, Bonaire, and Curacao, depend on income from oil refining and tourism. Aruba was granted independence in 1996.

Modern Legacy. Modern technology has added new dimensions to cultural change in Caribbean. Foreign corporations invest heavily in profitable agricultural goods, and a multibillion-dollar tourism industry has created new jobs for islanders. Like their forebears, however, many West Indians have continued to pursue employment opportunities outside of the Caribbean, taking their cultural heritage to other countries and people.

Suggested Readings. Two useful surveys of the Caribbean nations are *The Modern Caribbean* (1989), edited by Franklin W. Knight and Colin A. Palmer, and *A Brief History of the Caribbean: From the Arawak and the Carib to the Present* (1992), by Jan Rogozinski. As a case study in the history of a typical Caribbean nation, *The Making of a Transnational Community: Migration, Development, and Cultural Change in the Dominican Republic* (1990), by Eugenia Georges, is useful.—*Adolph Dupree*

White Paper of Canada (1969): Canadian federal government position paper on Native Canadian peoples. Officially called the "Statement of the government of Canada on Indian Policy," this government document called for an abrupt change in the way the government was to interact with Indians, Inuits, and Métis peoples. It took as its premise that the existing pattern of government policy—treating Native Canadians as wards of the state—was responsible for their grossly unequal and dependent status. The solution offered in the White Paper was to abolish the federal government's Department of Indian Affairs and Northern Development (DIAND) so that Native Canadians could be treated as any other citizens.

After the paper's publication, however, government officials were shocked at public reactions. Native Canadian groups agreed with the White Paper's assessment of existing problems but protested that the new policies it proposed were genocidal. Abolition of the DIAND would have meant the end of all government treaty obligations to native peoples, including health care and food and housing allotments. In 1970, the year after the White Paper was released, it was shelved and its proposals were never realized. Its most important legacy was the increased Native Canadian activism that it generated.—*Gretchen L. Green*

White Ribbon Campaign: Canadian antiviolence movement. The White Ribbon Campaign was created to commemorate the deaths of fourteen women who were shot to death in 1989 at Montreal's University of Quebec during a rampage by a disturbed gunman. The gunman, Marc Lepine, killed himself, leaving a suicide note expressing rage against women. The tragedy inspired a nationwide wave of protests against misogyny and violence against women. The campaign was founded as a national effort to remind the public of the incident and its significance; participants wear emblematic white lapel ribbons.—*Christopher E. Kent*

White supremacist movements: Alliances of people asserting their white Aryan descent, collectively subscribing to the ideology that their race is superior to others. White supremacists argue that because the Aryan race is endangered by nonwhite peoples, it must be defended; to achieve this end, they have targeted nonwhite peoples and carried out such violent hate crimes cross-burnings, church burnings, physical and verbal attacks, and other acts of intimidation. African Americans were long the primary targets of white supremacist violence, but members of other nonwhite minorities were increasingly targeted, as well, during the 1990's.

The Ku Klux Klan. The first major American white supremacist group was the Ku Klux Klan (KKK), which was first organized in 1865 in Pulaski, Tennessee. Initially composed mainly of disgruntled former Confederate soldiers who played pranks on the public for entertainment, the Klan evolved into a more serious movement, dedicated to terrorizing African Americans during Reconstruction and adopting a hierarchal quasi-military structure. When Klan members began using violence to intimidate black voters during the 1868 presidential election, Klan leader Nathan Bedford Forrest called for the organization's disbandment but was ignored. Klan violence moved President Ulysses S. Grant to send federal troops into the South to protect African Americans. Government action weakened the Klan's organization through the rest of the nineteenth century, but the group's racial ideology remained the philosophy of many white Americans into the twentieth century, when it periodically resurfaced as a component of new white supremacy movements. During the twentieth century white supremacist organizations arising from the original Klan included the United Klans of America and the Knights of the Ku Klux Klan (to which Louisiana state representative David Duke belonged).

Modern Nativism. Closely related to white supremacist beliefs was white American nativism, which might best be described as an attitude that opposed all things foreign. This belief was expressed in fear and hatred of immigrants, demands to close the U.S. borders, and demands for strict adherence to the literal words of the U.S. Constitution. A manifestation of this ideology was the myth of the international Jewish conspiracy—the belief that Jews have been trying to take over the world by controlling its international economy.

Another group advocating racial ideologies that formed during the early twentieth century was the Silver Shirts. Founded in 1933, when Adolf Hitler came to power in Germany, its avowed goal was to expose Jesus Christ's supposed militant beliefs while supporting Hitler and his anti-Semitic views. The ultra-right-wing John Birch Society, founded in 1958, professed

Tom Metzger (standing) and his son, John Metzger, on trial in Oregon, where in 1990 they defended themselves against the charge of inciting the bludgeoning death of an Ethiopian man by skinheads. (AP/Wide World Photos)

as its goal saving the Aryan race from international communism, a manifestation of which its leaders saw in the CIVIL RIGHTS MOVEMENT. The Minutemen, an underground army founded during the 1960's, was another white supremacist body devoted to combatting communism.

Many other white supremacist resurgences were violent white reactions to the Civil Rights movement of the 1960's. A public relations campaign led by David Duke during the 1970's and movements that began during the 1980's continuing through the 1990's entailed more expansive forms of outrage against all nonwhites.

Other white supremacist groups have emerged as manifestations of CHRISTIAN EXTREMISM, particularly in what has been called the "Christianity Identity" movement, whose members believe that Anglo-Saxons are God's chosen people. The Church of Jesus Christ Christian, for example, a Christian Identity body led by Wesley Swift, was a meeting point for men wanting to become leaders of the far-right political movement. It attracted Richard Butler—a former member of the Klan—Silver Shirts, and Posse Comitatus, who formed Aryan Nations in Hayden Lake, Idaho during the 1970's.

Members of the Posse Comitatus, formed in Portland, Oregon, during the 1960's, expressed their dislike for big government. They saw sheriffs as the highest power in local communities because they were not directly controlled by federal or state governments. They also subscribed to the ideology of nativism, asserting that the United States need not be so involved in world affairs. Posse ideology was particularly popular among bankrupted midwestern farmers, who had been hurt by high government-dictated interest rates and decreased land values.

White supremacist movements have varied in size and longevity, but only relatively minor ideological changes have separated different groups. The 1990's continued movement traditions with such new manifestations of white supremacism as SKINHEADS, the Order (a derivative of Aryan Nations), the American Nazi Party, NEO-NAZIS, the Populist Party, and the White Aryan Resistance. Mostly founded after 1980, these organizations have thrived in the United States.

Although a significant number of members

of so-called MILITIA groups follow the same religious beliefs as white supremacists, not all of them accept white supremacist ideology; their dominant ideology is opposition to big government. According to a study published in 1997, some white supremacist groups were losing members to militia groups. The different ideological bent of militia groups has made them somewhat more acceptable than white supremacist groups to mainstream Americans.

Religion. Concepts such as an "international Jewish Conspiracy," nativism, and fearing a New World Order are indications of how white supremacist religious thinking has often coincided with Christian Identity doctrine. Identity members belong to nondenominational churches proclaiming that the Aryan "race" is the Lost Tribe of Israel, making them genuine disciples of Christ. They depict all others—including Jews, blacks, and other people of colors—as inferiors sent to earth to challenge God's will. They believe that Jews are the literal offspring of Satan and Eve, with whom they must do battle in order to redeem the planet. These groups often cite biblical texts, in which they find interpretations significantly different from those of mainstream Christian faiths.

Society's Responses. Many human rights organizations have been formed to expose and combat white supremacist violence. For example, the Southern Poverty Law Center, founded in 1971, created a special "Klanwatch" task force to monitor violence against members of minority groups. Attorneys working for the center have forced into bankruptcy several major Klan organizations, including United Klans of America and White Aryan Resistance—actions that have helped to draw national attention to the threat of white supremacist activity. Other groups, including the Coalition for Human Dignity, Montana Human Rights Network, and the ANTI-DEFAMATION LEAGUE, have also monitored white supremacist activity and other expressions of far-right ideologies.

SUGGESTED READINGS. James Ridgeway's *Blood in the Face: The Ku Klux Klan, Aryan Nations, Nazi Skinheads, and the Rise of a New White Culture* (1990), examines white supremacist movement history. In *Religion and the Racist Right: The Origins of the Christian Identity Movement* (1994), Michael Barkun explores the movement's ideological and organizational components. James Aho theorizes overlapping ideologies of Idaho's New Christian Right in *The Politics of Righteousness: Idaho Christian Patriotism* (1990). —*Gina R. Terinoni*

Women, ordination of: Since the beginning of the Christian era, the role of women has been a source of controversy. The issue of women leaders was first addressed by the apostle Paul in his letters to the infant churches:

> Let your women keep silence in the churches: for it is not permitted unto them to speak; but they are commanded to be under obedience, as also saith the law. (1 Corinthians 14:34)

This admonition demonstrated his disapproval of women exercising leadership roles. He further forbade women "to teach or have authority over a man" (1 Timothy 2) and counseled women "to be subject to your husbands, as to the Lord. For the husband is the head of the wife as Christ is the head of the Church . . ." (Ephesians 5). Although some New Testament women, such as Dorcas and Priscilla, participated in church leadership, Paul's insistence upon the subordination of women to men effectively barred women from presiding over the Eucharist, baptism, or engaging in any other priestly function.

Paul's view that women were naturally subordinate to men was echoed by many early church fathers, including Irenaeus, Tertullian, and Thomas Aquinas. They believed that the hierarchy of authority between man and woman was intended by God from the beginning of Creation; that Christ validated patriarchy by choosing only male apostles, who in turn chose only men to succeed them; and that the Church did not have the authority to go against the tradition of the male priesthood initiated by Jesus Christ himself.

Protestant Denominations. The Christian church's suppression of women held sway for nineteen centuries. Until the mid-nineteenth century, only men served at Protestant, Anglican, and Orthodox and Roman Catholic altars. However, two conditions paved the way for the ordination of women in Protestant churches. The first was that most Protestant denominations were much less hierarchical than either the Anglican or Roman Catholic churches, which adhered to the episcopal structure of the early church. Although Protestant churches belong to general councils or assemblies of their denominations, individual churches have had the independence to govern their own affairs. Therefore many Protestant churches could decide whom they would call to their pulpits, even though their calls might be challenged by the governing bodies of their denominations.

The rise of the women's SUFFRAGE movement in

In 1994—twenty years after eleven women were ordained Episcopal priests in the United States—the thirty-two women in this photograph were the first to be ordained priests by the Episcopal Church's Anglican counterpart, the Church of England. (AP/Wide World Photos)

the United States also contributed to the case for ordaining women. In 1848 the SENECA FALLS CONVENTION for women's rights, meeting in a Wesleyan chapel in Seneca Falls, New York, condemned men for prohibiting women from serving as ministers. Five years later, Antoinette Louisa Brown was ordained as a Congregational minister in New York. Although the disapproval of her family and opponents of women's ordination caused her to leave the church (she was later ordained in the Unitarian Church), her ordination opened the door for women of other denominations to seek membership in the clergy.

In 1889 a Presbyterian church ordained Mrs. L. M. Woosley, but the Presbyterian Assembly later declared her ordination invalid. Finally in 1956, after years of bitter debate, the Presbyterians accepted women into the clergy. In the same year, the Methodists also granted women full clergy rights. The Lutherans followed in 1958.

The Episcopal and Catholic Churches. Because the hierarchical structure and theology of the Episcopal (Anglican) and Roman Catholic churches are similar, the struggle to ordain women in those churches proceeded at a slower pace. Until the mid-1970's both churches held to strict interpretations of apostolic succession. The belief that Christ gave his disciples power to administer the sacraments of the Church, which was transferred to subsequent generations of priests, was central to Anglican and Roman Catholic beliefs. Since Christ and the apostles were all males, and the priests were perceived to be Christ's representatives on Earth, the priesthood was traditionally restricted to men.

On July 29, 1974, in Philadelphia, the ordination of eleven Episcopal women by three retired bishops shocked the Anglican communion, and sent a strong message to both the Anglican and Roman Catholic hierarchies. Although the office of deacon had been open to Episcopal women for several years, the door to the priesthood had remained closed. A firestorm of controversy engulfed the church as the debate raged about whether to ratify the "irregular ordinations." The church faced schism as many lay people and clergy threatened to leave if the ordinations were approved. However, during the church's General Convention of 1976, the so-called Philadelphia Eleven were officially approved as members of the Episcopal clergy. Most Episcopalians eventually came to accept female clergy, but some individual congregations continued to refuse to allow women priests to serve at their altars. They retain the autonomy to choose their own clergy and are not forced by their dioceses or the national church to accept female priests as their rectors.

The Episcopalian decision to ordain women has influenced women's rights advocates within the Roman Catholic Church to fight for the ordination of Catholic women. However, each pope who has been petitioned on this issue has refused to sanction holy orders for women. On October 15, 1976, the Church issued the "Declaration on the Question of the Admission of Women to the Ministerial Priesthood." This document reiterated that the Church did not have the authority to admit women to the priesthood because Jesus did not call any woman to be one of the Twelve Apostles. It also emphasized the sacramental nature of the Church and the fact that the male priest mirrors the image of Christ on earth, especially as he celebrates the Eucharist. In spite of the Catholic Church's view that women cannot have a valid vocation to the priesthood, many prominent Catholic scholars and churchmen have called upon the Vatican to reconsider the issue.

SUGGESTED READINGS. *Feminist Ethics and the Catholic Moral Tradition* (1996), edited by Charles E. Curran, Margaret A. Farley, and Richard A. McCormick, and *Women Priests: A Catholic Commentary on the Vatican Declaration* (1977), edited by Leonard and Arlene Swindler, are excellent overviews of the Roman Catholic position. The essays in *The Ordination of Women Pro and Con* (1975), edited by Michael P. Hamilton and Nancy S. Montgomery debate the Episcopal viewpoint. *The Role of Women in the Ministry* (1990), by H. Wayne House, is written from a conservative Protestant perspective.—*Pegge Bochynski*

Women in the Senate and House (WISH List): National political organization established in December, 1991, to support pro-choice Republican women candidates for Congress and state governorships. WISH List was one of three new national women's political action committees (PACs) listed in 1992. The 1990's saw dramatic growth in the organized support for women candidates, both in numbers and in amounts of money raised and provided to support their political campaigns. In addition to more than a dozen national women's PACs, dozens of state-based organizations emerged during the 1990's. Along with the other large PACS, WISH List has sought women to be candidates, and it has provided campaign and leadership training as well as funding.

Ranked among the top national women's PACs, WISH List is the pre-eminent group supporting Republican women candidates. Other large national women's PACs have shown thrown their support almost exclusively to Democratic women candidates. None of the six largest PAC's have supported anti-choice woman candidates.—*Erika E. Pilver*

One of two women representing California in the U.S. Senate, Diane Feinstein speaks in behalf of fellow female members of the House and Senate calling for a ban on assault weapons in 1994. (AP/Wide World Photos)

Women of All Red Nations (WARN): Native American activist organization founded in 1978. WARN was founded by Lorelei Means and Madonna (Thunder Hawk) Gilbert, members of the Lakota Sioux Nation, to provide American Indian women with an institutional voice and a forum in which to address their concerns. WARN members challenged involuntary STERILIZATION OF WOMEN policies, protested instances of political imprisonment, and worked to resist the decline of Native American culture and family life.

In 1985 the group changed its name to Dakota Women of All Red Nations (DWARN) and began the process of establishing local chapters. DWARN has provided assistance to BATTERED WOMEN and fought to improve WOMEN'S HEALTH care. Members have also lobbied for the inclusion of American Indian courses and programs of study in colleges and universities.—*Alexander Scott*

The underlying goal of the Women's Educational Equity Act was to ensure that no form of sex discrimination deprives women of educational opportunities because of their sex. (James L. Shaffer)

Women's Airforce Service Pilots (WASP): Noncombat U.S. pilot program established for women in 1942. After the U.S. entrance into WORLD WAR II, the country had a critical need for pilots. Commanding General H. H. Arnold named Jacqueline Cochran director of a new unit called the Women's Flying Training Detachment in November, 1942. Originally at Houston Municipal Airport, the program was relocated to Avenger Field in Sweetwater, Texas, the following February.

Although the federal government gave them civil service status, the women pilots trained under military discipline. They flew tracking missions, ferried planes to various U.S. air bases, and gave instrument instruction. They also flew simulated bombing missions and flight-tested aircraft. Their seven-month training course included 118 hours of flying time, as well as 180 hours of ground school. The young learned to pilot every model of aircraft in the U.S. Army Air Corps inventory at that time.

Of the 25,000 applicants for the program, 1,830 were accepted and 1,074 earned wings. Thirty-eight WASPs died during World War II. A memorial at Avenger Field was dedicated to all WASPs on May 22, 1993. —*Mark Miller*

Women's Educational Equity Act (WEEA): U.S. federal law passed in 1974 to support efforts to eliminate sex discrimination in schools. In 1972 the U.S. Congress passed a series of laws regarding education, including EDUCATION AMENDMENTS, TITLE IX, which prohibited sex discrimination in schools receiving federal funds. Two years later Congress passed the WEEA to provide funds for research, materials, and training to help schools comply with Title IX. The WEEA also provided funds for programs to encourage female students to study subjects traditionally neglected by women, such as science and mathematics. One of the major activities of the WEEA was to review requests for grants to implement Title IX and to promote the academic achievement of female students. About one grant proposal in ten was selected for funding. Election of Ronald Reagan as president of the United States in 1980 led to more conservative leadership in the U.S. Department of Education and funding for WEEA was reduced.—*Rose Secrest*

Women's International League for Peace and Freedom (WILPF): Women's peace group founded in 1915. This transnational organization was established during WORLD WAR I by women from both neutral and belligerent countries to promote what many saw as women's special concern for peace issues. After its creation, the WILPF became an effective means through which women organized to address both pacifist and feminist goals. Its leaders have suggested that permanent peace can not be attained until women's views are integrated with men's in the political arena. Moreover, the league has continually advocated fundamental social changes—particularly racial justice and gender equality—that its members have maintained will lead to the abolition of war. Although the group has faced some public opposition, a strong indication of its success was awarding of Nobel Peace Prizes to Jane ADDAMS in 1931 and to Emily Greene BALCH in 1946, both of whom were active in the WILPF.—*Christy Jo Snider*

Women's Peace Party (WPP): U.S. pacifist organization founded in 1915. In January, 1915, six months after WORLD WAR I began in Europe, the WPP was formed in Washington, D.C., at the urging of well-known women's rights activists Jane ADDAMS and Carrie Chapman CATT. Its party platform called for democratic control of foreign policy, nationalization of arms manufacturing, and adoption of women's SUFFRAGE. During the following spring the party sent a delegation to The Hague International Congress of Women. The U.S. delegation played a leading role in the conference, becoming affiliated with the organization that would become the WOMEN'S INTERNATIONAL LEAGUE FOR PEACE AND FREEDOM (WILPF).

After the United States entered the war against Germany in April, 1917, the WPP became increasingly unpopular among the general American public; its members were harassed by the government and vilified in the press. After the war's end, WPP delegates attended the second International Congress of Women, and the group officially became known as the U.S. Section of the WILPF.—*Glenn Canyon*

Women's Sports Foundation (WSF): Advocacy organization founded in 1974 to promote equal opportunities for female athletes. The WSF was formed by leading female athletes, including tennis star Billie Jean KING and Olympic swimming champion Donna de Varona, to serve as an umbrella organization for the development of women's ATHLETICS AND SPORTS. A nonprofit organi-

zation, the WSF has been supported by foundation and corporate grants and by member donations.

The WSF has more than 2,300 individual and organizational members. It has maintained a speakers bureau; sponsored a national high-school awards program; published scholarship, camp, and organization guides; provided camp scholarships; offered development assistance to women's sports associations; and compiled statistics on women's sports. It has also worked actively to support enforcement of the EDUCATION AMENDMENTS, TITLE IX of 1972, which prohibited sex discrimination in athletics spending at federally funded educational institutions.—*Christopher E. Kent*

Woods, Eldrick "Tiger" (b. Dec. 30, 1975, Cypress, Calif.): American professional golfer. The son of an African American father and Thai mother, Woods began playing golf at the age of three under his father's tutelage. Success on the links came early and often. After winning

Shortly after turning pro in August, 1996, Tiger Woods played in the Greater Milwaukee Open, where he made a hole-in-one on the par-three fourteenth hole. (Archive Photos)

three U.S. Golf Association (USGA) junior amateur titles, he won the USGA's adult amateur title at eighteen—a feat that made him the youngest golfer ever to win that title. He repeated as amateur champion two more times—another feat that no one had previously accomplished. During two years as an undergraduate student at Stanford University he won additional golfing awards, while maintaining a solid academic record in economics. After turning professional in 1996, Woods won two tournaments during his first year as a pro. His most impressive early professional accomplishment was winning the 1997 Masters Tournament, setting a course record and simultaneously becoming the youngest player ever to win that prestigious competition.

In addition to garnering recognition for his remarkable golfing achievements, Woods has attracted national attention because of his mixed racial and ethnic background. His family background includes Thai, African, Chinese, American Indian, and European ancestors—a fact that has made him reluctant to be labeled only as an "African American" athlete. Already a living symbol of multiculturalism, Woods has worked with disadvantaged and minority children, whom he has introduced to the game of golf.—*Marc Alan Marsdale*

Workmen's Circle: Jewish labor benevolent and FRATERNAL ORGANIZATION. Founded in 1892, the Workmen's Circle became a national order in 1900. It had close ties with Jewish unions, especially in the garment industry, the Jewish labor press, and the Socialist Party. Membership grew from 879 in 1901 to a peak of more than 87,000 in 1925. The order offered health, death, and life insurance benefits and sponsored lectures and concerts for its members. It organized YIDDISH-language schools for children to ensure the transmission of secular Jewish culture. By 1950 some 38,000 students were enrolled in ninety-two schools. As the membership became older, more middle class, and less radical, the order reduced its stress on SOCIALISM.

In 1990 the order still claimed 50,000 members. It still had significant monetary resources permitting it to continue its educational and cultural activities, support Yiddish-language schools and a summer camp for adults and children, improve its health and insurance programs, and add activities for the retired.—*Milton Berman*

Wu, Harry (Wu Hongda; b. Feb. 8, 1937, Shanghai, China): CHINESE AMERICAN activist. The best-known American critic of human rights abuses by the government of the People's Republic of China, Wu began his career as an activist while he was a university student in Beijing, where he developed a reputation for expressing opinions with unusual openness. After he criticized the Soviet Union in 1960, he was imprisoned and spent nineteen years in labor camps. Upon his release, he emigrated to the United States, where he became a U.S. citizen and began a campaign to publicize human rights abuses in China. He secretly returned to China on several occasions to document abuses. On one such trip, in June, 1995, he was arrested at a remote border crossing. After being held for more than two months, he was tried on espionage charges, convicted, and sentenced to fifteen years imprisonment. His detention and trial provoked such strong protests from U.S. officials that he was expelled from China shortly after his conviction.—*Alexander Scott*

Wyatt v. Strickley (1971): Case that involved a federal district court in the daily operations of an Alabama state mental institution in order to improve the conditions therein.

The case originated as a class action initiated on behalf of a man named Ricky Wyatt and other patients involuntarily confined, through noncriminal proceedings, at a mental hospital in Tuscaloosa, Alabama. The local district court issued detailed orders specifying constitutional requirements for the hospital's physical plant and its staffing levels and quality. It further required individualized patient treatment plans.

This case touched off nation-wide reform in which the courts forced state legislatures either to improve conditions with their state psychiatric institutions or to release their inmates. These decisions served to help protect members of such groups as prisoners, poor people, minorities, and mental patients, who had traditionally lacked clout within the political system.

The district court followed with another decision, *Wyatt v. King* (1991), which further specified that mentally ill patients had a constitutionally protected interest in their own release from institutions when their condition no longer justified civil commitment, and that they also had full access to due process to secure such interests.—*Brian G. Tobin*

Encyclopedia of
MULTICULTURALISM

Time Line

Key Events in the History of American Multiculturalism

c. 43,000-13,000 B.C.E.	Estimated migration of ancestors of American Indians across Bering Strait to North America
c. 10,000-8,000 B.C.E.	First archaeological evidence of hunter-gatherer cultures in North America
c. 7,000 B.C.E.	Indians of Mexico begin agriculture
c. 4,000-2,000 B.C.E.	Estimated migration of ancestors of Inuits and Aleuts from Siberia
c. 2,000 B.C.E.	First evidence of permanent Indian villages in Mexico
c. 2,000-1,000 B.C.E.	Maize farmed by Indians in the Southwest
c. 100 B.C.E.-500	Mound builders flourish in Ohio region
c. 250-850	Mayan Indian civilization flourishes in Mexico (pyramids, astronomy, writing, calendar, etc.)
c. 700-1700	Growth of Indian ceremonial centers along Mississippi
c. 750-1250	Anasazi Indian civilization flourishes in the Southwest (permanent villages, communal architecture, cliff houses, farming)
c. 1000	Viking explorer Leif Ericson reaches coast of Canada
c. 1400-1500	Aztec Indians rule large empire in Mexico (develop cities, religion, warfare)
c. 1400-1600	Iroquois League formed among five tribes in Northeast
1492	Columbus makes contact with New World at Cuba and Hispaniola
1519-1521	Cortes conquers Mexico for Spain; fall of Aztec empire
1565	St. Augustine founded (oldest city in U.S., first permanent outpost of Spanish Empire)
late 1500's	Spanish missionaries begin work in New World
1600	Native population speaks 1,000 languages in at least 1,000 cultures
1607	English establish Jamestown colony
1610	Santa Fe founded by Spanish
1619	First Africans arrive in Jamestown as indentured servants
1620	Puritans (Pilgrims) arrive at Plymouth Rock
1639	Baptist church founded
1654	First Jews arrive in New Amsterdam, initially turned away
1664	First act requiring African servants to serve for life (begins slavery)
	First antimiscegenation law (Maryland)
1672-1677	King Philip's War against Indians in New England
1680	Pueblo Revolt against Spanish brings twelve years of independence for Pueblos
1706	Presbyterian church founded in America
c. 1720-1760	Great Awakening religious revival increases Protestant converts
1732	First foreign-language press in U.S. (German *Philadelphische Zeitung*)
1739	Stono Rebellion by Carolina slaves (seventy die)
1745	First elementary schools for blacks founded by Quakers
1754-1763	French and Indian War

1763-1766	Pontiac's Rebellion (Indians v. British)
1768	First Methodist church in America founded in New York City
1769-1830's	Spanish mission system in California
1775-1783	American Revolution: Soldiers of diverse backgrounds fight the British
1776	Declaration of Independence signed
1780	First state bans slavery (Pennsylvania)
1789	U.S. Constitution ratified
	Episcopal church founded in U.S. (independent of Anglican church)
1790	First U.S. Census (continues every decade thereafter)
1791	Bill of Rights ratified
1794	Eastern Orthodox church in North America established in Alaska
1803	Louisiana Purchase
1808	Slave trade officially outlawed (continues illegally)
1809	Sequoya begins to develop Cherokee written alphabet
c. 1810-1863	Underground Railroad helps slaves escape to freedom in North or Canada
1812	War of 1812
	Influx of African American slaves to Canada during and after war
1816	Independent African Methodist Episcopal (AME) church founded (Philadelphia)
1817	First of three Seminole wars in Florida against U.S.
1819	Spain cedes Florida to U.S.
1820	Missouri Compromise (Missouri declared slave state, Maine is free)
	Industrial Revolution begins
1821	Mexico wins independence from Spain
1824	Bureau of Indian Affairs established
1830	Indian Removal Act clears the way for forced relocation
1831	Nat Turner leads slave rebellion
1831-1834	Removal of Choctaws from Mississippi to Indian Territory (Oklahoma)
1833	American Anti-Slavery Society founded; abolitionist movement grows
	Oberlin College founded (first to admit women and all students regardless of race)
1836	Texas declares independence from Mexico; border conflicts
1837	First permanent women's college founded (Mount Holyoke, Mass.)
1838-1839	Removal of Cherokees from Georgia to Indian Territory in Trail of Tears
1839	Amistad slave revolt
	First Married Women's Property Act (Mississippi women may own slaves)
1841	First college degree awarded to a woman
1844	Philadelphia riots target Irish Catholic immigrants
1846-1848	Mexican-American War (U.S. gains territory from Mexico and residents may choose to be U.S. citizens in Treaty of Guadalupe Hidalgo)
1848	Seneca Falls, N.Y., Convention on woman suffrage
	California Gold Rush begins, prompts Chinese immigration

1849	Female doctors allowed to practice
1850	Fugitive Slave Law sets harsh penalties for runaway slaves
	First national women's rights convention (Worcester, Mass.)
1850's	Federally run Indian reservation system begins
1852	Harriet Beecher Stowe's novel *Uncle Tom's Cabin* published (draws European American sympathy for slaves)
1853	Gadsden Purchase of more territory from Mexico (Arizona, New Mexico)
1854	First African American college founded (Lincoln University, Penn.)
1857	Dred Scott decision makes slavery legal in territories, denies rights to blacks
1858	Fraser River Gold Rush begins Chinese immigration to Canada
1859	Abolitionist John Brown leads Harpers Ferry, Va., raid
1860	Black population of Canada is 50,000 (mostly former slaves from U.S.)
1860's	Married women allowed to own property and keep wages throughout U.S.
1861-1865	Civil War
1862	Mankato (Minnesota) massacre of Sioux Indians
1863	Draft riots in New York protest new military draft and target black residents as scapegoats of racial prejudice
	Emancipation Proclamation issued freeing slaves
1863-1864	Forced relocation of Indians with Long Walk of the Navajos
1863-1869	Building of transcontinental railroad by Chinese and other immigrant laborers
1864	Sand Creek (Colorado) massacre of 133 Indians
1865	Thirteenth Amendment outlaws slavery
	Ku Klux Klan formed
1865-1866	Black Codes instituted in southern states to block reforms
1865-1877	Reconstruction signals gains for blacks throughout the South
1866	Civil Rights Act of 1866 gives slaves citizenship, sets precedent for civil rights legislation in twentieth century
1868	Fourteenth Amendment guarantees "equal protection of the laws"; later used to protect minorities from discrimination
	Burlingame Treaty allows immigration of Chinese laborers
1869	National Woman Suffrage Association and American Woman Suffrage Association formed
	Red River Valley Rebellion by Canadian Métis for self-government
	Female lawyers licensed
1870	Wyoming women win right to vote and serve on juries
1870's-1880's	Period of anti-Chinese violence in the West
1871	End to treaty making between U.S. government and Indian tribes
1875	Native Sons of the Golden West founded; promotes nativist, anti-Japanese views
1876	Battle of Little Bighorn (Sioux defeat Custer) leads to federal retaliation against Plains Indians
	Indian Act begins era of social improvements for native Canadians
1877	Prominent Jewish banker refused lodging on grounds of "race"; marks start of modern American anti-Semitism
1878	Amendment for woman's suffrage first introduced in Congress

1881	American Federation of Labor formed from Knights of Labor
1882-1943	Chinese Exclusion Act bans Chinese immigration; need for labor prompts increased Mexican and Japanese immigration
1884-1918	Peak period for lynching of African Americans
1885	Japanese laborers arrive in Hawaii
	Native American Church established
	Canada passes measures to limit Chinese immigration
1887	Dawes Act allots land to Indians in assimilation scheme
1889	Anti-Japanese "Yellow Peril" campaign in California
	Ghost Dance religion wins many Indian adherents, threatens U.S. Army
1890	Battle of Wounded Knee (last major fight between Indians and U.S. Army)
1892-1943	Ellis Island, N.Y., becomes main port of entry for immigrants
1895	Chinese Americans found Native Sons of the Golden State to fight discrimination
1896	*Plessy v. Ferguson* sets "separate but equal" doctrine for blacks and whites in public accommodations that eventually allows segregation in all areas of life
1898	Spanish-American War; Hawaii, Puerto Rico, and the Philippines become U.S. territories
	Supreme Court rules that child born in U.S. to Chinese parents is a citizen (*U.S. v. Wong Kim Ark*)
1900	Indian population shrinks to 250,000 as a result of war, disease, and exploitation
1901-1910	Peak decade for immigration (nearly nine million arrivals, mostly southern and eastern Europeans)
1905	San Francisco School Board tries to establish separate schools for Japanese
	Niagara movement seeks civil rights for blacks
1907	Gentlemen's Agreement between U.S. and Japan bans immigration of Japanese laborers
1908	Production of the play *The Melting Pot*, by Israel Zangwill, popularizes idea of immigrants melding together to form a new nation
	Muller v. Oregon "protects" women in labor force (later seen as sex discrimination)
1909	National Association for the Advancement of Colored People (NAACP) founded
1910	Mexican Revolution begins, prompts increased immigration
	Angel Island opens in San Francisco Harbor to screen Chinese immigrants
1910-1920	Japanese "picture brides" arrive in U.S.
1911	Triangle Shirtwaist Company fire kills more than one hundred immigrant women, stimulates growth of labor movement
1913	Anti-Defamation League of B'nai B'rith founded to fight anti-Semitism
	First alien land laws (target Asians in West)
1914-1918	World War I
1915	First Jewish American lynched (Georgia)
1916	First Mexican American governor elected (Ezequiel Cabeza de Vaca in New Mexico)
1917	Immigration Act of 1917, first sweeping restrictive law (literacy test required)
	Jones Act gives U.S. citizenship to Puerto Ricans
	First woman elected to Congress (Jeanette Rankin)
1918	First rehabilitation acts for soldiers and workers with disabilities
	White women win right to vote in Canada

1920	Nineteenth Amendment grants women right to vote
	League of Women Voters founded
	Japanese Exclusion League founded
1920-1930	Great Migration: 750,000 blacks leave South for North and Midwest (one of two peak decades)
	Period of intense anti-Semitism (e.g. college admission quotas)
	Harlem Renaissance begins (black cultural and political activity flourishes in New York City)
1921	Italians Sacco and Vanzetti convicted of murder during Red Scare
	Sheppard-Towner Act funds prenatal and infant care
1922	*Ozawa v. U.S.* affirms only whites and blacks, not Asians, are eligible for citizenship
1923	First American birth control conference
	U.S. v. Bhagat Singh Thind strips an Asian Indian American of his citizenship
1924	Indian Citizenship Act gives citizenship to American Indians
	Immigration Act of 1924 sets national quotas to restrict immigration from eastern and southern Europe
	Border Patrol established to control illegal immigration
1929	League of United Latin American Citizens (LULAC) formed
1929-1939	Great Depression; large-scale repatriation/deportation of Mexican workers
1930	Japanese American Citizen's League (JACL) formed
	Nation of Islam black nationalist religious and social movement formed
1933	New Deal programs begin to help those hurt by Depression
1935	Social Security Act offers aid to the unemployed and retired
1938	Fair Labor Standards Act sets minimum wage, bans child labor
1939-1945	World War II, including Holocaust
1939	U.S. government refuses to admit 937 German Jewish refugees stranded off Cuba on the S.S. *St. Louis*
1940's	Second peak decade of Great Migration of blacks to North, Midwest, and West
1941	Japan attacks Pearl Harbor, U.S. declares war on Japan and enters World War II
1942	Congress of Racial Equality (CORE) established
1942-1945	Japanese American 442d Regimental Combat Unit most decorated such unit in U.S. history
1942-1946	Exclusion and internment of Japanese Americans in West
1942-1964	Bracero Program imports Mexican farm workers
1943	Zoot Suit riots by Anglo servicemen against Latinos in Los Angeles
1944	*Korematsu v. U.S.* upholds legality of Japanese American internment
1945	War Brides Act allows for immigration of foreign wives
1947	Restrictive covenants declared unconstitutional (formerly used to segregate housing)
	Jackie Robinson breaks color line in baseball
1948	Displaced Persons Act admits 400,000 European refugees to U.S.
	Desegregation of the military by Executive Order
	United Nations issues Universal Declaration of Human Rights
1950	McCarthy hearings in Senate target alleged communists
1950-1953	Korean War

1950's	Termination and relocation policies push many Indians into cities
1952	Puerto Rico becomes a commonwealth
	Immigration and Nationality Act of 1952 further restricts Asian immigration
1954	*Brown v. Board of Education* outlaws segregation in public schools
	Operation Wetback cracks down on illegal Mexican immigrants
1955-1956	Montgomery, Ala., bus boycott to protest segregation
1955-1975	Vietnam War (period of U.S. involvement)
1956	Little Rock, Ark., crisis over school desegregation
1957	Southern Christian Leadership Conference (SCLC) formed
	U.S. Commission on Civil Rights established
1959	First wave of Cuban refugees arrives
	Mexican American Political Association (MAPA) formed
	Hawaii becomes a state; elects first Japanese American to Congress (Daniel Inouye) and first Chinese American to Senate (Hiram Fong)
1960	First lunch counter sit-ins in Greensboro, N.C., by Civil Rights movement
	Sex discrimination banned in Canadian bill of rights
1960's	Large number of American women use birth-control pills, opening new opportunities for women
1961	CORE sponsors Freedom Rides throughout South to integrate buses
	President's Commission on the Status of Women founded
1962	United Farm Workers formed (first agricultural union)
1963	Equal Pay Act of 1963 first attempt to fight sex discrimination
	Betty Friedan's *Feminine Mystique* published, galvanizes women's movement
	Birmingham, Ala., civil rights demonstrations
	Assassination of NAACP official Medgar Evers
	March on Washington for civil rights attracts 250,000 people
	President John F. Kennedy assassinated
1964	Civil Rights Act of 1964 protects women and minorities in employment and public facilities; establishes Equal Employment Opportunity Commission (EEOC)
	First Mexican American elected to Senate (Joseph Montoya)
1965	Immigration and Nationality Act of 1965 removes national quotas, opens door to vastly increased Asian and Latin American immigration
	Voting Rights Act of 1965 removes poll tax and other barriers to minority voting participation
	Escalation of Vietnam War
	Black nationalist leader Malcolm X assassinated
	Watts (Los Angeles) riots
	Delano, Calif., grape strike by United Farm Workers
	Griswold v. Connecticut strikes down ban on contraception, affirms right to privacy
1965-1975	Peak of Chicano movement
1966	Black Panther Party founded
	Black Power movement begins
	National Organization for Women (NOW) founded

1967	Detroit riots and other civil disturbances leave one hundred dead
	First African American appointed to Supreme Court (Thurgood Marshall)
	New Canadian immigration law eases restrictions on Third World arrivals
1968	Kerner Report blames white racism for America moving toward "two societies, one black, one white, separate but unequal"
	Civil Rights Act of 1968 bans housing discrimination
	Bilingual Education Act, first law to require education of non-English speaking students in both English and their native language
	American Indian Civil Rights Act of 1968
	Architectural Barriers Act sets standards for accessibility for the disabled
	Civil rights leader Martin Luther King, Jr., assassinated
	Presidential candidate Robert Kennedy assassinated
	First African American woman elected to Congress (Shirley Chisolm)
	First tribal community college opened (Navajo Community College)
	American Indian Movement (AIM) founded
	Mexican American Legal Defense and Education Fund (MALDEF) formed
	Term "sexism" coined
1968-1971	Indian occupation of Alcatraz Island in San Francisco Bay
1969	Stonewall riots protesting closure of New York City gay bar spark gay liberation movement
1970	Gray Panthers formed to militantly defend rights of older Americans
1970's	Women integrated into all units of the military, female units abolished
1971	Alaska Native Claims Settlement Act (landmark compensation to indigenous peoples of Alaska)
	Canada's first multiculturalism policy supports cultural diversity and equity
	First busing plans approved by Supreme Court to achieve school desegregation
	National Women's Political Caucus founded
1972	Equal Rights Amendment (ERA) passes Congress (awaits state ratification)
	Equal Employment Opportunity Act puts affirmative action policies in place
	Trail of Broken Treaties protest march for Indian rights
1973	*Roe v. Wade* legalizes abortion
1974	*Lau v. Nichols* supports the right to bilingual education
1975	Education of All Handicapped Children Act guarantees free public education to disabled children
	First wave (125,000) of Vietnamese refugees arrives at end of Vietnam War
	Equal Credit Opportunity Act bans sex discrimination in lending
	Indian Self-Determination and Educational Assistance Act reverses prior assimilationist policy
1977	Television series based on Alex Haley's *Roots* promotes ethnic heritage revival
	Canada's Human Rights Act protects women and minorities
1978	Bakke case on reverse discrimination declares racial quotas unconstitutional
	Pregnancy Discrimination Act protects pregnant workers
1979	Tension between Vietnamese refugees and European Americans in Texas fishing industry leads to violence
1979-1981	Boat people exodus from Southeast Asia to U.S. and Canada

1980	Mariel boat lift brings new wave of Cubans to U.S.
	Refugee Act of 1980 redefines "refugee" more broadly; allows for entry of thousands of Vietnamese boat people and Cambodians fleeing the Pol Pot regime
	New disease type designated acquired immune deficiency syndrome (AIDS)
	Miami riots in response to policy brutality
1980's	First Mexican Americans appointed to Cabinet posts
1981	First woman appointed to the Supreme Court (Sandra Day O'Connor)
1982	ERA fails to meet deadline for ratification by states
	Chinese American Vincent Chin murdered by unemployed autoworkers when mistaken for Japanese
	Plyler v. Doe affirms right of illegal immigrants' children to education
1984	First woman candidate for vice president of a major party (Geraldine Ferraro)
	First African American presidential primary candidate of a major party (Jesse Jackson)
1985-1986	Conviction of key leaders of sanctuary movement for aiding illegal Central American immigrants
1986	Immigration Reform and Control Act of 1986 sets employer sanctions for hiring of illegal immigrants, offers amnesty to some undocumented residents
	African American Michael Griffith killed in Howard Beach, N.Y., incident
1988	Congress approves compensation to Japanese Americans who were unjustly interned during World War II
	Canadian Multiculturalism Act strengthened to combat racism
1989	Five Southeast Asian children killed in Stockton, Calif., schoolyard massacre
	Former Klan leader David Duke elected to Louisiana state legislature
	First African American governor elected (L. Douglas Wilder, Virginia)
	African American Yusef Hawkins killed in Bensonhurst (Brooklyn) incident
late 1980's	Debate on multiculturalism and "political correctness" within the academy begins (establishment of "hate speech" codes, revision of curriculum, etc.)
1990	Americans with Disabilities Act of 1990 offers sweeping protections
	Hate Crimes Statistics Act requires governments to monitor hate crimes, including acts against homosexuals
	Court orders INS to reconsider applications for political asylum by 150,000 Central Americans who had been denied fair treatment
1991	Gulf War
	Korean American shop owner Soon Ja Du kills African American teenager Latasha Harlins in dispute over bottle of orange juice
	Riots in Crown Heights section of Brooklyn, N.Y., reflect tensions between blacks and Jews (two people dead)
	Anita Hill testifies on sexual harassment charges at confirmation hearings for Supreme Court nominee Clarence Thomas
1992	Acquittal of four police officers accused of excessive force in beating of black motorist Rodney King
	Los Angeles riots, worst in U.S. history; smaller disturbances occur elsewhere
	"Year of the Woman" sees unprecedented election of women to office
	First American Indian elected to Senate (Ben Nighthorse Campbell)
	First Korean American elected to Congress (Jay C. Kim)

1992 (cont.)	Vietnamese American Luyen Phan Nguyen killed by mob in Florida
	Columbus Quincentennial protested by American Indian, Latino, and other groups
1993	Anti-abortionist murders doctor outside his clinic
	Gay rights march in Washington, D.C., attracts more than 250,000 people
	Clinton administration eases ban on homosexuals in U.S. military
	First woman prime minister elected in Canada (Kim Campbell)
	Vietnam Women's Memorial dedicated in Washington, D.C.
	Federal law enforcement agencies storm Branch Davidian compound near Waco, Texas
	Liberal Party wins Canadian national elections and Jean Chrétien becomes prime minister
	Shannon Faulkner files sex discrimination suit against the Citadel
	Jocelyn Elders becomes first African American surgeon general of the United States
	President Clinton signs Family and Medical Leave Act
	U.S. government apologizes for U.S. role in 1893 overthrow of Hawaiian Kingdom
	U.S. Holocaust Memorial Museum opens in Washington, D.C.
	Los Angeles Police officers charged with beating Rodney King convicted of violating his civil rights by federal court
1994	North American Free Trade Agreement (NAFTA) goes into effect
	Supreme Court of Colorado rules state's antigay Amendment 2 unconstitutional
	South Africa holds its first national nonrace elections
	U.S. Congress reauthorizes Bilingual Education Act
	Congressional Commission on Immigration Reform releases report calling for reduction in legal immigration
	Attorney General Janet Reno announces Operation Gatekeeper to control illegal immigration into United States
	California voters pass Prop 187, designed to restrict social services for illegal immigrants
1995	Slave-labor sweatshop exposed in Covina, California
	U.N Fourth World Conference on Women meets in Beijing, China
	President Bill Clinton authorizes $20 billion investment in bailout of Mexico
	Thousands of demonstrators commemorate twentieth anniversary of *Roe v. Wade* in Washington, D.C.
	Colin Ferguson shoots twenty-six persons on Long Island, New York, commuter train
	Myrlie Evers-Williams becomes national chairperson of National Association for the Advancement of Colored People
	Hundreds of thousands of African Americans gather in Washington, D.C., for Million Man March
	O. J. Simpson's criminal murder trial ends in acquittal
	U.S. Supreme Court tightens affirmative action guidelines in *Adarand Constructors v. Peña*
	Marion Berry reelected mayor of Washington, D.C., after serving prison sentence
	Willie Brown elected mayor San Francisco
	U.S. Supreme Court limits power of lower courts in school desegregation cases in *Missouri v. Jenkins*
	Smithsonian Institution drops plans for *Enola Gay* exhibition commemorating U.S. dropping of atomic bombs on Japan

1995 (cont.)	Quebec voters narrowly defeat referendum calling for sovereignty
	Oklahoma City, Oklahoma, federal building bombed
	Net Noir, an African American-oriented Internet Service, begins
1996	Kweisi Mfume becomes president of National Association for the Advancement of Colored People
	U.S. federal Welfare Reform bill alters provisions of food stamp program
	Hopwood v. Texas limits use of affirmative action in college admissions
	Madeleine Albright becomes first woman U.S. secretary of state
	Secretary of Commerce Ron Brown dies in plane crash in Bosnia
	California voters approve California Civil Rights Initiative (Prop 209)
	Defense of Marriage Act gives states power to prohibit same-sex marriages
	Oakland, California, school board recognizes Ebonics as a distinct language
	Texaco corporation settles racial discrimination suit by announcing plan to compensate minority employees for past discrimination, advance minority hiring and promotions, and increase dealings with minority-owned firms
1997	Members of Heaven's Gate cult commit mass suicide in Southern California
	Golfer "Tiger" Woods becomes youngest player to win Master's Tournament
	Rise in federal minimum wage to $5.15 per hour goes into effect

Selected Multicultural Resources

Compiled by K. L. A. Hyatt

CIVIL RIGHTS/ADVOCACY ORGANIZATIONS

African American/Jewish Coalition for Justice
116 21st Avenue
Seattle, WA 98122

Alaska Federation of Natives
See Manilaq Association

American Arabic Association
c/o Dr. Said Abu Zahra
29 Mackenzie Lane
Wakefield, MA 01880

American Jewish Committee
Institute of Human Relations
165 East Fifty-sixth Street
New York, NY 10022

American Jewish Congress
15 East Eighty-fourth Street
New York, NY 10028

Anti-Defamation League of B'nai B'rith
823 United Nations Plaza
New York, NY 10017

Asian American Curriculum Project (Japanese
   American Curriculum Project)
234 Main Street
P.O. Box 1587
San Mateo, CA 94401

Asian American Legal Defense and Education Fund
   (AALDEF)
99 Hudson Street
New York, NY 10013

Assembly of First Nations
55 Murray Street
Ottawa, ON K1N 5M3 Canada

Catholic League for Religious and Civil Rights
1011 First Avenue
New York, NY 10022

Center for Immigrant's Rights
48 Saint Marks Place
New York, NY 10003

Center for Women Policy Studies
2000 P Street, NW, Suite 508
Washington, DC 20036

Chinese Canadian National Council
386 Bathurst Street, Second Floor
Toronto, ON M5T 2S6 Canada

Coalition of Asian Pacific American Associations
240 East Seventy-sixth Street, Suite 3F
New York, NY 10021

Comision Femenil Mexicana Nacional, Inc.
379 South Loma Drive
Los Angeles, CA 90017

Congressional Black Caucus
2244 Rayburn Street
Washington, DC 20515

Congressional Hispanic Caucus
244 Ford House Office Building
Washington, DC 20515

Cuban American Legal Defense and Education Fund
2513 South Calhoun Street
Fort Wayne, IN 46807-1305

Ethnic Cultural Preservation Council (ECPC)
6500 South Pulaski Road
Chicago, IL 60629

Gray Panthers
P.O. Box 21477
Washington, DC 20009-9477

Human Rights Institute of Canada
77 Metcalfe Street, #201
Ottawa, ON K1P 5L6 Canada

Indochina Resource Action Center (IRAC)
See Southeast Asia Resource Action Center

International Gay and Lesbian Human Rights
  Commission
1360 Mission Street, Suite 200
San Francisco, CA 74103

Interracial Family Alliance (IFA)
P.O. Box 16248
Houston, TX 77222

Japanese American Citizens League (JACL)
1765 Sutter Street
San Francisco, CA 94115

Japanese American Curriculum Project
See Asian American Curriculum Project

League of United Latin American Citizens (LULAC)
221 North Kansas, Suite 1200
El Paso, TX 79901

League of Women Voters of the United States
1730 M Street, NW
Washington, DC 20036

Male Liberation Foundation
701 NE Sixty-seventh Street
Miami, FL 33138

Manilaq Association (Alaska Federation of Natives)
P.O. Box 256
Kotzebue, AK 99752

Mexican American Legal Defense and Educational
  Fund (MALDEF)
634 South Spring Street, Eleventh Floor
Los Angeles, CA 90014

Mexican American Unity Council
2300 West Commerce
San Antonio, TX 78207

National Alliance of Spanish-Speaking People for
  Equality
P.O. Box 2385
Washington, DC 20013

National Association for the Advancement of
  Colored People (NAACP)
4805 Mount Hope Drive
Baltimore, MD 21215

National Association of Arab Americans
1212 New York Avenue, NW, Suite 1225
Washington, DC 20005

National Association of Latino Elected and
  Appointed Officials
NALEO Education Fund
3409 Garnet Street
Los Angeles, CA 90023

National Black Coalition of Canada
2532 Main Street
Vancouver, BC V5T 3E4 Canada

National Center for Urban Ethnic Affairs (NCUEA)
P.O. Box 20, Cardinal Station
Washington, DC 20064

National Conference of Christians and Jews
71 Fifth Avenue, Suite 1100
New York, NY 10003-3095

National Congress of American Indians
2010 Massachusetts Avenue, NW, Second Floor
Washington, DC 20036

National Council of La Raza
810 First Street, NW, Third Floor
Washington, DC 20002

National Council of Negro Women, Inc.
1001 G Street, NW, Suite 800
Washington, DC 20006

National Gay and Lesbian Task Force
2320 Seventeenth Street, NW
Washington, D.C. 20009

National Immigration Law Center
1102 Crenshaw Blvd., Suite 101
Los Angeles, CA 90019

National Immigration Project of the National
    Lawyers Guild, Inc.
14 Beacon Street, Suite 506
Boston, MA 02108

National Institute Against Prejudice and Violence
See Prejudice Institute/Center for the Applied Study
    of Ethnoviolence

National Italian-American Foundation
1860 Nineteenth Street, NW
Washington, DC 20009

National Minority Business Council (NMBC)
235 East Forty-second Street
New York, NY 10017

National Organization for Men
11 Park Place
New York, NY 10007

National Organization for Women
1000 Sixteenth Street, NW, Suite 700
Washington, DC 20036

National Rainbow Coalition
1700 K Street, NW, Suite 800
Washington, DC 20006

National Urban Indian Council
10068 University Park Street
Denver, CO 80250-0168

National Urban League
500 East Sixty-second Street
New York, NY 10021

Native American Rights Fund
1506 Broadway
Boulder, CO 80302

Older Women's League (OWL)
666 Eleventh Street, NW, Suite 700
Washington, DC 20001

Organization of Chinese Americans
1001 Connecticut Avenue, NW, Suite 707
Washington, DC 20036

Prejudice Institute/Center for the Applied Study of
    Ethnoviolence (National Institute Against
    Prejudice and Violence)
Towson State University
Stephens Hall Annex
Towson, MD 21204-7097

Puerto Rican Legal Defense and Education Fund,
    Inc.
99 Hudson Street, Fourteenth Floor
New York, NY 10013

Southeast Asia Resource Action Center (Indochina
    Resource Action Center)
1628 Sixteenth Street, NW, Third Floor
Washington, DC 20009

Southern Christian Leadership Conference
334 Auburn Avenue, NE
Atlanta, GA 30303

Witches Anti-Discrimination Lobby
Hero Press
153 West Eightieth Street, Suite 1B
New York, NY 10024

Women of All Red Nations
4511 North Hermitage
Chicago, IL 60640

GOVERNMENT AGENCIES

Adminstration on Aging
330 Independence Avenue, SW
Washington, DC 20201

Alcohol, Drug Abuse, and Mental Health
    Administration
See Substance Abuse and Mental Health Services
    Administration

Bureau of Indian Affairs
500 Gold, SW, Sixth Floor
Albuquerque, NM 87103

Bureau of Labor Statistics
2 Massachusetts Avenue, NE
Washington, DC 20212

Bureau of the Census
Silver Hill and Suitland Roads
Washington, DC 20233

Canadian Heritage
15 Eddy Street
Hull, Quebec K1A 0M5 Canada

Canadian Human Rights Commission
Place de Ville, Tower A, #1300
320 Queen Street
Ottawa, ON K1A 1E1 Canada

Centers for Disease Control
Office of Assistant Secretary for Health
1600 Clifton Road, NE
Atlanta, GA 30333

Commission on Civil Rights
624 Ninth Street, NW
Washington, DC 20425

Department of Housing and Urban Development
451 Seventh Street, SW
Washington, DC 20410

Department of Veterans Affairs
801 Pennsylvania Avenue, SE
Washington, DC 20003

Equal Employment Opportunity Commission
1801 L Street, NW
Washington, DC 20507

Immigration and Naturalization Service
Tenth Street and Constitution Avenue, NW
Washington, DC 20530

Indian and Northern Affairs Canada
10 Wellington Street
Ottawa, ON K1A 0H4 Canada

Library of Congress
101 Independence Avenue, SE
Washington, DC 20540

Minority Business Development Agency
Department of Commerce
Fourteenth Street and Constitution Avenue, NW,
   Room 5053
Washington, DC 20230

National Archives and Records Administration
Seventh Street and Pennsylvania Avenue, NW
Washington, DC 20408

National Endowment for the Arts
1100 Pennsylvania Avenue, NW
Washington, DC 20506

National Endowment for the Humanities
1100 Pennsylvania Avenue, NW
Washington, DC 20506

National Institutes of Health
9000 Rockville Pike
Bethesda, MD 20892

National Labor Relations Board
1099 Fourteenth Street, NW
Washington, DC 20570

Office of Bilingual Education and Minority
   Language Affairs
Department of Education
600 Independence Avenue, SW
Washington, DC 20202-6510

Office of Minority Health Resource Center
8455 Colesville Road, Suite 910
Silver Springs, MD 20910

Office of Refugee Resettlement
Department of Health and Human Services, Family
   Support Administration
Aerospace Building, Sixth Floor
6401 Security Boulevard
Baltimore, MD 21235

Office of the Commissioner of Official Languages
110 O'Connor Street
Ottawa, ON K1A 0T8 Canada

Smithsonian Institution
1000 Jefferson Drive, SW, Room 2410
Washington, DC 20560

Social Security Administration
6401 Security Boulevard
Baltimore, MD 21235

Status of Women Canada
Constitution Square, Suite 700
360 Albert Street
Ottawa, ON K1A 1E1 Canada

Substance Abuse and Mental Health Services
    Administration (Alcohol, Drug Abuse, and
    Mental Health Administration)
5600 Fishers Lane
Rockville, MD 20857

Supreme Court of the United States
U.S. Supreme Court Building
1 First Street, NE
Washington, DC 20543

U.S. House of Representatives
The Capitol
Washington, DC 20515

U.S. Senate
The Capitol
Washington, DC 20510

INDEPENDENT MUSEUMS AND RESEARCH CENTERS

American Folklife Center, Library of Congress
10 First Street, SE
Washington, DC 20009

American Jewish Historical Society
2 Thornton Road
Waltham, MA 02154

Avery Institute of Afro-American History and
    Culture
58 George Street
Charleston, SC 29424

Balch Institute for Ethnic Studies
18 South Seventh Street
Philadelphia, PA 19086

Bethune Museum-Archives
1318 Vermont Avenue, NW
Washington, DC 20005

Cab Calloway Jazz Institute
Coppin State University
250 West North Avenue
Baltimore, MD 21216

California State Indian Museum
2618 K Street
Sacramento, CA 95816

Canadian Museum of Civilization
100 Laurier Street
Hull, Quebec K1A 0M5 Canada

Center for Migration Studies
209 Flagg Place
Staten Island, NY 10304

Chinatown Historical Museum
70 Mulberry Street
New York, NY 10013

Dusable Museum of African American History
740 East Fifty-sixth Place
Chicago, IL 60637

East-West Cultural Center
Sri Aurobindo Center
12329 Marshall Street
Culver City, CA 90230

Ellis Island Immigration Museum
Ellis Island
New York, NY 10004

Galeria Museo, Mission Cultural Center
2868 Mission Street
San Francisco, CA 94110

Hebrew Union College Skirball Museum
3077 University Avenue
Los Angeles, CA 90007

Indian Pueblo Cultural Center
2401 Twelfth Street, NW
Albuquerque, NM 87192

Italian-American Cultural Society
2811 Imperial Drive
Warren, MI 48093

Japanese American National Museum
941 East Third Street, Suite 201
Los Angeles, CA 90013

Jewish Museum, The
1109 Fifth Avenue
New York, NY 10128

Jewish Museum of San Francisco, The
121 Steuart Street
San Francisco, CA 94105

Latino Institute
228 South Wabash, Sixth floor
Chicago, IL 60604

Mexican American Cultural Center
3019 W. French Place
San Antonio, TX 78228

Mexican Museum, The
Fort Mason Center, Building D
San Francisco, CA 94123

Millicent Rogers Museum
P.O. Box A
Taos, NM 87571

Museo del Barrio, El
Fifth Avenue and 104th Street
New York, NY 10029

Museum of African American Art
4005 Crenshaw Boulevard, Third Floor
Los Angeles, CA 90008

Museum of Afro American History, Abiel Smith
   School
46 Joy Street
Boston, MA 02114

Museum of American Folk Art
107 West Palace
Santa Fe, NM 87503

Museum of American Folk Art
49 West Fifty-third Street
New York, NY 10019

Museum of the National Center of Afro-American
   Artists
300 Walnut Avenue
Boston, MA 02119

Museum of the Plains Indian and Crafts Center
Highway 89 and 2
Browning, MT 59417

Nana Museum of the Arctic
P.O. Box 49
Kotzebue, AK 99752

National Civil Rights Museum
450 Mulberry Street
Memphis, TN 38103-4214

National Cowgirl Hall of Fame & Western Heritage
   Center
111 West Fourth Street, Suite 300
Fort Worth, TX 76107

National Hall of Fame for Famous American Indians
Highway 62
Anadarko, OK 73005

National Museum of African Art, Smithsonian
   Institution
950 Independence Avenue
Washington, DC 20009

National Museum of American History,
   Smithsonian Institution
Fourteenth Street and Constitution Avenue, NW
Washington, DC 20560

National Museum of American Jewish History
55 North Fifth Street
Independence Mall East
Philadelphia, PA 19106

National Museum of the American Indian,
   Smithsonian Institution
470 L'Enfant Plaza, SW, Suite 7103
Washington, DC 20560

National Museum of Women in the Arts, The
1250 New York Avenue, NW
Washington, DC 20005

National Women's Hall of Fame
76 Fall Street
Seneca Falls, NY 13148

Navajo Nation Museum
P.O. Box 308
Window Rock, AZ 86515

Nordic Heritage Museum
3014 NW Sixty-seventh Street
Seattle, WA 98117

North American Black Historical Museum and
  Cultural Center
277 King Street
Amherstburg, ON N9V 2C7 Canada

Northwest Folklife
305 Harrison Street
Seattle, WA 98109

Polish Museum of America
984 North Milwaukee Avenue
Chicago, IL 60622

Schomburg Center for Research in Black Culture
515 Malcolm X Boulevard
New York, NY 10037

Simon Wiesenthal Center
Beit Hashoah Museum of Tolerance
9786 West Pico Boulevard
Los Angeles, CA 90035

Southwest Museum
234 Museum Drive
Los Angeles, CA 90065

Spertus Museum of Judaica
618 South Michigan Avenue
Chicago, IL 60605

Studio Museum in Harlem, The
144 West 125th Street
New York, NY 10027

Ukrainian Cultural and Educational Centre
184 Alexander Avenue, E.
Winnipeg, MB R3B 0L6 Canada

Ukrainian National Museum and Library
2453 West Chicago Avenue
Chicago, IL 60622

United States Holocaust Memorial Museum
100 Raoul Wallenberg Place, SW
Washington, DC 20024

Wing Luke Memorial Museum
414 Eighth Avenue S.
Seattle, WA 98104

Women's Canadian Historical Society of Toronto
153 Spadina Road
Toronto, On M5R 2T9 Canada

Women's Heritage Museum
1509 Portola Avenue
Palo Alto, CA 94306

NATIONAL EDUCATIONAL ORGANIZATIONS

American Association of University Women
1111 Sixteenth Street, NW
Washington, DC 20036

Canadian Ethnic Studies Association
University of Calgary
2500 University Drive, NW
Calgary, AB T2N 1N4 Canada

Canadian Immigration Historical Society
P.O. Box 9502
Ottawa, ON K1G 3V2 Canada

Center for Applied Linguistics (CAL)
1118 Twenty-second Street, NW
Washington, DC 20037

Center for Lesbian and Gay Studies
CUNY Graduate Center
33 West 42 Street
New York, NY 10036

Chinese Historical Society of America
650 Commercial Street
San Francisco, CA 94108

Duncan Black MacDonald Center for the Study of
  Islam and Christian/Muslim Relations
Hartford Seminary
77 Sherman Street
Hartford, CT 06105

Hispanic Public Relations Association
735 South Figueroa Street, Suite 818
Los Angeles, CA 92270

Homosexual Information Center
115 Monroe
Bossier City, LA 71111-4539

International Society of Intercultural Education,
  Training and Research
808 Seventeenth Street, NW, No. 200
Washington, DC 20006

Japanese American Cultural and Community Center
244 South San Pedro Street, Suite 505
Los Angeles, CA 90012

Multicultural History Society of Ontario
43 Queens Park Cres. East
Toronto, ON M5S 2C3 Canada

National Association for Bilingual Education
  (NABE)
1220 L Street, NW, Suite 605
Washington, DC 20005-4018

National Association for Chicano Studies (NACS)
c/o Dr. Carlos S. Maldonado
Eastern Washington University, Chicano Education
  Program
Monroe Hall 202, MS-170
Cheney, WA 99004

National Association for Ethnic Studies (NAES)
Arizona State University
Department of English
P.O. Box 870302
Tempe, AZ 85287-0302

National Council of Black Studies
Ohio State University
208 Mount Hall
1050 Carmack Road
Columbus, OH 43210

National Hispanic Institute
P.O. Box 220
Maxwell, TX 78656

National Institute on Age, Work and Retirement
c/o National Council on the Aging
409 Third Street, SW, Suite 200
Washington, DC 20024

National Japanese American Historical Society
1855 Folsom Street, Suite 161
San Francisco, CA 94103

National Multicultural Institute
3000 Connecticut Avenue, NW, Suite 438
Washington, DC 20008-2556

National Women's History Project
7738 Bell Road
Windsor, CA 95492

National Women's Studies Association (NWSA)
7100 Baltimore Avenue, Suite 301
College Park, MD 20740

United Negro College Fund
8260 Willow Oak Corp Drive
Fairfax, VA 22031

Filmography

Compiled by Wendy Sacket

SELECTED FEATURE FILMS

African American

Bird (1988): The life of legendary jazz musician Charlie Parker is the subject of this film. Directed by Clint Eastwood and starring Forrest Whittaker as Parker.

Birth of a Race (1918): Produced independently and made in response to D. W. Griffith's *The Birth of a Nation*, this film was one of the earliest attempts to provide a positive portrayal of African Americans.

Black Girl (1973): Ossie Davis directed this drama focusing on several generations of women in an African American family and the problems they face.

Blood of Jesus (1941): One of the few films to deal with religious life in the African American community, this film tells the story of a young woman whose faith aids her in times of crisis.

Boyz 'n the Hood (1990): John Singleton's impressive directorial debut focuses on life in South Central Los Angeles and one African American father's determination to safeguard his son's future.

Brother from Another Planet, The (1984): John Sayles' science fiction fantasy tells the story of a black space alien fleeing interplanetary slave traders who lands on Earth and finds himself in Harlem.

Claudine (1974): Diahann Carroll plays a cleaning woman struggling to raise her children as a single mother and James Earl Jones is the garbage collector with whom she falls in love.

Color Purple, The (1985): Adapted from Alice Walker's novel, this Steven Spielberg-directed film stars Whoopie Goldberg, Danny Glover, and Oprah Winfrey in a story of a young black woman's difficult journey from degradation to independence.

Cool World, The (1963): The first feature film shot in Harlem, Shirley Clarke's drama focuses on the lives of a group of young African Americans.

Cornbread, Earl and Me (1975): Moses Gunn and Rosalind Cash star in this drama centering on the death of a young African American basketball star at the hands of the police.

Darktown Jubilee (1914): This film sparked protests from some segments of the white community for its favorable portrayal of blacks. It is believed to be the first film to star an African American actor, Bert Williams.

Daughters of the Dust (1992): Julie Dash wrote and directed this story of a turn-of-the-century Gullah family who are planning to leave their isolated community on the Carolina Sea Islands for life on the mainland.

Fresh (1994): Coming-of-age story involving a twelve-year-old drug courier who uses mental skills developed through playing chess to mastermind a daring plan of vengeance against his employers.

Get on the Bus (1996): Director Spike Lee tackles various social issues facing the African American community by chronicling the interactions among a group of strangers traveling together by bus to attend the Million Man March in Washington, D.C., in October of 1995.

Glory (1989): This Civil War story draws on the long-neglected history of African Americans who fought for the North. Denzel Washington and Morgan Freeman play two of the black soldiers, and Matthew Broderick portrays the company's white commanding officer.

Go Tell It on the Mountain (1984): This powerful drama, based on the book by James Baldwin, tells the story of a young African American man's coming of age as he clashes with his domineering stepfather, a harsh, strong-willed preacher.

Hero Ain't Nothing But a Sandwich, A (1977): Cicely Tyson and Paul Winfield star in this story of an African American family's life in an urban ghetto.

Hollywood Shuffle (1989): Filmmaker Robert Townsend's low-budget comedy satirizes the experience of African American actors in Hollywood. Townsend also stars as the film's frustrated aspiring young actor.

Killer of Sheep (1977): Charles Barnett's documentary-like film focuses on the life of an African American slaughterhouse worker who finds that the emotional distance he needs at his job is carrying over into his personal life.

Lady Sings the Blues (1972): Diana Ross stars in this biographical film based on the musical career and troubled life of the legendary Billie Holliday.

Learning Tree, The (1969): Produced, directed, and written by Gordon Parks, the film traces the coming of age of an African American boy growing up in rural Kansas during the 1920's.

Malcolm X (1992): Spike Lee's epic screen biography of the murdered civil rights leader stars Denzel Washington in the title role. The film traces Malcolm X's life from early manhood through his religious conversion in prison to his emergence as one of the most powerful voices of black nationalism and self-sufficiency.

Milk and Honey (1989): This film follows a young woman who leaves Jamaica in search of a better life in Canada; she endures exploitation and hardship while trying to make it possible for her son to immigrate as well.

Mo' Better Blues (1990): Spike Lee's portrait of a talented jazz musician torn between two women stars Denzel Washington. The film's portrayal of two Jewish theater managers gave rise to controversy at the time of its release.

Native Son (1986): Based on the novel by Richard Wright, the film tells the story of Bigger Thomas, an African American teenager living with his mother (Oprah Winfrey) in a 1940's Chicago slum.

Nothin' but a Man (1963): A young African American man (Ivan Dixon) in the South enters into a troubled marriage with the better-educated daughter (Abbey Lincoln) of a minister.

Once Upon a Time . . . When We Were Colored (1996): Produced by noted television actor Tim Reid and based on the 1989 memoir by Clifton L. Taulbert, this film tells the story of a young boy's coming of age in the segregated environment of the 1940's Mississippi Delta. Cast includes Phylicia Rashad, Richard Roundtree, and Al Freeman, Jr.

187 (1997): Explores the problems faced by an inner–city high school teacher (Samuel L. Jackson) who survives a brutal gang attack and struggles to maintain his personal ethics in the face of escalating urban violence before taking matters into his own hands.

Panther (1995): Mario Van Peebles collaborated with his father on the script of this fictionalized account of the rise of the Black Panther Party in the years before external pressures and internal dissension led to its demise.

Porgy and Bess (1959): Gershwin's classic musical stars Sidney Poitier, Dorothy Dandridge, and Sammy Davis, Jr., in its story of the lives and loves of the inhabitants of a southern slum known as Catfish Row.

Ragtime (1981): Real and fictional characters are interwoven in this story of the events that radicalize a young black man (Howard Rollins).

Raisin in the Sun, A (1961): Sidney Poitier, Ruby Dee, and Diana Sands star in this screen version of Lorraine Hansberry's play, the story of an African American family living in a poor Chicago neighborhood.

River Niger, The (1976): James Earl Jones and Cicely Tyson star in this dramatization of the problems facing a working-class African American family in Los Angeles.

Rosewood (1997): Directed by John Singleton, this film dramatizes the destruction of the community of Rosewood, Florida, in 1923 by whites who believed that a white woman had been attacked by one of Rosewood's black residents.

School Daze (1988): Set on the campus of an all-black college, this Spike Lee musical focuses on the sensitive issue of color differentiation and discrimination within the African American community.

Shaft (1971): Gordon Parks directed this action picture that helped spark the trend toward black exploitation films in the 1970's. Richard Roundtree plays the title character.

She's Gotta Have It (1986): Spike Lee's first feature film tells the story of a young African American woman who refuses to choose among her three boyfriends.

Soldier's Story, A (1984): Set on a Louisiana army base in 1944, the film centers on a unit of African American soldiers and the murder of their black sergeant in a climate of extreme interracial tension.

Sounder (1972): Set during the Great Depression, this moving drama stars Paul Winfield and Cicely Tyson as black sharecroppers attempting to provide for their family.

Straight out of Brooklyn (1991): Set in the housing projects in Brooklyn, the film focuses on an African American family torn apart by poverty, unemployment, and alcohol abuse.

Sweet Sweetback's Baadasss Song (1971): Melvin Van Peebles produced, wrote, and directed this story of an African American man who runs afoul of the law when he comes to the aid of a man being beaten during an arrest.

To Sleep with Anger (1990): This offbeat film draws on elements of myth and magic in its story of an African American family disturbed by the presence of a strange visitor (Danny Glover).

Waiting to Exhale (1995): Adapted from the best-selling novel by Terry McMillan, this film was the first Hollywood production to explore the black experience from the perspective of four women struggling to establish their own self-worth.

Walking Dead, The (1995): One of the first Hollywood films to dramatize the horrific realities of the Vietnam War from the perspective of the numerous African American soldiers who fought in the war

American Indian

Apache (1954): Although it features white actors in American Indian roles, this Western takes a sympathetic tone toward the plight of the American Indian in the face of westward expansion. Burt Lancaster stars as Geronimo.

Black Robe (1991): Based on a best-selling novel, this drama, set in seventeenth century Canada, centers on a Jesuit priest (Lothaire Bluteau) who endures many hardships while traveling with his Algonquin guides to a remote Huron mission to convert the native people.

Broken Arrow (1950): Although it uses white actors in its leading roles, this film was one of the first to attempt a sympathetic portrayal of American Indians.

Dances with Wolves (1990): Kevin Costner directed and stars in this Oscar-winning story of a European American soldier sent to the West who is befriended, and later adopted, by a tribe of Sioux Indians.

Geronimo: An American Legend (1993): Originally aired as a made–for–television movie on Turner Network Television (TNT), this film stars Wes Studi as the famous Apache war leader who commands a group of renegades in raids against the white settlers who have evicted the tribe from their ancestral territories.

Last of the Mohicans, The (1992): Russell Means and Wes Studi star with Daniel Day-Lewis in the latest of many adaptations of the classic novel by James Fenimore Cooper. Director Michael Mann, best known for his work on the television series *Miami Vice*, emphasizes the action of the story through historical reenactment of battles between British colonists and their French and Indian opponents during the Seven Years' War in America.

Man Called Horse, A (1970): Richard Harris portrays an Englishman in the American West who joins an American Indian tribe. The film examines tribal culture in a manner rare in Hollywood feature films.

Map of the Human Heart (1992): Tells the story of an Inuit man who falls in love with a Metís girl in the 1930's and meets her again during World War II, when he serves as an airplane pilot.

Ramona (1936): Although old-fashioned and melodramatic in style, this film offers a sympathetic portrait of a young woman who is half American Indian and her resistance to the greed of white settlers.

Shadow of the Wolf (1993): An Inuit hunter (Lou Diamond Phillips) is tracked down by Canadian mounted police for killing a white trader in the 1930's.

Thunderheart (1992): A fictionalized account of the events surrounding the arrest of American Indian activist Leonard Peltier, the film centers on a part-Sioux FBI agent who is sent to a reservation to investigate the shooting deaths of two fellow agents.

Asian American

Alamo Bay (1985): Based on actual events, the film chronicles the clash between Vietnamese immigrants and local fishermen on the Gulf Coast of Texas.

Chan Is Missing (1982): As two taxi drivers search through San Francisco's Chinatown for their missing partner, they encounter a wide variety of Chinese Americans who defy stereotypes. Directed by Wayne Wang.

Combination Platter (1993): An illegal Chinese immigrant works as a waiter as he tries to obtain a green card.

Come See the Paradise (1990): This film focuses on the relationship between a European American man and a Japanese American woman who is sent to an internment camp during World War II.

Dim Sum: A Little Bit of Heart (1985): Examines the conflicts between traditional Chinese culture and modern American life that shape the relationship between a mother and daughter.

Eat a Bowl of Tea (1989): Set in New York's Chinatown in the late 1940's, Wayne Wang's adaptation of Louis Chu's novel focuses on the arranged marriage of a young man raised in America and his Chinese bride.

Flower Drum Song (1961): Although dated in its perspective, this adaptation of the popular Rodgers and Hammerstein musical was one of the first Hollywood films to focus on the lives of Chinese Americans.

Golden Gate (1993): David Henry Hwang wrote the script of this interracial love story between a Federal Bureau of Investigation agent (Matt Dillon) and the Chinese American daughter of a laundry worker whom he is investigating for alleged communist ties during the 1950's.

Great Wall, A (1986): Peter Wang's humorous film chronicles the encounter between a Chinese American family and their relatives in Beijing.

Heaven and Earth (1993): Director Oliver Stone dramatizes the life story of Le Ly Hayslip, who survived the privation and personal betrayal occasioned by the Vietnam War before coming to the United States as the bride of an American G.I.

Joy Luck Club, The (1993) Wayne Wang's film adaptation of Amy Tan's best–selling novel conveys the private triumphs and disappointments that shape the relationships among four Chinese immigrant mothers and their daughters, who have gone far in assimilating into American culture.

Masala (1993): This multicultural comedy set in Toronto deals with attempts by Asian Indian immigrants to adapt to life in Canada.

Thousand Pieces of Gold, A (1991): Rosalind Chao stars as Lalu Nathoy, a young woman sold into slavery by her father and sent to America, where she is purchased by a saloon keeper in a mining town who plans to force her into prostitution.

Wedding Banquet, The (1993): Taiwanese director Ang Lee stages a charming comedy that skewers ethnic stereotypes while telling the story of a gay man who invites his tradition-bound Chinese parents to America to witness his sham wedding with a beautiful young woman.

European American

America, America (1963): Elia Kazan wrote and directed this story of a young Greek man who emigrates to the United States.

Angelo My Love (1983): Robert Duvall directed this portrait of a street-smart Gypsy boy and the close-knit subculture in which he and his family live.

Avalon (1990): The American immigrant experience is the subject of this look at the Krichinskys, a multigenerational Eastern European family who settle in Baltimore.

Emigrants, The (1972) and *The New Land* (1973): These two films follow the fortunes of a family of Scandinavian settlers who leave a harsh life in their native land only to face more hardship as pioneers in America.

Godfather, The (1972), *The Godfather, Part II* (1974), and *The Godfather, Part III* (1990): Francis Ford Coppola's saga of the Corleone crime family traces the lives of Italian immigrant Vito Corleone and his son Michael within the violent world of organized crime.

Household Saints (1993): Director Nancy Savoca staged this film adaptation of Francine Prose's novel about an Italian American butcher who marries a woman he wins in an argument during a pinochle game and raises a daughter who believes she has visions of Catholic saints. This family drama captures the authentic flavor of American life during the years between 1949 and the 1960's.

King of the Gypsies (1978): This film, based on the ostensibly true stories in Peter Maas's novel, tells the story of three generations of Gypsies living in New York. It has been strongly criticized by the Gypsy community, however, as an inaccurate, stereotyped portrayal.

Molly Maguires, The (1970): Based on actual events in labor history, the film is set in a Pennsylvania coalmining community of Welsh immigrants and stars Sean Connery and Richard Harris.

Witness (1985): A young Amish boy witnesses a murder, and the police detective (Harrison Ford) assigned to the case is forced to hide within the isolated religious community when his life is threatened.

Jewish American

Chosen, The (1982): The friendship between two boys is threatened by the rifts between Hassidic and secular Jews in this drama set in New York.

Crossing Delancey (1988): A young Jewish woman is torn between her love for her grandmother and her desire to shed her immigrant heritage in favor of a more sophisticated lifestyle in contemporary New York.

Enemies, A Love Story (1989): Set in post-World War II New York, the film, based on a novel by Isaac Bashevis Singer, is a tragi-comic look at a Holocaust survivor and his complicated love life.

Gentleman's Agreement (1947): Gregory Peck stars as a reporter who pretends he is Jewish in order to research an article on anti-Semitism in America. The film received an Oscar as Best Picture.

Hester Street (1974): Set in the 1890's, this film explores the experiences of a family of Jewish immigrants adapting to life on the lower East Side of New York.

Jazz Singer, The (1927): Famous as the film that ushered in the era of talking pictures, this melodrama stars Al Jolson as a Jewish cantor's son who displeases his father by pursuing a career in show business. Remakes appeared in 1953 and 1980, the latter starring Neil Diamond.

Mourning Suit, The (1975): The story of a young musician, who befriends an elderly tailor. Contrasts traditional Jewish customs with modern secular life in Canada.

Stranger Among Us, A (1992): This suspense thriller stars Melanie Griffith as a police detective who goes undercover in New York's Hassidic Jewish community.

Latino

American Me (1992): Edward James Olmos stars as a Latino gang member who is sent to prison and attempts to change his life.

Ballad of Gregorio Cortez, The (1983): Set in south Texas around 1900, the film is based on the true story of a Mexican farmer (Edward James Olmos) who becomes the object of a manhunt.

Born in East L.A. (1987): Cheech Marin directed this comedy about a third-generation Mexican American who is deported to Tijuana in an immigration raid.

Bound by Honor (1993): Based on the life experiences of poet Jimmy Santiago Baca, this film chronicles the lives of Latino half brothers—one an artist who succumbs to drug addiction, the other an undercover narcotics detective who falls afoul of their cousin, a Latino gang leader and prison kingpin.

El Mariachi (1993): Robert Rodriguez directed this stylish debut film about a mariachi musician who is mistaken for an assassin.

El Norte (1984): Gregory Nava directed this moving look at the lives of a Guatemalan brother and sister who cross the U.S.-Mexico border as illegal immigrants.

El Super (1979): Roberto (Raymundo Hidalgo-Gato) is the Cuban superintendent of an apartment building in Manhattan. The film follows his problems at work and with his family.

La Bamba (1987): The film dramatizes the life of Latino rock and roll star singer Richie Valens (Lou Diamond Phillips), whose death in a plane crash cut short his promising career.

Mambo Kings, The (1992): Based on Oscar Hijuelos' Pulitzer Prize-winning novel, the film follows the fortunes of two Cuban brothers who come to New York in the 1950's to pursue careers as musicians.

Medal for Benny, A (1944): Based on a story by John Steinbeck, this wartime film tells the story of a young Latino man who leaves home after a brush with the law and enlists in the service.

Mi Vida Loca (1994): Docudrama based on the lives of young Latinas growing up in East Los Angeles. Director Allison Anders' decision to cast community members in the film adds authenticity to her story.

Milagro Beanfield War, The (1988): Robert Redford directed this story of an elderly farmer (Carlos Riquelme) who diverts water from a land development project to his small beanfield and sparks a controversy that ignites his southwestern community.

Salt of the Earth (1954): This film, the story of Mexican workers in a New Mexico mine who attempt to organize a union, was suppressed for many years after its director, Herbert Biberman, was blacklisted.

Stand and Deliver (1988): Edward James Olmos stars as real-life Los Angeles math teacher Jaime Escalante, whose determination to teach his inner-city students calculus brought him national acclaim.

Zoot Suit (1981): Luis Valdez wrote and directed this adaptation of his play, which tells the story of the 1942 Sleepy Lagoon murder case in Los Angeles. Edward James Olmos stars as "El Pachuco."

Women

Accused, The (1988): A young woman (Jodie Foster) who is gang-raped in a public bar finds that her own character is place on trial in the court case that follows.

Adam's Rib (1949): Spencer Tracy and Katharine Hepburn star in George Cukor's classic 1940's "battle-between-the-sexes" comedy about a feminist lawyer determined to prove women's equality to men.

Alice Doesn't Live Here Anymore (1975): Ellen Burstyn stars in Francis Coppola's film about a single mother's struggle for financial and emotional independence.

Ballad of Little Jo, The (1993): Tells the story of an orphaned young woman who poses as a man to survive on the western frontier, where she falls in love with a Chinese immigrant who works on her ranch.

Cimarron (1931): This Western epic based on Edna Ferber's popular novel follows forty years in the life of a frontierswoman—from young bride, to town leader, to newspaper editor, to congress-woman, to community matriarch.

First Wives' Club, The (1996): Goldie Hawn, Diane Keaton, and Bette Midler star as a trio of divorced women who exact clever revenge against their for-mer husbands and their new "trophy" wives.

Good Mother, The (1988): Adapted from the best-sell-ing novel by Sue Miller, this film tackles the issues that arise when a divorced mother must fight for custody of her eight-year-old daughter, whose father has accused her mother's boyfriend of inappropriate behavior.

Handmaid's Tale, The (1990): Futuristic fable based on the 1985 best-selling novel by Canadian author Margaret Atwood. A young woman is enslaved as a surrogate mother by the leader of a fundamentalist political state and his icy wife.

Julia (1977): This film, based on the memoirs of play-wright Lillian Hellman, chronicles the long friend-ship between the independent, liberated Hellman (Jane Fonda) and the radical, mysterious social re-former Julia (Vanessa Redgrave).

League of Their Own, A (1992): This comedy cele-brates the little-known history of the All-American Girls Professional Baseball League, which operated in the United States during World War II.

Norma Rae (1979): Sally Fields won an Oscar for her role as a poor southern factory worker transformed into a union organizer in this fictionalized account of strong female leadership and labor strife.

Swing Shift (1984): This film by Jonathan Demme shows how women went to work in factories during World War II, only to lose their jobs when the men came home.

Thelma and Louise (1991): This popular, controversial road movie follows the exploits of two women who head for Mexico after killing a man who has at-tempted to rape one of them.

Unmarried Woman, An (1978): Jill Clayburgh stars in this Paul Mazursky film about a woman coping with the trauma of divorce and her emotional growth from comfortable, affluent, supportive wife to a self-reliant unmarried woman.

Woman Rebels, A (1936): Adapted from Netta Syrett's novel *Portrait of a Rebel*, this film addresses the struggle of a woman (Katharine Hepburn) for eman-cipation in the Victorian era.

Other Minority Groups

Boys in the Band, The (1970): This groundbreaking portrayal of gay men is set in New York, where a group of friends representing various facets of gay life reveal their problems during the course of a party.

Children of a Lesser God (1986): Hearing-impaired actress Marlee Matlin received an Oscar for her por-trayal of a young deaf woman whose fierce inde-pendence brings her into conflict with the expecta-tions of hearing society.

Desert Hearts (1986): In this sympathetic portrait of a love affair between two women, a woman who has gone to Nevada to obtain a divorce finds herself falling in love with a young casino dealer.

Friendly Persuasion (1956): The events of the Civil War bring a Quaker family into conflict over their religion's belief in pacificism. Starring Gary Coo-per, Dorothy McGuire, and Anthony Perkins.

Heart Is a Lonely Hunter, The (1968): Allan Arkin stars as a lonely deaf mute isolated by his disability in this adaptation of Carson McCullers' novel.

If You Could See What I Hear (1982): Blind singer-songwriter Tom Sullivan is the subject of this film, which chronicles Sullivan's college years and early career.

Lianna (1983): John Sayles directed this exploration of a young wife and mother's gradual recognition of her homosexuality.

Longtime Companion (1990): This film takes a com-passionate look at the experiences of several gay men whose lives are devastated by the spread of the AIDS epidemic.

Miracle Worker, The (1962): This moving dramatiza-tion of Helen Keller's early life stars Patty Duke as the blind and deaf Keller and Anne Bancroft as her teacher, Annie Sullivan.

My Own Private Idaho (1991): Gus Van Sant directed this ambitious look at the lives of a group of street smart gay teenagers, basing his story in part on Shakespeare's *Henry IV*.

Nell (1994): An isolated backwoods woman who com-municates in her own language is discovered by a country doctor and a psychology student who have different reasons for facilitating the woman's tran-sition into mainstream society.

Other Side of the Mountain, The (1972): Based on the life of skier Jill Kinmont, the film follows her strug-gle to adjust after she is paralyzed in a skiing ac-cident.

Passion Fish (1992): John Sayles directed this drama about the growing friendship between two women, an actress (Mary McDonell) paralyzed in an accident and her attendant (Alfre Woodard).

Personal Best (1982): A young woman athlete enters into a lesbian relationship with another athlete in this sports drama written and directed by Robert Towne.

Philadelphia (1993): Tom Hanks won an Academy Award for his portrayal of a gay lawyer who is dismissed from his firm after he is diagnosed with AIDS; he then hires an African American lawyer (Denzel Washington) to help him prosecute his former employers for wrongful termination.

Rain Man (1988): Dustin Hoffman plays the autistic, but remarkably gifted, brother of a young man played by Tom Cruise in this moving exploration of how a family deals with disability.

Saint of Fort Washington, The (1993): Matt Dillon and Danny Glover star as two homeless men—one a white schizophrenic, the other a black Vietnam veteran—who overcome racial tensions and gang attacks in their struggle to survive on the streets of New York City.

Torch Song Trilogy (1988): This adaptation of Harvey Fierstein's play explores different aspects of the gay experience through its focus on its engaging central character.

Waterdance, The (1992): A young man struggles to adjust to life in a wheelchair following a devastating accident.

Intergroup Relations

Cat in the Sack, The (*Le Chat dans le sac*, 1964): A French Canadian film that points to the ambiguous place Quebec holds in Canada's national identity. It focuses on Barbara, who comes from an English-speaking family and pursues intellectual interests, and Claude, a product of Francophone culture, who struggles with the realities of current politics.

Do the Right Thing (1989): Spike Lee's powerful, controversial film takes place over the course of a hot summer day in the inner city as a small conflict between African Americans and Italian Americans escalates into a sudden riot.

Driving Miss Daisy (1989): This Academy Award-winning film traces the long, ambivalent relationship between an elderly southern Jewish woman and her African American chauffeur.

Goodbye, Columbus (1969): Based on Philip Roth's novel, the film takes a caustic look at the romance between a middle-class Protestant librarian and the spoiled daughter of a wealthy Jewish family. With Ali McGraw and Richard Benjamin.

Great White Hope, The (1970): James Earl Jones and Jane Alexander star in this drama based on the life of black boxer Jack Johnson, who outraged white society by his relationship with a white woman.

Guess Who's Coming to Dinner (1967): Sidney Poitier stars in one of Hollywood's first attempts to deal with interracial marriage.

I Like It Like That (1994): Notable as the first major Hollywood picture directed by an African American woman, this film chronicles the life of a young woman of mixed Latino and African American heritage as she struggles to keep her family together and succeed in the business world despite economic pressures and tense relations with her Latino mother-in-law.

In the Heat of the Night (1967): A police detective (Sidney Poitier) from the North finds himself aiding a bigoted local chief of police (Rod Steiger) with a murder investigation in a small southern town.

Isaac Littlefeathers (1985): This film tells of the difficulties experienced by a young boy—half American Indian and half white—who is being reared by a Jewish storekeeper in Alberta, Canada, during the 1950's.

Jungle Fever (1991): Spike Lee directed this exploration of the complex issue of interracial romance. The film also offers a powerful look at the devastating effect of drug use on both addicts and their families.

Little Big Man (1970): Dustin Hoffman stars in this story of a white man raised from childhood by an Indian tribe and his later encounters with white society. Chief Dan George plays Hoffman's mentor and teacher.

Long Walk Home, The (1990): Sissy Spacek and Whoopie Goldberg play a white woman and her African American cleaning woman whose lives are changed by the Montgomery bus boycott of 1955.

Losing Isaiah (1995): A recovering crack addict fights for custody of her son, who has been adopted by a well-meaning white family in this film which explores the controversies surrounding interracial adoption.

Mississippi Masala (1992): This film explores several aspects of American multiculturalism in its story of the romance between an African American man

(Denzel Washington) and a young Asian Indian woman whose family has emigrated from Uganda.

One Potato, Two Potato (1964): When a divorced white woman with a small daughter marries a black man, her former husband sues for custody of the child.

Patch of Blue, A (1965): A young blind woman (Elizabeth Hartman) is befriended by an African American man (Sidney Poitier). Raised by a bigoted mother (Shelley Winters), the blind woman is unaware that her new friend is black.

Shadows (1961): John Cassavetes' first feature film is a largely improvised drama centering on a light-skinned African American woman whose white boyfriend is unaware that she is black.

Six Degrees of Separation (1993): Film adaptation of John Guare's play about a young African American man who passes himself off as Sidney Poitier's illegitimate son in order to ingratiate himself with New York City's wealthy white elite.

Trouble-fete (1964): This story of a young Canadian student's revolt against conformity depicts Quebec's social unrest of the 1960's.

West Side Story (1961): This musical updating of the Romeo and Juliet story focuses on interracial romance and the clashes between two New York street gangs, one white and one Puerto Rican.

SELECTED DOCUMENTARIES

African American

Adam Clayton Powell (1989): A portrait of the controversial African American congressman, minister, and civil rights leader whose flamboyant lifestyle often drew criticism.

Bus, The (1964): Haskell Wexler directed this film record of one of the central events of the Civil Rights movement, the 1963 March on Washington.

Cassius the Great (1964): William Klein's film offers an early portrait of the great heavyweight champion who would later change his name to Muhammad Ali.

Eight Tray Gangster: The Making of a Crip (1993): The events and social conditions shaping the life of a Los Angeles gang member are the focus of this film.

Eldridge Cleaver (1970): The head of the Black Panther Party discusses his political and social views during his days in exile in Algeria.

Eyes on the Prize, Part I (1987) and Part II (1989): The acclaimed public television series takes an in-depth look at the history of the Civil Rights movement.

From Harlem to Sugar Hill (1968): Originally produced by CBS, this controversial film about the lives of middle-class black families was never broadcast on American television.

Fundi: The Story of Ella Baker (1981): A profile of civil rights leader Ella Baker, former executive director of the Southern Christian Leadership Conference and founder of the Student Nonviolent Coordinating Committee (SNCC).

Gospel (1982): A look at the world of gospel music and many of its greatest performers, the film includes footage of several rousing musical numbers.

Hail! Hail! Rock 'n' Roll (1987): The life, career, and musical influence of rock legend Chuck Berry is this film's focus.

Hoop Dreams (1994): Originally produced to be broadcast on the Public Broadcasting Service (PBS), this documentary about two Chicago teens who aspire to basketball careers beyond their inner-city neighborhoods received critical acclaim in theatrical release and stirred up controversy when it failed to be nominated for an Academy Award as best documentary.

King: A Filmed Record . . . Montgomery to Memphis (1970): Three hours in length, this film provides a penetrating look at the life and work of the late Martin Luther King, Jr.

Lady Day: The Many Faces of Billie Holliday (1992): This portrait of the great jazz singer includes rare film footage and interviews with colleagues and friends.

Last of the Blue Devils, The (1979): Rare performance footage highlights this profile of several influential jazz musicians, including the legendary Count Basie.

Listen Up: The Lives of Quincy Jones (1990): A look at the life and career of Quincy Jones and his influence on modern popular music.

Lorraine Hansberry: The Black Experience in the Creation of Drama (1976): This short film profiles the late playwright and explores how she drew on her own life in her plays.

Louie Bluie (1983): This profile of the life and career of musician Howard Armstrong examines the traditions and history of African American rural music.

Malcolm X (1972): Produced with the cooperation of his widow, Betty Shabazz, and author Alex Haley, this film chronicles the life of the slain civil rights leader.

March, The (1964): The 1963 March on Washington and Martin Luther King's "I Have a Dream" speech are the subject of this film by James Blue.

Negro Soldier, The (1943): Frank Capra directed this film chronicling the history of black soldiers in the U.S. military. Racial stereotypes mar its historical value and the practice of segregation within the armed forces is not addressed.

Nine from Little Rock (1963): Charles Guggenheim directed this film for the United States Information Agency profiling the later lives of the black students who first integrated an all-white Arkansas high school.

No Vietnamese Ever Called Me Nigger (1968): The experiences of African American soldiers during the Vietnam War is the subject of this film by David Loeb Weiss.

112th and Central: Through the Eyes of the Children (1993): Made in the wake of the 1992 Los Angeles riots, the film was shot by residents—many of them children—of the city's South Central area and offers a personal perspective on inner-city life.

Ornette . . . Made in America (1985): Shirley Clarke directed this look at the life and career of modern jazz great Ornette Coleman.

Paul Robeson: Tribute to an Artist (1979): A look at the life of the African American singer and actor, whose deeply held political convictions made him a source of controversy during his life.

Quiet One, The (1948): A touching look at the life of a young African American boy removed from his unhappy home and placed in a school for troubled boys. The film's thoughtful commentary was written by James Agee.

Spirit Moves, The (1981): Mura Dehn, an authority on modern dance, directed this historical overview of African American dance styles.

Study of Negro Artists, A (1937): Filmed during the 1930's, the film offers a rare look at the lives and work of African American artists of that era.

American Indian

Alaskan Eskimo, The (1953): Walt Disney produced this Academy Award-winning short film on the life of Alaska's indigenous people.

Broken Rainbow (1985): This Academy Award-winning film explores the motivations behind the forced relocation during the 1980's of thousands of Navajo Indians in Arizona.

Divided Trail: A Native American Odyssey, The (1978): This film explores the rarely examined plight of urban Indians, focusing on the lives of three members of the Chicago Indian Village.

Incident at Oglala (1992): Michael Apted's film questions the official account of the events on a Sioux reservation that resulted in the deaths of two FBI agents and the imprisonment of Indian activist Leonard Peltier.

Kwakiutl of British Columbia, The (n.d.): Documentary made by anthropologist Franz Boas in 1930-1931 of the cultural traditions of the Kwakiutl Indians of Vancouver Island.

Little Boy (1977): The destruction of American Indian culture in the Southwest is examined through a portrait of a troubled young man named Willie.

Nanook of the North (1921): Robert Flaherty's classic documentary explores the difficult life of an Eskimo family.

Native Awareness: Behind the Mask (1989): Introduction to native Canadian peoples and cultures for educators.

Navajo (1952): This film combines elements of both documentary and fiction in its story of a Navajo boy in Arizona who resists conforming to the demands of white society.

Seasons of the Navajo (1984): Follows a traditional Navajo family through the year. From the PBS "American Experience" series.

Winds of Change: A Matter of Choice (1989) and *A Matter of Promises* (1990): Two sixty-minute documentaries on the challenges of contemporary American Indian life from the PBS "American Experience" series.

Asian American

Becoming American (1981): Follows a Hmong family from a remote Thai refugee camp to settlement in Seattle.

Fire on the Water (1982): Documents prejudice against Vietnamese American fishermen on the Texas Gulf coast.

Forbidden City, USA (1989): Located in San Francisco's Chinatown, the first nightclub to feature exclusively Asian American acts is recalled through interviews and film clips.

From Hollywood to Hanoi (1992): A Vietnamese actress whose family emigrated to the United States following the Vietnam War travels back to her homeland and examines the historical events that have shaped her life.

Guilty by Reason of Race (1972): Traces the development of policies of exclusion and internment for Japanese Americans during World War II.

Inside Chinatown (1977): Portrait of Chinese Americans in the 1970's in San Francisco Chinatown.

Komagata Maru Incident, The (1985): Tells the story of Asian Indian immigrants who arrived in Canada by ship in 1914 but were not allowed to enter the country despite their British passports.

Nisei Soldier (1983): Loni Ding's film documents the heroism of the Japanese American 442d Regimental Combat Unit in World War II.

Ourselves (1979): Five women discuss growing up Asian American.

Overture: Linh from Vietnam (1981): Highlights the difficult adjustment to American life of Linh and her family.

Survival of Sontheary Sou, The (1984): Record of the sufferings of a Cambodian refugee under Pol Pot's regime in Cambodia and her passage to the United States.

Who Killed Vincent Chin? (1988): Produced as part of PBS's "Frontline" series, this film by Renee Tajima and Christine Choy examines the events surrounding the murder of a Chinese American man.

European American

Amish Portrait, An (1989): Interviews about cultural values with members of the Old Order Amish.

Irish, The (1977): Highlights the role of Irish Americans in building American cities and political structures.

Italianamerican (1974): Filmmaker Martin Scorsese interviews his parents about their lives in this affectionate portrait of the New York Italian American experience.

Northern Lights (1979): Documents the struggles of early Scandinavian immigrants and how they organized to promote their rights in rural America.

Village in Baltimore (1981): Looks at assimilation patterns in the city's Greektown through the life stories of four Greek American women.

Whitecomers, Episode I: The Magic Circle, 1600-1867 (n.d.): Examines the history of the French Canadians in Quebec.

Jewish American

Breaking the Silence: The Generation After the Holocaust (1984): Adult children of Holocaust survivors confront their family past.

In Her Own Time (1985): Cultural anthropologist Barbara Myerhoff explores her Jewish religious heritage in an attempt to come to terms with terminal cancer.

New Immigrants: Russian Jews in Philadelphia (1979): Highlights the newcomers' struggles to learn English and find work.

Number Our Days (1976): Lynne Littman directed this Academy Award-winning look at the lives of elderly Jewish men and women living in Los Angeles' Venice Beach area.

Shayna Maidels: Orthodox Jewish Teenage Girls (1992): This short film profiles several young women who have chosen to follow the teachings of Orthodox Judaism.

West of Hester Street (1984): Focuses on the efforts of the Galveston movement to encourage Jews to move to Texas.

Latino

Chicanas (1979): Traces the role of Mexican American women from pre-Columbian times to the 1970's.

Harvest of Shame (1960): A groundbreaking television documentary, this film drew attention to the deplorable living conditions of America's migrant workers. Narrated by Edward R. Murrow.

La Frontera (1982): Depicts life in towns along the U.S.-Mexico border.

Mexican-Americans: Viva La Raza (1972): View from Los Angeles of the early years of the Chicano movement.

New Underground Railroad, The (1986): Documents the efforts of the sanctuary movement to help a Salvadoran refugee family.

Women

Antonia: A Portrait of the Woman (1974): Jill Godmilow and Judy Collins' film centers on musical conductor Antonia Brico's life and her efforts to find acceptance in a male-dominated profession.

Daughter Rite (1972): Michelle Citron directed this innovative look at the complex relationships among mothers, daughters, and sisters.

Forbidden Love: The Unashamed Stories of Lesbian Lives (1993): This Canadian documentary presents the lesbian lifestyle of the 1950's; it combines interviews with nine women and the dramatization of a steamy lesbian novel.

Joyce at 34 (1972): Directors Joyce Chopra and Claudia Weill collaborated on this record of Chopra's last month of pregnancy and her efforts to combine work with motherhood after the birth of her child.

Mrs. Mary Norton, Socialist Suffragette (n.d.): Prominent suffragette from Vancouver recounts how Canadian women won the right to vote.

Not a Love Story: A Film About Pornography (1981): A stripper and a filmmaker explore the world of hardcore pornography and its influence on societal attitudes toward women.

Not a Pretty Picture (1974): Director Martha Coolidge films herself filming a fictional retelling of her own rape at the age of sixteen. Fictional and documentary footage combine to tell the story.

Rosie the Riveter (1980): The experiences of women who took over traditionally male jobs in wartime is the subject of this film by Connie Field.

Soldier Girls (1981): This film follows a group of female recruits through the rigors of boot camp and basic training.

Union Maids (1977): The involvement of women in the American labor movement is the subject of this film by James Klein and Julia Reichert.

When Abortion Was Illegal: Untold Stories (1992): This short film offers interviews with women who sought abortions before the procedure's legalization under *Roe v. Wade* in 1973.

With Babies and Banners: Story of the Women's Emergency Brigade (1978): The film recalls the women who participated in the strike against General Motors in the 1930's.

Other Minority Groups

Best Boy (1979): A mentally retarded man must try to achieve a measure of independence as his parents age in this Oscar-winning film.

Blind (1987): Set in the Alabama Institute for the Deaf and Blind, Frederick Wiseman's film looks at the lives of the school's blind students. Part of Wiseman's "Deaf and Blind" series, which also includes *Deaf, Adjustment and Work*, and *Multi-Handicapped*.

Children of Darkness (1983): A look at several children with mental or physical handicaps and the effect their disabilities have on their lives and their families.

Common Threads: Stories from the AIDS Quilt (1989): Using a memorial quilt as a starting point, this Oscar-winning film profiles several people with AIDS.

Educating Peter (1992): This short, engaging record of the attempt to "mainstream" a Down syndrome

boy into a grade school classroom received an Academy Award.

Gravity Is My Enemy (1977): Quadriplegic artist Mark Hicks, who learned to paint by holding a brush in his mouth, is the subject of this film made shortly before his death.

Green on Thursdays (1993): The issue of gay bashing is the subject of this disturbing film, shot in and around the Chicago area.

Helen Keller in Her Story (1955): This Academy Award-winning film features Helen Keller in a retelling of her triumph over the dual handicaps of deafness and blindness.

It Was a Wonderful Life (1993): Jodie Foster narrates this look at the lives of several formerly well-to-do women who find themselves homeless in Los Angeles.

Living Proof (1993): A film chronicle of several people with AIDS and their determination to live their lives to the fullest despite their illness.

Paris Is Burning (1991): The film's subject is the lives of the African American and Latino gay men who participate in Harlem drag balls.

Silent Pioneers (1984): The film offers portraits of older gay leaders whose efforts in more repressive times helped bring about the gay rights movement.

Silverlake Life: The View from Here (1992): A powerful film documenting the lives of two gay men with AIDS. The film, which records the progression of their illness, was shot by the men themselves with a video camera.

Times of Harvey Milk, The (1984): This Oscar-winning film recalls the life and political career of San Francisco's first openly gay city supervisor, who was assassinated in 1978.

Titicut Follies (1967): Frederick Wiseman's exposé of conditions at the Bridgewater State Mental Hospital was banned for many years because of its harrowing depiction of patient treatment.

Word Is Out (1978): Produced by a gay collective, the film interviews a wide variety of gay men and lesbian women about the experience of being homosexual.

Intergroup Relations

Days of Waiting (1990): A Caucasian woman married to a Japanese American man recalls her life in a World War II internment camp after she chose to remain with her husband.

It Is Necessary to Be Among the Peoples of the World to Know Them (*Faut aller parmi le monde pour le savoir*, 1971): This long cinema-verité documentary film expounds on the grievances of certain groups in Quebec; the primary complaint is that General Motors refuses to recognize French as the working language of the company.

Liberators: Fighting on Two Fronts in World War II (1992): Holocaust survivors and African American World War II veterans recall the story of the black troops who aided in the liberation of the concentration camps. Narrated by Denzel Washington.

Métis, The (1978): Portrait of the Métis of Canada who are descended from Europeans and native Canadians.

Mississippi Triangle (1984): Christine Choy's film explores the long history of ethnic conflicts among the white, black, and Asian communities of the Mississippi Delta.

My Childhood: Hubert Humphrey's South Dakota and James Baldwin's Harlem (1964): A look at the contrasting childhood experiences of former vice-president Hubert Humphrey and African American writer James Baldwin.

Tell Me Who I Am (1985): Canadian film exploring ethnic identity in a multicultural society.

Time for Burning, A (1966): Set in Omaha, Nebraska, the film focuses on a white Lutheran minister who is dismissed from his position for attempting to foster communication between his congregation and their African American neighbors.

Bibliography

General Sources on American Multiculturalism

Compiled by Kevin J. Bochynski

CIVIL RIGHTS, DISCRIMINATION, AND SOCIAL MOVEMENTS

Albert, Peter J., and Ronald Hoffman, eds. *We Shall Overcome: Martin Luther King and the Black Freedom Struggle.* New York: Pantheon Books, 1990.

Altschiller, Donald, ed. *Affirmative Action.* New York: H. W. Wilson, 1991.

Berkowitz, Edward D. *Disabled Policy: America's Programs for the Handicapped.* New York: Cambridge University Press, 1987.

Bradley, David, and Shelley Fisher Fishkin, eds. *The Encyclopedia of Civil Rights in America.* Armonk, N.Y.: M. E. Sharpe, 1997.

Branch, Taylor. *Parting the Waters: America in the King Years, 1954-63.* New York: Simon & Schuster, 1988.

Commission on Wartime Relocation and Internment of Civilians. *Personal Justice Denied: Report of the Commission on Wartime Relocation and Internment of Civilians.* Washington, D.C.: Government Printing Office, 1982.

Cone, James H. *Martin and Malcolm and America: A Dream or a Nightmare.* Maryknoll, N.Y.: Orbis Books, 1991.

Cornell, Stephen. *The Return of the Native: American Indian Political Resurgence.* New York: Oxford University Press, 1988.

Cruikshank, Margaret. *The Gay and Lesbian Liberation Movement.* New York: Routledge, 1992.

Curry, George E. and Cornel West, eds. *The Affirmative Action Debate.* Reading, Mass.: Addison-Wesley, 1996.

Davis, Abraham L., and Barbara L. Graham. *The Supreme Court, Race, and Civil Rights.* Thousand Oaks, Calif.: Sage Publications, 1995.

Deloria, Vine, Jr. *Behind the Trail of Broken Treaties: An Indian Declaration of Independence.* Austin: University of Texas Press, 1985.

Dreyfuss, Joel, and Charles Lawrence III. *The Bakke Case: The Politics of Inequality.* New York: Harcourt Brace Jovanovich, 1979.

Eastland, Terry. *Ending Affirmative Action: The Case for Colorblind Justice.* New York: Basic Books, 1996.

Freedman, Jo, ed. *Social Movements of the Sixties and Seventies.* New York: Longman, 1983.

Garrow, David J., ed. *We Shall Overcome: The Civil Rights Movement in the United States in the 1950's and 1960's.* 3 vols. New York: Carlson Publishing, 1989.

Gates, Henry Louis, Jr., ed. *Speaking of Race, Speaking of Sex: Hate Speech, Civil Rights, and Civil Liberties.* New York: New York University Press, 1994.

Graham, Hugh D., ed. *Civil Rights in the United States.* University Park, Pa.: Pennsylvania State University Press, 1994.

Grossman, Mark. *The ABC-CLIO Companion to the Native American Rights Movement.* Santa Barbara, Calif.: ABC-Clio, 1996.

Hampton, Henry, and Steve Fayer, with Sarah Flynn, comps. *Voices of Freedom: An Oral History of the Civil Rights Movement from the 1950's Through the 1980's.* New York: Bantam Books, 1990.

Harding, Vincent. *There Is a River: The Black Struggle for Freedom in America.* 2d ed. New York: Harcourt Brace Jovanovich, 1993.

Haskins, James, with J. M. Stifle. *The Quiet Revolution: The Struggle for the Rights of Disabled Americans.* New York: Thomas Y. Crowell, 1979.

Irons, Peter. *The Courage of Their Convictions: Sixteen Americans Who Fought Their Way to the Supreme Court.* New York: Free Press, 1988.

Kluger, Richard. *Simple Justice: The History of "Brown v. Board of Education" and Black America's Struggle for Equality.* New York: Alfred A. Knopf, 1976.

Levine, Michael L. *African Americans and Civil Rights: From 1619 to the Present.* Phoenix, Ariz.: Oryx Press, 1996.

Levy, Leonard W., et al, eds. *Civil Rights and Equality: Selections from the Encyclopedia of the American Constitution.* New York: Macmillan, 1989.

Loevy, Robert D. *To End All Segregation: The Politics of the Passage of the Civil Rights Act of 1964.* Lanham, Md.: University Press of America, 1990.

Luker, Ralph. *Historical Dictionary of the Civil Rights Movement*. Lanham, Md.: Scarecrow Press, 1997.

Olson, James S., and Mark Baxter, eds. *Encyclopedia of American Indian Civil Rights*. Westport, Conn.: Greenwood Press, 1997.

Rasmussen, R. Kent. *Farewell to Jim Crow: The Rise and Fall of Segregation in America*. New York: Facts on File, 1997.

Robinson, Cedric J. *Black Movements in America*. New York: Routledge, 1997.

Rosales, Francisco A. *Chicano!: The History of the Mexican American Civil Rights Movement*. Houston, Tex.: Arte Publico Press, 1996.

Schwartz, Bernard. *Behind Bakke: Affirmative Action and the Supreme Court*. New York: New York University Press, 1988.

U.S. Commission on Civil Rights. *Civil Rights Issues Facing Asian Americans in the 1990's*. Washington, D.C.: Government Printing Office, 1992.

CULTURAL PLURALISM, ASSIMILATION, AND INTERGROUP RELATIONS

Allen, Irving L. *The Language of Ethnic Conflict*. New York: Columbia University Press, 1983.

Allport, Gordon W. *The Nature of Prejudice*. Reprint. Reading, Mass.: Addison-Wesley, 1979.

Aufderheide, Patricia, ed. *Beyond PC: Toward a Politics of Understanding*. Saint Paul, Minn.: Graywolf Press, 1992.

Banks, Stephen P. *Effective Multicultural Public Relations: A Social-interactive Approach*. Thousand Oaks, Calif.: Sage Publications, 1995.

Bernstein, Richard. *Dictatorship of Virtue: Multiculturalism and the Battle for America's Future*. New York: Alfred A. Knopf, 1994.

Bissoondath, Neil. *Selling Illusions: The Cult of Multiculturalism in Canada*. Toronto: Penguin, 1994.

Blank, Renee, and Sandra Slipp. *Voices of Diversity: Real People Talk About Problems and Solutions in a Workplace Where Everyone Is Not Alike*. New York: Amacom, 1994.

Bork, Robert H. *Slouching Towards Gomorrah: Modern Liberalism and American Decline*. New York: Regan Books, 1996.

Boyd, Alex, Curt Idrogo, Lotsee Patterson, and Kenneth Yamashita, eds. *Guide to Multicultural Resources 1997/1998*. Fort Atkinson, Wis.: Highsmith Press, 1997.

Burayidi, Michael A. *Multiculturalism in a Cross-national Perspective*. Lanham, Md.: University Press of America, 1997.

Burke, Ronald K., ed. *American Public Discourse: A Multicultural Perspective*. Lanham, Md.: University Press of America, 1992.

Carnevale, Anthony P., and Susan C. Stone. *The American Mosaic: An In-depth Report on the Advantage of Diversity in the U.S. Work Force*. New York: McGraw-Hill, 1995.

Costa, Janeen A., and Gary J. Bamossy, eds. *Marketing in a Multicultural World: Ethnicity, Nationalism, and Cultural Identity*. Thousand Oaks, Calif.: Sage Publications, 1995.

Cox, Taylor. *Cultural Diversity in Organizations: Theory, Research, and Practice*. San Francisco: Berrett-Koehler, 1993.

Dana, Richard H. *Multicultural Assessment Perspectives for Professional Psychology*. Boston: Allyn & Bacon, 1993.

Dathorne, O. R. *In Europe's Image: The Need for American Multiculturalism*. Westport, Conn.: Bergin & Garvey, 1994.

Davey, Frank. *Cultural Mischief: A Practical Guide to Multiculturalism; Sketches, Texts and Stories*. Vancouver: Talonbooks, 1996.

Devine, Philip E. *Human Diversity and the Culture Wars: A Philosophical Perspective on Contemporary Cultural Conflict*. Westport, Conn.: Praeger, 1996.

D'Souza, Dinesh. *The End of Racism: Principles for a Multicultural Society*. New York: Free Press, 1995.

Dugan, Romano. *Intercultural Marriage: Promises and Pitfalls*. Yarmouth, Maine: Intercultural Press, 1988.

Dunn, Susan, and Gary J. Jacobsohn, eds. *Diversity and Citizenship: Rediscovering American Nationhood*. Lanham, Md.: Rowman & Littlefield, 1996.

Eoyang, Eugene Chen. *Coat of Many Colors: Reflections on Diversity by a Minority of One*. Boston: Beacon Press, 1995.

Ewalt, Patricia L., ed. *Multicultural Issues in Social Work*. Washington, D.C.: NASW Press, 1996.

Fay, Brian. *Contemporary Philosophy of Social Science: A Multicultural Approach*. Cambridge, Mass.: Blackwell, 1996.

Fine, Marlene G. *Building Successful Multicultural Organizations: Challenges and Opportunities*. Westport, Conn.: Quorum Books, 1995.

Fisher Fishkin, Shelley. *Was Huck Black? Mark Twain and African American Voices*. New York: Oxford University Press, 1993.

Foster, Lawrence, and Patricia S. Herzog, eds. *Defend-

ing Diversity: Contemporary Philosophical Perspectives on Pluralism and Multiculturalism. Amherst: University of Massachusetts Press, 1994.

Frideres, James, ed. *Multiculturalism and Intergroup Relations.* New York: Greenwood Press, 1989.

Gay, Kathlyn. *"I Am Who I Am": Speaking Out About Multiracial Identity.* New York: Franklin Watts, 1995.

Gentile, Mary C., ed. *Differences That Work: Organizational Excellence Through Diversity.* Boston: Harvard Business School, 1994.

Giroux, Henry A. *Living Dangerously: Multiculturalism and the Politics of Difference.* New York: P. Lang, 1993.

Gitlin, Todd. *The Twilight of Common Dreams: Why America Is Wracked by Culture Wars.* New York: Metropolitan Books, 1995.

Glazer, Nathan. *We Are All Multiculturalists Now.* Cambridge, Mass.: Harvard University Press, 1997.

Glazer, Nathan, and Daniel P. Moynihan. *Beyond the Melting Pot: The Negroes, Puerto Ricans, Jews, Italians, and Irish of New York City.* Cambridge, Mass.: MIT Press, 1963.

Gordon, Avery F., and Christopher Newfield, eds. *Mapping Multiculturalism.* Minneapolis: University of Minnesota Press, 1996.

Gordon, Jacob U., ed. *Managing Multiculturalism in Substance Abuse Services.* Thousand Oaks, Calif.: Sage Publications, 1994.

Gordon, Milton. *Assimilation in American Life: The Role of Race, Religion, and National Origins.* New York: Oxford University Press, 1964.

Green, James W. *Cultural Awareness in the Human Services: A Multi-Ethnic Approach.* 2d ed. Boston: Allyn & Bacon, 1995.

Hall, Peter M., ed. *Race, Ethnicity, and Multiculturalism: Policy and Practice.* New York: Garland, 1997.

Henderson, George. *Cultural Diversity in the Workplace: Issues and Strategies.* Westport, Conn.: Quorum Books, 1994.

Hendricks, James E., and Bryan Byers, eds. *Multicultural Perspectives in Criminal Justice and Criminology.* Springfield, Ill.: Charles C. Thomas, 1994.

Herrnstein, Richard J., and Charles A. Murray. *The Bell Curve: Intelligence and Class Structure in American Life.* New York: Free Press, 1994.

Hess, David J. *Science and Technology in a Multicultural World: The Cultural Politics of Facts and Artifacts.* New York: Columbia University Press, 1995.

Higham, John. *Strangers in the Land: Patterns of American Nativism, 1860-1925.* Reprint. New York: Atheneum, 1963.

Hing, Bill Ong. *To Be an American: Cultural Pluralism and the Rhetoric of Assimilation.* New York: New York University Press, 1997.

Hollinger, David A. *Postethnic America: Beyond Multiculturalism.* New York: Basic Books, 1995.

Jackson, Sandra, and Jose Solis, eds. *Beyond Comfort Zones in Multiculturalism: Confronting the Politics of Privilege.* Westport, Conn.: Bergin & Garvey, 1995.

Jacoby, Russell, Naomi Glauberman, and Richard J. Herrnstein, eds. *The Bell Curve Debate: History, Documents, Opinions.* New York: Times Books, 1995.

Kahn, Joel S. *Culture, Multiculture, Postculture.* Thousand Oaks, Calif.: Sage Publications, 1995.

Kallen, Horace. *Culture and Democracy in the United States.* Reprint. New York: Arno, 1970.

Kanpol, Barry, and Peter McLaren, eds. *Critical Multiculturalism: Uncommon Voices in a Common Struggle.* Westport, Conn.: Bergin & Garvey, 1995.

Kaufman, Jonathan. *Broken Alliance: The Turbulent Times Between Blacks and Jews in America.* New York: Scribner, 1988.

Kiselica, Mark S. *Multicultural Counseling with Teenage Fathers: A Practical Guide.* Thousand Oaks, Calif.: Sage Publications, 1995.

Kreps, Gary L., and Elizabeth N. Kunimoto. *Effective Communication in Multicultural Health Care Settings.* Thousand Oaks, Calif.: Sage Publications, 1994.

Kymlicka, Will. *Multicultural Citizenship: A Liberal Theory of Minority Rights.* New York: Oxford University Press, 1995.

Lassiter, Sybil M. *Multicultural Clients: A Professional Handbook for Healthcare Providers and Social Workers.* Westport, Conn.: Greenwood Press, 1995.

Lind, Michael. *The Next American Nation: The New Nationalism and the Fourth American Revolution.* New York: Free Press, 1995.

Locke, Don C. *Increasing Multicultural Understanding: A Comprehensive Model.* Newbury Park, Calif.: Sage Publications, 1992.

McLennan, Gregor. *Pluralism.* Minneapolis: University of Minnesota Press, 1995.

Naylor, Larry L. *Cultural Diversity in the United States.* Westport, Conn: Bergin & Garvey, 1997.

Norgren, Jill, and Serena Nanda. *American Cultural Pluralism and Law.* 2d ed. Westport, Conn.: Praeger, 1996.

Oleksy, Elzbieta H., ed. *American Cultures: Assimilation and Multiculturalism.* San Francisco: International Scholars Publications, 1996.

Paniagua, Freddy A. *Assessing and Treating Culturally Diverse Clients: A Practical Guide.* Thousand Oaks, Calif.: Sage Publications, 1994.

Parillo, Vincent N., ed. *Strangers to These Shores: Race and Ethnic Relations in the United States.* 3d ed. New York: Macmillan, 1989.

Polenberg, Richard. *One Nation Divisible: Class, Race, and Ethnicity in the United States Since 1938.* New York: Viking Press, 1980.

Ponterotto, Joseph G., et al, eds. *Handbook of Multicultural Counseling.* Thousand Oaks, Calif.: Sage Publications, 1995.

Prasad, Pushkala, et al, eds. *Managing the Organizational Melting Pot: Dilemmas of Workplace Diversity.* Thousand Oaks, Calif.: Sage Publications, 1997.

Reed, Ishmael, ed. *MultiAmerica: Essays on Cultural Wars and Cultural Peace.* New York: Viking Press, 1997.

Rogers, Mary F., and George Ritzer, eds. *Multicultural Experiences, Multicultural Theories.* New York: McGraw-Hill, 1996.

Rose, Peter I. *They and We: Racial and Ethnic Relations in the United States.* 2d ed. New York: Random House, 1990.

Rossman, Marlene L. *Multicultural Marketing: Selling to a Diverse America.* New York: American Management Association, 1994.

Roy, Donald H. *The Reuniting of America: Eleven Multicultural Dialogues.* New York: Peter Lang, 1996.

Sackmann, Sonja, ed. *Cultural Complexity in Organizations: Inherent Contrasts and Contradictions.* Thousand Oaks, Calif.: Sage Publications, 1997.

Salins, Peter D. *Assimilation, American Style.* New York: Basic Books, 1996.

Schlesinger, Arthur. *The Disuniting of America.* New York: W. W. Norton, 1992.

Schmidt, Alvin J. *The Menace of Multiculturalism: Trojan Horse in America.* Westport, Conn.: Praeger, 1997.

Simons, George F., Bob Abramms, L. Ann Hopkins, and Diane J. Johnson. *Cultural Diversity Fieldbook: Fresh Visions and Breakthrough Strategies for Revitalizing the Workplace.* Princeton, N.J.: Peterson's/Pacesetter Books, 1996.

Simonson, Rick, and Scott Walker, eds. *The Graywolf Annual Five: Multi-cultural Literacy.* St. Paul, Minn.: Graywolf Press, 1988.

Spickard, Paul R. *Mixed Blood: Intermarriage and Ethnic Identity in Twentieth Century America.* Madison: University of Wisconsin Press, 1989.

Suzuki, Lisa A., Paul J. Meller, and Joseph G. Ponterotto, eds. *Handbook of Multicultural Assessment: Clinical, Psychological, and Educational Applications.* San Francisco: Jossey-Bass, 1996.

Taylor, Charles, and Amy Gutmann, eds. *Multiculturalism: Examining the Politics of Recognition.* Princeton, N.J.: Princeton University Press, 1994.

Trager, Oliver, ed. *America's Minorities and the Multicultural Debate.* New York: Facts on File, 1992.

Tsongas, Paul E. *Journey of Purpose: Reflections on the Presidency, Multiculturalism, and Third Parties.* New Haven, Conn.: Yale University Press, 1995.

Tully, James. *Strange Multiplicity: Constitutionalism in an Age of Diversity.* New York: Cambridge University Press, 1995.

Villa, Carlos., Reagan Louie, and David Featherstone, eds. *Worlds in Collision: Dialogues on Multicultural Art Issues.* San Francisco: International Scholars Publications, 1995.

Walton, Sally J. *Cultural Diversity in the Workplace.* Burr Ridge, Ill.: Irwin Professional/Mirror Press, 1994.

Wieland, Darryl, et al, eds. *Cultural Diversity and Geriatric Care: Challenges to the Health Professions.* New York: Haworth Press, 1994.

Yetman, Norman. *Majority and Minority: The Dynamics of Race and Ethnicity in American Life.* Boston: Allyn & Bacon, 1991.

Zhou, Min, and Carl L. Bankston III. *Growing Up American: The Adaptation of Vietnamese Children to American Society.* New York: Russell Sage Foundation, 1998.

CULTURE AND COMMUNITY

Aguero, Kathleen, ed. *Daily Fare: Essays from the Multicultural Experience.* Athens: University of Georgia Press, 1993.

Ammons, Elizabeth, and Annette W. Parks, eds. *Tricksterism in Turn-of-the-century American Literature: A Multicultural Perspective.* Hanover, N.H.: University Press of New England, 1994.

Appiah, Kwame Anthony, and Henry Louis Gates, Jr., eds. *The Dictionary of Global Culture.* New York: Alfred A. Knopf:, 1997.

Ashe, Arthur. *A Hard Road to Glory: A History of the African-American Athlete.* New York: Warner Books, 1988.

Auerbach, Susan, ed. *Encyclopedia of Multiculturalism.* 6 vols. New York: Marshall Cavendish, 1994.

Backus, Karen, and Julia C. Furtaw, eds. *Asian Americans Information Directory.* Detroit: Gale Research, 1992.

Bak, Hans, ed. *Multiculturalism and the Canon of American Culture.* Amsterdam: VU University Press, 1993.

Bernheimer, Charles, ed. *Comparative Literature in the Age of Multiculturalism.* Baltimore: The Johns Hopkins University Press, 1995.

Black Americans Information Directory. Detroit: Gale Research, 1990.

Boswell, Thomas D., and James R. Curtis. *The Cuban-American Experience: Culture, Images, and Perspectives.* Totowa, N.J.: Rowman & Allanheld, 1984.

Brooks, Tilford. *America's Black Musical Heritage.* Englewood Cliffs, N.J.: Prentice-Hall, 1984.

Bruchac, Joseph, ed. *Breaking Silence: An Anthology of Contemporary Asian American Poets.* Greenfield Center, N.Y.: Greenfield Review Press, 1983.

Chan, Jeffery Paul, et al., eds. *The Big Aiiieeeee! An Anthology of Chinese American and Japanese American Literature.* New York: Meridian, 1991.

Cohen, Hennig, and Tristan Potter Coffin, eds. *The Folklore of American Holidays.* Detroit: Gale Research, 1987.

Cordry, Harold V. *The Multicultural Dictionary of Proverbs: Over 20,000 Adages from More Than 120 Languages, Nationalities and Ethnic Groups.* Jefferson, N.C.: McFarland, 1997.

Davis, Arthur P., and Michael W. Peplow, eds. *The New Negro Renaissance: An Anthology.* New York: Holt, Rinehart and Winston, 1975.

Day, Frances A. *Multicultural Voices in Contemporary Literature: A Resource for Teachers.* Portsmouth, N.H.: Heinemann, 1994.

Emery, Lynne Fauley. *Black Dance: From 1617 to Today.* 2d rev. ed. Princeton, N.J.: Princeton Book Company, 1988.

Finazzo, Denise A. *All for the Children: Multicultural Essentials of Literature.* Albany, N.Y.: Delmar, 1997.

Frosch, Mary, ed. *Coming of Age in America: A Multicultural Anthology.* New York: New Press, 1994.

Gillan, Maria M., and Jennifer Gillan, eds. *Unsettling America: An Anthology of Contemporary Multicultural Poetry.* New York: Viking Press, 1994.

Goldberg, David T. *Multiculturalism: A Critical Reader.* Cambridge, Mass.: Blackwell, 1994.

Harris, Dean A., ed. *Multiculturalism from the Margins: Non-dominant Voices on Difference and Diversity.* Westport, Conn.: Bergin & Garvey, 1995.

Haskins, James. *Black Music in America.* New York: Thomas Y. Crowell, 1987.

Heartney, Eleanor. *Critical Condition: American Culture at the Crossroads.* New York: Cambridge University Press, 1997.

Helbig, Alethea K., and Agnes Perkins. *This Land Is Our Land: A Guide to Multicultural Literature for Children and Young Adults.* Westport, Conn.: Greenwood Press, 1994.

Highwater, Jamake. *Arts of the Indian Americas.* New York: Harper & Row, 1983.

_____. *The Sweetgrass Lives On: Fifty Contemporary North American Indian Artists.* New York: J. B. Lippincott and Thomas Y. Crowell, 1980.

Hispanic Americans Information Directory. Detroit: Gale Research, 1990.

Huerta, Jorge. *Chicano Theater: Themes and Forms.* Ypsilanti, Mich.: Bilingual Press, 1982.

Jay, Gregory S. *American Literature and the Culture Wars.* Ithaca, N.Y.: Cornell University Press, 1997.

Johns, Stephani Bernardo. *The Ethnic Almanac.* Garden City, N.Y.: Doubleday, 1981.

Kim, Elaine H. *Asian American Literature: An Introduction to the Writings and Their Social Context.* Philadelphia: Temple University Press, 1982.

King, Laurie. *Hear My Voice: Bibliography; An Annotated Guide to Multicultural Literature from the United States.* Menlo Park, Calif.: Addison-Wesley, 1994.

King, Russell, John Connell, and Paul D. White, eds. *Writing Across Worlds: Literature and Migration.* New York: Routledge, 1995.

Kollar, Judith L. *An Annotated Bibliography of Multicultural Literature.* Huntington Beach, Calif.: Teacher Created Materials, 1993.

Kymlicka, Will, ed. *The Rights of Minority Cultures.* New York: Oxford University Press, 1995.

Levine, Lawrence W. *The Opening of the American Mind: Canons, Culture, and History.* Boston: Beacon Press, 1996.

Levine, Peter. *Ellis Island to Ebbets Field: Sport and the American Jewish Experience.* New York: Oxford University Press, 1992.

Lippard, Lucy. *Mixed Blessings: New Art in a Multicultural America.* New York: Pantheon Books, 1990.

Miller, Sally, ed. *The Ethnic Press in the United States: A Historical Perspective.* Westport, Conn.: Greenwood Press, 1987.

Miller-Lachmann, Lyn. *Global Voices, Global Visions: A Core Collection of Multicultural Books.* New Providence, N.J.: R. R. Bowker, 1995.

Newman, Jacqueline M. *The Melting Pot: An Annotated Bibliography and Guide to Food and Nutrition Information for Ethnic Groups in America.* New York: Garland, 1986.

Niatum, Duane, ed. *Harper's Anthology of Twentieth Century Native American Poetry.* San Francisco: Harper & Row, 1987.

O'Brien, James P. *Music in World Cultures: Understanding Multiculturalism Through the Arts.* Dubuque, Iowa: Kendall/Hunt, 1994.

Olney, James, ed. *Afro-American Writing Today.* Baton Rouge: Louisiana State University Press, 1989.

Pack, Robert, and Jay Parini, eds. *American Identities: Contemporary Multicultural Voices.* Hanover, N.H.: University Press of New England, 1994.

Pankratz, David B. *Multiculturalism and Public Arts Policy.* Westport, Conn.: Bergin & Garvey, 1993.

Parasnis, Ila, ed. *Cultural and Language Diversity and the Deaf Experience.* New York: Cambridge University Press, 1996.

Rochman, Hazel. *Against Borders: Promoting Books for a Multicultural World.* Chicago: American Library Association, 1993.

Root, Maria P. P., ed. *Filipino Americans: Transformation and Identity.* Thousand Oaks, Calif.: Sage Publications, 1997.

Russell, Cheryl. *The Official Guide to Racial and Ethnic Diversity: Asians, Blacks, Hispanics, Native Americans, and Whites.* Ithaca, N.Y.: New Strategist, 1996.

Seller, Maxine Schwartz, ed. *Ethnic Theater in the United States.* Westport, Conn.: Greenwood Press, 1983.

Shaw, Arnold. *Black Popular Music in America.* New York: Schirmer Books, 1986.

Shohat, Ella, and Robert Stam. *Unthinking Eurocentrism: Multiculturalism and the Media.* New York: Routledge, 1994.

Siemerling, Winfried, and Katrin Schwenk, eds. *Cultural Difference and the Literary Text: Pluralism and the Limits of Authenticity in North American Literatures.* Iowa City: University of Iowa Press, 1996.

Storm, John S. *The Latin Tinge.* New York: Oxford University Press, 1979.

Straub, Deborah G., ed. *Voices of Multicultural America: Notable Speeches Delivered by African, Asian, Hispanic, and Native Americans, 1790-1995.* New York: Gale Research, 1996.

Taylor, Charles A. *Guide to Multicultural Resources: The Source for Networking with Minority Groups.* Madison, Wis.: Praxis, 1989.

Vecoli, Rudolph J., Judy Galens, Anna J. Sheets, and Robyn V. Young, eds. *Gale Encyclopedia of Multicultural America.* 2 vols. Detroit: Gale Research, 1995.

Velez-Ibanez, Carlos G. *Border Visions: Mexican Cultures of the Southwest United States.* Tucson: University of Arizona Press, 1996.

Vlach, John Michael. *By the Work of Their Hands: Studies in Afro-American Folklife.* Charlottesville: University Press of Virginia, 1991.

Wasserman, Paul, and Alice Kennington, eds. *Ethnic Information Sources of the United States.* 2d ed. 2 vols. Detroit: Gale Research, 1995.

Weatherford, Jack. *Native Roots: How the Indians Enriched America.* New York: Crown, 1991.

West, Cornel. *Beyond Eurocentrism and Multiculturalism.* 2 vols., Monroe, Maine: Common Courage Press, 1993.

EDUCATION

Abalos, David T. *Strategies of Transformation Toward a Multicultural Society: Fulfilling the Story of Democracy.* Westport, Conn.: Praeger, 1996.

Adams, Maurianne, ed. *Promoting Diversity in College Classrooms: Innovative Responses for the Curriculum, Faculty, and Institutions.* San Francisco: Jossey-Bass, 1992.

Amerasia Journal. Los Angeles: UCLA Asian American Studies Center.

Anderson, Talmadge, ed. *Black Studies: Theory, Method, and Cultural Perspectives.* Pullman: Washington State University Press, 1990.

Arthur, John, and Amy Shapiro, eds. *Campus Wars: Multiculturalism and the Politics of Difference.* Boulder, Colo.: Westview Press, 1995.

Aztlán: A Journal of Chicano Studies. Los Angeles: UCLA Chicano Studies Research Center.

Baker, Gwendolyn C. *Planning and Organizing for Multicultural Instruction.* 2d ed. Menlo Park, Calif.: Addison-Wesley, 1994.

Banks, James A., and Cherry A. Banks, eds. *Handbook of Research on Multicultural Education.* New York: Macmillan, 1995.

————. *Multicultural Education: Issues and Perspectives.* Boston: Allyn & Bacon, 1989.

Berman, Paul, ed. *Debating PC: The Controversy over Political Correctness on College Campuses.* New

York: Dell Books, 1992.

Block, Cathy C., and Jo Ann Zinke. *Creating a Culturally Enriched Curriculum for Grades K-6.* Boston: Allyn & Bacon, 1995.

Bloom, Allan. *The Closing of the American Mind: How Higher Education Has Failed Democracy and Impoverished the Souls of Today's Students.* New York: Simon & Schuster, 1987.

Border, Laura L. B., and Nancy V. Chism, eds. *Teaching for Diversity.* San Francisco: Jossey-Bass, 1992.

Bowser, Benjamin P., Terry Jones, and Gale A. Young, eds. *Toward the Multicultural University.* Westport, Conn.: Praeger, 1995.

Bull, Barry L., Royal T. Fruehling and Virgie Chattergy. *The Ethics of Multicultural and Bilingual Education.* New York: Teachers College Press, 1992.

Byrnes, Deborah A., and Gary Kiger, eds. *Common Bonds: Anti-bias Teaching in a Diverse Society.* 2d ed. Wheaton, Md.: Association for Childhood Education International, 1996.

Carson, Diane, and Lester D. Friedman, eds. *Shared Differences: Multicultural Media and Practical Pedagogy.* Urbana: University of Illinois Press, 1995.

Cheatham, Harold E., et al. *Cultural Pluralism on Campus.* Alexandria, Va.: American College Personnel Association, 1991.

Ch'maj, Betty E. M., et al, eds. *Multicultural America: A Resource Book for Teachers of Humanities and American Studies.* Lanham, Md.: University Press of America, 1993.

Cornbleth, Catherine, and Dexter Waugh. *The Great Speckled Bird: Multicultural Politics and Education Policymaking.* New York: St. Martin's Press, 1995.

Cummins, Jim, and Dennis Sayers. *Brave New Schools: Challenging Cultural Illiteracy Through Global Learning Networks.* New York: St. Martin's Press, 1995.

Davidman, Leonard, and Patricia T. Davidman. *Teaching with a Multicultural Perspective: A Practical Guide.* 2d ed. New York: Longman, 1997.

Delpit, Lisa D. *Other People's Children: Cultural Conflict in the Classroom.* New York: New Press, 1995.

DeVillar, Robert A., Christian Faltis, and James P. Cummins, eds. *Cultural Diversity in Schools: From Rhetoric to Practice.* Albany: State University of New York Press, 1994.

D'Souza, Dinesh. *Illiberal Education: The Politics of Race and Sex on Campus.* New York: Free Press, 1991.

Dubin, Fraida, and Natalie A. Kuhlman, eds. *Cross-cultural Literacy: Global Perspectives on Reading and Writing.* Englewood Cliffs, N.J.: Regents/Prentice-Hall, 1992.

Dublin, Thomas, ed. *Becoming American, Becoming Ethnic: College Students Explore Their Roots.* Philadelphia: Temple University Press, 1996.

Duhon-Sells, Rose M., and Emma T. Pitts, eds. *A Vision of Multicultural Education for the Year 2000.* Lewiston, N.Y.: Edwin Mellen Press, 1994.

Du Mont, Rosemary R., Louis Buttlar, and William A. Caynon. *Multiculturalism in Libraries.* Westport, Conn.: Greenwood Press, 1994.

Dunn, Rita S., and Shirley A. Griggs. *Multiculturalism and Learning Style: Teaching and Counseling Adolescents.* Westport, Conn.: Praeger, 1995.

Dyson, Anne H., and Celia Genishi, eds. *The Need for Story: Cultural Diversity in Classroom and Community.* Urbana, Ill.: National Council of Teachers of English, 1994.

Fiol-Matta, Liza, and Mariam Chamberlain, eds. *Women of Color and the Multicultural Curriculum: Transforming the College Classroom.* New York: Feminist Press at the City University of New York, 1994.

Flaxman, Erwin, and A. Harry Passow, eds. *Changing Populations, Changing Schools.* Chicago: University of Chicago Press, 1995.

Fullinwider, Robert K., ed. *Public Education in a Multicultural Society: Policy, Theory, Critique.* New York: Cambridge University Press, 1996.

Garcia, Eugene E, et al., eds. *Chicano Studies: A Multidisciplinary Approach.* New York: Teachers College Press, 1984.

_____, ed. *Meeting the Challenge of Linguistic and Cultural Diversity in Early Childhood Education.* New York: Teachers College Press, 1995.

_____. *Understanding and Meeting the Challenge of Student Cultural Diversity.* Boston: Houghton Mifflin, 1994.

Gates, Henry Louis, Jr. *Loose Canons: Notes on the Culture Wars.* New York: Oxford University Press, 1992.

Gollnick, Donna M., and Philip C. Chinn. *Multicultural Education in a Pluralistic Society.* 3d ed. Columbus, Ohio: Charles E. Merrill, 1990.

Graff, Gerald. *Beyond the Culture Wars: How Teaching the Conflicts Can Revitalize American Education.* New York: W. W. Norton, 1992.

Grant, Carl A., ed. *Educating for Diversity: An Anthology of Multicultural Voices.* Boston: Allyn & Bacon, 1995.

Grant, Carl A., and Susan Millar. *Research and Multicultural Education: From the Margins to the Mainstream.* Philadelphia: Falmer, 1992.

Gray, Robin F., Jose A. Ballester y Marquez, and Judith Frediani. *Race to Justice: A Racial Justice and Diversity Program for Junior High.* Boston: Unitarian Universalist Association, 1995.

Guyette, Susan, and Charlotte Heth, eds. *Issues for the Future of American Indian Studies: A Needs Assessment and Program Guide.* Los Angeles: UCLA American Indian Studies Center, 1985.

Hale-Benson, Janice E. *Black Children: Their Roots, Culture, and Learning Styles.* Rev. ed. Baltimore: The Johns Hopkins University Press, 1986.

Harbeck, Karen, ed. *Coming Out of the Classroom Closet: Gay and Lesbian Students, Teachers, and Curricula.* New York: Haworth Press, 1992.

Harris, Violet J., ed. *Teaching Multicultural Literature in Grades K-8.* Norwood, Mass.: Christopher-Gordon, 1993.

Harvey, Carol P., and M. June Allard. *Understanding Diversity: Readings, Cases, and Exercises.* New York: HarperCollins, 1995.

Hayden, Carla D., ed. *Venture into Culture: A Resource Book of Multicultural Materials and Programs.* Chicago: American Library Association, 1992.

Herring, Roger D. *Multicultural Counseling in Schools: A Synergetic Approach.* Alexandria, Va.: The Association, 1997.

Hilgers, Thomas, Marie Wunsch, and Virgie Chattergy, eds. *Academic Literacies in Multicultural Higher Education: Selected Essays.* Honolulu: Center for Studies of Multicultural Higher Education, University of Hawaii at Manoa, 1992.

Hoffman, Charlene, et al., eds. *Historically Black Colleges and Universities, 1976-1990.* Washington, D.C.: National Center for Education Statistics, 1992.

Indian Studies. Ithaca, N.Y.: Cornell University American Indian Program.

Irvine, Janice M. *Sexuality Education Across Cultures: Working with Differences.* San Francisco: Jossey-Bass, 1995.

Journal of American Indian Education. Tempe, Ariz.: Arizona State University Center for Indian Education.

Journal of Black Studies. Beverly Hills, Calif.: Sage Publications.

Journal of Ethnic Studies. Bellingham: Western Washington University.

Journal of Negro Education. Washington, D.C.: Howard University.

King, Edith W., Marilyn Chipman, and Marta Cruz-Janzen. *Educating Young Children in a Diverse Society.* Boston: Allyn & Bacon, 1994.

King, Joyce E., and Etta R. Hollins, and Warren C. Hayman, eds. *Preparing Teachers for Cultural Diversity.* New York: Teachers College Press, 1997.

Kirp, David. *Just Schools: The Idea of Racial Equality in American Education.* Berkeley: University of California Press, 1982.

Kozol, Jonathan. *Savage Inequalities: Children in America's Schools.* New York: Crown, 1991.

Kramer, Martin, and Stephen S. Weiner, eds. *Dialogues for Diversity: Community and Ethnicity on Campus.* Phoenix, Ariz.: Oryx Press, 1994.

La Belle, Thomas J., and Christopher R. Ward. *Ethnic Studies and Multiculturalism.* Albany: State University of New York Press, 1996.

_____. *Multiculturalism and Education: Diversity and Its Impact on Schools and Society.* Albany: State University of New York Press, 1994.

Larkin, Joseph M., and Christine E. Sleeter, eds. *Developing Multicultural Teacher Education Curricula.* Albany: State University of New York Press, 1995.

Lee, Courtland C., ed. *Counseling for Diversity: A Guide for School Counselors and Related Professionals.* Boston: Allyn & Bacon, 1995.

Levine, David P., ed. *Rethinking Schools: An Agenda for Change.* New York: New Press, 1995.

Lutzker, Marilyn. *Multiculturalism in the College Curriculum: A Handbook of Strategies and Resources for Faculty.* Westport, Conn.: Greenwood Press, 1995.

McCormick, Theresa M. *Creating the Nonsexist Classroom: A Multicultural Approach.* New York: Teachers College Press, Teachers College, Columbia University, 1994.

Martin, Rebecca R. *Libraries and the Changing Face of Academia: Responses to Growing Multicultural Populations.* Metuchen, N.J.: Scarecrow Press, 1994.

Martin, Renee J., ed. *Practicing What We Teach: Confronting Diversity in Teacher Education.* Albany: State University of New York Press, 1995.

Massaro, Toni Marie. *Constitutional Literacy: A Core Curriculum for a Multicultural Nation.* Durham, N.C.: Duke University Press, 1993.

Morris, Libby V., and Sammy Parker. *Multiculturalism in Academe: A Source Book.* New York: Garland, 1996.

MultiCultural Review. Westport, Conn.: GP Subscription Publications, Greenwood Publications Group.

Nava, Alfonso. *Educating Americans in a Multicultu-*

ral Society. 2d ed. New York: McGraw-Hill, 1994.

Nieto, Sonia. *Affirming Diversity: The Sociopolitical Context of Multicultural Education.* New York: Longman, 1992.

Nomura, Gail, et al., eds. *Frontiers of Asian American Studies: Writing, Research, and Commentary.* Pullman: Washington State University Press, 1989.

Pedersen, Paul, and John C. Carey, eds. *Multicultural Counseling in Schools: A Practical Handbook.* Boston: Allyn & Bacon, 1994.

Perry, Theresa, and James W. Fraser, eds. *Freedom's Plow: Teaching in the Multicultural Classroom.* New York: Routledge, 1993.

Peterson, Reece L., and Sharon Ishii-Jordan, eds. *Multicultural Issues in the Education of Students with Behavioral Disorders.* Cambridge, Mass.: Brookline Books, 1994.

Power, F. Clark, and Daniel K. Lapsley, eds. *The Challenge of Pluralism: Education, Politics, and Values.* Notre Dame, Ind.: University of Notre Dame Press, 1992.

Ray, Douglas, and Deo H. Poonwassie, eds. *Education and Cultural Differences: New Perspectives.* New York: Garland, 1992.

Reissman, Rose. *The Evolving Multicultural Classroom.* Alexandria, Va.: Association for Supervision and Curriculum Development, 1994.

Renyi, Judith. *Going Public: Schooling for a Diverse Democracy.* New York: New Press 1993.

Rhoads, Robert A., and James R. Valdez. *Democracy, Multiculturalism, and the Community College: A Critical Perspective.* New York: Garland, 1996.

Riggs, Donald E., and Patricia A. Tarin, eds. *Cultural Diversity in Libraries.* New York: Neal-Schuman, 1994.

Rivera-Batiz, Francisco L., ed. *Reinventing Urban Education: Multiculturalism and the Social Context of Schooling.* New York: IUME Press, 1994.

Roberts, Helen R. *Teaching from a Multicultural Perspective.* Thousand Oaks, Calif.: Sage Publications, 1994.

Rothstein, Stanley W., ed. *Class, Culture, and Race in American Schools: A Handbook.* Westport, Conn.: Greenwood Press, 1995.

Saravia-Shore, Marietta, and Steven F. Arvizu, eds. *Cross-cultural Literacy: Ethnographies of Communication in Multiethnic Classrooms.* New York: Garland, 1992.

Schuster, Marilyn R., and Susan R. Van Dyne, eds. *Women's Place in the Academy: Transforming the Liberal Arts Curriculum.* Totowa, N.J.: Rowman & Allanheld, 1985.

Sellers, M. N. S., ed. *An Ethical Education: Community and Morality in the Multicultural University.* Providence, R.I.: Berg, 1994.

Shapiro, Joan P., Trevor E. Sewell, and Joseph P. DuCette. *Reframing Diversity in Education.* Lancaster, Pa.: Technomic, 1995.

Siccone, Frank. *Celebrating Diversity: Building Self-Esteem in Today's Multicultural Classrooms.* Boston: Allyn & Bacon, 1995.

Simmons, Ron. *Affirmative Action: Conflict and Change in Higher Education After Bakke.* Cambridge, Mass.: Schenkman, 1982.

Sims, Serbrenia J. *Diversifying Historically Black Colleges and Universities: A New Higher Education Paradigm.* Westport, Conn.: Greenwood Press, 1994.

Sleeter, Christine E., ed. *Empowerment Through Multicultural Education.* Albany: State University of New York Press, 1991.

Sleeter, Christine E., and Carl A. Grant. *Making Choices for Multicultural Education: Five Approaches to Race, Class, and Gender.* 2d ed. New York: Maxwell Macmillan International, 1994.

Sleeter, Christine E., and Peter McLaren, eds. *Multicultural Education, Critical Pedagogy, and the Politics of Difference.* Albany: State University of New York Press, 1995.

Spindler, George D., and Louise S. Spindler. *Pathways to Cultural Awareness: Cultural Therapy with Teachers and Students.* Thousand Oaks, Calif.: Corwin Press, 1994.

Spring, Joel H. *Deculturalization and the Struggle for Equality: A Brief History of the Education of Dominated Cultures in the United States.* 2d ed. New York: McGraw-Hill, 1997.

_____. *The Intersection of Cultures: Multicultural Education in the United States.* New York: McGraw-Hill, 1995.

Stimpson, Catharine R. *Women's Studies in the United States.* New York: Ford Foundation, 1986.

Tiedt, Pamela, and Iris M. Tiedt. *Multicultural Teaching; A Handbook of Activities, Information, and Resources.* 3d ed. Boston: Allyn & Bacon 1989.

Vogt, W. Paul. *Tolerance and Education: Learning to Live with Diversity and Difference.* Thousand Oaks, Calif.: Sage Publications, 1997.

Vold, Edwina B., ed. *Multicultural Education in Early Childhood Classrooms.* Washington, D.C.: National Education Association, 1992.

Weis, Lois, and Michelle Fine, eds. *Beyond Silenced Voices: Race, Class, and Gender in American Schools.* Albany: State University of New York Press, 1993.

Wilson, John K. *The Myth of Political Correctness: The Conservative Attack on Higher Education.* Durham, N.C.: Duke University Press, 1995.

Wlodkowski, Raymond J., and Margery B. Ginsberg. *Diversity and Motivation: Culturally Responsive Teaching.* San Francisco: Jossey-Bass, 1995.

Women's Studies Quarterly. New York: Feminist Press at City University of New York.

Wurzel, Jaime S. *Toward Multiculturalism: Readings in Multicultural Education.* Yarmouth, Maine: Intercultural Press, 1988.

Yeo, Frederick L. *Inner-City Schools, Multiculturalism, and Teacher Education: A Professional Journey.* New York: Garland, 1997.

ETHNIC GROUPS AND ETHNICITY

Acuña, Rodolfo. *Occupied America: A History of Chicanos.* 3d ed. New York: Harper & Row, 1987.

Alba, Richard D. *Ethnic Identity: The Transformation of White America.* New Haven, Conn.: Yale University Press, 1990.

_____. *Italian Americans: Into the Twilight of Ethnicity.* Englewood Cliffs, N.J.: Prentice-Hall, 1985.

Allen, James P., and Eugene J. Turner, eds. *We the People: An Atlas of America's Ethnic Diversity.* New York: Macmillan, 1988.

Bachelis, Faren. *The Central Americans.* New York: Chelsea House, 1990.

Bahr, Howard M., et al. *Native Americans Today: Sociological Perspectives.* New York: Harper & Row, 1972.

Bataille, Gretchen M., and Kathleen M. Sands. *American Indian Women Telling Their Lives.* Lincoln: University of Nebraska Press, 1984.

Bataille, Gretchen M., and Charles L. P. Silet, eds. *The Pretend Indians: Images of Native Americans in the Movies.* Ames: Iowa State University Press, 1980.

Bayes, Jane H. *Minority Politics and Ideologies in the United States.* Novato, Calif.: Chandler & Sharp, 1982.

Benjamin, Lois. *The Black Elite.* Chicago: Nelson-Hall, 1991.

Blackwell, James E. *The Black Community: Diversity and Unity.* 3d ed. New York: HarperCollins, 1991.

Brettschneider, Marla, ed. *The Narrow Bridge: Jewish Views on Multiculturalism.* New Brunswick, N.J.: Rutgers University Press, 1996.

Buenker, John D., and Lorman A. Ratner, eds. *Multiculturalism in the United States: A Comparative Guide to Acculturation and Ethnicity.* New York: Greenwood Press, 1992.

Burnet, Jean R., with Howard Palmer. *Coming Canadians: An Introduction to Canada's Peoples.* Toronto: McClelland and Stewart, 1988.

Catalano, Julie. *The Mexican Americans.* New York: Chelsea House, 1988.

Chabran, Richard, and Raphael Chabran, eds. *The Latino Encyclopedia.* 6 vols. New York: Marshall Cavendish, 1996.

Champagne, Duane, ed. *The Native North American Almanac: A Reference Work on Native North Americans in the United States and Canada.* Detroit: Gale Research, 1994.

Choy, Bong-Youn. *Koreans in America.* Chicago: Nelson-Hall, 1979.

Dallmayr, Fred R. *Beyond Orientalism: Essays on Cross-cultural Encounter.* Albany: State University of New York Press, 1996.

Estell, Kenneth, ed. *The African American Almanac.* Detroit: Gale Research, 1994.

Fitzpatrick, Joseph P. *Puerto Rican Americans: The Meaning of Migration to the Mainland.* 2d rev. ed. Englewood Cliffs, N.J.: Prentice-Hall, 1987.

Foster, Carol, et al., eds. *Minorities: A Changing Role in America.* Wylie, Tex.: Information Plus, 1992.

Franklin, John Hope, and Genna Rae McNeil, eds. *African Americans and the Living Constitution.* Washington, D.C.: Smithsonian Institution Press, 1995.

Freeman, James M. *Hearts of Sorrow: Vietnamese-American Lives.* Stanford, Calif.: Stanford University Press, 1989.

Friedman, Lester D., ed. *Unspeakable Images: Ethnicity and the American Cinema.* Urbana: University of Illinois Press, 1991.

Fuchs, Lawrence. *The American Kaleidoscope: Race, Ethnicity, and the Civic Culture.* Hanover, N.H.: University Press of New England, 1990.

Garcia, Maria C. *Havana USA: Cuban Exiles and Cuban Americans in South Florida, 1959-1994.* Berkeley: University of California Press, 1996.

Garwood, Alfred N, ed. *Black Americans: A Statistical Sourcebook.* Boulder, Colo.: Numbers and Concepts, 1991.

_____. *Hispanic Americans: A Statistical Sourcebook.* Boulder, Colo.: Numbers and Concepts, 1991.

Gernand, Renee. *The Cuban Americans.* New York: Chelsea House, 1988.

_____. *Ethnic Dilemmas, 1964-1982.* Cambridge, Mass.: Harvard University Press, 1983.

Gomez-Quinones, Juan. *Chicano Politics: Reality and Promise, 1940-1990.* Albuquerque: University of New Mexico Press, 1990.

Gonzales, Juan L., Jr. *The Lives of Ethnic Americans.* Dubuque, Iowa: Kendall/Hunt, 1991.

Gudykunst, William B., and Tsukasa Nishida. *Bridging Japanese/North American Differences.* Thousand Oaks, Calif.: Sage Publications, 1994.

Gutierrez, David G., ed. *Between Two Worlds: Mexican Immigrants in the United States.* Wilmington, Del.: Scholarly Resources, 1996.

Habenstein, Robert, Charles Mindel, and Roosevelt Wright, Jr., eds. *Ethnic Families in America: Patterns and Variations.* 3d ed. New York: Elsevier, 1988.

Harlan, Judith. American Indians Today: Issues and Conflicts. New York: Franklin Watts, 1987.

Hertzberg, Hazel W. *The Search for an American Indian Identity: Modern Pan-Indian Movements.* Syracuse, N.Y.: Syracuse University Press, 1971.

Higham, John, ed. *Ethnic Leadership in America.* Baltimore: The Johns Hopkins University Press, 1978.

Hirschfelder, Arlene B., and Martha K. De Montano. *The Native American Almanac: A Portrait of Native America Today.* New York: Prentice-Hall General Reference, 1993.

Hirschfelder, Arlene B., and Paulette Fairbanks. *The Encyclopedia of Native American Religions: An Introduction.* New York: Facts on File, 1992.

Holli, Melvin G., and Peter d'Alroy Jones, eds. *Ethnic Chicago: A Multicultural Portrait.* 4th ed. Grand Rapids, Mich.: Wm. B. Eerdmans, 1994.

Holte, James Craig. *The Ethnic I: A Sourcebook for Ethnic-American Autobiography.* Westport, Conn.: Greenwood Press, 1988.

Hurtado, Aida. *Redefining California: Latino Social Engagement in a Multicultural Society.* Los Angeles: Chicano Studies Research Center, University of California, 1992.

Josephy, Alvin M. *Now That the Buffalo's Gone: A Study of Today's American Indians.* New York: Alfred A. Knopf, 1982.

Kanellos, Nicolas, ed. *The Hispanic American Almanac: A Reference Work on Hispanics in the United States.* Detroit: Gale Research, 1993.

Kinton, Jack, ed. *American Ethnic Revival: Group Pluralism Entering America's Third Century.* Aurora, Ill.: Social Science and Sociological Resources, 1977.

Laguerre, Michel S. *American Odyssey: Haitians in New York City.* Ithaca, N.Y.: Cornell University Press, 1984.

Lee, Joan F. J. *Asian American Experiences in the United States: Oral Histories of First to Fourth Generation Americans from China, the Philippines, Japan, India, Pacific Islands, Vietnam and Cambodia.* New York: McFarland, 1991.

Malson, Micheline Ro., et al., eds. *Black Women in America: Social Science Perspectives.* Chicago: University of Chicago Press, 1990.

Markowitz, Harvey, ed. *Ready Reference: American Indians.* 3 vols. Pasadena, Calif.: Salem Press, 1995.

Melendy, H. Brett. *Asians in America: Filipinos, Koreans, and East Indians.* New York: Hippocrene Books, 1981.

Melville, Margarita B., ed. *Twice a Minority: Mexican American Women.* St. Louis: C. V. Mosby, 1980.

Mindel, Charles H., and Robert Habenstein. *Ethnic Families in America: Patterns and Variations.* New York: Elsevier, 1976.

Mirande, Alfredo, and Evangelina Enriquez. *La Chicana: The Mexican-American Woman.* Chicago: University of Chicago Press, 1979.

Moore, Joan W., and Harry Pachon. *Hispanics in the United States.* Englewood Cliffs, N.J.: Prentice-Hall, 1985.

Ng, Franklin, ed. *The Asian American Encyclopedia.* 6 vols. New York: Marshall Cavendish, 1996.

O'Brien, David J., and Stephen S. Fugita. *The Japanese American Experience.* Bloomington: Indiana University Press, 1991.

O'Leary, Timothy J., and David Levinson, eds. *Encyclopedia of World Cultures.* Vol. 1, *North America.* Boston: G. K. Hall, 1991.

Olson, James S., and Raymond Wilson. *Native Americans in the Twentieth Century.* Provo, Utah: Brigham Young University Press, 1984.

Patterson, E. Palmer. *Indian Peoples of Canada.* Toronto: Grolier, 1982.

Rippley, La Vern J. *The German Americans.* Lanham, Md.: University Press of America, 1984.

Rodriguez, Clara E. *Puerto Ricans: Born in the U.S.A.* Boston: Unwin Hyman, 1989.

Root, Maria P. P., ed. *Racially Mixed People in America.* Newbury Park, Calif.: Sage Publications, 1992.

Saran, Parmatma. *The Asian Indian Experience in the United States.* Cambridge, Mass.: Schenckman, 1985.

Schaefer, Richard T. *Racial and Ethnic Groups*. 6th ed. New York: HarperCollins, 1996.

Shapiro, Ian, and Will Kymlicka, eds. *Ethnicity and Group Rights*. New York: New York University Press, 1997.

Shorris, Earl. *Latinos: A Biography of the People*. New York: W. W. Norton, 1992.

Silberman, Charles. *A Certain People: American Jews and Their Lives Today*. New York: Summit Books, 1985.

Thernstrom, Stephan, ed. *Harvard Encyclopedia of American Ethnic Groups*. Cambridge, Mass.: Harvard University Press, 1980.

Trigger, Bruce G., et al, eds. *The Cambridge History of the Native Peoples of the Americas*. 3 vols. Cambridge: Cambridge University Press, 1996.

Walker-Moffat, Wendy. *The Other Side of the Asian American Success Story*. San Francisco: Jossey-Bass, 1995.

Weyr, Thomas. *Hispanic U.S.A.: Breaking the Melting Pot*. New York: Harper & Row, 1988.

Wilkinson, J. Harvie, III. *One Nation Indivisible: How Ethnic Separatism Threatens America*. Reading, Mass.: Addison-Wesley, 1997.

Williams, Michael W., ed. *The African American Encyclopedia*. 8 vols. New York: Marshall Cavendish, 1993.

Yinger, J. Milton. *Ethnicity: Source of Strength; Source of Conflict*. New York: State University of New York Press, 1994.

Zhou, Min, and Carl L. Bankston III. *Growing Up American: The Adaptation of Vietnamese Children to American Society*. New York: Russell Sage Foundation, 1998.

GENDER AND SEXISM

Albrecht, Lisa, and Rose M. Brewer. *Bridges of Power: Women's Multicultural Alliances*. Philadelphia: New Society, 1990.

Benokraitis, Nijole V., and Joe R. Feagin. *Modern Sexism: Blatant, Subtle, and Covert Discrimination*. Englewood Cliffs, N.J.: Prentice-Hall, 1986.

Boston Women's Health Book Collective. *The New Our Bodies, Ourselves: A Book by and for Women*. Rev. ed. New York: Simon & Schuster, 1992.

Buechler, Steven M. *Women's Movements in the United States: Woman Suffrage, Equal Rights, and Beyond*. New Brunswick, N.J.: Rutgers University Press, 1990.

Burke, Phyllis. *Gender Shock: Exploding the Myths of Male and Female*. New York: Anchor Books, 1996.

Caraway, Nancie. *Segregated Sisterhood: Racism and the Politics of American Feminism*. Knoxville: University of Tennessee Press, 1991.

Castro, Ginette. *American Feminism: A Contemporary History*. Translated by Elizabeth Loverde-Bagwell. New York: New York University Press, 1990.

Davis, Flora. *Moving the Mountain: The Women's Movement in American Since 1960*. New York: Simon & Schuster, 1991.

Dines, Gail, and Jean M. Humez, eds. *Gender, Race, and Class in Media: A Text-Reader*. Thousand Oaks, Calif.: Sage Publications, 1995.

Ellis, Angele, and Marilyn Llewellyn. *Dealing with Differences: Taking Action on Class, Race, Gender, and Disability*. Thousand Oaks, Calif.: Corwin Press, 1997.

Faludi, Susan. *Backlash: The Undeclared War Against American Women*. New York: Crown, 1991.

Feminist Studies. College Park, Md.: University of Maryland Women's Studies Program.

Friedan, Betty. *The Feminine Mystique*. New York: W. W. Norton, 1963.

_____. *The Second Stage*. New York: Summit Books, 1981.

Giddings, Paula. *When and Where I Enter: The Impact of Black Women on Race and Sex in America*. New York: William Morrow, 1984.

Hanmer, Trudy J. *Taking a Stand Against Sexism and Sex Discrimination*. New York: Franklin Watts, 1990.

Huang, Fung-Yea. *Asian and Hispanic Immigrant Women in the Work Force: Implications of the United States Immigration Policies Since 1965*. New York: Garland, 1997.

Ingoldsby, Bron B., and Suzanna D. Smith, eds. *Families in Multicultural Perspective*. New York: Guilford Press, 1995.

Landes, Alison, Carol D. Foster, and Norma H. Jones, eds. *Women's Changing Role*. Wylie, Tex.: Information Plus, 1992.

Landrine, Hope, ed. *Bringing Cultural Diversity to Feminist Psychology: Theory, Research, and Practice*. Washington, D.C.: American Psychological Association, 1995.

Lynch, Frederick R. *The Diversity Machine: The Drive to Change the "White Male Workplace"*. New York: Free Press, 1997.

McFadden, Margaret, ed. *Ready Reference: Women's Issues*. 3 vols. Pasadena, Calif.: Salem Press, 1997.

Maggio, Rosalie. *The Dictionary of Bias-free Usage:*

A Guide to Nondiscriminatory Language. Phoenix: Oryx Press, 1991.

Morraga, Cherrie, and Gloria Anzaldua, eds. *This Bridge Called My Back: Writings by Radical Women of Color.* Watertown, Mass.: Persephone Press, 1981.

Nelson, Adie, and Barrie W. Robinson, eds. *Gender in the 1990s: Images, Realities, and Issues.* 2d ed. Toronto: Nelson Canada, 1995.

Newton, David E. *Gay and Lesbian Rights: A Reference Handbook.* Santa Barbara, Calif.: ABC-Clio, 1994.

Pal, Leslie A. *Interests of State: The Politics of Language, Multiculturalism, and Feminism in Canada.* Buffalo, N.Y.: McGill-Queen's University Press, 1993.

Ruiz, Vicki, and Ellen C. DuBois, eds. *Unequal Sisters: A Multicultural Reader in U.S. Women's History.* 2d ed. New York: Routledge, 1994.

Sobejano-Moran, Antonio, ed. *Feminism in Multicultural Literature.* Lewiston, N.Y.: The Edwin Mellen Press, 1996.

Steinem, Gloria. *Outrageous Acts and Everyday Rebellions.* New York: Holt, Rinehart and Winston, 1983.

Stetson, Dorothy McBride. *Women's Rights in the U.S.A.* Pacific Grove, Calif.: Brooks/Cole, 1991.

Taylor, Ronald L., ed. *Minority Families in the United States: A Multicultural Perspective.* Englewood Cliffs, N.J.: Prentice-Hall, 1994.

Valdivia, Angharad N.,ed. *Feminism, Multiculturalism, and the Media: Global Diversities.* Thousand Oaks, Calif.: Sage Publications, 1995.

Zack, Naomi, ed. *Race/Sex: Their Sameness, Differences and Interplay.* New York: Routledge, 1997.

HISTORY

Abdul-Jabbar, Kareem and Alan Steinberg. *Black Profiles in Courage: A Legacy of African American Achievement.* New York: William Morrow, 1996.

Archdeacon, Thomas J. *Becoming American: An Ethnic History.* New York: Free Press, 1983.

Asante, Molefi. *Afrocentricity.* Rev. ed. Trenton, N.J.: Africa World Press, 1988.

Bennett, Lerone, Jr. *Before the Mayflower: A History of Black America.* 6th ed. Chicago: Johnson, 1987.

Bowden, Henry Warner. *American Indians and Christian Missions.* Chicago, Ill.: University of Chicago Press, 1981.

Boxberger, Daniel L., ed. *Native North Americans: An Ethnohistorical Approach.* Dubuque, Iowa: Kendall/Hunt, 1990.

Brown, Dee. *Bury My Heart at Wounded Knee: An Indian History of the American West.* New York: Holt, Rinehart and Winston, 1974.

Cao, Lan, and Himilce Novas. *Everything You Need to Know About Asian American History.* New York: Plume, 1996.

Champagne, Duane, ed. *Chronology of Native North American History: From Pre-Columbian Times to the Present.* Detroit: Gale Research, 1994.

Chan, Sucheng. *Asian Americans: An Interpretive History.* Boston: Twayne, 1991.

Christian, Charles M., and Sari Bennett. *Black Saga: The African American Experience.* Boston: Houghton Mifflin, 1995.

Clayton, Lawrence A., ed. *The Hispanic Experience in North America: Sources for Study in the United States.* Columbus: Ohio State University Press, 1992.

Cullen-DuPont, Kathryn. *The Encyclopedia of Women's History in America.* New York: Facts on File, 1996.

Curtis, Nancy C. *Black Heritage Sites: An African American Odyssey and Finder's Guide.* Chicago: American Library Association, 1996.

Daniels, Roger. *Asian America: Chinese and Japanese in the United States Since 1850.* Seattle: University of Washington Press, 1988.

D'Emilio, John. *Sexual Politics, Sexual Communities: The Making of a Homosexual Minority in the United States, 1940-1970.* Chicago: University of Chicago Press, 1983.

Dinnerstein, Leonard. *Natives and Strangers: Blacks, Indians, and Immigrants in America.* Reprint. New York: Oxford University Press, 1990.

Duberman, Martin B., et al., eds. *Hidden from History: Reclaiming the Gay and Lesbian Past.* New York: New American Library, 1989.

Dubois, Ellen Carol, and Vicki L. Ruiz, eds. *Unequal Sisters: A Multi-cultural Reader in U.S. Women's History.* New York: Routledge, Chapman & Hall, 1990.

Fernandez-Shaw, Carlos M. *The Hispanic Presence in North America from 1492 to Today.* New York: Facts on File, 1991.

Flexner, Eleanor, and Ellen F. Fitzpatrick, eds. *Century of Struggle: The Woman's Rights Movement in the United States.* Cambridge, Mass.: The Belknap Press of Harvard University Press, 1996.

Franklin, John Hope, and Alfred A. Moss, Jr. *From Slavery to Freedom: A History of Negro Americans.* 6th ed. New York: Alfred A Knopf, 1988

Gann, L. H., and Peter J. Duignan. The *Hispanics in the United States: A History.* Boulder, Colo.: Westview Press, 1986.

Genovese, Eugene D. *From Rebellion to Revolution: Afro-American Slave Revolts in the Making of the Modern World.* Baton Rouge: Louisiana State University Press, 1979.

_____. *Roll, Jordan, Roll: The World the Slaves Made.* New York: Pantheon Books, 1974.

Gerber, David A., ed. *Anti-Semitism in American History.* Chicago: University of Illinois Press, 1986.

Goings, Kenneth W., and Raymond A. Mohl, eds. *The New African American Urban History.* Thousand Oaks, Calif.: Sage Publications, 1996.

Harrison, Alferdteen, ed. *Black Exodus: The Great Migration from the American South.* Jackson: University Press of Mississippi, 1991.

Herzberg, Arthur. *The Jews in America: Four Centuries of Uneasy Encounter.* New York: Simon & Schuster, 1989.

Hoxie, Frederick E., ed. *Indians in American History: An Introduction.* Arlington Heights, Ill.: Harlan Davidson, 1988.

Hutton Frankie, and Barbara S. Reed, eds. *Outsiders in 19th-Century Press History: Multicultural Perspectives.* Bowling Green, Ohio: Bowling Green State University Popular Press, 1995.

Johnson, Berman E. *The Dream Deferred: A Survey of Black America, 1840-1896.* 2d ed. Dubuque, Iowa: Kendall/Hunt, 1996.

Kanellos, Nicolas, and Cristelia Perez. *Chronology of Hispanic-American History: From Pre-Columbian Times to the Present.* New York: Gale Research, 1995.

Kanellos, Nicolas, and Bryan Ryan, eds. *Hispanic American Chronology.* New York: UXL, 1996.

Kerber, Linda K., Alice Kessler-Harris, and Kathryn K. Sklar, eds. *U.S. History as Women's History: New Feminist Essays.* Chapel Hill: University of North Carolina Press, 1995.

Konig, Hans. *Columbus: His Enterprise, Exploding the Myth.* New York: Monthly Review Press, 1991.

Krause, Corinne. *Grandmothers, Mothers, and Daughters: An Oral History of Three Generations of Ethnic Women.* Boston: Twayne, 1991.

Lai, Him Kark, Joe Huang, and Don Wong, eds. *The Chinese of America, 1785-1980.* San Francisco: Chinese Culture Foundation, 1980.

Lemann, Nicholas. *The Promised Land: The Great Black Migration and How It Changed America.* New York: Vintage Books, 1992.

Lunardini, Christine A. *Women's Rights.* Phoenix, Ariz.: Oryx Press, 1996.

McHenry, Robert, ed. *Famous American Women: A Biographical Dictionary from Colonial Times to the Present.* New York: Dover, 1980.

McKissack, Patricia C., and Fredrick McKissack, Jr. *Black Diamond: The Story of the Negro Baseball Leagues.* New York: Scholastic, 1994.

Meier, Matt S., and Feliciano Rivera, eds. *Dictionary of Mexican American History.* Westport, Conn.: Greenwood Press, 1981.

Minkoff, Debra C. *Organizing for Equality: The Evolution of Women's and Racial-Ethnic Organizations in America, 1955-1985.* New Brunswick, N.J.: Rutgers University Press, 1995.

Moses, L. G., and Raymond Wilson, eds. *Indian Lives.* Albuquerque: University of New Mexico Press, 1985.

Nabokov, Peter, ed. *Native American Testimony: A Chronicle of Indian-White Relations from Prophecy to the Present, 1492-1992.* New York: Viking Press, 1991.

Nalty, Bernard C. *Strength for the Fight: A History of Black Americans in the Military.* New York: Free Press, 1986.

Nash, Gary. *Red, White, Black: The Peoples of Early America.* 2d ed. Englewood Cliffs, N.J.: Prentice-Hall, 1982.

Nieman, Donald G., ed. *The African American Family in the South, 1861-1900.* New York: Garland, 1994.

Nies, Judith. *Native American History: A Chronology of the Vast Achievements of a Culture and Their Links to World Events.* New York: Ballantine Books, 1996.

Okihiro, Gary Y. *Margins and Mainstreams: Asians in American History and Culture.* Seattle: University of Washington Press, 1994.

Olson, James S., and Raymond Wilson. *Native Americans in the Twentieth Century.* Urbana: University of Illinois Press, 1984.

Orfalea, Gregory. *Before the Flames: A Quest for the History of Arab Americans.* Austin: University of Texas Press, 1988.

Prucha, Francis Paul. *The Great Father: The United States Government and the American Indians.* 2 vols. Lincoln: University of Nebraska Press, 1984.

Ross, Leon T., and Kenneth A. Mimms. *African American Almanac: Day-by-Day Black History.* Jefferson, N.C.: McFarland, 1997.

Smith, Jessie C. and Carrell P. Horton, eds. *Historical Statistics of Black America*. New York: Gale Research, 1995.

Southern, Eileen. *The Music of Black Americans: A History*. 3d ed. New York: W. W. Norton, 1997.

Sowell, Thomas. *Ethnic America: A History*. New York: Basic Books, 1981.

Stampp, Kenneth. *The Peculiar Institution: Slavery in the Ante-bellum South*. New York: Alfred A. Knopf, 1961.

Stokes, Melvyn, and Rick Halpern, eds. *Race and Class in the American South Since 1890*. Providence, R.I.: Berg, 1994.

Sturtevant, William C., ed. *Handbook of North American Indians*. Washington, D.C.: U.S. Government Printing Office, 1978.

Takaki, Ronald. *A Different Mirror: A History of Multicultural America*. Boston: Little, Brown, 1993.

_____. *Strangers from a Different Shore: A History of Asian Americans*. Boston: Little, Brown, 1989.

Van Deburg, William L., ed. *Modern Black Nationalism: From Marcus Garvey to Louis Farrakhan*. New York: New York University Press, 1997.

Vaz, Kim Marie, ed. *Black Women in America*. Thousand Oaks, Calif.: Sage Publications, 1995.

Velie, Alan R., ed. *Native American Perspectives on Literature and History*. Norman: University of Oklahoma Press, 1995.

Vigil, Diego. *From Indians to Chicanos: A Sociocultural History*. St. Louis: C. V. Mosby, 1980.

Ware, Susan, comp. *Modern American Women: A Documentary History*. 2d ed. New York: McGraw-Hill, 1997.

Warhus, Mark. *Another America: Native American Maps and the History of our Land*. New York: St. Martin's Press, 1997.

Weatherford, Doris. *Milestones: A Chronology of American Women's History*. New York: Facts on File, 1997.

Weber, David J., ed. *Foreigners in Their Native Land: Historical Roots of the Mexican Americans*. Albuquerque: University of New Mexico Press, 1973.

_____. *The Spanish Frontier in North America*. New Haven, Conn.: Yale University Press, 1992.

White, Deborah Gray. *Ar'n't I a Woman?: Female Slaves in the Plantation South*. New York: W. W. Norton, 1985.

Woloch, Nancy. *Women and the American Experience*. New York: Alfred A. Knopf, 1984.

Yung, Judy. *Chinese Women of America: A Pictorial History*. Seattle: University of Washington Press, 1986.

Zinn, Howard. *A People's History of the United States*. New York: Harper & Row, 1990.

Zophy, Angela Howard, ed. *Handbook of American Women's History*. Hamden, Conn.: Garland Reference Library of the Humanities, 1990.

IMMIGRANTS AND IMMIGRATION

Ashabranner, Brent K. *Still a Nation of Immigrants*. New York: Cobble Hill Books/Dutton, 1993.

Bean, Frank D., Barry Edmonston, and Jeffrey S. Passel, eds. *Undocumented Migration to the United States: IRCA and the Experience of the 1980's*. Santa Monica, Calif.: Rand, 1990.

Bodnar, John. *The Transplanted: A History of Immigrants in Urban America*. Bloomington: Indiana University Press, 1985.

Briggs, Vernon M., and Stephen Moore. *Still an Open Door?: U.S. Immigration Policy and the American Economy*. Washington, D.C.: American University Press 1994.

Brimelow, Peter. *Alien Nation: Common Sense About America's Immigration Disaster*. New York: Random House, 1995.

Capaldi, Nicholas, ed. *Immigration: Debating the Issues*. Amherst, N.Y.: Prometheus Books, 1997.

Chiswick, Barry, ed. *Immigration, Language, and Ethnicity: Canada and the United States*. Washington, D.C.: AEI Press, 1992.

Cummings, Scott, ed. *Self-Help in Urban America*. Port Washington, N.Y.: Kennikat, 1980.

Daniels, Roger. *Coming to America: A History of Immigration and Ethnicity in American Life*. New York: HarperCollins, 1990.

Davis, Marilyn P. *Mexican Voices, American Dreams: An Oral History of Mexican Immigration to the United States*. New York: Henry Holt, 1990.

Diner, Hasia R. *Erin's Daughters in America: Irish Immigrant Women in the Nineteenth Century*. Baltimore: The Johns Hopkins University Press, 1982.

Dinnerstein, Leonard, and David M. Reimers. *Ethnic America: A History of Immigration*. 3d ed. New York: Harper & Row, 1988.

Ferraro, Thomas J. *Ethnic Passages: Literary Immigrants in Twentieth Century America*. Chicago: Chicago University Press, 1993.

Fitzpatrick, Joseph P. *Puerto Rican Americans: The Meaning of Migration to the Mainland*. 2d rev. ed.

Englewood Cliffs, N.J.: Prentice-Hall, 1987.

Glazer, Nathan. *Clamor at the Gates: The New American Immigration.* San Francisco: ICS Press, 1985.

Haines, David. *Refugees as Immigrants: Cambodians, Laotians, and Vietnamese in America.* Totowa, N.J.: Rowman & Littlefield, 1989.

_____, ed. *Refugees in the United States: A Reference Handbook.* Westport, Conn.: Greenwood Press, 1985.

Hamamoto, Darrell Y., and Rodolfo D. Torres, eds. *New American Destinies: A Reader in Contemporary Asian and Latino Immigration.* New York: Routledge, 1997.

Handlin, Oscar. *A Pictorial History of Immigration.* New York: Crown, 1972.

_____. *The Uprooted: The Epic Story of the Great Migrations that Made the American People.* 2d ed. Boston: Little, Brown, 1990.

Henderson, George, and Thompson D. Olasiji. *Migrants, Immigrants, and Slaves: Racial and Ethnic Groups in America.* Lanham, Md.: University Press of America, 1995.

Howe, Irving. *World of Our Fathers: The Journey of the East European Jews to America and the Life They Found and Made.* New York: Simon & Schuster, 1976.

Ichioka, Yuji. *The Issei: The World of the First Generation Japanese Immigrants, 1885-1924.* New York: Free Press, 1988.

Knoll, Tricia. *Becoming Americans: Asian Sojourners, Immigrants, and Refugees in the Western United States.* Portland, Oreg.: Coast to Coast Books, 1982.

Lissak, Rivka Shpak. *Pluralism and Progressives: Hull House and the New Immigrants, 1890-1919.* Chicago: University of Chicago Press, 1989.

Loveless, Stephen C. *Immigration and Its Impact on American Cities.* Westport, Conn.: Praeger, 1996.

Masud-Piloto, Felix R. *From Welcomed Exiles to Illegal Immigrants: Cuban Migration to the U.S., 1959-1995.* Lanham, Md.: Rowman & Littlefield, 1996.

Miller, E. Willard and Ruby M. Miller. *United States Immigration: A Reference Handbook.* Santa Barbara, Calif.: ABC-Clio, 1996.

Myers, Ernest R., ed. *Challenges of a Changing America: Perspectives on Immigration and Multiculturalism in the United States.* San Francisco: Austin & Winfield, 1994.

Palmer, Ransford R., ed. *In Search of Better Life: Perspectives on Migrations from the Caribbean.* New York: Praeger, 1990.

Portes, Alejandro and Ruben G. Rumbaut. *Immigrant America: A Portrait.* 2d ed. Berkeley, Calif.: University of California Press, 1996.

Pozzetta, George, ed. *Folklore, Culture, and the Immigrant.* New York: Garland, 1991.

Riemers, David M. *Still the Golden Door: The Third World Comes to America.* New York: Columbia University Press, 1985.

Roitman, Joel M. *The Immigrants, the Progressives, and the Schools: Americanization and the Impact of the New Immigration Upon Public Education in the United States, 1890-1920.* Stark, Kans.: De Young Press, 1996.

Santoli, Al. *New Americans: An Oral History of Immigrants and Refugees in the United States Today.* New York: Viking Penguin, 1988.

Stave, Bruce M., John F. Sutherland, and Aldo Salerno. *From the Old Country: An Oral History of European Migration to America.* New York: Twayne, 1994.

Tripp, Eleanor B. *To America: The Story of Why People Left Their Homes for the New Land.* New York: Harcourt, Brace & World, 1969.

Ungar, Sanford J. *Fresh Blood: The New American Immigrants.* New York: Simon & Schuster, 1995.

Wasserman, Fred, ed. *Ellis Island: An Illustrated History of the Immigrant Experience.* New York: Macmillan, 1991.

Weatherford, Doris. *Foreign and Female: Immigrant Women in America, 1840-1930.* New York: Schocken Books, 1986.

Weinberg, Sidney Stahl. *The World of Our Mothers: The Lives of Jewish Immigrant Women.* Chapel Hill: University of North Carolina Press, 1988.

Weisberger, Bernard A. *Many People, One Nation.* Boston: Houghton Mifflin, 1987.

Zhou, Min, and Carl L. Bankston III. *Growing Up American: The Adaptation of Vietnamese Children to American Society.* New York: Russell Sage Foundation, 1998.

RACE AND RACISM

Ashmore, Harry S. *Hearts and Minds: The Anatomy of Racism from Roosevelt to Reagan.* New York: McGraw-Hill, 1982.

Beals, Ivan A. *Our Racist Legacy: Will the Church Resolve the Conflict?* Notre Dame, Ind.: Cross Cultural, 1997.

Bell, Derrick. *Race, Racism, and American Law.* 2d ed. Boston: Little, Brown, 1980.

Brooks, Roy. *Rethinking the American Race Problem.* Berkeley: University of California Press, 1990.

Bullard, Sara, et al., eds. *The Ku Klux Klan: A History of Racism and Violence.* 3d ed. Montgomery, Ala.: Klanwatch, 1988.

Carlisle, Rodney. *The Roots of Black Nationalism.* Port Washington, N.Y.: Kennikat Press, 1975.

Cashmore, E. Ellis. *Dictionary of Race and Ethnic Relations.* 2d ed. London: Routledge, 1988.

Dijk, Teun A. van, ed. *Communicating Racism: Ethnic Prejudice in Thought and Talk.* Newbury Park, Calif.: Sage Publications, 1987.

Doob, Christopher B. *Racism: An American Cauldron.* New York: HarperCollins, 1993.

Dudley, William, and Charles Cozic, eds. *Racism in America: Opposing Viewpoints.* San Diego: Greenhaven Press, 1991.

Edwards, Jefferson D., Jr. *Purging Racism from Modern Christianity: Freedom and Purpose Through Identity.* Grand Rapids, Mich.: Zondervan, 1996.

Fetzer, Philip L., ed. *The Ethnic Moment: The Search for Equality in the American Experience.* Armonk, N.Y.: M. E. Sharpe, 1997.

Flynn, Kevin, and Gary Gerhardt. *The Silent Brotherhood: Inside America's Racist Underground.* New York: Free Press, 1989.

Foner, Philip S. and Daniel Rosenberg, eds. *Racism, Dissent, and Asian Americans from 1850 to the Present: A Documentary History.* Westport, Conn.: Greenwood Press, 1993.

Gates, E. Nathaniel, ed. *Racial Classification and History.* New York: Garland, 1997.

Giovanni, Nikki. *Racism 101.* New York: William Morrow, 1994.

Gossett, Thomas. *Race: The History of an Idea in America.* 1963. Rev. ed. Edited by Arnold Rampersad and Shelley Fisher Fishkin. New York: Oxford University Press, 1997.

Gregory, Steven and Roger Sanjek, eds. *Race.* New Brunswick, N.J.: Rutgers University Press, 1994.

Hacker, Andrew. *Two Nations: Black and White, Separate, Hostile, Unequal.* Rev. ed. New York: Ballantine Books, 1995.

Harris, Fred, and Roger Wilkins, eds. *Quiet Riots: Race and Poverty in the United States.* New York: Pantheon Books, 1988.

Hawley, Willis D., and Anthony Jackson, eds. *Toward a Common Destiny: Improving Race and Ethnic Relations in America.* San Francisco: Jossey-Bass, 1995.

Herbst, Philip, comp. *The Color of Words: An Encyclopedic Dictionary of Ethnic Bias.* Yarmouth, Maine: Intercultural Press, 1997.

Hill, Herbert, and James E. Jones, Jr., eds. *Race in America: The Struggle for Equality.* Madison: University of Wisconsin Press, 1993.

hooks, bell. *Killing Rage: Ending Racism.* New York: Henry Holt, 1995.

Horsman, Reginald. *Race and Manifest Destiny: The Origins of American Racial Anglo-Saxonism.* Cambridge, Mass.: Harvard University Press, 1981.

Huff, Delores J. *To Live Heroically: Institutional Racism and American Indian Education.* Albany: State University of New York Press, 1997.

Lubiano, Wahneema H., ed. *The House that Race Built: Black Americans, U.S. Terrain.* New York: Pantheon Books, 1997.

McKenzie, Steven L. *All God's Children: A Biblical Critique of Racism.* Louisville, Ky.: Westminster John Knox Press, 1997.

McKissack, Patricia. *Taking a Stand Against Racism and Racial Discrimination.* New York: Franklin Watts, 1990.

Newton, Michael, and Judy Newton. *Racial and Religious Violence in America: A Chronology.* New York: Garland, 1991.

Page, Clarence. *Showing My Color: Impolite Essays on Race and Identity.* New York: HarperCollins, 1996.

Pascoe, Elaine. *Racial Prejudice.* Issues in American History series. New York: Franklin Watts, 1985.

Powell, Thomas F. *The Persistence of Racism in America.* Lanham, Md.: Littlefield Adams, 1993.

Root, Maria P. P., ed. *The Multiracial Experience: Racial Borders as the New Frontier.* Thousand Oaks, Cal.: Sage Publications, 1996.

Ropers, Richard B. and Daniel J. Pence. *American Prejudice: With Liberty and Justice for Some.* New York: Insight Books, 1995.

Rothenberg, Paula S., ed. *Race, Class, and Gender in the United States: An Integrated Study.* 3d ed. New York: St. Martin's Press, 1995.

Russell, Kathy, Midge Wilson, and Ron Hall. *The Color Complex: The Last Taboo Among African-Americans.* New York: Harcourt Brace Jovanovich, 1992.

Shipman, Pat. *The Evolution of Racism: Human Differences and the Use and Abuse of Science.* New York: Simon & Schuster, 1994.

Shropshire, Kenneth L. *In Black and White: Race and*

Sports in America. New York: New York University Press, 1996.

Smith, Robert C. *Racism in the Post-Civil Rights Era: Now You See It, Now You Don't.* Albany: State University of New York Press, 1995.

Sowell, Thomas. *Race and Culture: A World View.* New York: Basic Books, 1994.

Steele, Shelby. *The Content of Our Character: A New Vision of Race in America.* New York: St. Martin's Press, 1990.

Takaki, Ronald T., ed. *From Different Shores: Perspectives on Race and Ethnicity in America.* 2d ed. New York: Oxford University Press, 1994.

Taylor, Jared. *Paved with Good Intentions: The Failure of Race Relations in Contemporary America.* New York: Carroll & Graf, 1992.

Terkel, Studs. *Race: How Blacks and Whites Think and Feel About the American Obsession.* New York: New Press, 1992.

Thernstrom, Stephan, and Abigail M. Thernstrom. *America in Black and White: One Nation, Indivisible.* New York: Simon & Schuster, 1997.

Tuch, Steven A., and Jack K. Martin. eds. *Racial Attitudes in the 1990s: Continuity and Change.* Westport, Conn.: Praeger, 1997.

Vaughan, Alden T. *Roots of American Racism: Essays on the Colonial Experience.* New York: Oxford University Press, 1995.

Weinberg, Meyer, comp. *Racism in Contemporary America.* Westport, Conn.: Greenwood Press, 1996.

_____. *Racism in the United States: A Comprehensive Classified Bibliography.* Westport, Conn.: Greenwood Press, 1990.

West, Cornel. *Race Matters.* New York: Beacon Press, 1993.

Wilson, Carter A. *Racism: From Slavery to Advanced Capitalism.* Thousand Oaks, Calif.: Sage Publications, 1996.

Wilson, Clint C., II, and Felix Gutierrez. *Race, Multiculturalism, and the Media: From Mass to Class Communication.* 2d ed. Thousand Oaks, Calif.: Sage Publications, 1995.

Yancey, George A. *Beyond Black and White: Reflections on Racial Reconciliation.* Grand Rapids, Mich.: Baker Books, 1996.

Zack, Naomi, ed. *American Mixed Race: The Culture of Microdiversity.* Lanham, Md.: Rowman & Littlefield, 1995.

_____. *Race and Mixed Race.* Philadelphia: Temple University Press, 1993.

RELIGIOUS GROUPS AND RELIGION

Bellah, Robert N., and Frederick E. Greenspahn, eds. *Uncivil Religion: Interreligious Hostility in America.* New York: Crossroad, 1987.

Cantor, David and Alan M. Schwartz, eds. *The Religious Right: The Assault on Tolerance and Pluralism in America.* New York: Anti-Defamation League, 1994.

Cenkner, William, ed. *The Multicultural Church: A New Landscape in U.S. Theologies.* New York: Paulist Press, 1996.

DeYoung, Curtiss P. *Coming Together: The Bible's Message in an Age of Diversity.* Valley Forge, Pa.: Judson Press, 1995.

Foster, Charles R., and Theodore Brelsford. *We Are the Church Together: Cultural Diversity in Congregational Life.* Valley Forge, Pa.: Trinity Press International, 1996.

Gaede, S. D. *When Tolerance Is No Virtue: Political Correctness, Multiculturalism and the Future of Truth and Justice.* Downers Grove, Ill.: InterVarsity Press, 1993.

Gill, Sam D. *Native American Religions: An Introduction.* Belmont, Calif.: Wadsworth, 1982.

Hollenbach, David. *Justice, Peace, and Human Rights: American Catholic Social Ethics in a Pluralistic World.* New York: Crossroad, 1988.

Law, Eric H. F. *The Bush Was Blazing But Not Consumed: Developing a Multicultural Community Through Dialogue and Liturgy.* St. Louis: Chalice Press, 1996.

Lee, Jung Young. *Marginality: The Key to Multicultural Theology.* Minneapolis, Minn.: Fortress Press, 1995.

Lincoln, C. Eric, and Laurence H. Mamiya. *The Black Church in the African American Experience.* Durham, N.C.: Duke University Press, 1990.

Lippy, Charles, and Peter Williams, eds. *Encyclopedia of the American Religious Experience: Studies of Traditions and Movements.* 3 vols. New York: Charles Scribner's Sons, 1988.

Liptak, Dolores Ann. *Immigrants and Their Church.* New York: Macmillan, 1989.

McGuire, Meredith B. *Religion: The Social Context.* 3d ed. Belmont, Calif.: Wadsworth, 1992.

Rhoads, David M. *The Challenge of Diversity: The Witness of Paul and the Gospels.* Minneapolis, Minn.: Fortress Press, 1996.

Wald, Kenneth D. *Religion and Politics in the United States.* 2d ed. Washington, D.C.: Congressional Quarterly, 1992.

Subject List

This section lists the entries of the entire eight-volume encyclopedia by various subjects and topic headings. The first part of the list is arranged by population groups, which include:

The second part lists entries under these twenty subject areas:

Entries printed in ordinary roman or italic characters appear in the first six volumes of the encyclopedia. Those printed in **boldface** are in the supplement—volumes 7 and 8; boldface entries followed by asterisks (*) are supplement updates of topics that also appear in the original six volumes.

Entries By Population Group

AFRICAN AMERICANS
A. Philip Randolph Institute
Aaron, Hank
Abdul-Jabbar, Kareem
Abolitionist movement

Affirmative action*
African American-American Indian relations
African American farmers
African American-Jewish relations
African American-Korean American relations*

Tyson, Mike
Ujamaa
Underground Railroad
United Negro College Fund
Universal Negro Improvement Association
Vesey, Denmark
Voting Rights Act of 1970
Voting Rights Act of 1975
Voting Rights Act of 1982
Walker, Alice
Walker, Madame C. J.
Washington, Booker T.
Washington Urban League v. Washington
   Metropolitan Area Transit
Watts riots
Wellesley College
West, Cornel
West Indian culture
Wheatley, Phillis
Wilkins, Roy
Williams, Daniel Hale
Wilson, William Julius
Winfrey, Oprah
Wonder, Stevie
Woods, Eldrick "Tiger"
Woodson, Carter Godwin
Wright, Richard
Young, Andrew Jackson, Jr.
Young, Charles

AMERICAN INDIANS, INUITS, and ALEUTS
Acoma, Battle of
African American-American Indian relations
Alaska Native Claims Settlement Act
Alcatraz Island, occupation of
Aleuts in the United States
American Indian assimilation
American Indian Civil Rights Act of 1968
American Indian cultural contributions
American Indian demography
American Indian gambling
American Indian games
American Indian hunting and fishing
American Indian languages
American Indian migration legends
American Indian Movement
American Indian Religious Freedom Act
American Indian revitalization movements
American Indian studies programs
American Indian trade

American Indian-U.S. government relations
American Indian-U.S. government treaties
American Indian water rights
American Indian women
American Indians—contemporary social
   conditions
American Indians—rural
American Indians of California
American Indians of the Great Lakes
American Indians of the Great Plains
American Indians of the Northeast
American Indians of the Pacific Northwest
American Indians of the Southeast
American Indians of the Southwest
Americans for Indian Opportunity
Anasazi
Apaches
Arapahos
Architecture and dwellings—American Indian
Articles of Agreement
Arts and crafts—American Indian
Assembly of First Nations
Bacon's Rebellion
Banks, Dennis
Bannock War
Big Foot
Bison and American Indians
Black Kettle
Bureau of Indian Affairs
Business and corporate enterprise
Camp Grant Massacre
Campbell, Ben Nighthorse
Captain Jack
Carlisle Indian School
Cherokee Tobacco case
Cherokees
Cheyennes
Choctaw Nation of Oklahoma
Choctaws, Mississippi band
Cíbola, Seven Cities of
Cochise
Colonial America
Colonialism
Columbus, Christopher
Columbus Day celebrations
Comanches
Council of Energy Resource Tribes
Councils, tribal
Crazy Horse
Creation myths—American Indian

Creek War
Curtis, Edward Sheriff
Dancing Rabbit Creek, Treaty of
Dawes Act
Deloria, Ella Cara
Deloria, Vine, Jr.
Department of Indian Affairs and Northern Development
Education—American Indian
Erdrich, Louise
Exploration and explorers of the New World
Fetterman Massacre
Five Civilized Tribes
French and Indian War
Friends of the Indian
Gall
Geronimo
Ghost Dance religion
Hayes, Ira
Health and medicine—American Indian
Heat-Moon, William Least
Hopis
Indian Act of 1876
Indian Act of 1951
Indian Act of 1985
Indian Arts and Crafts Board
Indian Child Welfare Act
Indian Citizenship Act of 1924
Indian Claims Commission
Indian Education Acts
Indian hobbyist movement
Indian Removal Act of 1830
Indian Reorganization Act
Indian rights movement
Indian Rights Association
Indian Self-Determination and Education Assistance Act of 1975
Indian Territory
Indian Wars
Institute of American Indian Arts
Inuits
Iroquois League
Joseph, Chief
Kachinas
King Philip's War
Little Bighorn, Battle of the
Little Turtle
Lone Wolf v. Hitchcock
Long Walk of the Navajos
Longest Walk

Lord Dunmore's War
Mankato, Minn.—mass executions
Mankiller, Wilma
Manuelito
Medicine men—traditional American Indian
Mesa Verde
Métis
Missionaries and American Indians
Momaday, N. Scott
Mound builders
Music—American Indian
Natchez Revolt
National Congress of American Indians
National Council of American Indians
National Indian Association
National Indian Youth Council
Native American Church
Native American Grave and Burial Protection Act
Native American land claims
Native American Programs Act of 1974
Native American Rights Fund
Native Hawaiian Health Care Act of 1988
Navajo Code Talkers
Navajo-Hopi Land Dispute
Navajo Rehabilitation Act
Navajo War
Navajos
Nez Perce
Oklahoma Indian Welfare Act
Oklahoma land runs
Osceola
Pan-Indianism
Parker, Ely Samuel
Parker, Quanah
Pequot War
Peyote
Pocahontas
Pontiac
Pontiac's Rebellion
Popé
Potlatches and giveaways
Powhatan
Powhatan Confederacy
Powwows
Pueblo Revolt of 1680
Pueblos
Pushmataha
Rain Dance
Red Cloud
Red River War

ASIAN and PACIFIC ISLANDER AMERICANS

National Democratic Council of Asian and Pacific Americans

Native Sons of the Golden West

Nativism

Ng Poon Chew

Ngor, Haing

Nisei

Onizuka, Ellison

Organization of Chinese American Women

Organization of Chinese Americans

Organization of Pan Asian American Women

Ozawa, Seiji

Ozawa v. United States

Pacific Islander Americans

Pakistani Americans

Paper sons

Pei, I. M.

Picture brides

Plyler v. Doe

Post-traumatic stress disorder—Indochinese refugees

Refugee Act of 1980

San Francisco, Calif.

Sansei

Saund, Dalip Singh

Shima, George

Shintoists

Singh, Jag Jeet

Sojourners and Asian immigration

Southeast Asia Resource Action Center

Sri Lankan Americans

Sun Yat-sen

Tagalog language

Taiwanese Americans

Takaki, Ronald

Takamine, Jokichi

Takei, George

Tan, Amy

Thai Americans

Tien, Chang-lin

Tongs

Toyama, Tetsuo

Triads

Tydings-McDuffie Act

Uchida, Yoshiko

United States v. Bhagat Singh Thind

Vietnamese Americans

Wang, An

Wang, Wayne

Wards Cove Packing Co. v. Atonio

Wong, Anna May

Wong, Jade Snow

Yamaguchi, Kristi Tsuya

Yamasaki, Minoru

Yang, Chen Ning

Yashima, Taro

Yellow peril

Yep, Laurence Michael

Yonsei

Yung Wing

EUROPEAN and MIDDLE EASTERN AMERICANS

Acadians in the United States

Afghan Americans

Albanian Americans

American-Arab Anti-Discrimination Committee

American Turners

Amish

Ancient Order of Hibernians in America

Anglo-Saxons in colonial America

Arab Americans

Architecture—Spanish influence

Armenian Americans

Australian Americans

Austrian Americans

Bacon's Rebellion

Basque Americans

Belgian Americans

Belorussian Americans

Benevolent and fraternal organizations

Black Hand conspiracy

Bulgarian Americans

Canadians in the U.S.

Cart War of 1857

Celtic and Ceilli Music

Colonial America

Columbus, Christopher

Croatian Americans

Czech Americans

Danish Americans

Del Amo Foundation

Displaced Persons Act

Dutch Americans

Egyptian Americans

English Americans

Estonian Americans

Exploration and explorers of the New World

Ferraro, Geraldine

Fetterman Massacre

Finnish Americans

Hadassah
Hanukkah
Hasidism
Hebrew language
Hebrew Union College
Holocaust, the
Holocaust denial
Holocaust Memorial Museum, U.S.
Israeli Americans
Jewish American communities
Jewish American women
Jewish Americans
Jewish Defense League
Jewish immigrants
Jewish philanthropy
Jewish Theological Seminary
Jews—Conservative
Jews—Orthodox
Jews—Reconstructionist
Jews—Reform
Jews and intellectual life
Kosher
Labor movement
Landsmannschaften
Lerner, Michael
Passover
Restrictive covenants
Rosh Hashanah
Russian Jews
Sephardic Jews
Skirball Museum and Cultural Center
United Hebrew Trades Union
Wirth, Louis
Workmen's Circle
Yeshiva University
Yiddish language
Yom Kippur
Young Men's/Women's Hebrew Association
Zionism

LATINOS
Adarand Constructors v. Pena
Alatorre, Richard
Alianza Hispano-Americana, La
Alien Contract Labor Law
Alien smuggling
Alliance for Progress
Alvarez, Luis Walter
American G.I. Forum
Anaya, Rudolfo A.

Anaya, Toney
Argentinean Americans
Arnaz, Desi
Association of Puerto Rican Executive Directors
August 29th Movement
Aztlán
Badillo, Herman
Báez, Joan
Ballet Hispanico
Banco Popular
Barrios*
Bilingual education*
Bilingual Education Act of 1968
Bilingual Foundation for the Arts
Bilingual Review Press
Bilingualism
Blades, Rubén
"Blowout"
Border control
Border culture
Border Folk Festival
Border Patrol, U.S.
Bracero program
Brazilian Americans
Brown Berets
Brown Power movement
Brown Scare
Bujones, Fernando
Business and corporate enterprise
California
Carr, Vikki
Cart War of 1857
Castañeda, Carlos
Catholic Youth Organization
Católicos por la Raza
Cavazos, Lauro Fred
Central American Refugee Center
Chávez, César Estrada
Chávez, Linda
Chicanismo
Chicano Moratorium
Chicano movement
Chicano studies programs
Chilean Americans
Cholos
Cinco de Mayo
Cisneros, Evelyn
Cisneros, Henry Gabriel
Clemente, Roberto
Code switching

Mexico, bailout of
Miami, Fla.
Migrant workers
Molina, Gloria
Montalbán, Ricardo
Montoya, Joseph Manuel
Moreno, Rita
Mothers of East L.A.—Santa Isabel
Mount Pleasant riots
Movimiento Estudiantil Chicano de Aztlán
Murals
Music—Latino
National Alliance of Spanish-Speaking People for
  Equality
National Association of Hispanic Journalists
National Association of Hispanic Publications
National Association of Latino Elected and
  Appointed Officials
National Association of Latino Elected and
  Appointed Officials Education Fund
National Chicano Health Organization
National Chicano Moratorium on Vietnam
National Conference of Puerto Rican Women
National Congress for Puerto Rican Rights
National Council of Hispanic Women
National Council of La Raza
National Hispanic Media Coalition
National Puerto Rican Coalition
National Puerto Rican Forum
Nicaraguan Americans
North American Free Trade Agreement
Novello, Antonia Coello
Nuyoricans
Olmos, Edward James
Operation Bootstrap
Operation Gatekeeper
Operation Wetback
Ortega, Katherine Davalos
Pachuco
Panamanian Americans
Paredes, Américo
Partido de la Raza Unida
Pecan shellers' strike
Penitentes
Peruvian Americans
Plyler v. Doe
Political Association of Spanish-Speaking
  Organizations
Posadas, Las
Proposition 187

Puerto Rican Family Institute
Puerto Rican Legal Defense and Education Fund
Puerto Rican nationalism
Puerto Rican Traveling Theater
Puerto Ricans
Quinceañera
Quinn, Anthony
Quinto Sol Publications
Raza Unida Party, La*
Repatriation program
Rescate, El
Reynoso, Cruz
Rivera, Diego
Rivera, Geraldo Miguel
Rodríguez, Richard
Ronstadt, Linda Marie
Roybal, Edward R.
Salinas lettuce strike
Salsa music
Salvadoran Americans
San Jacinto, Battle of
San Joaquin cotton strike
San Pascual, Battle of
Sanctuary movement
Santa Fe, N.Mex.
Santa Fe Fiesta
Santana, Carlos
Santayana, George
Santería
Serra, Junípero
Sierra, Paul Alberto
Sixty-fifth Infantry Regiment
Sleepy Lagoon case
Sociedad Nacional Hispánica Sigma Delta Pi
Society of Hispanic Professional Engineers
Southwest Voter Registration Education Project
Spanglish
Spanish Empire and the New World
Spanish International Network
Spanish language
Suarez, Xavier
Taos Rebellion
Teatro Campesino, El
Texas Folklife Festival
Texas Revolt
Tex-Mex music
Tijerina, Reies López
Tonatiuh International
Trevino, Lee
Undocumented persons

United Farm Workers
United States v. Lopez
Valdez, Luis Miguel
Valens, Ritchie
Valenzuela, Fernando
Vaquero
Young Lords
Zoot-suit riots

OTHER MARGINALIZED GROUPS

Acquired immune deficiency syndrome*
Age Discrimination in Employment Act
Ageism and age discrimination
AIDS quilt project
Air Carriers Access Act
Alcoholism
American Association of Retired Persons
Americans with Disabilities Act of 1990
Architectural Barriers Act
Bill of Rights for the Handicapped
Biracial and mixed race children
Bisexuality
Braille
Child abuse
Children's Defense Fund
Children's rights movement
Christian extremism
Civil rights
Civil rights legislation*
Civil Rights Restoration Act of 1987
Colorado Constitution Ballot Amendment 2
Coming out
Declaration of the Rights of the Child
Declaration on the Rights of Disabled Persons
Disability rights movement
Dix, Dorothea Lynde
"Don't ask, don't tell"
Education for All Handicapped Children Act
Education of the Handicapped Act
Elderly abuse
Elementary and Secondary Education Act
Employment Equity Act of 1986
Environmental racism
Equal Educational Opportunity Act
Equal Employment Opportunity Act of 1972
Equal opportunity programs
Equal protection
Ethnic cleansing
Ethnic identity
Eugenics

Foxworthy, Jeff
Frank, Barney
Fundamentalism, religious
Gay and lesbian activism
Gay and lesbian parents
Gay and lesbian rights movement
Gay and lesbian studies programs
Gay bashing
Gay Liberation Front
Gray Panthers
Haig v. The Queen
Haymarket Affair
Homophobia
Homosexuality, religion and
In re Gault
Independent living movement
Individuals with Disabilities Education Act
Industrial Workers of the World
Infant mortality
Intelligence and achievement tests, bias in
Keller, Helen
Kuhn, Maggie
Lesbians
McKinney v. University of Guelph
Mainstreaming
Mapplethorpe, Robert
Marriages, same-sex
Migrant Children Education Assistance Act of 1960
Military, homosexuals in
Mills v. Board of Education of District of Columbia
Minimum wage laws for women and children
Miscegenation
Mossop v. Attorney General of Canada
National Center for Lesbian Rights
National Coalition for Haitian Rights
National Council of Senior Citizens
National Gay and Lesbian Task Force
National Institute on Aging
New Age movement
Nuns and priests
Older Americans
Orphans and orphanages
PARC v. Commonwealth of Pennsylvania
Rehabilitation Act
Religious right
Retirement Equity Act
Self-Help for the Elderly
Selph v. Council of the City of Los Angeles
Sex-change operations

Sign language
Skinheads
Social Security Disability Insurance
Soldiers Rehabilitation Act
Special Olympics
Stonewall riots
Transcendental meditation
Transsexuals
Vocational rehabilitation legislation
**Voting Accessibility for the Elderly and
 Handicapped Act**
White supremacist movements
Widows
Wyatt v. Strickley

WOMEN
Abortion
Abzug, Bella
Academies—female
Addams, Jane
African American women
African American women—matriarchy debate
*Akron v. Akron Center for Reproductive Health,
 Inc.*
Albright, Madeleine
Alcott, Louisa May
Alimony
All-American Girls Professional Baseball League
Alternative music, women in
American Association of University Women
American Indian women
American Woman Suffrage Association
Anderson, Mary
Anthony, Susan B.
Antiabortion protests and violence
Antifeminism
Arden, Elizabeth
Army Nurse Corps
Asian American women
Association for Intercollegiate Athletics for Women
Atkinson, Ti-Grace
Atwood, Margaret
Baby M case
Baby Richard case
Balch, Emily Greene
Barbie dolls
Barnard College
Barrymore, Ethel
Barton, Clara
Battered women

Battle of the Sexes
Beauty pageants
Beecher, Catharine Esther
Berenson, Senda
Bethune, Mary McLeod
Biased language
Biological clock
Birth control and family planning
Black feminism
Blackwell, Elizabeth
Bobbitt case
Bourke-White, Margaret
Brandeis Brief
Braun, Carol E. Moseley*
Breast cancer
Breast-feeding
Breast implants
Breckenridge, Mary
Brooks, Allen, and Dixon v. Canada Safeway
Brown, Helen Gurley
Brown, Rita Mae
Brownmiller, Susan
Bryn Mawr College
Bulimia nervosa
Business and corporate enterprise
Cabrini, Mother
Call Off Your Old Tired Ethics
Campbell, Kim
Caraway, Hattie
Carson, Rachel
Cassatt, Mary
Cather, Willa
Catholics for a Free Choice
Catt, Carrie Chapman
Cesarean Prevention Movement
Cesarean sections
Chesnut, Mary Boykin
Child, Lydia Maria
Chisholm, Shirley
Citadel case
Civil Rights Act of 1964
Civil rights legislation*
Clark, Marcia
Clearinghouse on Women's Issues
Clinton, Hillary Rodham
Colleges—women's
Colored Women's League
Combat, women in
Commission on Civil Rights
Common-law marriage

Women's Peace Party
Women's Reserve in the Marine Corps
Women's Sports Foundation
Women's studies programs
Wong, Anna May

Wong, Jade Snow
World War II—civilian roles
Yamaguchi, Kristi Tsuya
Year of the Woman
Zaharias, "Babe" Didrikson

Entries by Subject

AMERICAN HISTORY (pre-World War I)
Abolitionist movement
Acadians in the United States
Acoma, Battle of
African American-American Indian relations
African American studies programs
African Americans—early history and cultural
  contributions
Alamo, Battle of the
Alien and Sedition Acts
American Colonization Society
American Indian assimilation
American Indian cultural contributions
American Indian demography
American Indian studies programs
American Indian trade
American Indians of California
American Indians of the Great Lakes
American Indians of the Great Plains
American Indians of the Northeast
American Indians of the Pacific Northwest
American Indians of the Southeast
American Indians of the Southwest
American Indian-U.S. government relations
American Indian-U.S. government treaties
American Revolution
Amistad slave revolt
Anasazi
Anglo-Saxons in colonial America
Anti-Chinese violence
Apaches
Arab Americans
Arapahos
Architecture—Spanish influence
Architecture and dwellings—American Indian
Armenian Americans
Articles of Agreement
Ashkenazic Jews
Asia-Pacific Triangle
Asian American studies programs
Asiatic Exclusion League

Austrian Americans
Back to Africa movement
Bacon's Rebellion
Bannock War
Belgian Americans
Belorussian Americans
Bison and American Indians
Black Codes
Black History Month
Blasphemy laws
Brook Farm
Buffalo soldiers
Bureau of Colored Troops
Bureau of Indian Affairs
Burlingame Treaty
Calvinists
Camp Grant Massacre
Canadians in the United States
Carlisle Indian School
Carson, Kit
Cart War of 1857
Catholic-Protestant relations
Catholics, Roman
Central Pacific Railroad—Chinese workers
Cherokees
Chesnut, Mary Boykin
Cheyennes
Chicano studies programs
Chinatowns
Chinese Americans
Chinese boycott of 1905
Chinese Consolidated Benevolent Association
Chinese Exclusion Act
Chinese Hand Laundry Alliance
Chivington, John Milton
Choctaw Nation of Oklahoma
Choctaws, Mississippi band
Church and state, separation of
Cíbola, Seven Cities of
Civil rights legislation*
Civil service

CULTURE and COMMUNITY

EMPLOYMENT, BUSINESS, LABOR, and the ECONOMY

Manlapit, Pablo
Maquiladoras
Migrant workers
Minimum wage laws*
Minimum wage laws for women and children
Molly Maguires
Mommy track
Motown Industries
Muller v. Oregon
National Association of Female Executives
National Association of Manufacturers
National Consumers League
National Negro Business League
National Women's Trade Union League
Negro American Labor Council
New Deal
Nontraditional Employment for Women Act of 1992
North American Free Trade Agreement
Office of Minority Business Enterprise
Old boys' network
Operation Bootstrap
Ortega, Katherine Davalos
Padrone system
Parker, Quanah
Pecan shellers' strike
Perkins, Frances
Pregnancy and employment
Pregnancy Discrimination Act
Protective legislation for women*
Randolph, A. Philip
Repatriation program
Retirement Equity Act
Salinas lettuce strike
San Joaquin cotton strike
Sexual harassment
Sharecropping
Shima, George
Socialism
Society of Hispanic Professional Engineers
Sweatshops
Thai garment workers slavery case
Triangle Shirtwaist Company fire
Two-tiered wage system
United Auto Workers
United Farm Workers
United Hebrew Trades Union
United Mine Workers of America
United Steelworkers
Wages

War Labor Board and women
Women's Bureau of the Department of Labor
World War I
World War II—civilian roles

ETHNIC GROUPS and ETHNICITY
Acadians in the United States
Afghan Americans
African American population—diversity within
Aleuts in the United States
Alianza Hispano-Americana, La
Amerasians
American Indian assimilation
American Indian demography
American Indian revitalization movements
American Indians—contemporary social conditions
American Samoa
Americans for Indian Opportunity
Arab Americans
Argentinean Americans
Armenian Americans
Asian American movement
Asian American population, diversity within
Asian Indian Americans
Assimilation
Australian Americans
Austrian Americans
Balch, Emily Greene
Basque Americans
Belgian Americans
Belorussian Americans
Black-on-black violence
Brazilian Americans
Bulgarian Americans
Cambodian Americans
Canadians in the United States
Chilean Americans
Chinese Americans
Colombian Americans
Croatian Americans
Cuban Americans
Cultural pluralism
Cultural relativism
Czech Americans
Danish Americans
Discrimination—ethnic
Dominican Americans
Dutch Americans
Ecuadoran Americans
Egyptian Americans

Puerto Rican nationalism
Puerto Ricans
Raza Unida Party, La*
Romanian Americans
Russian Americans
Russian Jews
Salvadoran Americans
Samoan Civic Association
Sansei
Saudi Americans
Scots-Irish Americans
Scottish Americans
Serbian Americans
Sioux
Skinheads
Slovak Americans
Slovenian Americans
Society of American Indians
Spanish Americans—contemporary
Sri Lankan Americans
Swedish Americans
Swiss Americans
Syrian Americans
Taiwanese Americans
Thai Americans
Tribes
Turkish Americans
Ukranian Americans
Vietnamese Americans
Welsh Americans
West Indian culture
White Anglo-Saxon Protestant
Yonsei

FAMILY LIFE
Abortion
Adoption
African American women
African American women—matriarchy debate
Alimony
American Indian women
Antifeminism
Antimiscegenation laws
Asian American women
Baby M case
Baby Richard case
Biracial and mixed race children
Birth control and family planning
Blended families
Breast-feeding

Cesarean sections
Child abuse
Child care
Child custody and visitation rights
Childbirth and child rearing
Common-law marriage
Cult of True Womanhood
Day care
Divorce
Domestic violence
Eating disorders
Family and Medical Leave Act
Family life
Family planning services
Family Protection Act of 1979
Family Support Act of 1988
Fatherlessness
Feminism
Friedan, Betty
Griswold v. State of Connecticut
Head of household, female
Housework
Hyphenated names
Hysterectomies
Infanticide
Intermarriage
Irish American women
Jewish American women
Latinas
Marriage
Maternity leave
Matriarchy
Men's movement
Midwives
Mommy track
Motherhood
Mothers Against Drunk Driving
Orphans and orphanages
Picture brides
Planned Parenthood Federation of America
Poverty, feminization of
Property rights—married women's
Protective legislation for women*
Puerto Rican Family Institute
Reed v. Reed
Reproductive rights
Sanger, Margaret
Scandinavian women
Schlafly, Phyllis
Sexism

Protective legislation for women*
Rainbow Coalition
Rape
Rape trauma syndrome
Rich, Adrienne
Roe v. Wade
Schlafly, Phyllis
Seneca Falls Convention
Sexism
Sexist language
Sexual harassment
Shaw, Anna Howard
Stanton, Elizabeth Cady
Steinem, Gloria
Sterilization of women
Stone, Lucy
Suffrage movement and suffragists
Supreme Court rulings—women's's issues*
Surrogate mothers
Tailhook scandal
Teenage pregnancy
Title IX of the Education Amendments
Transsexuals
Truth, Sojourner
United Nations Decade for Women
**United Nations Fourth World Conference on
  Women**
Violence Against Women Act
Voting patterns
War Labor Board and women
Webster v. Reproductive Health Services
Willard, Frances Elizabeth
Women of All Red Nations
Women's Equity Action League
Women's liberation movement
Women's studies programs
Year of the Woman

HEALTH, SCIENCE, and TECHNOLOGY
Abortion
Acquired immune deficiency syndrome*
Acupuncture and moxibustion
AIDS quilt project
Alcoholism
Alcoholism and drug abuse
Alternative medicine
Alvarez, Luis Walter
Army Nurse Corps
Banneker, Benjamin
Barton, Clara

Battered child syndrome
Biological clock
Blackwell, Elizabeth
Breast cancer
Breast implants
Breckenridge, Mary
Bulimia nervosa
Carver, George Washington
Cesarean Prevention Movement
Cesarean sections
Child Protection and Toy Safety Act
Childbirth and child rearing
Curanderas
Dalkon Shield
Depo-Provera
Drew, Charles Richard
Earhart, Amelia
Eating disorders
Elders, Joycelyn
Fossey, Dian
Foster, Henry, Jr.
Genital mutilation and clitoridectomy
Gynecology
Hale House
Health and medicine
Health and medicine—American Indian
Health and medicine—women's
Hysterectomies
Infant mortality
Intrauterine devices
Lee, T. D.
McCoy, Elijah
Medicine men—traditional American Indian
Midwives
Morning-after pill
National Chicano Health Organization
Native Hawaiian Health Care Act of 1988
Novello, Antonia Coello
Ochoa, Severo
Office of Research on Women's Health
Onizuka, Ellison
Our Bodies, Ourselves
Planned Parenthood Federation of America
Plastic surgery
Post-traumatic stress disorder—Indochinese refugees
Premenstrual syndrome
Prenatal care
Race—scientific theories*
Ride, Sally
Roe v. Wade

Hong Kong, Chinese Americans from
Hungarian Americans
Icelandic Americans
Illegal aliens
Immigration—illegal
Immigration Act of 1882
Immigration Act of 1907
Immigration Act of 1917
Immigration Act of 1924
Immigration Act of 1943
Immigration Act of 1990
Immigration and Nationality Act of 1952
Immigration and Nationality Act of 1965
Immigration and Naturalization Service
Immigration Convention of 1886
Immigration legislation*
Immigration Reform and Control Act of 1986
Immigration Restriction League
In Re Ah Moy, on Habeas Corpus
Indochina Migration and Refugee Assistance Act of 1975
Indonesian Americans
Internal Security Act of 1950
Iranian Americans
Iraqi Americans
Irish Americans
Israeli Americans
Issei
Italian Americans
Jamaican Americans
Japanese Americans
Jewish Americans
Jewish immigrants
Johnson, Albert
Jordanian Americans
Korean Americans
Landsmannschaften
Laotian Americans
Latino population—diversity within
Latvian Americans
Lebanese Americans
Ling Sing v. Washburn
Literacy testing
Lithuanian Americans
Mail-order brides
Mariel boat lift
Maroons
Melting pot theory
Mexican Americans
Migrant Health Act

Migration and Refugee Assistance Act
Mutual aid societies and organizations
Names and name changes
National Coalition for Haitian Rights
National Immigration Forum
Nationality parishes
Native Sons of the Golden West
Nativism
Naturalization
Naturalization Act of 1790
New Zealander Americans
Nicaraguan Americans
Norwegian Americans
Operation Gatekeeper
Operation Wetback
Oral history
Organic Act of Guam of 1950
Pacific Islander Americans
Padrone system
Pakistani Americans
Palestinian Americans
Panamanian Americans
Paper sons
Peruvian Americans
Picture brides
Polish Americans
Political asylum
Portuguese Americans
Post-traumatic stress disorder—Indochinese refugees
Puerto Ricans
Quotas—immigration
Refugee Act of 1980
Refugee Relief Act
Refugees
Rescate, El
Return migration
Romanian Americans
Russian Americans
Russian Jews
Salvadoran Americans
Sanctuary movement
Saudi Americans
Scots-Irish Americans
Scottish Americans
Serbian Americans
Slovak Americans
Slovenian Americans
Sojourners and Asian immigration
Southeast Asia Resource Action Center
Spanish Americans—contemporary

Sri Lankan Americans
Swedish Americans
Swiss Americans
Syrian Americans
Taiwanese Americans
Takaki, Ronald
Terminal Island
Thai Americans
Tongs
Turkish Americans
Ukranian Americans
Undocumented persons
Vietnamese Americans
War Brides Act
War Refugee Board
Welsh Americans
Xenophobia
Yellow peril

POLITICS, GOVERNMENT, LAW, and MILITARY

Activist and protest organizations
Age Discrimination in Employment Act
Aid to Families with Dependent Children
Air Carriers Access Act
Alaska Native Claims Settlement Act
Alatorre, Richard
Albright, Madeleine
Alien and Sedition Acts
Alien land laws
Amerasian Homecoming Act of 1987
American Civil Liberties Union
American Indian-U.S. government relations
American Indian-U.S. government treaties
American Indian water rights
American Legion
American Revolution
Americans with Disabilities Act of 1990
Anaya, Toney
Antimiscegenation laws
Arendt, Hannah
Ariyoshi, George Ryoichi
Army Nurse Corps
Asia-Pacific Triangle
At-large elections
Attorneys
Badillo, Herman
Barry, Marion
Bay of Pigs invasion
Bill of Rights

Blasphemy laws
Bond, Julian
Bradley, Tom
Brandeis Brief
Braun, Carol E. Moseley*
Brown, Ron
Brown, Willie L., Jr.
Brownsville incident
Buffalo soldiers
Bunche, Ralph Johnson
Bureau of Colored Troops
Bureau of Indian Affairs
Campbell, Ben Nighthorse
Campbell, Kim
Caraway, Hattie
Catt, Carrie Chapman
Cavazos, Lauro Fred
Census, Bureau of the
Census of 1990, U.S.
Chang Yin-huan
Chávez, Linda
Chesnut, Mary Boykin
China lobby
Chinese Exclusion Act
Chisholm, Shirley
Chivington, John Milton
Church and state, separation of
Cisneros, Henry Gabriel
Civil rights
Civil Rights Act of 1964
Civil rights legislation*
Civil service
Clinton, Hillary Rodham
Cold War
Combat, women in
Commission on Civil Rights
Communist Party
Congressional Black Caucus
Congressional Caucus for Women's Issues
Congressional caucuses
Congressional Hispanic Caucus
Conservatives
Constitution, U.S.
Councils, tribal
Counter Intelligence Program
Custer, George Armstrong
Davis, Benjamin O., Jr.
Davis, Benjamin O., Sr.
Dawes Act
Declaration of Independence

**PREJUDICE, DISCRIMINATION, CIVIL
    RIGHTS, and SOCIAL JUSTICE**

Oklahoma land runs
Older Americans
Operation PUSH
Organization of Afro-American Unity
Ozawa v. United States
Pan-Africanism
Pan-Indianism
Parks, Rosa
Peace activism
Persecution
Plessy v. Ferguson
Political correctness
Prejudice
Priests and social activism
Protective legislation for women*
Puerto Rican Legal Defense and Education Fund
Quakers
Quotas—admissions
Quotas—immigration
Quotas—racial
Race—scientific theories*
Race—sociological debate
Racism
Rainbow Coalition
Reconstruction
Red scare
Redlining
Regents of the University of California v. Bakke
Removal and relocation of American Indians
Restrictive covenants
Reverse discrimination
Richmond v. J. A. Croson Co.
Roosevelt, Eleanor
St. Francis College v. Al-Khazraji
Sanctuary movement
Scapegoat
Scott v. Sandford
Segregation, desegregation, and integration
Sexism
Sit-ins
Social Darwinism
Social organizations
Southern Christian Leadership Conference
Southwest Voter Registration Education Project
Spingarn Medal and medal winners*
Stanton, Elizabeth Cady
Steinem, Gloria
Stereotype
Stonewall riots
Stowe, Harriet Beecher

Student Nonviolent Coordinating Committee
Supreme Court rulings—discrimination and minority status*
Supreme Court rulings—women's issues*
Thirteenth Amendment
Tijerina, Reies López
Trail of Broken Treaties
Truth, Sojourner
Tubman, Harriet
Turner, Nat
Underground Railroad
United Nations Commission on Human Rights
United States v. Bhagat Singh Thind
Universal Declaration of Human Rights
Universal Negro Improvement Association
Voting patterns
Voting Rights Act of 1965
Wages
Wards Cove Packing Co. v. Atonio
Watts riots
Weeks v. Southern Bell
Wells, Ida Bell
Wilkins, Roy
Women's liberation movement
Wounded Knee, confrontation at
Wright, Richard
Yellow peril
Young, Andrew Jackson, Jr.
Zoot-suit riots

PROFESSIONS
Academics
Art and artists
Attorneys
Civil service
Dramatists and drama
Fiction writers and fiction
Journalists and journalism
Judges
Librarians
Musicians and composers
Poets and poetry
Social work
Spingarn Medal and medal winners*
Teachers
Theologians and theology

RACE, RACISM, and SLAVERY
A. Philip Randolph Institute
Abolitionist movement

Affirmative action*
African American-American Indian relations
African American-Jewish American relations
African American-Korean American relations*
African American population—diversity within
African American studies programs
African American women
Alexander v. Holmes County Board of Education
Alien land laws
American Civil Liberties Union
American Colonization Society
American Indian women
Anti-Asian violence, contemporary
Anti-Chinese movement
Anti-Chinese violence
Anti-Filipino violence
Anti-Japanese Laundry League
Anti-Japanese movement
Anti-Korean incidents
Antimiscegenation laws
Anti-Semitism
Anti-Southeast Asian incidents
Apartheid
Asian American studies programs
Asian American women
Asiatic Exclusion League
Assimilation
Athletics and sport
Authoritarian personality
Back to Africa movement
Baldwin, James Arthur
Baraka, Amiri
Baseball
Benevolent and fraternal organizations
Bigotry
Birmingham demonstrations
Black Codes
Black nationalism
Black Panther Party
Black Power movement
Black United Front
Brown, H. Rap
Brown Berets
Brown Power movement
Brown Scare
Camp Grant Massacre
Carmichael, Stokely
Chavis, Benjamin Franklin, Jr.
Chicano movement
Chicano studies programs

Church fires
Civil rights
Civil Rights Act of 1964
Civil Rights movement
Civil War
Civilian Exclusion Orders
Cleaver, Eldridge
Colleges—African American
Commission on Civil Rights
Congress of Racial Equality
Critical Race Theory
Cultural pluralism
Detroit riots
Discrimination—business and employment
Discrimination—ethnic
Discrimination—housing
Discrimination—laws
Discrimination—public education
Disfranchisement
Du Bois, W. E. B.
Duke, David
Education
Equal Employment Opportunity Commission
Ethnic cleansing
Ethnic studies movement
Eugenics
Evers, Medgar W.
Farrakhan, Louis Abdul*
Feminism
Fifteenth Amendment
Fourteenth Amendment
Free Soil Party
Freedom Rides
Fugitive Slave Act
Furman v. Georgia
Garner v. Louisiana
Garvey, Marcus
Georgia v. McCollum
Gerrymandering
Ghetto
Gong Lum v. Rice
Gonzáles, Rodolfo "Corky"
Grandfather clause
Gregg v. Georgia
Griggs et al. v. Duke Power Company
Higher education
Japanese Exclusion League of California
Jeffries, Leonard
Kansas-Nebraska Act
King, Rodney, case

Ku Klux Klan
Latinas
Ling Sing v. Washburn
Little Rock crisis
Long Island Railroad Murder Case
Malcolm X
Marshall, Thurgood*
Melanin theory
Middle Passage
Military
Milliken v. Bradley
Million Man March
Miner, Myrtilla
Minority group
Miscegenation
Missouri Compromise
Montgomery bus boycott
Multicultural education
Multiculturalism
Multiculturalism—Canadian policy
Nation of Islam
National Association for the Advancement of Colored People*
National Urban League
Neo-Nazis
Niagara movement
Northwest Ordinance
Operation PUSH
Pan-Africanism
Parks, Rosa
Plessy v. Ferguson
Political correctness
Prosser, Gabriel
Quotas—admissions
Quotas—immigration
Quotas—racial
Race—scientific theories*
Race—sociological debate
Race riots
Racism
Rainbow Coalition
Reconstruction
Regents of the University of California v. Bakke
Resegregation
Reverse discrimination
Scott v. Sandford
Scottsboro Nine
Segregation, desegregation, and integration
Self-segregation
Sit-ins

Slavery
Southern Christian Leadership Conference
Student Nonviolent Coordinating Committee
Supreme Court rulings—discrimination and minority status*
Texaco boycott
Thirteenth Amendment
Truth, Sojourner
Turner, Henry McNeal
Universal Negro Improvement Association
Vesey, Denmark
Washington Urban League v. Washington Metropolitan Area Transit
Watts riots
White supremacist movements
Wilkins, Roy
Wirth, Louis
Women's liberation movement
Wright, Richard
Young Lords
Zoot-suit riots

RELIGIOUS GROUPS and RELIGION

African American-Jewish American relations
African Methodist Episcopal church
Amana Colonies
American Indian Religious Freedom Act
American Jewish Committee
American Protective Association
Amish
Ancestor worship
Anti-Defamation League
Anti-Semitism
Ashkenazic Jews
Baha'is
Baptists
Bar/bat mitzvah
Blasphemy laws
Blue laws
B'nai B'rith, Independent Order of
Branch Davidians
Brook Farm
Buddhists
Cabrini, Mother
Calvinists
Catholic-Protestant relations
Catholic Youth Organization
Catholics, Roman
Catholics for a Free Choice
Católicos por la Raza

Christian extremism
Christian-Jewish relations
Christian Scientists
Christmas
Christmas decoration controversies
Church and state, separation of
Church fires
Chy Lung v. Freeman
Conference of Catholic Bishops, U.S.
Confucian tradition
Congregationalists
Creation myths—American Indian
Creationism and evolution teaching
Crummell, Alexander
Day, Dorothy
Día de los Muertos
Discrimination—religious
Eastern European Jews
Eastern Orthodox churches
Eastern Rite churches
Ecumenical movement
Eddy, Mary Baker
Episcopalians
Evangelical and Pentecostal congregations—African
  American
Farrakhan, Louis Abdul*
Festival of Our Lady of Guadalupe
Fundamentalism, religious
German Jews
Ghost Dance religion
Gospel music—African American
Great Awakening
Hasidism
Hindus
Homosexuality, religion and
Huguenots
Hutchinson, Anne
Hutterites
International Society for Krishna Consciousness
Jehovah's Witnesses
Jewish American communities
Jewish Americans
Jewish Theological Seminary
Jews—Conservative
Jews—Orthodox
Jews—Reconstructionist
Jews—Reform
Kachinas
Kosher
Liberation theology

Lutherans
Maryland Act of Religious Toleration
Medicine men—traditional American Indian
Mennonites
Methodists
Missionaries and American Indians
Moon, Sun Myung
Mormons
Muhammad, Elijah
Muslims
Nation of Islam
**National Council of Churches of Christ in the
  U.S.A.**
Nationality parishes
Native American Church
New Age movement
New Harmony, Ind.
Nuns and priests
Oneida Community
Penitentes
Pentecostals
Peyote
Philadelphia riots of 1844
Pietists
Popé
Posadas, Las
Presbyterians
Priests and social activism
Protestants
Puritans
Quakers
Quinceañera
Rabbis, women as
Rastafarianism
Religion
Religion and mythology—American Indian
Religious Freedom Restoration Act
Religious organizations
Religious right
Religious Roundtable
Russian Jews
Sanctuary movement
Santería
School prayer
Self-Realization Fellowship
Sephardic Jews
Seton, Elizabeth Ann Bayley
Seventh-day Adventists
Shakers
Shamanists

Shintoists
Sikhism
Snake Dance
Southern Christian Leadership Conference
Spanish Empire and the New World
Spanish missions
Spirituals
Sun Dance
Theologians and theology
Transcendental meditation
Turner, Henry McNeal
Unification church
Unitarians
Vatican II
White Anglo-Saxon Protestant
Women, ordination of
Women's Christian Temperance Union
Wovoka
Young Men's Christian Association
Young Women's Christian Association

SOCIAL CONDITIONS, PROTEST, and REFORM

Abolitionist movement
Acquired immune deficiency syndrome*
Activism in the 1960's—student
Activist and protest organizations
Adarand Constructors v. Pena
Addams, Jane
Affirmative action*
African American studies programs
Akron v. Akron Center for Reproductive Health, Inc.
American Citizens for Justice
American Friends Service Committee
American Indian assimilation
American Indian Movement
American Indian studies programs
American Indians—contemporary social conditions
American Indians—rural
American Woman Suffrage Association
Antiabortion protests and violence
Asian American studies programs
Atkinson, Ti-Grace
Attica prison riot
Balch, Emily Greene
Banks, Dennis
Barrios
Battered women
Bill of Rights for the Handicapped

Birth control and family planning
Black Power movement
Bloody Sunday
"Blowout"
Bobbitt case
Brown Berets
Brown Power movement
Brown Scare
Busing
California Civil Rights Initiative
California Rural Legal Assistance
Call Off Your Old Tired Ethics
Chicano studies programs
Child, Lydia Maria
Child abuse
Children's Defense Fund
Children's rights movement
Chu, Louis
Citadel case
Civil rights
Civil rights legislation*
Civil Rights movement
Clark, Marcia
Class
Clearinghouse on Women's Issues
Cochran, Johnnie L., Jr.
Columbus Day celebrations
Consciousness-raising
Cuffee, Paul
Culture of poverty thesis
Darden, Christopher A.
Davis, Angela
Delano grape strike
Detroit riots
Dewson, Molly
Discrimination—housing
Dix, Dorothea Lynde
Draft riots
Earned income tax credit
Eastman, Crystal
Ecofeminism
Edelman, Marian Wright*
Eisenstadt v. Baird
Elderly abuse
Enola Gay **exhibit controversy**
Entitlement programs
Environmental racism
Equal opportunity programs
Evacuation Claims Act of 1948
Federal assistance programs

Food stamps
Freedmen's Bureau
Frontiero v. Richardson
Gangs and crime
Gay Liberation Front
Ghetto
Goldman, Emma "Red Emma"
Great Migration
Hague Women's Peace Conference
Hale House
Harlem riots
Hawaiian Renaissance
Hawaiian reparations
Haymarket Affair
Head of household, female
Head Start
Henry Street Settlement
Holocaust denial
Homelessness
Hoyt v. Florida
Hull House Association
Hyde Amendment
In re Gault
Indian rights movement
Industrial Workers of the World
Infanticide
Inner city
Internal colonialism
Jones v. Alfred H. Mayer Co.
Kelley, Florence
King, Martin Luther, Jr.
King, Rodney, case
Kit Carson National Forest takeover
Koreagate
Kuhn, Maggie
Labor movement
Lerner, Michael
Long Island Railroad Murder Case
Los Angeles riots
March First movement
March on Washington
March to Austin
March to Sacramento
Mexico, bailout of
Miami riots
Militias
Million Man March
Miss Saigon controversy
Montgomery bus boycott
Mothers Against Drunk Driving

Mount Pleasant riots
Moynihan Report
National Abortion and Reproductive Rights Action League
National Association for the Advancement of Colored People*
National Chicano Moratorium on Vietnam
National Coalition Against Domestic Violence
National Coalition for Redress/Reparations
National Council of Senior Citizens
National Gay and Lesbian Task Force
National Institute on Aging
National Welfare Rights Organization
Navajo-Hopi Land Dispute
New Deal
Niagara movement
No-no boys
Ohio v. Akron Center for Reproductive Health
Older Americans
Olympic Games*
Operation Rescue
Organization of Afro-American Unity
PARC v. Commonwealth of Pennsylvania
Planned Parenthood Federation of America
Planned Parenthood v. Ashcroft
Police-community relations
Poverty
Poverty, feminization of
Prenuptial agreements
Priests and social activism
Proposition 187
Prostitution
Protective legislation for women*
Public housing developments
Race—sociological debate
Reproductive rights
RU-486
Rural life and culture
Rust v. Sullivan
Salinas lettuce strike
Sanctuary movement
Sanger, Margaret
Self-Help for the Elderly
Selph v. Council of the City of Los Angeles
Sentencing Project Report
Settlement houses
Simpson, O. J., case
Sit-ins
Sleepy Lagoon case
Social Security Act

Social work
Steel Strike of 1919
Suburbanization
Tailhook scandal
Termination and urbanization—American Indian
Terrell, Mary Church
Texaco boycott
Thai garment workers slavery case
Trail of Broken Treaties
Underclass
United Farm Workers
United States v. Lopez
Upward Bound program
Urban life and culture
Urbanization
Voting Accessibility for the Elderly and Handicapped Act
Voting Rights Act of 1970
Voting Rights Act of 1975
Voting Rights Act of 1982
War on Poverty
Watts riots
Women's Christian Temperance Union
Women's International League for Peace and Freedom
Women's Peace Party
Wounded Knee, confrontation at
Wu, Harry
Wyatt v. Strickley

SPORTS
Aaron, Hank
Abdul-Jabbar, Kareem
Ali, Muhammad
All-American Girls Professional Baseball League
American Turners
Ashe, Arthur R., Jr.
Association for Intercollegiate Athletics for Women
Athletics and sport
Baseball
Basketball
Battle of the sexes
Berenson, Senda
Chang, Michael
Clemente, Roberto
Education Amendments, Title IX
Flores, Thomas Raymond
Football
Gibson, Althea
Gonzalez, Pancho*

Harlem Globetrotters
Image Awards, NAACP
Joe Louis memorial sculpture
Johnson, Earvin "Magic"
Jordan, Michael
King, Billie Jean
Lee, Bruce
López, Nancy
Negro League baseball
Negro League Baseball Museum
Olympic Games*
Peck, Annie Smith
Robeson, Paul
Robinson, Jackie
Rudolph, Wilma
Skateboarding
Sokol
Special Olympics
Thorpe, Jim
Trevino, Lee
Tyson, Mike
Valenzuela, Fernando
Wightman, Hazel
Women's Sports Foundation
Woods, Eldrick "Tiger"
Yamaguchi, Kristi Tsuya
Zaharias, "Babe" Didrikson

URBAN, RURAL, and REGIONAL LIFE
African American-Jewish American relations
African American population—diversity within
American Indians—rural
American Indians of California
American Indians of the Great Lakes
American Indians of the Great Plains
American Indians of the Northeast
American Indians of the Pacific Northwest
American Indians of the Southeast
American Indians of the Southwest
Amish
Asian American population—diversity within
Barrios*
Border culture
Border Folk Festival
California
California Rural Legal Assistance
Cart War of 1857
Census, Canadian
Chicago, Ill.
Chinatowns

Encyclopedia of

MULTICULTURALISM

INDEX